"This book deals with the deep and disturbing issu bashing, and brainwashing, violence and vengeance, retaliativ... parental alienation, false allegations of abuse. Easy to read and understand cases reveal the seamy side of post-divorce relations and amply illustrate the damage parents can inflict on their children. Specific rules and recommendations, based on the author's extensive clinical experience and warm wisdom, provide guidance for how parents can avoid such divorce poison. This book should be required reading for every parent, the week after they leave divorce court. It will help them protect their children's interests from their own retaliatory impulses or their ex-spouse's vengeful behavior."

> —Alison Clarke-Stewart, Ph.D., associate dean for research, School of
> Social Ecology, University of California, Irvine, and author of Daycare

"In this engaging book, Richard Warshak skillfully draws attention to the devastating consequences of a poorly recognized form of child abuse: parental alienation. He has filled *Divorce Poison* with clear, poignant, concrete, and well-reasoned advice for parents who must confront the malignant effects of parental alienation on relationships with their children and on the children themselves. Every divorcing parent should read *Divorce Poison* closely, examine their own behavior critically, and take steps to minimize alienation and its effects."

> —Michael E. Lamb, Ph.D., National Institute of Child Health and
> Human Development

"Family courts struggle daily to address the needs of children who reject a parent after divorce or separation, but there are few resources to help parents deal with day-to-day situations. Dr. Warshak provides skillful coaching to parents who are the targets of divorce poison on how to protect their relationships with their children. His book will prove equally valuable to those who advise parents, including family lawyers, therapists, mediators, and parent educators. Dr. Warshak also helps parents distinguish divorce poison from other relationship difficulties and advises parents who are falsely accused of alienating their children from the other parent."

> —Leslie Ellen Shear, J.D., certified family law specialist, State Bar of
> California Board of Legal Specialization

"A great book for both parents and professionals on a previously neglected topic by an outstanding clinician/researcher."

> —Henry Biller, Ph.D., professor of psychology, University of Rhode Island,
> and author of The Father Factor

"Always painful, divorce can turn lethal when one parent attempts to poison the children against an ex-spouse. In this balanced, compassionate book, Richard Warshak offers vital advice to those caught in the emotional maelstrom of a bitter divorce."

> —Mark Pendergrast, author of Victims of Memory

"*Divorce Poison* is long overdue. The mere fact of a divorce does not have to damage children; however, an all-out war between the parents has a very good chance of wreaking havoc. This book recognizes the critical importance of every child's having a relationship with both parents."

> —*Karen DeCrow, attorney and past president, National Organization for Women*

"This incredible book extends our understanding of parental alienation in a meaningful way. Every parent—even if not separated or divorced—will see himself or herself in this book and learn from it. This powerful book will influence parents, professionals, courts, and legislatures for years to come."

> —*David L. Levy, J.D., president, Children's Rights Council*

"Just about every parent who's been through a divorce knows how tempting it is to say something nasty to the kids about the other parent. But blinded by their anger, too few of these parents realize the damage they're doing to their children. *Divorce Poison* is an absolute must-read for any parent going through a divorce. In it, Warshak lays bare the evils of parental alienation and gives readers the knowledge they need to defend themselves—and their children—against it."

> —*Armin Brott, author of* The Expectant Father *and* The Single Father

"This book is a testament to Dr. Warshak's vast experience, erudition, and deep commitment to the prevention, diagnosis, and treatment of the various categories of alienated children."

> —*Richard A. Gardner, M.D., clinical professor of child psychiatry, Columbia University College of Physicians and Surgeons*

"This book fills a need for those concerned with divorce in our culture, particularly divorces that have resulted in extreme hostility, which is so harmful to children and others involved. It is a much-needed wake-up call for neglectful parents and a supportive resource for parents who are striving to meet their children's needs."

> —*Emily B. Visher, Ph.D., and John S. Visher, M.D., cofounders of Stepfamily Association of America and authors of* How to Win as a Stepfamily

"Richard Warshak's *Divorce Poison* is a must-read for every parent involved in a hostile divorce. He clearly spells out the problems and the devastating effects vindictiveness can have on the child, then provides a wealth of information to help parents change for the better."

> —*Dr. John W. Santrock, professor of psychology, University of Texas at Dallas*

"Divorce can be ugly, and in the ugliest divorces, one parent destroys children's relationships with their mother or father. *Divorce Poison* offers clear, practical, and even-handed advice on this incredibly difficult problem. The first step? Look inward. Protect your children by finding an antidote for your own poison and by swallowing a little more from your ex."

> —*Robert E. Emery, Ph.D., Director of the Center for Children, Families, and the Law, University of Virginia, and author of* Renegotiating Family Relationships

DIVORCE POISON

Also by Dr. Richard A. Warshak

The Custody Revolution

DIVORCE POISON

Protecting the Parent-Child Bond
from a Vindictive Ex

DR. RICHARD A. WARSHAK

HARPER

NEW YORK . LONDON . TORONTO . SYDNEY

IN MEMORY OF
my father, Henry L. Warshak,
Grandma and Grandpa Ades,
Aunt Danny, Aunt Helen and Uncle Morris, Uncle Nat,
Uncle Rene, Uncle Barney,
cousins Nancy, Nazira, Alan, and Andy,
Grandma and Grandpa Warshak,
Aunt Estelle and Uncle Ralph, Aunt Evelyn and Uncle Arthur,
and C. G. and Allie B. Brock

IN MEMORY OF THE CHILDREN MURDERED IN THE HOLOCAUST,
WHOSE CRIES WE MUST NEVER FORGET

and to

Nicole	Aaron
Richard	Shaun
David	Callie

WHOSE PRECIOUS LIVES FILL ME WITH HOPE,
AND WHOSE SMILES BRING ME MORE JOY THAN THEY WILL EVER KNOW

What goes on in your heart?
What goes on in your mind?
You are tearing me apart,
When you treat me so unkind.
What goes on in your mind?

—John Lennon, Paul McCartney, and Ringo Starr

CONTENTS

ACKNOWLEDGMENTS

I was lucky to be born into a very large extended family. This good fortune fuels my passion about actively helping children remain connected to their parents and other relatives rather than passively allowing them to lose these ties.

I am grateful to the families who have shared with me their painful experiences. They have taught me much about how parent-child conflicts develop and about how to protect children from their parents' battles. Some of their stories are told in these pages with details changed to preserve anonymity.

Every field has its pioneers who make the initial contributions that form the foundation for subsequent work. I have learned much from the work of Dr. Richard A. Gardner, Dr. Stanley S. Clawar, and Dr. Brynne V. Rivlin who first brought the problem of alienated children to the attention of the legal and mental health professions.

Special thanks go to Dr. John A. Zervopoulos, who took time from his busy schedule to read the entire manuscript and offer excellent suggestions for improvement. My understanding of the problems of alienated children has been enriched by discussions with him and with Dr. Mark R. Otis, Dr. Donald R. Lammers, and Dr. Anna Beth Benningfield.

My brother, Alan Warshak, earns my gratitude for educating me about Judaism's prohibitions against bad-mouthing and securing for me, on short notice, a very hard to find videotape.

Susan Ginsburg encouraged me to write the book and then connected me with Simon Lipskar, whose wise guidance helped shape the book proposal so that it would be welcomed into a good home. He then found just the right home with Judith Regan, whose enthusiasm for the book is deeply appreciated. Tia Maggini made valuable suggestions that improved the structure of the book and made it more reader-friendly.

Working with Cassie Jones was a pleasure. She set a high standard for the book, never allowing my wish to be finished overcome her gentle but firm judgment that there was still more to do. Her eye for details was matched by a keen attention to the flow of the manuscript. If the book grabs and holds the reader's attention, she deserves the credit.

I have lived and breathed this book for more years than I care to acknowledge, and my wife, Sandra, has lived and breathed it with me. She has done so with grace, warmth, and love. Her empathy for the pain that leads to divorce poison and the anguish that results from it, and her conviction that this was a book that should be written, gave me the inspiration to take on the project. Her unflagging enthusiasm gave me the fuel to persist to the end. Her professional insights, based on her own work with alienated children and their parents, have enriched the book. I thank her for all this, and for enriching my life beyond my wildest dreams.

INTRODUCTION
STEALING THE SOUL

Your ex-spouse is bad-mouthing you to the children, often or constantly portraying you in a negative light, perhaps even trying to turn the children against you. What should you do? If you handle the situation ineffectively, your relationship with your children could suffer. You could lose their respect. You could lose their affection. Or, in severe cases, you could lose contact with them altogether.

The conventional advice is to do nothing. Psychologists caution parents to avoid criticizing the other parent in front of the children. They fear that such criticism could be misinterpreted to mean "fighting fire with fire" and result in greater injury to the children. After years of consulting on cases where parents had heeded advice to be passive and had no success, I am convinced that the standard approaching is wrong. It does not work. Often, it makes things worse. As relationship with their children progressively deteriorate, parents usually try desperately to reason with them. Such efforts inevitably meet with failure and leave parents feeling helpless and hopeless.

This book explains why the common approaches are impotent, why doing nothing will accomplish nothing, and why relying primarily on reasoning is an unreasonable approach to the problem. It offers a blueprint for an effective response grounded in a solid understanding of the techniques and dynamics of parents who poison their children's relationships with loved ones.

After reading this book you will be able to distinguish different types of criticism, ranging from occasional mild bad-mouthing to severe and systematic brainwashing. You will know why and how parents manipulate their children. You will know how to detect subtle psychological maneuvers in various guises. You will learn how these practices—even those that seem innocuous—damage children. And you will discover powerful strategies to preserve or rebuild loving relationships with your children.

Divorce does not always damage children. But when children are caught in the crossfire of their parents' hostility, it usually does. It hurts just to stand on the sidelines and watch parents trade shots. It hurts even more when parents enlist children as allies in the battle. And it hurts the most when one parent engages in a systematic campaign to turn the children against the other parent.

When I began my studies on divorce, more than twenty-five years ago, psychologists were most concerned about the damage to children when a parent, usually the father, walked out of their lives. We had discovered that a father's abandonment made it much more likely that his children would suffer psychological problems. We also found that children generally did better after divorce when both parents continued to participate in child-rearing. I wrote about these discoveries, and their implications for parents and for public policy, in my book *The Custody Revolution*.

In that book I mentioned, very briefly, my concern for children whose parents coach and brainwash them during a custody dispute. That one sentence, though, touched a nerve in parents and grandparents around the world. They called and wrote, desperate for solutions to the problem, and their desperation became the inspiration for this book.

The problem they face is the exact opposite of what I have written so much about. In these families children do not crave more time with an absent parent. In these families parents do not reject their children. Instead, children reject their parents. I heard repeatedly about children who express contempt for or fear of a parent who had always been devoted to them. About children who lambaste their parents in a most unchildlike manner. About children who will have nothing to do with the parent, who refuse even to talk on the phone with the parent.

In most cases the rejection is not a reaction to gross mistreatment by the parent. That would be understandable, and this book shows how to distinguish such children from those whose rejection of a parent is unreasonable. The focus here is on those children whose rejection of one parent results primarily from the other parent's influence. One parent may berate the other parent directly in front of the children, or allow them to overhear put-downs. In some cases the children are exposed to a relentless barrage of harsh criticisms of their other parent. They may be actively encouraged to join in the put-downs. Some unfortunate children are subjected to a deliberate and intensive effort on the part of one parent to alienate them from the other parent. These children are, in a word, brainwashed. What is washed out of their brains is any awareness of positive, loving feelings for a parent. These children disown the need and desire for contact with the parent. All that remains is a catalog of complaints that is supposed to justify the dramatic change in attitude about a parent who, in the past, had been a source of love and comfort.

There are degrees of alienation. In the worst cases it is so complete that the relationship is totally severed. After years of commitment—years of emotional and financial support, years of loving and worrying—parents find themselves reviled or ignored by their children. They are unwelcome at graduation ceremonies. They are excluded from weddings. They have no contact with their grandchildren.

In most families, though, the estrangement is only partial. The bad-mouthing does not sever ties between parents and children, but it does taint the quality of their relationship. It creates unnecessary tension for children and more conflict in their relationship with both parents. The tension and conflict may result in children who are more withdrawn and reluctant to discuss their thoughts and feelings, or children who have less respect for their parents' authority. Though these children may be less affectionate and more reserved, they are still able to find some enjoyment in the relationship. This is especially true when they are given enough time to relax their guard and experience the parent as more positive than they have been led to believe.

Parents are not the only targets of bad-mouthing, bashing, and brain-washing—what I have come to call *divorce poison*. Grandparents, and sometimes an entire extended family, receive the same treatment. This problem cuts across gender lines. Women and men in their roles as parents, stepparents, aunts, uncles, and grandparents are all vulnerable. And, in all cases, the children suffer.

We hear a lot about manipulation by leaders of religious cults. Bad-mouthing and brainwashing by divorced parents, however, have claimed far more victims than the headline-grabbing mass suicides. Several million people are affected, and more are added to the roster every day. Yet, until now, the problem has received little attention. Most books for divorced parents admonish them not to place children in the middle of their conflicts. But they provide little guidance on when it is appropriate to criticize a parent to a child and when it is destructive. None discuss the systematic process of psychological manipulation and how to help children resist and reverse its influence. Search the index of every parent guidance book, as I did one day in a bookstore, and you will find only one with entries on brainwashing or alienation. This is not meant as a critique of these books. It merely illustrates that we are at a very early stage in recognizing and learning how to cope with parental manipulation. In fact, parents who consult mental health professionals most often receive advice that, though well-intentioned, is not only inadequate and ineffective but shortchanges the children and may even intensify the alienation.

This book does not claim to have all the answers, or even most of them. It does offer insights that my wife and I have gained in our psychology practices as we struggled to help children caught in the crossfire of their parents' battles. I expect future research to discover even more effective strategies for rescuing children from divorce poison. Consider this a work in progress. I hope it will provide a lifeboat for families in which a child's relationship with a formerly loved adult is in danger of drowning. My aim is to help parents, grandparents, and other relatives better understand bad-mouthing, bashing, and brainwashing and to share with them practical advice that has helped other families in similar circumstances. You have the best chance of success if you follow this advice under the guidance of a competent therapist who understands the problems of alienated children.

Some parents whose behavior undermines their children's affection for the other parent are only dimly aware of their intentions. Other parents may be struggling with temptations in this direction. By exposing the true motives behind such behavior, and the damage it causes, I hope my work will dissuade these parents from acting on their destructive impulses.

Millions of adults, when they were children, suffered some degree of estrangement from loved ones in the aftermath of their parents' divorce.

This book will help them make sense of what was done to them. It will help them heal ruptured relationships.

Increased recognition of parental manipulation has brought with it an increase in false accusations of brainwashing. Innocent parents are losing custody of their children after being accused of fomenting alienation. This book shows how to defend oneself effectively against such accusations. Judges, lawyers, and mental health professionals who are involved with families in which there have been accusations of alienation and brainwashing, whether true or false, will find suggestions for safeguarding the welfare of children from divorced homes.

Divorce Poison was written primarily on behalf of children. The failure of their parents' marriage is a chilling lesson that we cannot always count on love. At such a vulnerable time in their lives, children especially need and deserve as much love as they can get. Those who close off avenues of love and support detour children from their pursuit of emotional security. When they manipulate children into erecting the barriers themselves, when they enlist them as agents in their own deprivation, they violate their children's trust in a most cruel manner. It is a form of kidnapping; stealing the soul.

I wrote this book to help lost souls find their way back to the hearts that await them. I wish them a successful journey.

CHAPTER 1
THE DELICATE BALANCE

Let us raise a standard to which the wise and honest can repair.
—George Washington

Fred slammed down the phone after his ex threatened to take him to court if he did not pay his child support on time. He turned to five-year-old Marty and said, "We can't go fishing this weekend. I have to work because your selfish mom is spending too much money."

Fred regretted his words almost as soon as they left his lips. The divorce was hard enough on the boy; hearing such criticisms of his mother only added to his stress. The hurt look on Marty's face confirmed that Fred had, in that moment, failed his son. The father resolved to do better in the future. The divorce was not Fred's idea and he was still bitter about it. Every now and then he would burden his son with some barb directed at the boy's mother, often blaming her for "leaving us." Each time he did this he was sorry afterward. But he never spoke with Marty about the harsh words. Marty's mom, who knew Fred spoke ill of her, never said anything to Marty about it. The little boy was left on his own to deal with the bad-mouthing.

Meryl hated Doug, the father of her twin eight-year-old boys, and took every opportunity to let them know it. Doug refused to marry her after she became pregnant. Ever since then she wished he would just disappear from her life. But he didn't. He was actively involved with his boys and he paid his child support regularly.

Meryl's anger did not dissipate over time. She constantly maligned Doug in front of his sons. When Doug was a few minutes late to pick up the children, Meryl told them he was irresponsible. She belittled the gifts he bought. She told the boys their dad was a loser because he was a high school band teacher and could not afford to take them on expensive vacations. When Doug had to lead the band at Friday-night football games, he asked his sister to pick up the boys and bring them to the stadium. Even though the boys enjoyed the games and liked watching their father at work, Meryl complained. She told them that it was too bad they didn't have a father who could pay more attention to them. She even went back to court to ask the judge to eliminate the Friday-night contacts if Doug would not personally pick up his children. (She was unsuccessful.) When the boys told their mother that their dad was proud about winning the all-state band competition, she told them that he bragged too much. When Doug did nice things for the children that she could not think of how to criticize, she dismissed these by saying, "He's just trying to make himself look good."

When Meryl became engaged to be married, Doug hoped that this would help her get past her anger and stop bashing him. Instead, she became worse. She started pressuring her sons to call her fiancé Dad. At the same time she began referring to Doug by first name when talking to the boys. "Doug's on the phone," she would say. "Do you want to speak to him or should I tell him you're too busy?" "Doug's probably going to be late again." "Don't tell Doug where Dad and I are going on our honeymoon."

Meryl returned to court, this time hoping to reduce the boys' time with Doug so that they could spend more time with "their own family," by which Meryl meant herself, her fiancé, and his son from a previous marriage. Despite the twins' strong attachment to their father, she did not want them to regard him as part of their family. Hoping to please their mother, the boys began telling her that they really didn't have such a good time with Doug. She exploited this by telling them about the fun things that she and her fiancé and his son would be doing while the boys were with Doug.

Doug worried when the boys began calling him Doug instead of Dad and asking to return home earlier than scheduled. He was not sure how to respond. His attorney advised him not to say anything that could be construed as criticizing Meryl because it might make him look bad in court. So Doug said nothing. The boys were given no help in coping with their mother's bashing of their father.

Richie and his new wife, Janice, were determined to move out of state with Richie's twelve-year-old daughter, Meadow, but first they had to win custody away from Giselle. Richie had always denigrated Giselle in front of their daughter, but now he intensified his campaign of hatred. He hoped that Meadow would share his hatred of her mother and ask to live with him.

One day Richie asked Meadow if she remembered the time her mother beat her with a belt. Meadow didn't remember. This was no surprise because the event never occurred. Richie brought up the event-that-never-was several times during the next few weeks. It was beginning to seem real to Meadow, although she wasn't sure if she actually remembered it or if she just remembered her father's account of it. Richie began casually referring to Giselle's violent temper. Although Meadow had never before thought of her mom in those terms, the more her dad and Janice talked about it, the more it seemed it must be true.

When Meadow complained that her mom wouldn't let her watch television until she completed her homework, Richie sympathized with her and told her that Giselle treated her too much like a kid. He continued to undermine Meadow's respect for her mother by referring to Giselle either as "the boss" or by her first name. At the same time, he and Janice indulged Meadow with material possessions and privileges. The contrast with Giselle's treatment made her seem excessively strict and depriving.

Richie's maneuvers had their intended effect. One day when Meadow was being particularly disrespectful, her mom lost her patience and yelled at her. Meadow ran to the bathroom, locked the door, and said in a panicked voice, "Don't beat me!" Giselle was flabbergasted.

"What would make you think I would do a thing like that?" Giselle asked.

Meadow answered, "I know how you get when you're mad. I'll tell Dad if you touch me."

Giselle said, "I think your dad and Janice have brainwashed you."

Meadow was offended. "No they haven't," she said. "I can think for myself. I'm not a kid anymore."

Later that evening Meadow called her dad and told him, "Giselle almost hit me, but I got away." He offered to come to pick her up right away. She said she would be all right for one more day. For the rest of the night and the next day she avoided her mother.

In subsequent weeks Meadow complained to her mom about all the rules in her home. Janice didn't enforce such rules. Janice treated Meadow with respect. Things got to a point where Giselle was reluctant to set reasonable limits because it made her look like a bad parent in her daughter's eyes. She knew that Meadow's preferences could play a key role in the custody decision. In fact, when Meadow had not been suffi- ciently critical of her mother during an interview with the court- appointed custody evaluator, Richie and Janice reprimanded Meadow. They told her that if she didn't do her part to help them win custody, and tell the psychologist what a bad mother Giselle was, it would be her fault if she had to stay with Giselle and not be able to move with them.

By this time Richie and Janice had talked so much about the benefits of the proposed move (e.g., they would buy a house with a swimming pool) that Meadow was convinced that she would be much happier if she could go with them. She was so focused on the benefits that she failed to think much about the impact of leaving her friends, school, dance instruc- tor, and close relatives. Meadow was thinking exactly as her dad and step- mom wanted her to think, yet she insisted that her negative thoughts and feelings about her mother were her own and not influenced by anyone.

Bad-mouthing, bashing, and brainwashing. All are ways that parents who live apart from each other hurt their children just as surely as if they laced their milk with a poison intended to jeopardize their emotional health. These three families have one more thing in common: No one came to the children's rescue. No one helped them cope with the toxic criticism. Each maligned parent thought it was best to say nothing. Having witnessed the damage caused by their ex's destructive criticism, they each assumed that the right thing to do was to avoid any criticism of their own. They were wrong.

THE UNITED FRONT

"We try to present a united front to our children," one mother told me. "When we reprimand the children, he backs me up and I back him up.

Even when we disagree about how to handle the children, we don't let them know."

"What about when you and your husband have conflicts about other matters?" I asked. "Do you ever argue in front of the children?"

"Never. That's our private business. The children never learn about it."

The "united front" approach is the traditional gold standard of good parenting. Experts agree that one of the best ways to help your children survive your divorce is to keep them out of the line of fire. If more parents lived up to this standard, there would be less need for this book. But it is equally true that too many parents slavishly follow this tradition, and avoid criticizing their ex, even when their children could profit from hearing valid criticisms expressed in a constructive manner.

How do we know when to criticize and when to keep silent? The key is in understanding how each approach can help or hurt children.

Maintaining a united front usually results in more secure and better-behaved children. We all know that children don't like to witness their parents arguing or saying bad things about each other. I have never met a child who enjoyed the spectacle. It seems paradoxical that children are quick to complain about the way their parents treat them, yet they take offense when other people say bad things about their parents.

Can you recall how, when you were a child, the worst insults your playmates could deliver were put-downs of your parents? In my day we called it "ranking out" a kid's parents. Stephen King referred to this as breaking "the cardinal rule for kids." In *The Body* (the story on which the film *Stand By Me* was based), King explained, "You could say anything about another kid, you could rank him to the dogs and back, but you didn't say a word ever about his mom and dad. . . . If a kid ranked out your mom and dad, you had to feed him some knuckles."

Children put their parents on a pedestal, and then vigorously resist efforts to topple the pedestal prematurely. When peers attack your parent, it is a simple matter of protecting the parent's honor. When the attack comes from the other parent, though, the situation becomes complicated. If a child sides with her critical father, her image of her mother suffers. If she opposes the father, her image of him suffers. Even if she tries to stay out of the conflict she will feel guilty for failing to defend her mother.

Eight-year-old Adrian was so troubled by her father's put-downs of her mother that she tuned out reality. When he went into angry tirades about all her mother's faults, she numbed herself to her feelings. She pretended that what she heard with her ears did not register in her brain. This strategy provided temporary relief. But there was a cost. In the long run, the more she shrank her awareness of reality, the less equipped she was to cope with it.

When a child no longer needs to keep her parents on a pedestal, she will begin to see them more realistically. But this process takes time. And it should be the child who sets the timetable, not an angry parent.

Adrian's father was so intent on bad-mouthing his ex-wife that nothing would deter him from his destructive goal. But some parents in his position will restrain themselves when they have a clearer understanding of the damage they are inflicting. If you think your ex is open to such examination, share this book with him or her.

Tearing down a child's positive image of a parent is one big risk of dropping the united front. Another risk is that it sets an example that your children may emulate. Belinda consulted me with a problem shared by many single mothers. Her twelve-year-old son, Chad, was becoming increasingly disrespectful to her. He felt no need to comply with her simplest requests. She asked him if he finished his homework, and he told her to shut up. She told him that he couldn't go outside after dinner, and he said he didn't have to listen to a crazy lady. "Crazy lady" was the term his father used freely around Chad. The more Chad identified with his father's put-downs of Belinda, the freer Chad felt to defy her authority.

Belinda needed her ex-husband to join forces with her to control their son. Instead, Chad's father aligned himself with his son against Belinda. This is what psychologists call a weak parental coalition, and it is a poor environment in which to raise children. The healthiest families are those in which the parents exercise authority together. Though they respect their children's feelings, the parents operate with clear lines drawn between the generations. The parents are a joint force to be reckoned with, they are co-leaders. As a result, their children cannot divide and conquer, and their parents do not encourage that type of manipulation.

Of course, even in the best marriages and most amicable divorces, conflict and anger are inevitable. It isn't so much the presence of conflict that harms children. It is the way parents deal with their conflicts. Shield-ing children from hostile and bitter confrontations is certainly desirable. But allowing children to observe how their parents accommodate differ-ences and resolve disputes in a nonviolent and nonadversarial manner can be helpful, instructive, and reassuring.

What hurts children the most is when parents place children in the middle of their battles. In some cases children witness their parents' vio-lent disputes. Or their parents encourage them to take sides, deliver angry messages, or spy on the other parent. Taken to extremes, such practices may be part of a systematic effort to turn children against the other par-ent. Even in less extreme cases, this type of behavior will harm children. Protecting your children from such harm is one justification for dropping the united front, despite the risks we have discussed.

WHEN SILENCE IS NOT GOLDEN

Many well-intentioned parents steadfastly adhere to a united front at all costs. This is a big mistake. At times children need to hear constructive criticisms of their other parent. I am not advocating open season on your ex. Before criticizing, you must be convinced that it is primarily for your children's welfare, and not primarily for your own satisfaction, and that the disclosure primarily helps your children rather than hurts them.

There are two circumstances in which it is a mark of good parenting to drop the united-front approach. The first is when you are the target of malignant criticism.

After months of arguing, Denise asked her husband, Evan, to move out of the house, and he did. Whenever he phoned to speak with his sons, Denise took the call and launched into a tirade about what a bad husband and father he was. What bothered Evan the most is that he could hear the boys in the background and knew they overheard their mother. When his sons came to his apartment, they told him that Mommy said he abandoned his family and didn't care about them any-more. They also said that she told them he was lazy and stupid. Evan sim-ply ignored these comments. He was determined not to stoop to her level. He would take the high road. Besides, they were disputing custody, and Evan's attorney warned him that if the children heard him say anything critical of their mother, this could reflect poorly on him during the custody trial.

Using some of the techniques exposed in chapter 6, "The Corruption of Reality," Denise succeeded in manipulating the children so that they began to protest spending time with their dad. They said they wanted to see him when they were ready, and that he should stop forcing them to spend time with him. The phrase *forced visitation* became a familiar refrain. By the time the case reached court, the boys were well on their way to being totally estranged from their father.

By failing to take a more active approach, Evan deprived his children of an effective defense against their mother's brainwashing. The boys and their father were not the only ones to suffer. In what Dr. Richard Gardner calls the "spread of animosity," the boys began to denigrate all of Evan's family. Doting grandparents and favorite uncles were now regarded as unwelcome intruders.

Experts regard the attempt to poison a child's relationship with a loved one as a form of emotional abuse. As with other forms of abuse, our first priority must be to protect children from further damage. This is not a time for silence. Exactly what we should do depends on the motives and means behind the destructive criticism, which we discuss in chapters 4–6.

Even when a parent has not bad-mouthed us, we may need to discuss his faults with our children. Frank was an angry, depressed man who would periodically lash out at his daughter with harsh disapproval for normal childlike behavior. When Gail forgot to hang her coat in the closet, Frank yelled at her and called her a slob. Gail was too young to understand that her father's outbursts were a symptom of emotional disturbance. Instead, Gail came to think of herself as a bad child. Gail's mother said nothing. She subscribed to the idea that you should never say anything bad about the other parent. By withholding her opinion of Frank's behavior, she compounded Gail's suffering.

All parents sometimes behave in irrational ways that are confusing and troubling to their children. If we say nothing about this irrational behavior, we give our children no help in understanding it. We leave them on their own to cope. And when our children lack an accurate understanding of a parent's troubling behavior, they may blame themselves for it as Gail did. Helping children in Gail's position is the second circumstance that justifies dropping the united front.

HOW TO DISTINGUISH BETWEEN HELPFUL AND HARMFUL CRITICISM

Contrary to the "do nothing" approach, I believe it *may be appropriate*, at times, for one parent to acknowledge the other parent's shortcomings and help the children make sense of the behavior and place it in proper perspective. Note the key phrase *may be appropriate*. Whether or not it is appropriate depends on a very careful and sensitive assessment of the situation. If we are not careful, we may cause as much damage as the parent we are criticizing. The need to respond effectively to denigration is never a license for unbridled retaliation.

First and foremost we must maintain a steadfast commitment to shield our children from unnecessary stress and destructive communications. Some parents never make this commitment. Others lose it somewhere in the tangle of the disappointment and anger of a failed marriage. They allow their impulse to indulge personal wrath to take priority over concern for their children. So, for example, they run down their ex in front of the children, with total disregard for the children's need to maintain a positive image of that parent. They may try to justify their destructive behavior by hiding behind superficial rationalizations. Some common excuses: "I'm just telling him the truth about his mother," or "She needs to know what her father is really like."

Before discussing with your children, or even mentioning, alleged flaws of their other parent, you should consider your motives. And you should weigh the potential benefits and risks to your children. If this sounds like too much work, if you do not have the patience to think critically about such matters, if you just want to get on with the business of telling the children how bad the other parent is, then your motives are not good. Rather than acting like a responsible parent you are indulging your whims. Most likely your children will be harmed rather than helped by your revelations.

Some parents do not distinguish between their own desires and the needs of their children. Essentially such parents operate under the credo that "What I want must be what my children want." Other parents are so intent on poisoning their children's relationship with the ex that the idea of censoring their disdain for the other parent would never occur to them. They want their children to share their hatred. I will have more to say about all of these behaviors in chapter 4, "Malignant Motives."

Even parents with good intentions are often unsure about when they should criticize and when they should remain silent. Separated and divorced spouses struggle with heavy doses of anger, fear, uncertainty, and hurt, along with the very human temptation to express such feelings in destructive and irrational ways. Resisting this temptation is a genuine challenge. Occasionally parents succumb.

Most children can withstand their parents' isolated mistakes and lapses of good judgment. Repeated mistakes, though, can be damaging, especially when they become a familiar pattern of behavior. The following test gives parents a tool to help them judge whether their criticisms are likely to help or hurt their children.

A TEST

When faced with the impulse to present a parent or grandparent in a negative light, do some serious soul-searching. The following five questions will help you cut through self-deception, expose irrational motives that could be fueling your behavior, and focus attention on your children's genuine welfare. Of course it is best to review the questions before exposing your children to criticisms of their loved ones. The more you do so, the more you will avoid destructive communications. But lapses in judgment are inevitable. Every breakup has such moments. This test can serve as a reminder to be careful about what you say. When you do slip up, reviewing these questions can help strengthen your resolve to do better in the future. If you believe that you are the target of bad-mouthing, these questions will help you clarify what is wrong with your ex's behavior.

The test sets a high standard by which parents can evaluate their past and future behavior. The closer parents come to meeting the standard, the more they will shield their children from the harmful effects of acrimony.

1. *What is my real reason for revealing this information to the children?*

   You may think of more than one reason. But if any one of these does not concern their best interests, think again about whether the children will truly benefit from what you plan to say. If you decide to tell them, you will need to make sure that you do so in a manner that does not serve motives other than their best interest. Review the malignant motives discussed in chapter 4. Make sure that your criticisms do not serve one of these purposes.

2.   *Are my children being harmed by the behavior I am about to criticize? Or are they being harmed by not having the information I am about to reveal?*

You may have a legitimate grievance about your ex-spouse, but there is no reason to share this with the children if they are not hurt by the behavior in question. For example, a man wanted to tell his children, who were raised Catholic, that their mother had an abortion years earlier. He insisted that they had a right to know the truth. But when asked how his children were harmed by withholding this information, he drew a blank.

3.   *How will it help the children to hear what I am about to tell them?*

Even if the children are being harmed by their other parent's behavior, before discussing it with them you should be convinced that your revelations will actually benefit the children. A woman believed that her ex-husband had been stingy in the divorce settlement. She knew that more money would enable her to provide better for her children. But she decided not to complain to the children about their father because she could not think of how it would help them to hear her opinion that their father was a cheapskate. There was nothing the children could do about the situation. Her revelations would only place the children in the middle of an adult conflict and perhaps diminish their respect for their father.

4.   *Do the possible benefits of revealing this to the children outweigh the possible risks?*

In many situations there is reason to believe that the revelations might benefit the children, but at the same time might create problems for them. An honest discussion of the other parent's flaws might help the children have more realistic expectations. But it might also poke holes in their idealization of the parent before they are emotionally prepared to give this up. Or it might lead to greater conflict in the parent-child relationship. If, after weighing the benefits and risks, you decide to share your criticisms with the children, you will want to do so in a manner that maximizes the benefits while minimizing the harm. The next question will help you accomplish this goal.

5. *If I were still happily married to my spouse, and I wanted to protect our children's relationship with him or her, how would I handle the situation?*

This question helps raise your consciousness so that the content and style of your communications with your children avoids the influence of irrational motives. It challenges you to think of the most constructive course to take. If, when happily married, you would not want your children to have the information you are about to give, why do you think they need to know it now? And if, when happily married, you would find a way to discuss it that minimized harm to their relationship with the other parent, an approach that did not undermine their general respect and regard for that parent, that same discretion is called for after divorce.

Remember, it is easy to fool ourselves into thinking that bad-mouthing is justified. Because of the potential damage to our children, we should be convinced that what we say, and how we say it, meets the test of the five questions.

What if we are unsure about whether to include a particular observation or opinion in our conversations with the children? Here is a simple rule to follow: *When in doubt, leave it out.*

Test Applications

To illustrate the use of this test, let us look at two typical scenarios that often prompt divorced parents to criticize their ex-spouses to their children: (1) reacting to a parent who is chronically late and (2) explaining the reasons for the divorce.

A father is always late to pick up his children. This often disrupts his ex-wife's schedule. After repeated instances of such inconvenience, she may want to berate him in front of the children by saying such things as "You can't count on your father" or "He's so irresponsible" or "Your father cares more about his girlfriend than he does about you."

When this mother asks herself question 1 of our test, *What is my real reason for revealing this information to the children?* she realizes that she has mixed motives. On the one hand, she feels bad for the children and angry at the man who disappoints them. On the other hand, she is angry that he is inconsiderate of her needs. She concludes that her concern for the children is genuine, but that if she decides to talk with them about their father's lateness, she will need to be cautious not to allow her anger at him to influence the way she handles the situation.

Next she asks, *Are my children being harmed by the behavior I am about to criticize?* Yes, they are being harmed. They are constantly disappointed when he does not come to get them on time and they are anxious that he will fail to show up. Not only are they disappointed and anxious, but they may assume that their father is late because they are not important enough to him. This could hurt their self-esteem.

The next question is *How will it help the children to hear what I am about to tell them?* It could help them to have a different mind-set while waiting for their father so that they can avoid excessive disappointment and worry. If the issue is discussed openly, their mother could help them find a healthy way to cope with his lateness. It could also help them place their father's behavior in perspective so that they do not regard it as an index of their worth to him.

Question 4 is *Do the possible benefits of revealing this to the children outweigh the possible risks?* The risks are the discomfort they could feel when their mother criticizes their father. Their mother's criticisms could cut deeper than their father's lateness. Nevertheless, if she chooses her words with discretion, she can help the children while minimizing the likelihood of stressing them even further. It is important to keep in mind your child's age when you decide what to say and how to say it. For instance, some children may be too young or immature to benefit from such a discussion.

The question that helps her the most is question 5: *If I were still happily married to my husband, and I wanted to protect our children's relationship with him, how would I handle the situation?* This forces her to think about the best way to discuss the issue with her children. She realizes that she

actually handled the same issue during the marriage in a different manner. And she can think of no reason not to handle it in a similar fashion
now. While she was married, her husband's lateness was a chronic irritant
to her. But the children always showed much more tolerance of this trait.
By the way, this is true in general: *Children are more able and willing to tolerate faults in their parents than spouses are with each other.*

Armed with this perspective the mother realizes that it will not help
the children to hear her berate their father as irresponsible or inconsiderate. And it could undermine their respect for him. Instead, she tells them,
"You may have noticed that Dad is usually late to pick you up. I know he
loves spending time with you, but Dad has always been late for things,
even things that are very important to him. A lot of people have a problem being on time. I wish Dad did not have this problem, but it does not
have to be a big deal. Instead of just waiting by the door for him each
time, find something to do that will keep you occupied and take your
mind off the time. That way you won't have to worry so much. You know
he always shows up and then you have a great time together." It would
not have been wrong if she also encouraged the children to tell their
father how they felt about his lateness.

None of the above discussion is meant to justify the father's lateness or
to minimize the inconsiderateness of his behavior. His ex-wife had good
reason to resent his irresponsible handling of his time with the children.
His behavior hurt the children. It caused her to be late for her own appointments. Time is a precious commodity, especially for a single parent.

This mother deserves our respect because she handled the situation
in a constructive manner. She carefully balanced her children's need to
respect and admire their father with their need for assistance in coping
with his lateness. She did not allow her resentment to dictate her behavior. The result is that she remained focused on what was most important
to her—her children's welfare.

It is a more difficult challenge for parents to explain to their children reasons for the divorce. Children will ask why, and they need and deserve an
explanation that takes into account their intellectual and emotional maturity. In some situations, the reasons for the divorce will necessarily include
facts that will lead the children to hold one parent more responsible than

the other. As I write this chapter I am consulting on one such case. The mother became pregnant in the course of an extramarital affair and decided to leave her husband and three sons to move to another city and marry her lover. Naturally, the children know what their mother has done. And they are liable to blame the divorce on her behavior. But even in this situation, the information can be conveyed to the children in a manner that does not encourage them to reject their mother. Without condoning the mother's behavior, the father can explain to his sons that he was not able to make their mother happy enough to stay in the marriage.

If we feel wronged, or do not want the divorce, we may want to tell the children that the divorce is all the other parent's fault. Question 1's search for motives will usually reveal that our wish to blame the divorce entirely on the other parent has less to do with our children's needs than our own.

At least three motives drive our desire to assign blame. First, we want to deflect blame from ourselves. We want to avoid accepting responsibility for the failure of our marriage. We do not want our children to be angry with us and we do not want to feel guilty for hurting them. Second, we want our children's sympathy and alliance. And third, we want to punish our spouse. By making the other parent the bad guy, we manipulate the children to be angry with, perhaps even turn against, the other parent.

The message that our spouse is to blame for the divorce, therefore, carries three hidden requests: "Don't be mad at me. Pity me. Join me in being angry at your other parent." None of these serves our children.

Perhaps even more to the point, many people are wrong in blaming the failure of their marriage entirely on their ex-spouse. Though the initial decision to divorce might not have been their own, in the majority of cases both spouses contributed to the marital difficulties.

An honest answer to question 1, therefore, puts us on notice that we may be about to indulge our destructive urges under the guise of helping our children. Question 2 also produces no justification for telling the children that their other parent is fully responsible for the divorce: How can we say that they will be harmed by not hearing this? And, in response to question 3, it is difficult to think of any clear benefit they would gain by hearing our opinion that the other parent is totally at fault. (This does not mean that we should deprive children of an explanation for the divorce.) Our response to question 4, concerning the benefits and risks of the proposed revelations, forces us to acknowledge that placing blame gives our children no particular advantage in coping with the divorce, and it creates a clear risk. The children may share our anger. And this will add unnecessary strain to their relationship with their other parent, thereby impeding their adjustment to the divorce.

Question 5 helps us identify the type of explanation that would best suit the needs of our children and protect their relationship with both parents. There are various possible explanations, depending on the circumstances of the marital conflict. But most helpful accounts of the divorce will avoid laying exclusive blame on one parent. The children will learn that their parents have decided to end their marriage. They may hear that the parents do not get along, or make each other unhappy. They may even learn of extramarital affairs. But they will be reassured that the divorce is not their fault. And they will not be asked to take sides in the conflict. They will not have to view either parent as "the bad guy."

Understanding our true motives, the goal of question 1, is the key to successfully navigating the delicate balance between helpful and harmful criticism. But it is easy to fool ourselves. We can shrink our awareness of malevolent intentions by hiding them behind noble-sounding rationalizations. Alice Miller has shown how parents heap even the worst abuses on their children while telling them, "This is for your own good."

To get beyond such rationalizations, it will be helpful to review the malignant motives discussed in chapter 4. Ask yourself whether any of these could be influencing your decision to portray your ex or a grandparent in a negative light. It may help to discuss your intentions with a friend whom you can trust to be objective. Be honest. Instead of quickly dismissing the likelihood of ulterior motives, stretch your awareness to detect even the hint of their presence. These efforts will pay off. The more we are in touch with our true feelings, the more control we have over their expression. When we surrender this control, we are more likely to act destructively and sabotage our children's relationships with loved ones.

Divorce is one of life's most painful passages. It is painful for the spouse who wants it, painful for the spouse who feels rejected, and painful for the children.

We can understand and empathize with the spouse who feels

wronged and wants revenge, or the spouse who is overwhelmed with anxiety at the thought of losing the children, or the spouse who prefers to forget that the marriage ever was. But using the children to get revenge, to cope with anxiety, to erase the past, is unacceptable. Parents must hold themselves to a higher standard. They must have the courage to face what they are doing to their children. They must honor their mission to safeguard their children's welfare, even when the darkest feelings beckon them to dim their awareness of their betrayal of their children. Divorce poison must be left in the bottle. Children deserve no less.

CHAPTER 2

BAD-MOUTHING, BASHING, AND BRAINWASHING

I can see that your head
Has been twisted and fed
By worthless foam from the mouth.
—BOB DYLAN, "TO RAMONA"

Divorce poison comes in different concentrations. In mild form it consists of occasional blaming and bad-mouthing. In its more potent form it constitutes full-fledged brainwashing. Each requires a different antidote. An effective response to bad-mouthing will be ineffective in the face of brainwashing.

BAD-MOUTHING

The period immediately before and after the marital separation is usually the most volatile time in the divorce process. It is the time children are most likely to witness each parent laying blame on the other. You or your spouse may be so tempted to demean each other that you find it difficult to restrain yourself around the children. At times you may speak directly to them. More often, though, your children will overhear hostile communications not intended for them.

Ellen felt so betrayed by her husband's affair that she felt compelled to tell everyone what a louse he was. For a period of about two weeks she bad-mouthed him, often within earshot of her preschool son. Then one day, while her son was playing with his action figures, Ellen overheard him call the bad guy "a worthless piece of trash." This was the exact phrase Ellen repeatedly used to describe his father. In that instant she realized how her bad-mouthing was affecting her son, and Ellen resolved to be more careful about what she said when he was around.

Preoccupied with their own distress, recently separated parents find their anger and anguish pressing for expression to sympathetic listeners—friends, relatives, and attorneys. Like Ellen, they sometimes overlook the fact that their children are also listening. If "little pitchers have big ears," never are their ears so big as during a family crisis. At these times, children's attention is inevitably drawn to adult conversations. They want both to hear and not to hear. They want to learn the details of their parents' struggles. So they collect bits of information like pieces of a puzzle, trying to assemble a clear picture of the turmoil surrounding them. But they don't like what they hear, and often attempt to bury it in the recesses of their minds.

A spouse or ex-spouse who is occasionally bad-mouthing you or your relatives but was previously very protective of the children's feelings may need someone to provide the type of jolt Ellen received when she overheard her son parroting her hostility. Of course, we can't expect your ex to be receptive to your advice. But perhaps you can enlist the support of someone he or she trusts: a relative, friend, member of the clergy, or therapist. This person should confront both parents with their obligation to protect the children from their conflicts. Sometimes, all that bad-mouthing parents need is to have their attention drawn to their destructive behavior. If they fail to recognize the harm in bad-mouthing, they should think about the fact that children identify with both parents. This means that children experience bad-mouthing of a parent as a personal attack. It is a put-down of that aspect of themselves that identifies with the maligned parent. This is one reason divorce poison diminishes your child's self-esteem. *Bad-mouth your ex and you simultaneously bad-mouth your child.*

If you are the target of occasional bad-mouthing, don't ignore it, but don't overreact. Comments such as "Mom ruined the family" may be an expression of pain by an ex who was emotionally unprepared for the divorce. When these sentiments resonate with your children's natural reactions to the divorce, it may seem as if your ex is deliberately drawing the children into an alliance against you. This is certainly one possibility, but you shouldn't assume that this is your ex's intention, or that the bad-mouthing will result in such an alliance.

Even if your children repeat something bad that your ex has said about you, don't assume that they are turning against you. Children often repeat such comments because they are troubling. Your children may be seeking help from you.

When you know your children have heard your ex bad-mouthing you, ask them how they feel about what they heard. Let them know that you understand how disturbing it was for them to hear such unkind words. Showing such empathy helps children face and express their feelings rather than deny and repress them. It gives them the sense that their pain can be understood and resolved rather than stored up to cause havoc in the future. If what they heard about you is true, even if it would have been better for them not to know, you have no choice but to acknowledge the facts. Let them know you are sorry they had to hear it. If they repeat things about you that are untrue, simply explain that their other parent is mistaken and clarify the reality. Explain that the harsh words were said in anger. Help them understand by calling attention to the many times in the past when they were angry and said something they didn't truly mean. Reassure them that things will probably get better in the future as everyone gets used to the divorce.

Most likely this will be sufficient if you are still in the early stages of your separation, if the bad-mouthing is occasional rather than frequent, and if the children maintain close to their usual level of affection and respect for you (some increase in anger and misbehavior is expected in the immediate aftermath of the separation). You can help them most by continuing to support their relationship with your ex while providing as much affection, attention, and understanding as you can.

Above all, don't retaliate. *The obligation to help children cope with bad-mouthing is not a license to bad-mouth in return.* Such behavior would merely multiply your children's distress. In fact, your best chance of reducing bad-mouthing may be to consistently acknowledge the specific things that your ex does for the children and express your appreciation. It is more difficult to bad-mouth someone who frequently says nice things about you.

If you become aware that you have been guilty of bad-mouthing, first acknowledge to your children that you made a mistake and then apologize. As with your ex's bad-mouthing, show empathy for the discomfort your remarks caused (e.g., "I'll bet that made you feel real bad when I said those mean things about Mommy.") and explain that the harsh words were said in anger.

Make it very clear that it would please you most if they did not let *your* anger interfere with their love and affection for the other parent. Tell them that they deserve to have two parents and two sets of extended families that they can love, and you want them to feel very free in showing that love. In fact, you *expect* them to show love and respect.

By labeling occasional bad-mouthing as "mild" I do not mean that children are unaffected by it. Unwelcome words always leave their mark. I will have more to say about this later in the book. But for now I would like my readers to observe the discomfort many children of divorce feel when in the presence of both parents. *Bad-mouthing kills spontaneous displays of affection as children inhibit their behavior toward one parent for fear of disappointing the other, or appearing disloyal.* They develop the guilty sense that they must keep their love for the maligned parent a closely guarded secret. This is what parents do to children when they fail to give them unconditional permission to love both of their parents.

Bad-mouthing can leave a more severe and lasting impression when the criticism is particularly harsh, the child is very young, and the parent makes no attempt to offset the impact of the ill-chosen words. One year after divorce, a rejected father told his four-year-old daughter that Mommy's boyfriend, Ira, was "sent by the devil." A year later the father had become resigned to the presence of Ira in his daughter's life, but he had never said anything to her about the "devil" comment. No apology. No retraction. No explanation. When her mother and Ira announced their engagement, the girl's first reaction was: "Daddy said Ira was sent by the devil." She was still clearly troubled by this. A single mean-spirited remark, made to a child at a very impressionable age, more than one year earlier, was enough to introduce an unwarranted wariness toward her future stepfather. This example, though, is the exception to the rule. In general, infrequent bad-mouthing, while never good for children, does not create severe harm.

BASHING

Unfortunately, many parents go beyond occasional blaming and bad-mouthing. In these families, virtually everything the children hear one parent say about the other is a harsh, snide, or sarcastic put-down. When destructive criticism reaches this level, when it is particularly vicious and predominant, bad-mouthing is too mild a term to accurately describe the behavior. Instead, I call it "bashing."

If we think of infrequent bad-mouthing as occasional potshots in an otherwise demilitarized zone, bashing is an artillery barrage in an ongoing war. Neither situation is suitable for children, but the risk of injury is obviously much greater with bashing. When verbal attacks reach the level of bashing, they leave a trail of emotional carnage.

A few children find a way to withstand the onslaught. How do they cope? It has a lot to do with the conclusions these children draw about their parents' irrational behavior. How we think about a situation makes a big difference in how it affects us. The same is true for children.

Take the case of two brothers whose alcoholic father beats them regularly. Both boys become accustomed to their father's outbursts; they regard them as unwelcome, fearful, yet inevitable events in their lives. The first brother, despite his anger and protests, believes, at some level of consciousness, that his father is acting appropriately. He concludes that he is a bad boy, worthy of his father's harsh treatment. The thought that his father is actually irrational and out of control is just too frightening to entertain. The boy prefers to accept the blame for his father's behavior, rather than face the unsettling reality that he is living with a parent whose behavior makes no sense.

The second brother understands that his father's punishments are not warranted. Most important, he believes that the punishments are a reflection of his father's disturbance rather than an index of his own worth. This boy concludes that his situation is terribly unfortunate and he tries to keep out of his father's way as much as possible. And he vows to treat his own children better when he becomes a father. The two brothers draw different conclusions as a result of exercising different levels of awareness and courage in facing harsh realities.

Similar considerations apply to children exposed to bashing. All children dislike the behavior and wish it would stop. Many try not to think about the bashing. Usually they develop troubling conflicts in their feelings about their parents and about themselves. But a few children seem unaffected. They remain in touch with the reality of their parent's behavior. If asked, they will tell you that the behavior is disturbed and wrong. They usually discuss the bashing in a matter-of-fact tone. They dislike it but accept the fact that they are powerless to change it. They take it in stride.

Curiously, they maintain a positive regard for *both* parents. They recognize that the bashing parent has a major problem when it comes to the target, but they dismiss it as a mental aberration in an otherwise sane parent whom they continue to love. Older children may occasionally defend the target of the bashing. But most learn that life is easier if they keep their expressions of affection for the target out of earshot of the bashing parent. All the while, they maintain an undiminished love for the target of the bashing.

Unfortunately, these children are in the minority. I believe that most children are unable to cope in this manner without adult assistance. Most are unable to perform the mental gymnastics that allow them to retain love for both parents while escaping substantial compromises in their psychological development. Even those who appear to be coping well are not necessarily free from suffering and harm caused by exposure to bashing.

If your children understand that the bashing is unjustified, help them understand that this is an adult problem. It is not their job to correct the parent doing the bashing or to defend the target of the bashing. Let them know that you will understand their reluctance to show affection for you in the presence of their other parent. Assure them that you will always know they love you, even when they do not show it.

Teach the children how to accept the reality of the bashing rather than pretend it does not exist. The healthiest stance is to adopt a matter-of-fact attitude. The bashing exists. It is irrational. It is unpleasant. And they can't do anything about it.

Compare the bashing episodes to thunderstorms. We do not like being exposed to rain, thunder, and lightning, but we do not deny their unpleasant reality. If we pretended the storm did not exist we would do nothing to protect ourselves. Instead we accept the fact of the storm's existence and its inevitability. We also accept that we are powerless to control the storm. We ease our fear through better understanding of the phenomena. And we protect ourselves by taking cover, or removing ourselves from the storm's path.

In the same manner children can tell themselves, "Uh-oh, Dad's at it again. Let's get out of his way and find something else to do until the storm blows over."

If you are the target of bashing, you must respond in a knowledgeable and effective manner. If you fail to do so, you may be allowing an even more harmful process to take root.

BRAINWASHING

Bashing becomes more destructive when it continues unchecked, it is repetitive, and the children are programmed, through a variety of techniques, to join in the vilification of a parent, grandparent, or other relative. At this point it becomes brainwashing.

You might think that brainwashing is too strong a term to apply to your own family's situation. But if your children are turning against you with the support and encouragement of their other parent—if they are withdrawing or expressing fear or hatred that is unjustified by anything you have done—the term *brainwashing* aptly describes what is happening to them. As we will see, the conditions that foster children's estrangement, and the techniques that parents use to poison their children's relationships, have much in common with the type of mind control that we usually think of in regard to brainwashed prisoners of war and members of cults. Parents who are the target of brainwashing can easily describe the changes in their children's responses to them. It is as if the children have become different people.

Every brainwashed child once expressed love and affection for the target of brainwashing; once felt safe with, looked forward to seeing, even craved attention from the target. Every such child had a history of gratifying memories that bound the child to the target. All of that is gone—disconnected from the child's thoughts, feelings, and behavior. In its place is a child who spouts only fear and hatred for the formerly loved adult; a child who recalls few of the good times, and defensively dismisses those that are recalled with some version of "I was just pretending to enjoy myself with you."

The story of how this egregious transformation takes place is told later in the book. In chapters 5 and 6 we see how bad-mouthing and bashing, in concert with certain critical conditions and tactics, if not understood and stopped, will likely result in relationships that are at best tainted, and at worst totally lost. We describe these damaged relationships as alienated.

But here we must proceed with caution. For not everything that looks like alienation is alienation. And alienation is not always the result of bad-mouthing, bashing, and brainwashing. If you have accused your ex of fostering alienation in your children, or you have been accused of this yourself, these distinctions become crucial to your case.

PARENTAL ALIENATION SYNDROME

Tina was shocked and angry when her ex-husband filed a motion to deprive her of custody of their son, Vince. Wesley accused Tina of brainwashing Vince. He claimed that, as a result of Tina's mistreatment, the boy suffered from a disturbance known as parental alienation syndrome. After Tina spoke with her attorney, she was worried. Her attorney told her that the judge might transfer custody to Wesley if a mental health expert diagnosed Vince as exhibiting this syndrome.

Tina had unwillingly become caught up in a storm of controversy that has been brewing for several years among divorce lawyers and therapists. At the center of the storm is a distinguished and creative child psychiatrist by the name of Richard A. Gardner, M.D.

In 1971, Dr. Gardner wrote *The Boys and Girls Book About Divorce*, the first book on divorce written for children. Its honest and engaging style, and its practical solutions to the most common dilemmas that children of divorce face, made it an instant hit among critics, parents, and children. It was featured in *Time* magazine and *The New York Times Sunday Magazine*, is now in its twenty-eighth printing, has been translated into six languages, and is considered a classic in its field. Dr. Gardner has since published forty-two more books for parents, children, and therapists, and his therapeutic techniques and games have become standard tools for child psychotherapists.

After all this acclaim, how did this respected doctor become a controversial figure? In the 1980s Dr. Gardner began seeing more cases of severe divorce poisoning that arose during child custody disputes. In some of these families, the children joined forces with one parent to denigrate the other parent. As Dr. Gardner worked with these families, he noticed certain similarities among children who rejected a parent. Many, for example, expressed hatred not just toward a parent but toward the parent's entire family. Most would give trivial or absurd explanations for why they now hated people they formerly loved. "Mom embarrassed me at Little League practice," said one child, "when she sprayed us with stuff that kills bugs."

Because these children shared a common pattern of behaviors that was related to their rejection of a parent, Dr. Gardner introduced a term to describe their disturbance. He called it parental alienation syndrome—PAS for short. Dr. Gardner's detailed account of the origin, course, and manifestations of the phenomenon, along with his guidelines for intervention by courts and therapists, has captured the attention of the mental health and legal professions. Even Gardner's critics acknowledge that his formulation of PAS has brought a great deal of attention to the problem of alienated children. The term has made it easier for therapists throughout the world to communicate about the disturbance and to propose strategies to help PAS children and their families.

Some therapists, however, object to the label PAS. Indeed, some mental health professionals oppose the use of any diagnostic terms for family disturbances. They agree that parents sometimes poison their children's affections for the other parent. They agree that many of these children previously enjoyed a healthy loving relationship with the parent they now reject. They even agree on the behaviors that characterize alienated children. But they do not believe that this disturbance warrants a separate label or the term "syndrome." And they fear that the term will be misused in court. More than other newly proposed diagnoses, PAS has provoked great controversy. Readers interested in a detailed analysis of this controversy will find more information on my website: www.warshak.com.

When Dr. Gardner first wrote about PAS, he saw more mothers than fathers who were programming their children against the other parent. This became one source of controversy. Critics attacked the doctor as being against mothers. These attacks continue, despite the fact that Dr. Gardner has often testified on behalf of women, and despite his position that changes in divorce practices have now resulted in as many fathers as mothers who foster PAS.

Some critics believe that PAS unfairly holds one parent responsible for a problem that has many facets. As we will see in the next chapter, some children become alienated as a result of several factors, with no one element predominating over the others. A therapist who understands PAS would not use the term to describe this type of alienation. When a child's alienation is independent of divorce poison—when it would have occurred without the influence of the favored parent—this is not a valid case of PAS. Other critics fear that men whose own behavior has pushed away their children will shirk responsibility for the problems and instead blame their wives. These women must then defend themselves against false allegations of promulgating PAS. If the court holds the mother responsible for the children's poor relationship with their father, she could lose custody, just as Tina feared. PAS experts, including Dr. Gardner, apply the term only to children who reject a parent without justification and under the influence of the other parent. But therapists with a poor understanding of PAS may recommend placing children in the custody of a parent whom they have good reason to reject.

More than one hundred articles have been published by professionals who, like Dr. Gardner, see PAS in their practices. The scientific community, though, still awaits the extent of research that will determine whether the problem should be labeled a "syndrome" and whether it will take its place in the official manual of diagnoses. Until then, experts will continue to disagree about the use of this term. Many parents, though, find it reassuring to learn that therapists are aware of the problem and working to develop effective treatments. A recent E-mail from a mother expressed this attitude: "I didn't even know there was an official name for what was happening until this had gone on for two years. It must have taken ten lawyers before I found one who told me what was going on. Plus, I was blindsided by my divorce and could not believe Dad would stoop so low, especially since he's an educator. I was just way behind from the get-go." Another mother wrote: "It has been such an eye-opener to read about this. I had felt so alone for so long. I knew what was going on but had no way to prove it. I just now have learned about PAS."

One of the advantages of a term like *PAS* is that it is brief and much less cumbersome than the phrase "children who are irrationally alienated as a result of divorce poison" or "alienated children who previously had a good relationship with a rejected parent." For this reason, if you occasionally see the term in this book, please understand that it refers only to children whose alienation is clearly and primarily the result of divorce poison.

I share others' concerns about the misuse of the term *PAS* and take this up next. Misdiagnosis is not unique to PAS. All mental health disturbances can be and often are mistakenly dignosed. The solution is not to abandon diagnoses; it is to better educate the people who use them. In chapter 3, "Alienated Children," I discuss in greater detail how to identify irrational alienation accurately and how to recognize when it is misdiagnosed. But I do not want us to get too preoccupied with the label. Even PAS critics agree that divorce poison often damages parent-child relationships. Regardless of what we call it, the disturbance exists and it is serious.

CHILDREN WHO RESIST DIVORCE POISON

Some children are easily drawn into what Dr. Janet Johnston and Dr. Linda Campbell call "unholy alliances" with a parent. Other children resist pressure to join in their parents' battles and instead maintain a steadfast refusal to take sides. Can you predict if your child will be immune to attempts to poison her relationship with you? Not with 100 percent certainty. But certain factors do increase the odds in your favor.

The formula for predicting success in resisting alienation has four key components:

1. The environment and manner in which the bad-mouthing, bashing, and brainwashing takes place

2. Your prior relationship with your child

3. Specific characteristics of your child

4. Your response to divorce poison

1. The Habitat of Alienation

Of the four protective factors, this is most central. Divorce poison is easiest to neutralize when three conditions are met:

-   The child remains in sufficient physical contact with the target

-   The child maintains a psychological connection with the target

-   The child is not excessively afraid of the alienating parent

These conditions make it easier for a child to resist becoming alienated, and make it easier to help a child overcome alienation that has already occurred. When these conditions are absent, divorce poison has a much greater chance of taking root and crowding out loving memories. Chapter 5, "The Alienating Environment," explains exactly how physical isolation, psychological dependence, and fear lay the groundwork for brainwashing, and how you can protect your children.

2. Prealienation Relationship

It would be only fair if a long history of a tender relationship with a loving, involved, understanding parent insulated your child from divorce poison. Unfortunately, it does not work this way. A child may be willing to denigrate the parent whose love is easily granted, in exchange for conditional acceptance from a parent who was previously uninvolved or harshly punitive and rejecting. A child who fears a parent may become that parent's willing ally in order to avoid the parent's wrath. A child who felt neglected by a parent may welcome that parent's newfound interest and generosity rather than recognize or acknowledge that the parent is attempting to buy his child's allegiance through overindulgence. A child may feel obliged to show loyalty to an emotionally fragile parent, even when that means participating in a war against the other parent. These are just some of the reasons why placing children in the middle of their parents' battles can demolish even the best parent-child relationships.

Parent-child relationships are particularly vulnerable when children are first informed of the impending separation, or when one parent actually leaves the home. If your spouse manipulates the children to blame you for the divorce, or to believe you have abandoned them, affection can dissolve overnight as their distress and hurt feelings are channeled into hatred. The risk becomes multiplied if, for any reason, you have no communication or contact with the children after you leave the home. This keeps you from reassuring the children of your love and helping them understand that they do not have to choose between their parents.

By now it should be clear that a close relationship with your child offers no guarantee against alienation. Nevertheless, it may improve the odds in your favor. It stands to reason that it will be easier to turn a child against a parent who has been relatively uninvolved than against one who has been extremely involved. It will be easier to turn a child against a parent who usually disregards her children's feelings than one who is usually empathic. Children are less likely to resist efforts to turn them against a parent with whom they are already angry or distant. And there are some children whose love and trust in a parent runs so deep that it renders divorce poison impotent. For these reasons, notwithstanding the observations made above, I regard a history of a warm, positive, mutually affectionate parent-child relationship as a protective factor against alienation.

3. Children Predisposed to Alienation

Certain characteristics in children may make alienation less likely. In general, the better the child's psychological development, the better able she will be to maintain affectionate relationships with both parents. It is easier to make a child afraid of the target when the child is fearful by nature.

A child who has confidence in her own judgment, who is used to thinking critically and independently, will resist attempts at manipulation. She will remain aware of her own experiences. When one parent bad-mouths the other, she will trust her own perceptions rather than automatically absorb the alienating parent's view.

Nine-year-old Karen told her therapist, "My mom is so mad at Dad. She's always telling me how bad he is and that she's sorry I have him for a father. I know she wants me to be mad at him too. But he's really a nice dad. I have fun with him. He taught me how to ride a bike. He coaches my soccer team. All my friends like him too. I don't know why Mom hates Dad so much, but that's her problem. When she starts going on about how bad he is, I just ignore her. Sometimes I go to my room or go outside and play. It usually doesn't last long. I wish she would stop, because it's really embarrassing. But she's not gonna get me to say he's a bad daddy. I know better."

Karen's attitude reveals an exceptionally high level of self-esteem, a hallmark of a psychologically healthy child. In *The Art of Living Consciously*, Dr. Nathaniel Branden, a leading authority on self-esteem, advises, "Parents who love their children with wisdom and not merely with feelings encourage independent, critical thinking. They teach them that the unexamined idea is not worth holding." This type of parenting not only inoculates children against divorce poison, it helps them resist any attempt to bypass their rational faculty, whether from a peer encouraging drug use or a politician spouting propaganda. Karen's parents treated her in this manner prior to the separation. It is one reason Karen could display such a healthy response when her mom bad-mouthed her dad. Like many otherwise benevolent and sensible people, though, Karen's mother sometimes lost her perspective, showed poor judgment, and abandoned good parenting practices under the pressure of the anxi-ety, hurt, and anger triggered by divorce.

Children who are overly dependent or too close to a parent will be more susceptible to that parent's negative attitudes about the other par-ent. I once worked with a boy who was so dependent on his mother that at the age of ten he was still calling her into the bathroom to wipe him after he defecated. Even during the marriage, this boy and his mother often teamed up against the father. When the father finally had enough of his unrewarding marriage and called it quits, the boy refused all con-tact with his father. His mother saw nothing wrong with this, and instead labeled the father's attempts to see his son as "harassment."

By discussing traits in children that protect or predispose them to alienation, I do not mean to imply that we should hold children fully responsible for their alienation. Though it is important to learn how we can guide children to resist divorce poison, we must not lose sight of the fact that the children are victims.

Some experts believe that younger children are more resistant to alienation than older children because they cannot be relied upon to sus-tain a consistently negative stance toward the target. Once they leave the orbit of the programming parent, they "forget" that they are supposed to be afraid of or angry with the target parent. Although this may be true of some children, as a general rule this has not been my experience. In fact, research confirms the commonsense notion that younger children are generally more malleable than older children. It is easier, for example, for a parent to implant false memories of abuse in younger children. Once these take hold, the child may be quite resistant to any overtures from the alleged abuser. On the other hand, research by Dr. Judith Wallerstein and Dr. Joan Kelly found that children between the ages of nine and twelve years are most likely to join forces with one parent against the other. This is clearly an area in which more research is needed before drawing any firm conclusions. Perhaps readers of this book will assist by letting me know of their own experiences.

4. The Burden of the Rejected Parent

When children begin to show signs of succumbing to divorce poison, the target parent's reactions may play a crucial role in determining the ultimate outcome. Parents who practice the advice given earlier in this chapter will improve their children's chances of resisting alienation. They must exercise self-restraint and show empathy for the children's feelings despite their obnoxious and belligerent behavior. But they must also do everything possible to maintain contact with the children. To increase the chances of reversing alienation, follow these seven rules, which are described in greater detail in chapter 7, "Poison Control":

1. Don't lose your temper, act too aggressive, or harshly criticize your children.

2. Don't counterreject your children by telling them that if they don't want to see you, you don't want to see them.

3. Don't passively allow the children and your ex to dictate the terms of your contact with them. Don't wait patiently until the children feel "the time is right" for them to see you. Alienated parents learn too late that the time is never right.

4. Don't spend your time with the children trying to talk them out of their negative attitudes. Engage in conflict-free, pleasurable interaction instead.

5. Don't dismiss the children's feelings or tell them that they're not really angry or afraid of you. Although this may be true, the children will merely feel that you don't understand them.

6. Don't accuse the children of merely repeating what the other parent has told them. Again, although this may be true, the children will vehemently deny it and feel attacked by you.

7. Don't bad-mouth your ex.

It is important to keep in mind that target parents generally have had no prior experience dealing with this degree of disrespect and rejection from their children. In some ways, the difficulties alienated children present are similar, though more intense and unexpected, than the difficulties teenagers present when they begin to devalue their parents. It is the rare parent who grasps the process of alienation early enough to avoid all the mistakes listed above. Most target parents benefit from specific coaching on how to respond effectively to divorce poison.

CHAPTER 3
ALIENATED CHILDREN

How sharper than a serpent's tooth it is to have a thankless child.
—William Shakespeare, *King Lear*

At age eleven, Jeremy was as close to his father as a boy can be. He told his sixth-grade teacher that he was going to attend his father's college, enlist in the navy, and then work for the State Department, just as his dad had done. Within two months of his parents' separation, Jeremy insisted that he hated his father and never wanted to see him again. His hatred spread like a virus to encompass everyone associated with his father. He didn't want to play with his cousins, and he rejected the grandmother who had been his favorite person in the world.

Divorce poison works fast—so fast that it catches target parents off guard, leaving them confused about exactly what is happening and bewildered about why it is happening. Learning about pathological alienation and the typical behaviors of alienated children helped Jeremy's father and his relatives understand exactly what they were up against. It was reassuring to know that others had similar experiences, and that the problem has been recognized and described by mental health professionals.

Experts disagree about how to label and treat this disturbance. Despite their differences, though, most experts agree that alienated children share certain traits and behaviors first identified by Dr. Richard

Gardner. Whether you are the target of attempts to poison the children's affection, or have been accused of making such attempts, it is essential that you become familiar with these characteristics.

THE HATE CAMPAIGN

This goes far beyond the usual type and amount of criticisms and complaints that children heap upon their parents. You will see a degree of contempt and cruelty reserved for one's worst enemies. The children treat the target parent as unworthy of even the smallest amount of regard and respect. Their obnoxious behavior commonly prompts others to remark that the children are acting like spoiled brats. One child poured soup over his father's head in a restaurant. Another child punished her mother by always ordering the most expensive item on a menu and then not eating any of it. Some of these children threaten to kill the parent. Formerly compliant children now scream profanities at the parent, confident that this will please their other parent, who will champion the children's "right to express themselves." In less extreme cases, children merely shun the target parents; they fail to greet them, avoid conversation and eye contact, and leave without saying good-bye. These can be easily recognized as signs of alienation because they represent abrupt departures from the child's usual behavior.

Normally, children who treat a parent with gross disrespect understand that they are violating acceptable manners and rules; they feel guilty for their transgressions. By contrast, alienated children engage in all sorts of sadistically cruel behaviors toward a parent without expressing the slightest bit of guilt. The children act as if they are entitled to receive material benefits from the target parent while treating the same parent with malice, disregarding his or her feelings, and exhibiting no gratitude for past or current contributions to their welfare. It is as if the parent has been relegated to a status of subhuman scapegoat and thereby fair game for any mistreatment. One study described these children as "pitiless in their condemnation."

TRIVIAL EXPLANATIONS FOR THE HATRED

Ask these children why they hate their parents and most cite common minor grievances that couldn't possibly account for the extreme turnabout in their feelings. "She's always telling me to brush my teeth," a little girl whined. "That's why I don't want to be with Mom." Alienating parents usually accept such complaints, though absurd, as reasonable explanations for why the child would not want to associate with the other parent.

"This letter is to inform you that I am not going to see you anymore. I don't love you anymore," a twelve-year-old girl wrote to her mother, with her father's support.

What did this mother do to lose her precious daughter's love? What horrible abuse did she visit on her child? The letter continued, "You don't respect me. You treat me like a baby. You don't care about how I think or how I feel."

Sound familiar? It will to every parent of a preteeen or teenager, or to anyone who remembers how she felt during those years. If such feelings were grounds for terminating parent-child relationships, all children in junior high school would be living on their own.

Unfortunately, therapists who are inexperienced in this area may accept the child's reasoning. In the case of our twelve-year-old letter writer, the court's social worker wrote a report that referred to this child as a "young adult" and castigated the mother for not treating her as such. The social worker recommended that the mother get counseling to learn how to deal with teenagers. What is frightening is that such reports wield great power over custody decisions in our courts. I do not know this social worker, but, given her overidentification with the child, I would not be surprised if she had some unresolved issues from her own adolescence. The result of her report was the complete cessation of the mother-daughter relationship. Seven years later this bereaved mother sought my help in reuniting with her estranged daughter.

To justify their wish to stop seeing a parent, children often recite a litany of that parent's past mistakes, errors in judgment, and minor personality weaknesses. They magnify the rejected parent's negative traits and behavior, and treat the parent as though he or she lacks any redeeming virtues. In an intact family, normal parents would consider it preposterous if their children wanted to disown a parent for such frivolous reasons. Prior to the onset of divorce poison, most alienated children showed respect and affection for both parents, regardless of the parents' alleged faults. Certainly, prior to the marital separation, no court would terminate parental rights based on the type of insignificant allegations lodged by alienated children. And no therapist would recommend that a parent give up her relationship with the children because of her children's complaints. Despite normal parent-child conflicts, children continue to sleep in their parents' home, have meals with parents, talk to parents, vacation with them, and so on. When children become alienated in the aftermath of their parents' separation, their explanations for the sudden and complete hatred or fear of the parent rarely make sense in light of their past history of treating that same parent with love and affection.

One of the most common excuses children give for rejecting a parent is that the parent refuses to accept the rupture of the relationship and continues to press for contact with the children. A father received the following letter from his thirteen-year-old daughter, "I do not wish to visit you at all this summer. The more you demand and force me, the stronger I will resist you. Every time you force me to go with you, I lose more respect for you. So now I wish to end my relationship, or what is left of my relationship with you."

A mother learned that her ex-husband and his new wife were planning to relocate to another part of the country with her daughter. When this mother sought legal help to prevent the move, the girl held this against her and refused any contact with her. Of course, these parents would not have to force contact if their children were not resisting it in the first place. But the children's circular reasoning casts the parents' refusals to accept alienation as the cause of, and excuse for, the alienation. Some children claim that they intend to renew contact with the alienated parent "when the time is right." From parents' bitter experiences I have learned that very often the time is never "right." Though some children try to reconcile after years of alienation, many do not. Either way, nothing can replace the lost years.

TAKE ACTION

Exercise self-restraint

Alienated children repay years of a parent's love, compassion, and hard work with the most unbelievably rude and obnoxious behavior. In the face of such abuse, it is natural to want to retaliate, to lash out physically or verbally against the children or the parent fomenting the behavior. DON'T. *Why?*

- Harsh punishment and angry exchanges will escalate hostility rather than relieve it.

- Remember that your children are being manipulated to serve as vehicles to express their other parent's hostility. Don't punish them for the sins of the alienating parent. ✳

- The children are primed to see you in a bad light and are looking for excuses to justify their rejection of you. Don't help them.

- Your punitive reactions and loss of temper will play directly into the hands of the alienating parent. Even one lapse of judgment can be raised repeatedly in court and exaggerated to create the impression that it is typical of how you mistreat your children. Your behavior will then be mistaken as the cause of alienation rather than an isolated, desperate reaction to it.

Maintain contact

When children repeatedly complain about being forced to see the alienated parent, many parents make the crucial mistake of telling them, in effect, "If you are so unhappy being here with me, stop coming. Return when you have a more positive attitude." Usually occurring in the early stages of alienation, this approach grows out of frustration and anger as well as an inadequate understanding of the potency of divorce poison. If your goal is to improve your relationship with your children, ceasing contact will not bring you any closer. *Why?*

- Maintaining contact is crucial for reversing alienation. We take this up in greater detail in chapter 5.

- Even when they seem to have no use for you, the children have a long history of depending on you for love and care. Surprisingly, if you counterreject them, on some level they will feel hurt and abandoned, and will channel their pain into more anger and alienation.

- Years later, children remember the perceived abandonment and blame the alienated parent for the ruptured relationship: "You said you didn't want to see us anymore."

- The absence of contact can be distorted in court to argue that you caused the alienation by your rejection of the children.

- As long as the children are dependent on the alienating parent, they may not be able on their own to resist divorce poison. When you lose contact with them, you lose the opportunity to help them escape or withstand the noxious environment. In too many families, when children are allowed to determine when to contact the alienated parent, they never see or talk to that parent again.

Develop a thick skin

To survive a campaign of hatred, you must learn to withstand high levels of verbal aggression and provocative behavior. If you allow yourself to feel crushed by the children's rejection, it will be very difficult for you to demonstrate the self-restraint and commitment necessary to see the problem through to a successful resolution. As in most interpersonal conflicts, you would be wise to remember that cooler heads prevail. Cultivate the habit of reminding yourself that the children who inflict pain on you are themselves victims. Like brainwashed soldiers and brainwashed cult members, your children's hostility is not fully their own. In a very real sense, they are not in their right mind.

Avoid getting drawn into a debate about the reasons for the hatred

It is tempting to dispute the rationalizations the children give for their newfound hatred. Resist this temptation and instead concentrate on having pleasant experiences with the children. *Why?*

- It is a debate you cannot win. The children believe their reasons are sound and will resent the implication that they are being absurd.

FALSE ABUSE ACCUSATIONS

Children who are irrationally alienated usually give trivial—even ridiculous—excuses for rejecting a parent. A small percentage of children, though, give reasons that are anything but trivial. These children launch what are known in family law circles as "the nuclear weapons" of custody litigation: accusations of physical or sexual abuse.

These accusations are so extremely powerful that they usually result in an immediate court-ordered ban on all normal contact between the accused and his or her children. When the children are true victims of abuse, the court's actions protect them from further harm. But *when the children have been manipulated to make false reports of abuse, the ban on contact intensifies alienation, sometimes striking the death blow to the relationship.*

Some people insist that children never make false reports of abuse. They are wrong. False reports do occur. They range from innocent misunderstandings to deliberate attempts to alienate children, sometimes in order to win custody.

A young child mentions that her father touched her "privates." Her mother becomes concerned enough to make a report to the proper authorities. An investigation reveals that the girl had just participated in a program at preschool intended to help children protect themselves against sexual abuse. The warnings of the instructor were still on the child's mind when her father bathed her that night and the result was the child's alarming report to her mother. When false accusations stem from such misunderstandings, the accusing parents do not want to believe that their children have been abused. They express relief upon learning that the abuse did not take place, and they willingly reestablish contact between the exonerated accused and the children. In these cases, the children generally do not become alienated.

The situation is entirely different when false accusations are made by children who are alienated as a result of divorce poison. In such cases the children generally have some of the other characteristics discussed in this chapter. Sometimes, but not always, the details of the abuse accusation stretch credulity. Even after investigations establish the innocence of the target parent, the children and the favored parent may cling to the charges of abuse.

Some children are aware that they are giving a false report. Either on their own, or with a parent's coaching, they have decided to lie. Other

alienated children magnify an isolated act of physical restraint or discipline into an accusation of physical abuse. And still others, through
repeated and suggestive questioning, are manipulated not only to make
false allegations of physical or sexual abuse but to actually believe they
have been victims of abuse. In other words, they are not consciously
lying. They believe their false stories.

The Genesis of a False Accusation

An award-winning book published by the American Psychological Association shows just how easily children can be manipulated to give false
accounts that bad things have happened to them. In *Jeopardy in the Courtroom*, Cornell University professor Dr. Stephen Ceci and his colleague Dr.
Maggie Bruck describe studies that reveal the type of conversations with
children that can lead to false allegations.

In one study children were simply asked to repeatedly think about
whether different events had ever happened to them, such as getting their
finger caught in a mousetrap and going to the hospital to get the trap off.
After ten sessions, more than half the children told false stories about fictitious events in their lives. In fact, their stories were so elaborately embellished with details that experts could not detect which events were real and
which were not. Even more remarkable, after the researchers told the children that the events never really happened, many of the children continued to insist that they remembered the fictitious events occurring. ABC
news correspondent John Stossel interviewed some of these children for
the show *20/20*. One four-year-old-boy had already been told by his parents that the whole mousetrap story was just in his imagination and that
nothing like this had ever happened. Yet when Stossel asked the boy if he
ever got his finger caught in a mousetrap, with his parents there beside
him, this child said he remembered the event and then gave a detailed
account. Stossel reminded him that his parents already said that it never
happened, but the boy protested, "It really did happen. I remember it!"

In another study, a stranger named "Sam Stone" visited a preschool
classroom. He said hello, walked around the room for two minutes, then
said good-bye and left. That was it. He touched nothing. During the next
ten weeks, the children were interviewed four times and asked to describe
Sam Stone's visit. One month following the fourth interview, another

adult interviewed the children, this time asking about two events which did not occur, "Did Sam Stone do anything to a book or a teddy bear?"

The investigators learned that they could produce false reports of Sam Stone's behavior both by bad-mouthing Sam Stone and by asking the children leading, suggestive questions. The bad-mouthing took the form of telling stories to the children, prior to Sam Stone's visit, about Sam Stone's clumsiness. For example:

You'll never guess who visited me last night. [pause] That's right. Sam Stone! And guess what he did this time? He asked to borrow my Barbie and when he was carrying her down the stairs, he tripped and fell and broke her arm. That Sam Stone is always getting into accidents and breaking things!

The day after Sam Stone's visit, the children were shown a soiled teddy bear that had not even been in the room during Sam's visit. They were asked if they knew how the teddy bear had been soiled. An example of a suggestive question was the following: "Remember that time Sam Stone visited your classroom and spilled chocolate on that white teddy bear? Did he do it on purpose or was it an accident?"

By the time of the final interview, an astounding 72 percent of the youngest preschoolers falsely incriminated Sam Stone. Like the children in the mousetrap study, they embellished their stories with fabricated details, such as reporting that they saw Sam Stone on his way to the store to buy chocolate ice cream. Once again, the children fooled the experts.

The investigators showed videotaped interviews of the children to specialists who interview children for purposes of criminal investigations and who treat children suspected of having been abused. These experts were confident in their judgments about which events really occurred and which were made up. But the experts were wrong. In fact, the very children they rated as most accurate were the children who were least accurate. Substitute Mommy or Daddy for Sam Stone and you begin to see how children can be manipulated to give convincing, yet false, negative reports about a parent.

False beliefs about abuse hurt children beyond the damage done by the alienation. A child who believes that she has been sexually abused by a relative can develop problems similar to those of a child who has actually suffered abuse. The child comes to distrust her caretakers in the same way she would if actually abused. Her view of sexuality is corrupted at an early age, and this may lead to problems in sexual adjustment as an adult. Her ability to trust in close relationships is impaired. This may interfere with her relationships throughout her life.

Exploiting Abuse to Produce Alienation

Some cases are complicated because they involve both abuse and divorce poison. In these cases, a child has been abused in a parent's home. But the alienation that follows results more from the influence of the other parent than the abuse incident. Consider the following.

A divorced mother's date deliberately exposed himself to her young daughter. When the father learned of this incident, his first reaction was not concern for his daughter but outrage at his ex-wife. He saw this as an opportunity to exact revenge on his ex for leaving him. Even though she had no more contact with the perpetrator, the father took her to court to try to restrict her access to their child. He argued that his daughter was now afraid to see her mother. To support this position, he tried to convince the girl that her mother's house was unsafe and that her mother was unable to protect her from bad things. Rather than help his child move past the unfortunate episode, he exploited the episode. He repeatedly brought it up, acted as though she was irreparably damaged by the isolated incident, and did all that he could to keep it fresh in her mind.

By the time the court evaluator interviewed the child, she was certainly alienated from her mother. But the father's negative behavior played a much larger role in the alienation than the interaction with her mother's date. The mother had the good fortune to be assigned a custody evaluator who looked beyond the father's explanation and recognized that the child's rejection of her mother was not reasonable or normal. Because the abusive incident was not typical of the environment provided by this mother, the evaluator recommended no change in custody. Another evaluator might well have assumed that the child's alienation was justified and that the child's reluctance to be in her mother's home deserved respect and accommodation. In such a case, the professional might have recommended extremely restricted contact between mother and daughter to take place in an artificial, court-supervised setting. The complicated nature of so many of these cases dictates the need for specialized expert examinations of all children who report abuse.

In some cases, although children have no direct experience with abuse, they have witnessed physical altercations between their parents. As tensions heat up in a deteriorating marriage, isolated acts of domestic violence, unfortunately, are all too common. These frighten children. If they perceive one parent as the aggressor, their sympathies will naturally lie with the other parent.

Let us suppose that a husband and wife's argument escalates to the point of mutual shoving, grabbing, and pushing. Each receives minor bruises. The wife calls the police, who come to the home and ask the husband to leave for the night. The children have had ringside seats to the entire shameful spectacle.

It is now up to the mother to talk to the children about the incident. She can express her regret that they had to see their parents acting in this manner. She can remind them that this is not typical of how their parents behave. She can reassure them that they will be seeing their father very soon, that the hostility is between the parents and does not involve the children, and that both parents love them very much.

Or the mother can exploit the incident in a bid to gain the children's alliance with her and against their father. She can send the message that, because she is so angry with their father, they should be too. She can exaggerate the severity of the aggression. She can speak about their father as a violent man from whom they all need protection. She can make the children afraid to see him again.

Even without the mother's programming, the children's reunion with their father is apt to begin awkwardly. If he handles the moment with sensitivity to their feelings, before long their relationship is back to normal. But if the children are out of contact with their father for a prolonged period of time, they are more likely to adopt their mother's viewpoint. Their last contact with their father will leave a disproportionate imprint on their thoughts and feelings about him. Love and comfort built up over years of living together will be erased by an isolated incident that lasted a few minutes. In such a case, the children will cite the episode of domestic violence as the reason for their hatred and fear of their father. A careful investigation, though, will reveal the mother's role in fostering the alienation. As we will see later in this chapter, the situation is very different when domestic violence has been chronic. In such families children may develop an aversion to a violent parent that is reasonable and would not qualify as pathological alienation.

Responding to Children's Reports of Abuse

I must emphasize that reports of child abuse need to be taken seriously. Adults abuse children at an alarming rate and our society has historically been reluctant to acknowledge the problem. Some of this abuse undoubtedly occurs in families with high levels of parental animosity. It would be a serious mistake, then, to automatically dismiss reports of abuse merely because they emerge during acrimonious divorce disputes.

This point merits emphasis. We should not assume that all children in divorced families who allege abuse and reject the alleged abuser are acting under the influence of divorce poison. Children who actually are treated cruelly or witness a parent's repeated and excessive violence or out-of-control behavior have good reasons to avoid contact with the perpetrator. This should never be confused with alienation resulting from divorce poison. In one case, the responsibility for alienation lies with alienated parents whose own behavior has pushed away their children. In the other case children's alienation is aided and abetted by the favored parent. In both cases, the guilty parties may shirk responsibility for their children's alienation and blame the other parent. But no therapist who truly understands the type of alienation being discussed in these pages would mistake the two situations.

TAKE ACTION

When a child makes a claim of abuse, as soon as possible seek a professional evaluation of the child, the alleged perpetrator, and the person to whom the child reported the incident. The more time that elapses between the original report and the professional examination, and particularly the more times a child has talked with an adult about the incident, the more likely that the accuracy of the child's report will be suspect. Including all parties to the allegation allows the evaluator to investigate more of the factors that will help determine whether or not the child's report is likely to be accurate. The evaluator should have experience with abused children and with irrationally alienated children. It is best if the initial evaluation is videotaped, with the camera capturing both the interviewer and the child. A videotaped evaluation will allow other experts who may subsequently become involved to reach opinions about the accuracy of the child's report without subjecting the child to a series of examinations. The videotape will also reveal the extent to which an examiner has used or avoided suggestive and coercive interview techniques that could taint a child's ultimate credibility and testimony. (Parents should not conduct their own taped interviews of their children.)

POLARIZING PARENTS: SAINTS AND SINNERS

"I don't want you to have any part in my life because everything in my life has been good except when you have forced me to go with you," a ten-year-old boy told his father.

Ordinarily children have mixed feelings about their parents. They like certain things; they don't like others. Even children who have suffered abuse from a parent can think of positive things to say about the abuser and have some good memories of better times spent with that parent.

When a child has been poisoned against a parent, that parent is all bad in the child's mind. By contrast, the other parent is all good. In any conflict between the favored parent and the target parent, the children automatically take the side of the favored parent. These situations bear a striking resemblance to the behavior of a racial bigot who is primed to believe anything negative about members of the hated race. Alienated children uncritically accept every allegation the favored parent makes against the other parent, even when there is obvious contradictory evidence. One mother told me that her ex moved their daughter to another country in order to keep the mother from seeing her child. After years of being brainwashed, the girl actually accused the mother of moving away.

TAKE ACTION

Expose the children to people who treat you with positive regard. When you are with your children, spend time with others who treat you with respect and affection. Especially try to surround yourself with other children, such as nieces and nephews, who demonstrate their love. Observing other people valuing you will help offset the exclusively negative image held by your children. Also, it will be more difficult for the children to maintain their rudeness in an environment that regards such behavior as aberrant. As a result of wanting to fit in, the children may begin to treat you better. In turn, positive behavior can awaken positive attitudes.

PARROTING ADULTS

Not only do the children endorse every complaint made by the favored parent, they incorporate the parent's words into their own descriptions and catalog of complaints. This is most obvious when the language goes far beyond the child's normal vocabulary and understanding, or expresses attitudes that are decidedly unchildlike. When asked why she did not want to see her father, one five-year-old explained, "He buys me too many toys. He's just trying to spoil me." A six-year-old boy complained about his mother, "She keeps violating my privacy."

DECLARATION OF INDEPENDENCE

Even when using adult language, alienated children never recognize that their hatred is the result of manipulation. They resent any suggestion that their opinions are influenced by the other parent. In this respect they are like adolescents who emphasize their independence while wearing exactly the same clothes as all their friends. "No one told me what to say" is a popular refrain.

Older children appreciate that a parent's bad-mouthing could meet with disapproval from outside observers, such as a therapist or judge. Although these children do not believe their negative attitudes have been influenced by the favored parent, they nonetheless seek to protect that parent from criticism by denying that the parent has ever bad-mouthed the other parent. The children insist that their hatred and rejection is their autonomous response to the alienated parent's mistreatment.

I consulted in a Canadian case in which a psychologist asked a boy what his dad thought of his mom. The boy replied, "I have no idea. I never asked him." He was lying. Numerous taped phone calls caught the father bashing the mother in the most explicit and crude language and coaching his son to make false allegations against the mother. Moreover, the boy was well aware that his father was seeking to prevent the mother from ever seeing her son again.

Once the children are successfully poisoned, the offending parent may, in fact, tone down the bad-mouthing, confident that the goal has been accomplished. When the children object to seeing their other parent, the favored parent can then pay lip service to the importance of the children's relationship with the rejected parent. They claim either that they are helpless to change their children's negative attitudes or that they believe they must "respect" their children's choices.

Naive court-appointed evaluators who examine the children at this later stage of alienation mistakenly conclude that the children's rejection of a parent is indeed independent of the other parent's behavior or wishes. One therapist concluded that the children's rejection of their father was not influenced by the mother because, during an interview, the children expressed their hatred for their father without looking to their mother for cues.

TAKE ACTION

Resist the temptation to argue with your children about the origin of their criticisms of you even when they use exactly the same words your ex does. If you attribute their attitudes to your ex, whether or not they realize what they are doing (and many times they do not), they will feel dismissed. You will only incur further resentment. Instead, briefly acknowledge their complaints and then try to change the mood with a fun activity. Before the children can acknowledge that they have been influenced by their other parent they will need to understand the general concept of mental persuasion. Chapter 7, "Poison Control," describes a strategy you can use, preferably with the guidance of a therapist, to lay this groundwork.

HATRED BY ASSOCIATION

"I don't understand. What do you mean, 'He doesn't want to see his grandma ever again'?" The elderly woman was understandably bewildered. Her relationship with her eldest grandson had always been marked by mutual love, affection, and enjoyment, spared the ambivalence that characterizes children's relationships with parents. Now he wanted to have nothing to do with her, and she could not think of a single thing that she had done to warrant excommunication. What this grandmother thought must surely be a temporary aberration became an estrangement made permanent by her death a few years later.

Divorce poison delivers a cruel blow to the extended family. In what Dr. Richard Gardner calls the "spread of animosity," children regard as enemies not only the hated parent but everyone associated with that parent, including grandparents, aunts, uncles, cousins, and friends. As a result, children lose contact with one-half of their family and their heritage.

One of the key benefits to children of an extended family, especially grandparents, is that these people usually love and are loved with much less ambivalence than parents. They don't have to place as many restrictions on children and are usually delighted to see them. The result is that children normally have a reservoir of love for healthy grandparents that is undiluted by the frustrations that parents and children visit daily upon each other. Parents do well to support this unambivalent love, especially embattled divorced parents, because the grandparent-grandchild relationship may be the only one in which children experience themselves as a source of joy. I wrote about this in *The Custody Revolution* and feel strongly about it. My convictions are undoubtedly shaped by my own experiences growing up. Both my parents gave me the strong sense that my grandparents were to be accorded only love and respect. If my parents had criticisms of my grandparents, I never heard them. I checked with my older brother and his memory matches mine. Despite slight and infrequent frustration with my grandparents' minor and quite reasonable restrictions (no ball playing in the house; keep the noise level down), I never recall feeling anything other than love and affection for them. They were solid presences in my life—adored, respected, and venerated.

When divorce poison enters the equation, children face their grandparents with hatred or at least with a great deal of conflict about showing their love. Even when the result is not the complete loss of contact, the relationships are tainted with discomfort, hesitation, inhibition, and the loss of the specialness that comes with relatively unconditional positive regard.

The spread of animosity extends even to pets! I recall watching a videotape of a child who was described by her mother and her teachers as a sweet girl who loved animals. When the father's little dog sought her attention, this "sweet" child could not summon up even the slightest affection for this cute dog. The dog made repeated efforts to snuggle, and the girl rebuffed the dog, and even pushed the dog away. The dog clearly did not understand such irrational behavior, and continued repeatedly to seek affection. Like members of an alienated extended family, the dog must have wondered (if dogs can wonder) what he did to deserve such contempt. This video was a poignant testament to the extent to which everything associated with the target parent becomes tainted in the child's mind.

The spread of hatred is one of the best ways to distinguish between children who are the victims of divorce poison and those whose alienation is a response to mistreatment by the hated parent. Children who are severely abused by their fathers, for example, generally welcome the loving involvement of their father's relatives. Victims of divorce poison, though, act as if every relative of the hated parent has behaved in an equally offensive manner deserving of swift and total abandonment. In this respect the children are following the lead of the favored parent.

Some parents and professionals resist the notion that one parent can be primarily responsible for a child's alienation. They believe that both parents must play a significant role. I think the spread of hatred is the clearest indication that a child's alienation can be, and often is, independent of the behavior of the people being rejected. Very often the child goes from loving to shunning a relative without having had any contact with the relative in the intervening period. No one could attribute such alienation to the behavior of the relative.

One woman told me that shortly following her brother's separation from his wife, her nephew stopped speaking to her. The last thing he said to her was that his mother told him and his siblings that when they saw their aunt and uncle they no longer needed to kiss them or say hello because "they are strangers to you." As far as his mother was concerned they did not exist. His mother took the separation from his father as a reason to essentially declare war on the father's entire extended family, despite the close ties that existed between her children and their aunts, uncles, and cousins.

In a surprising number of families, divorce results in the total rupture of relations between an ex-spouse and the former in-laws. At first, the children shun the extended family in order to show loyalty to the favored parent. Over time, the children come to believe that the rejected family is truly deserving of contempt.

A boy in rural Kansas was raised by his paternal grandmother from the age of two to twelve, even though his parents were married for five of these years and lived next door. Four years after the divorce, when the boy's mother learned that her ex had a girlfriend, she began bad-mouthing the man and his entire family. She told her former mother-in-law that she wanted to have nothing to do with her anymore. The next time the boy visited his grandmother, he walked in the house without greeting her, kept his head down, avoided eye contact, and went straight to his room, where he stayed for several hours.

How do children justify rejecting their grandparents? In some cases they offer no reasons. The alienating parent decides to break relations with his former in-laws and the children merely follow suit. Often, though, children do give a reason for their negative opinion of their grandparents. They usually recall an episode in which the grandparents defended the alienated parent against the children's criticisms. After that, the grandparents were enemies.

Alienated children succumb to a type of tribal warfare. They categorize every relative as either ally or enemy. No one can be neutral. Failing to take a stand against the alienated parent is equivalent to siding with that parent against the other parent and the children.

In the typical scenario, the alienated parent has confided in her family that the children have been denigrating her. But not having seen it themselves, the family is ill prepared for the harshness of the children's negative attitudes and the dramatic change in their behavior. When the relatives witness it firsthand, they are appalled. They respond as they would to any other instance of the children acting rudely and disrespect-fully. They try to reason with the children and they reprimand them. When the children give trivial reasons for their newly acquired attitudes, the relatives dismiss these as ridiculous. If the children claim that they have been abused, they are called liars. In turn, the children feel misunderstood and they resent the implication that they are distorting reality.

The children respond by rejecting the relatives. Before they know what has happened, the relatives have lost the children's affection. In many cases that is the last time they ever see or speak to the children. *Alienation often strikes with vicious speed and little advance warning.*

One little girl said she didn't like Grandma anymore because

Grandma yelled at her for being mean to Mommy. The girl called her mother a retard and butthole and said that she didn't have to do anything her mother asked. Prior to the alienation this girl would have acted contrite after a reprimand from her grandmother for such obnoxious misbehavior. But the rules are different for alienated children. They have learned that they can get away with disrespectful behavior when it is encouraged and sanctioned by the other parent. When this girl told her father how Grandma reacted to her criticisms of Mommy, the father said Grandma didn't love them anymore and he would try to protect her from having to go to see her "mean" grandparents ever again.

This grandmother reacted naturally, but ineffectively, to her granddaughter's rude behavior. Many relatives of alienated parents make the same mistake. They fail to recognize that the alienated children and their favored parent are sitting in judgment of them. Relatives who defend the target are guilty of siding with the enemy. This places relatives in a difficult bind: To maintain a relationship with the children they are asked to agree that the target parent is not worthy of love and respect. But there is a way to escape this bind.

Strike While the Iron Is Cold

The first step calls for restraint. When the child is rude and hateful to the parent, you can say that you are sorry to see this. But don't try to "talk sense" into the children. Don't criticize them. Don't punish them for their obnoxious behavior toward the rejected parent. These types of well-intentioned reactions only serve to convince the children that you do not understand their position. They will conclude that your loyalty to the rejected parent blinds you to the gross mistreatment they are convinced this parent has inflicted on them.

Following a course of restraint is difficult for two reasons. First, the children may not accept your position of neutrality. They may insist on your explicit allegiance. Second, it is natural to feel a strong urge to defend the maligned parent. If you give in to this urge, however, the children will reject you and you will have lost the opportunity to influence them in a positive direction.

Restraint does not mean passivity. While avoiding confrontations about the alienation, you need to inoculate the children against the spread of animosity. Try to postpone any conversations about the alienation until you and the child are engaged in an enjoyable activity. Child psychiatrist Dr. Fred Pine calls this approach "striking while the iron is cold." Children are more receptive to our communications when they are in a good mood. At the right time, comment on how much fun you have together. Reminisce about past good times. Ask the child what her favorite time was with you in the past. Then ask her to tell you what made that time so much fun. Give your understanding of what she is saying and ask if you are correct: "So you enjoyed planting the flowers with me because I let you get your hands in the dirt and we laughed a lot." The purpose here is not merely to reinforce the good memories. It is to get the child to acknowledge the good times and give enough details so that it will later be more difficult for her to rewrite the history of the relationship and discount the fun she had in the past. Often, when confronted with the evidence of a better past relationship with the target, children give excuses such as "I was just pretending to have a good time" or "I only smiled in the picture because you made me" or "I only liked the trip to Disney World because Daddy [if Mom is the alienated parent] was there."

Once you have emphasized the good relationship you enjoy, let the child know that you are aware that she no longer likes her mom or wants to be around her, and add that you hope she doesn't stop loving you. If this is brought up before the hatred has spread, she will most likely protest that this could never happen.

The next step is to tell her that sometimes when parents are angry with each other they try to get their kids to take sides. Then tell her something like the following: "I'm afraid that because Dad is so angry with Mom right now, and you are so angry with Mom, that Dad may try to get you to be angry with me. What will you do if Daddy tries to get you to stop loving me?"

The basic idea is to help the child anticipate the pressure that might be brought to bear on her to renounce you, and then give her some tools to cope with the pressure. Preventing alienation is easier than reversing it. As with most of the advice in this book, it is preferable first to seek guidance from a therapist who understands these problems. In many cases, the helpful messages will be better received and more effective if they come from a therapist whom the child trusts.

The best coping tools depend on the specific circumstances. The child might simply observe to herself that the father is trying to manipulate her and remind herself that she can continue to love you. Or, if she is able to assert herself with her father without fear of his retaliation, she can defend her love for you and ask him to please stop trying to get her to dislike you. In general, it is best if children learn to tell their parents that they do not want to be placed in the middle of their battles. Dr. Gardner's classic book, *The Boys and Girls Book About Divorce*, might be helpful for children six years of age and older. The book advises children to think for themselves when it comes to their parents' criticisms about each other. One important caveat: Some children will experience the instruction to assert themselves in this manner as an additional and oppressive burden. This is another reason to enlist the aid of a therapist who might be able to work with the parents to help them understand their child's feelings and needs.

Create a Demilitarized Zone

If a child's alienation from a parent is severe, as a relative you must do everything possible to maintain some degree of affection with the child. A cordial relationship with the child gives you more leverage to help reverse the alienation. What this means is that you may have to bite your tongue when the children bad-mouth your relative until you can formulate a comprehensive plan along the lines suggested in chapter 7, "Poison Control."

Using this approach, you agree with the child that, because she feels so strongly about the alienated parent, you won't discuss that parent while the child is with you. You must avoid any hint of criticism of the favored parent. Such criticism will make it impossible for an alienated child to behave affectionately with you without feeling disloyal toward the criticized parent and fearing reprisals for "consorting with the enemy." Instead, concentrate on creating positive experiences with the child.

This does not mean that you will never try to actively reverse the alienation. It means that you are letting the child know that your home is a safe haven outside the battle zone. In your home the child is free to put aside the hostilities and simply enjoy your company. This allows you to maintain a positive connection with them that positions you to help reverse the alienation. Later in this book you will learn many subtle ways to chip away at this problem.

IS YOUR CHILD IRRATIONALLY ALIENATED?

Most professionals recognize that some children reject a parent for no good reason. Although professionals disagree about what to call this problem, they agree on the characteristics to look for in children suffering from this disturbance. If your child has several of the symptoms listed below (there is no exact cut-off), it is likely that she should be evaluated for pathological alienation. If her behavior does not conform to this list, then she is not exhibiting signs of irrational alienation.

- ☐ A campaign of hatred with no gratitude for the target parent's contributions

- ☐ No guilt for treating the parent with malice and disregarding the parent's feelings

- ☐ Trivial explanations for the hatred (or false allegations of abuse)

- ☐ Polarized views of parents: Instead of the ambivalence that characterizes normal human relationships, the children describe the alienated parent only in negative terms, can think of nothing good to say about that parent, and may have few, if any, positive memories of the parent. By contrast, in many cases the children regard the other parent as perfect.

- ☐ In any conflict between the favored parent and the target parent, the children automatically take the side of the favored parent, sometimes without hearing the target's response, and sometimes in the face of obvious contradictory evidence.

- ☐ Parroting adult language: The children's expressions echo those of the alienating parent and are often clearly beyond the children's normal vocabulary and understanding.

- ☐ Declaration of independence: The children profess that their rejection of the target parent is their own decision and that the other parent has exercised no influence or contribution to the alienation.

- ☐ Hatred by association: The child denigrates and rejects relatives, friends, even pets associated with the target parent, despite a previous history of gratifying relations.

ALIENATION WITHOUT DIVORCE POISON

Before proceeding further, we must be clear that divorce poison is not the only cause of alienation. Children can reject one parent when the other parent has done little or nothing to foster alienation. In some cases the alienation is justified. In other cases the alienation reflects a child's exaggerated response to a difficult situation.

> One cannot conclude, merely by knowing that a child is alienated from a parent, that brainwashing has occurred.

JUSTIFIED ALIENATION

Ever since Ira moved out of his house in a Chicago suburb, his two teenage daughters have refused to spend time with him. Ira blamed this on his wife, and hired a lawyer to defend his parental rights. The lawyer asked if I would help convince the court to force the girls to see their father.

After investigating the situation I told the lawyer that my testimony would not favor his client's position. I had learned that Ira suffered from a serious psychiatric disturbance. For years he had intimidated and behaved sadistically toward his wife and children. After Ira left, his wife hired an attorney, filed for divorce, and began to assert herself. The girls realized that they now had a chance to protect themselves from further abuse.

This was a case in which the children's alienation was clearly warranted by their father's behavior. They had good reasons for resenting and fearing him. In fact, Ira had become more volatile since the separation, due in part to the stress of living alone and the divorce litigation. I thought that Ira would need to make major changes before his daughters would reasonably want to renew their relationship.

Like many abusive parents, Ira was unable or unwilling to acknowledge his responsibility for the problems in his relationship with his children. Instead he accused his wife of poisoning the children against him. Although in some cases it is difficult to determine each parent's contribution to alienation, it was clear to me that Ira's daughters were not victims of divorce poison. First, there was clear evidence of Ira's abuse. Second, there was no evidence that Ira's wife did anything to undermine the girls'

affection for their father. And third, the girls lacked most of the characteristics of children who have been manipulated to turn against a parent.
They did not talk about their parents in black-and-white terms. In fact,
they were quite angry with their mother for being so passive and submis-
sive over the years and not protecting them better. Also, their rejection of
their father did not extend to his relatives. The presence or absence of the
spread of animosity is often the best way to discriminate between children who are suffering from divorce poison and those who are responding to genuine abuse. Victims of abuse generally maintain contact with
the abuser's extended family, unless the relatives defend the abuser. In
this case, Ira's parents had sympathy for their grandchildren and daughter-in-law and the girls maintained cordial contact with them.

Ira's relationship with his daughters was the sort of parent-child relationship that usually becomes alienated even in the absence of divorce.
As adults, children of such abusive parents learn to avoid their parents or
see them only under strictly limited circumstances.

Even when a parent does not physically or sexually abuse the children,
alienation can occur if the children witness domestic violence, frightening
displays of rage, or the aftermath of violence. Severe emotional abuse, neg-
lect, abandonment, or very poor treatment by a chronically angry, rigidly
punitive, intimidating, extremely self-centered, or substance-abusing parent can also result in alienation. In such cases, the children may not be
ready to cast aside their resentment merely because the parent has decided
to come back into their lives or treat them better.

The fact that children have good reasons for rejecting a parent does not
rule out the possibility that the favored parent also contributes to the alienation. Talk to child protection workers and you will learn that most abused
children never give up their quest for acceptance and love from the abuser. I
have seen this in my own work with many abused children. Some of these
children suffered acts of unspeakable cruelty that no person should have to
endure. Many had to be taken from their homes to protect them from further
harm. In the early stages of my career I was puzzled that so many of these
children wanted to return to the homes in which they were so severely mistreated. In fact, child protection agencies are reluctant to remove a child permanently from an abusive home if they believe a chance exists to improve
family functioning while ensuring the child's safety. The loss of a parent,
even an abusive one, is not taken lightly. When divorce poison enters the
equation, though, the favored parent may welcome the child's total repudia-

tion of the other parent. He or she never entertains the possibility of repairing the relationship and sparing the child the loss of the parent.

TAKE ACTION

The presence or absence of the spread of animosity is often the best way to discriminate between children who are suffering from divorce poison and those who are responding to genuine abuse. Abused children generally welcome love and affection from all sources, including relatives of the abuser who have caused them no harm.

CHILD-DRIVEN ALIENATION

Up to this point we have discussed alienation that results from the destructive behavior of parents: either the favored parent or the rejected parent. Some cases of alienation have less to do with the behavior of parents than with mistakes children make themselves. *Rejecting a parent may be a child's misguided way of coping with difficult feelings.*

Consider the case of a woman who endured years of suffering in an unhappy, conflict-ridden marriage. Following her divorce she fell in love with a man who lived in another state. He was unable to relocate his work and he did not want to move away from his two young children, so, when they married, the woman moved in with him. In what was the most difficult decision of her life, she agreed that her two teenage children could remain with their father so that they would not have to make all the adjustments required by a move: changing schools, giving up friends, living apart from extended family, joining new athletic leagues, finding new music teachers, and so on. She made arrangements to see the children during all school holidays, three-day weekends, and most of the summer.

Her son, Jeff, was not happy with this arrangement. He didn't want to move, but he was hurt and angry that his mother did. He felt rejected by her and complained that she put her own needs and those of her new husband ahead of those of her family. Why, he asked, was it more important that her husband live near his children than it was for her to live near hers? Of course, he had a point.

It became a serious problem, though, when Jeff's anger and disappointment in his mother snowballed into complete rejection. He refused to see her. He refused her phone calls. He deleted her E-mail. He ignored her on Mother's Day. He said he no longer would have anything to do with her.

Jeff's father tried to reason with his son. He talked about the close relationship the boy and his mother shared prior to her decision to move. He explained that in two years, when Jeff went off to college, he would be separated from his mother regardless of where she lived. The father reminded Jeff of the many things his mother did to show her love over the years. Jeff's dad supported the mother's right to find happiness and encouraged his children to have sympathy for her decision. Nevertheless, Jeff held stubbornly to his position that his mother's actions were inexcusable and that she no longer deserved his love and affection. He was adamant about having no more contact with her.

Given the history of their relationship, Jeff's sweeping condemnation and repudiation of his mother was unreasonable and was not shared by his sibling. Whether or not she did the right thing in moving away, she clearly did not deserve the degree of scorn and rejection coming from her son. And the father certainly was not contributing to the alienation. This is an example of what I call "child-driven alienation." It was not justified by the behavior of the rejected parent, and it was not promoted by the behavior of the favored parent.

There were no villains in this drama, only a child struggling with difficult feelings and seeking to assuage his disappointment by closing his heart.

In Jeff's case, further exploration of his feelings revealed that it was not so much his mother's move that was at the root of his complaints. Had his mother been offered a great job opportunity in another state, he might well have given his blessings to the move. Jeff was most upset about her remarriage. Like most children, he harbored a secret hope that his parents would reconcile. The remarriage dashed this hope. Psychotherapy helped Jeff form a more balanced view of his mother's behavior, and recover his love for her.

Parents' reactions can help alleviate or aggravate instances of child-driven alienation. Favored parents can do their best to counter their children's irrational attitudes. Or, if they are gratified by the children's anger at the other parent, they can passively accept their children's position and do nothing to improve the situation. Or they can welcome, approve, and reinforce their children's negative attitudes, thereby entrenching the alienation. In such a case the children may have their own reasons for being angry with a parent, but without the contributions of the favored parent, the anger would dissipate over time and not result in the total rupture of the relationship. In an intact family children get angry with their parents without rejecting them entirely. After a divorce, though, one parent may sanction the children's disowning the other parent. This may temporarily gratify the favored parent, but in the long run he or she must demonize the ex to justify the alienation or else face the fact that he has visited a terrible deprivation upon their children.

Target parents, too, can have an impact on child-driven alienation. The more they follow the seven rules discussed on page 38, the more likely rejected parents will recover their children's affection. The more they react with rigid, counterrejecting, insensitive behavior, the more likely their children's negative attitudes will harden and become permanent.

Exclusively child-driven alienation—those in which neither parent contributes significantly to the problem—is the least frequent path to parental alienation. In my experience, when it occurs, the most common triggers are a parent's relocation, remarriage, extramarital affair, or religious conversion of the parent or child.

Most instances of exclusive child-driven alienation involve older children. Younger children are more susceptible to their parents' influence. But teens often assume that their parents are stupid dolts whose opinion is worth less than that of a perfect stranger. Like Jeff, they will defend their mistaken beliefs rigidly and self-righteously while stonewalling their parents' attempts at persuasion. Also, children who are themselves adults at the time of their parents' divorce sometimes take sides in the dispute and refuse to have any further contact with the parent they blame for the divorce.

TAKE ACTION

If your alienated teen is unreceptive to parental input, ask a person whom your child respects to intervene. This can be a favorite relative, teacher, religious leader, coach, scoutmaster, the parent of one of your child's close friends, or even the friend himself. Teens often are more willing to entertain ideas that come from people other than their parents.

UNDERSTANDING THE ROOTS OF ALIENATION

When a child is severely alienated, we must identify the roots of the problem if we are to have the best chance of helping the child. This lets us know where to concentrate our efforts.

In many cases it is easy to determine when a child's alienation is primarily the result of the favored parent's influence, when it is a reasonable response to the alienated parent's mistreatment of the child, and when it is driven mainly by the child's own motives. In other cases, though, understanding the roots of alienation is complicated because there's a mixture of causes with no one clear primary element. Of course, this does not stop parents locked in a vicious custody dispute from blaming each other for their child's troubles. Frequently each parent accuses the other of brainwashing. It can be difficult to sort out each parent's contribution. Sometimes both parents are engaged in a battle for their child's mind and soul. Each is guilty of brainwashing in an effort to win the child's allegiance. But often one parent is more actively engaged in brainwashing. What looks like the other parent's brainwashing may be a frustrated reaction to alienation or a desperate or crude attempt to resist or reverse it.

Relief from alienation requires an understanding of all the contributing factors. The child may have her own motives, the rejected parent may be responding in a rigid manner that reinforces the negative attitudes, and the favored parent may be actively or passively supporting the rupture of the parent-child relationship. In addition to the actions of the parents and child, sometimes the circumstances of the marriage and divorce play a key role.

Problematic parent-child relationships during the marriage can pave the way for alienation when the marriage fails. The mother and child, for example, may have always had an overly close relationship that excluded the father. During the marriage the mother subtly undermined the father's authority or openly disparaged him. Following the separation, the father had trouble eliciting the child's respect.

In one family, sixteen-year-old Janet had been distant from her father for five years prior to the marital separation. Her dad, Gerald, was somewhat introverted, not very sociable, and not very warm. Gerald rarely told his daughter he loved her, but he did show his love in nonverbal ways. When his daughter was younger, they played together. He took the family on several enjoyable vacations. He worked long hours and went without many material things so that he could support Janet in private school and extracurricular activities that were really beyond his means. But he failed to attend many of these activities. When he was laid off from his job, Gerald was so depressed that he withdrew even more and became short-tempered with his wife and child. He began to feel like an outsider in his own family. In truth, his wife and daughter did act as though he were superfluous. This family pattern actually went back several generations in the mother's family. She grew up in a home with her mother, aunt, and grandmother, but no father. When she left Gerald, she and Janet moved into a house with her mother, sister, and grandmother. Her family had little use for men, and now Janet was being raised in the same tradition.

The seeds for Janet's alienation from her father were sown in their distant relationship, for which Gerald certainly had to take some responsibility. With daily contact, and her mom's limited support, Janet had been able to sustain a relationship with her dad. But the relationship was too weak to withstand the strain of her parents' divorce. With her father's absence and the mother's complete lack of support, Janet became increasingly alienated.

When her dad insisted on some minimal contact, Janet said she was scared of him, although she admitted that he had never physically hurt her or even threatened to hurt her. She told a judge that she was unnerved by his presence at school games where she was a cheerleader. Although Janet thought her stance was reasonable, it was really quite irrational. Here was a man who had dedicated himself to her welfare all of her life, and she claimed to feel safer in the presence of strangers than with her own father.

Dr. Gardner's organ-transplant principle comes to mind, because it underscores the unique and indispensable role that each parent occupies in the child's life. Dr. Gardner points out that if a child needed a kidney transplant, the target parent would be one of the very few people on earth who would volunteer to give up one of his kidneys. It makes no sense to banish from your life one of the two people among the billions on earth who has this level of commitment to your welfare. Gerald may not have been father-of-the-year material, but he was Janet's only father. In any reasonable accounting of his role in her life, the assets certainly outweighed the liabilities. Janet's alienation from her father was not justified by his behavior, yet it was not solely the result of her mother's manipulations. Each member of the family, and the divorce itself, played a significant role in creating the problem.

In another family, a teenager succumbed to her father's influence, denigrated her mother, refused to see her, and testified against her in court. Although the mother had been much more involved in raising her daughter, there was a significant factor that accounted for the girl's willingness to side with her father against her mother. When this girl was five years old, her father had abandoned the family. The girl did not see him again for three years. This episode left her with a fragile sense of her importance to her father. When he demanded allegiance from her in a war against her mother, she viewed this as an opportunity to solidify their bond. Though her father was certainly guilty of dispensing divorce poison, we should not overlook the girl's own psychological makeup as a central contributing factor to her alienation. The search for the roots of alienation is not a quest to place blame but to find effective solutions to this tragic problem.

When parents or judges ask therapists to treat alienated children, the therapist's understanding of the roots of the problem will guide the treatment. Is the alienation justified or unjustified? Is it primarily the result of divorce poison, mistreatment by the target parent, or the child's own mistaken decisions?

In cases of child-driven alienation, it would be insufficient to work exclusively with the favored parent, because that parent is not the source of the problem. The primary work has to be with the child. On the other hand, with children who are frightened to be with a parent because of the parent's violent behavior, it makes little sense to try to help the children overcome their fears without first helping the parent develop better self-control and providing a setting in which the parent-child contacts can take place safely. When a parent tries to poison his child against the other parent and the child succumbs by becoming severely alienated, it makes little sense to work exclusively with the child without removing her from the noxious environment. This requires legal assistance, which is discussed in chapter 8, "Getting Professional Help." Even the most skilled therapist will have a slim chance of reversing the alienation by meeting exclusively with the child for one forty-five-minute session a week, and then returning the child to the brainwashing parent.

TAKE ACTION

Don't overlook your own possible contributions to your child's alienation. If you are working with a therapist who has sufficient understanding and experience in working with alienated children, pay careful attention if the therapist tries to explain how you have contributed to the alienation. If your behavior has legitimately turned off your children, it won't help merely to blame your ex and deny your culpability; this will only complicate the problem. Instead, learn what you can do personally to help your children recover their affection, respect, and trust. Chapter 7 gives more specific advice along these lines.

IS IT ALIENATION OR NOT?

Before searching for the roots of alienation, it is necessary to determine whether the child is truly alienated. A child's hostility, reluctance to spend time with a parent, or even refusal to see the parent does not always mean that alienation is present. We must be careful not to confuse situations that superficially resemble alienation with the real thing. Some parents make this mistake innocently. Others knowingly raise false aliegations of alienation to support their bid for custody. Parents, therapists, and judges who misidentify alienation will aggravate rather than relieve a child's distress.

To avoid this error, keep in mind that alienated children relate to one parent, but not the other, in a *consistently* negative manner. As we will see in the following sections, a child is not severely alienated when the hostility and apparent rejection

- is temporary and short-lived rather than chronic (not to be confused with intermittent alienation that returns when in the presence of the favored parent)
- is occasional rather than frequent
- occurs only in certain situations
- coexists with expressions of genuine love and affection
- is directed at both parents

Normal Reactions to Divorce

Divorcing parents worry about how their breakup will affect their relationship with their children. Their worry might lead them to be oversensitive to any negative behavior on the children's part.

Occasional hostility from children is normal, and parents should expect more of it in the early weeks following the breakup. This is a time when children most need their parents' attention, patience, sensitivity, compassion, and reassurance. And it is a time when parents, preoccupied with their own distress, are least able to call upon these qualities. Many children express their sadness and uncertainty by becoming more defiant and belligerent. Unless their difficult behavior becomes chronic, and is directed at only one parent, it probably does not represent true alienation. It would be a mistake to assume that temporary and occasional displays of hostility mean that the children are being subjected to divorce poison, just as it would be a mistake to assume that they are reacting to mistreatment by a parent. The more likely explanation is that the difficult behavior represents a reaction to the divorce itself.

It takes children time to get used to the idea of seeing their parents in two different homes. Kyle was a clever ten-year-old boy. After his parents announced their intention to divorce, and his father moved out of the house, Kyle refused to meet with his father for lunch unless his mother was present. This was his way of registering his objection to the divorce: He would not cooperate with the transitions between parents necessitated by the divorce. He also hoped that he could engineer a reconciliation, like the girls did in his favorite film, *The Parent Trap*. Because his parents did not go along with his plan, Kyle's manipulations were short-lived and in no way resembled the chronic hatred expressed by alienated children.

How tolerant should parents be of their children's refusal to cooperate with scheduled times of contact? As in most dilemmas of parenting, there is no absolute and universal prescription. It is best to avoid the extremes of being overly harsh and punitive or overly lax and passive. Ask yourself whether your child is staying in touch with you in other ways and whether the general tone of your relationship has remained positive or is growing more negative. Is your child receptive to a suggestion to make up the time or to meet for dinner? Parents of teenagers should be aware that their children may have outgrown the parenting plan that was established when they were younger. Teenagers normally choose to spend more time with peers and less time with both parents. Don't mistake this natural process, which affects both parents, for the type of rejection exhibited by alienated children.

As a general rule, absent clear signs of divorce poison, I recommend that parents regard a child's first two consecutive refusals of contact as temporary reactions (unless contacts are scheduled very infrequently, such as when a parent lives in another state). Beyond this, parents should take active steps to understand the basis for the child's refusal and to ensure contact. The principle is the same as if your child refused to attend school. You would insist on attendance while trying to get to the root of the problem.

Parents should be even more lenient regarding phone contact. Children differ in their enjoyment of phone conversations, and the same child will react differently from one call to the next. If the call comes at a time when she is involved in an enjoyable activity, she may not want to stop what she is doing to come to the phone. Accept this normal behavior. Don't let your feelings be hurt. And don't leap to the conclusion that your child is alienated. With computer-literate children, try communicating through E-mail and instant messaging. Incidentally, I regard computer communication as one of the greatest boons to relationships between divorced parents and their children, especially when the parent lives far away.

TAKE ACTION

If your child occasionally refuses a scheduled contact, avoid overreacting or underreacting. Don't rigidly insist on each contact regardless of extenuating circumstances. Express your disappointment in a mild tone, and let her know that you are looking forward to the next time. Unless you live far away from your child and contacts are relatively rare, allow two consecutive refusals before taking more active steps to understand the problem and to ensure contact. Don't assume, without other evidence, that she is becoming alienated. But don't naively overlook this possibility either. Refusing a scheduled contact may be your child's way of asserting some control as a means of managing the initial anxiety triggered by your separation. If you fail to show some flexibility, your child may become more anxious and become even more uncomfortable about the contacts. When refusal of contact becomes more frequent, though, it is clear that your child needs help to resolve the difficulty. Ignoring repeated refusals of contact will establish a pattern that can harden into alienation if not understood and corrected.

Separation Anxiety

Lois was seventeen months old when her parents separated. She got along very well with each parent when she was in their care. But when it was time to leave one home for the other, she screamed and clung to the parent she was leaving. Fortunately, her parents knew that children between fifteen and twenty-four months of age are often anxious about separations, and they regarded Lois's vehement protests as normal. Neither parent accused the other of fostering alienation.

Mindy, fifteen months old, cried and hid behind her mother's legs when her father came to the door to take her for the day. Mindy's mother thought it would be traumatic to insist on the exchange when the girl was so frightened. This was not a case of divorce poison. The mother would have done the same if her daughter refused to attend day care. We wouldn't even say Mindy was alienated from her father, because her protests were specific to the exchanges. When her mother was present, Mindy loved playing with her father. In this case, all it took to resolve the problem was some brief education for the parents about normal child development.

In some families, a mother who has no difficulty leaving her protesting child with the baby-sitter allows her anger at her ex to create a blind spot when it comes to fostering the child's contact with the father. When these situations are mishandled, they can result in alienation, manifested in the child's chronic anxiety around the absent parent. I have worked with families in which the young child's normal separation protests resulted in the cessation of contact with the father. Because the child was given no opportunity to become secure with the father, the relationship was compromised even when the child outgrew the toddler years.

Parents, experts, and even cultures disagree about how best to help children with separation anxiety. Some advocate a quick parting, and point out that the child's protest is short-lived. Others advocate a gradual approach, giving the child time to get used to the separation. Using this approach, parents may enact an elaborate routine around separations with frequent hugs and kisses. Other parents adopt a strategy somewhere between these two extremes.

For a funny depiction of the gradual approach, watch Steve Martin in the movie, *A Simple Twist of Fate*. His daughter was anxious about attending kindergarten. To relieve her anxiety, the character played by Martin sat directly behind the girl the entire first day of school, and throughout the week he gradually moved further and further back until she no longer required his presence. The gradual approach is more the custom in cultures such as Japan that show greater tolerance for a young child's dependence on a parent.

TAKE ACTION

Prepare young children for transitions to the other parent with only a little advance notice, using a relaxed and matter-of-fact tone, much as you would announce a pending trip to the store. Use the same tone to let them know when they will return. Young children are very sensitive to a parent's moods. If a parent conveys anxiety about an upcoming separation, either by tone of voice or by too many reassurances, the child will "absorb" the parent's anxiety and have more difficulty with the separation. If the children's distress at the time of the exchange worries you, ask the other parent to call fifteen minutes later (or use a third party if direct communication between parents is a problem) to let you know whether they have calmed down.

Another situation in which separation anxiety might be mistaken for alienation is when a child protests contact with a parent who is unfamiliar, as in the case of a divorced father returning from an overseas military or work assignment. The mother may have done everything possible to promote the child's bond to the absent parent. The child may even be excited at the prospect of seeing his father. Nevertheless, when it comes time to separate from the mother, the boy is scared. If the parents are sensitive to the child's anxiety and allow the relationship to develop gradually, he will become more secure with the father. If, however, the parents are impatient for the child to be with the father, or the father assumes that the mother has programmed the son against him, he will react in ways that complicate the situation and may provoke the child's alienation.

Similar considerations apply to a young child who is afraid to spend the night with his father because he has never slept away from home. Rather than accept the child's rejection of overnights or ignore the child's feelings, the parents should work to help the child feel comfortable in his father's new home. Without this assistance, the resistance to overnights may become more entrenched. When children act on their fears, the fear usually grows stronger. Although not initially an alienation problem, if handled incorrectly by either parent, this situation could develop into a more pervasive rejection of the father.

Difficult, Troubled, and Shy Children

Some children, by temperament, have more difficulty adjusting to stress, new situations, or transitions. They may show this difficulty with defiant, oppositional, or withdrawn behavior when having to switch from one activity to another at home or in school. When this problem occurs during exchanges between parents' homes, it is important not to mistake this for alienation. The negative behavior is temporary, the child is able to show affection for the parent once he or she adjusts to the transition, and the same negative behavior occurs with both parents.

Children who are depressed may withdraw from both parents or act irritable with both. If divorced parents don't communicate with each other about their experiences with their children, they may falsely conclude that the negative behavior occurs only in their home, and that their children are becoming alienated.

Children prone to explosive outbursts, such as those suffering from a bipolar disorder, may say mean and hateful things and act aggressively in the midst of an emotional meltdown. At these times they are acting irrationally and do not discriminate the object of their attacks. They are just as likely to treat the other parent or a sibling in the same manner. This should not be confused with alienation.

Nine-year-old Nolan came to his father's home with a chip on his shoulder. He refused all the father's suggestions for enjoyable activities. When his favorite television show was preempted by a news bulletin, Nolan went into a rage. He broke his Game Boy and cussed at his father, telling him he hated him and never wanted to see him again. Had he been unaware of Nolan's bipolar disorder, this father might have worried that his son was being alienated. Instead, Nolan's dad was certain that his ex was not dispensing divorce poison. He knew she needed and looked forward to a break from caring for this difficult child. She certainly wouldn't do anything to make Nolan reluctant to be with his father. She did have a better feel for managing her son in a way that reduced the frequency of meltdowns. For this reason, Nolan was more comfortable with her and less eager to leave her home. But he was not alienated from his father. Nolan wanted to see his father and, when he was calm, usually enjoyed being with his dad.

Avoiding the War Zone

Some parents fight with each other every chance they get. Exchanges of the children take place in a climate of great tension, ranging from smoldering but obvious resentment to screaming, cursing, shoving, and outright violence. In such cases, at least one parent has no hesitancy about exposing the children to the awful hostilities.

To protect themselves from tension, fear, and embarrassment, children in explosive families sometimes tell one parent that they no longer want to see the other parent. The rejected parent, aware that the children receive a steady diet of divorce poison, assumes that the children's withdrawal from contact means they are alienated. This may not be true. Many of these children continue to feel love for the rejected parent. But they feel a desperate need to get out of the crossfire, and they don't know how else to do it except to cut ties with one of the warring factions.

Aware of the damage caused by exposure to high conflict, some therapists believe it is best to spare children such exposure, even when this means losing contact with a parent and often that parent's entire extended family. I think they are mistaken. Of course, parents' battles can devastate a child's sense of security and well-being; that's why I wrote this book. But so can the loss of a parent. As the child gets older, he will become better able to protect himself from his parents' animosity. He may never recover, though, from the rupture of the parent-child relationship and the loss of the extended family. So I advise maintaining the relationship while doing everything possible to shield the child from the shrapnel of his parents' attacks.

TAKE ACTION

To protect children from exposure to destructive tension, transfers should be arranged so that both parents are not present at the same time. This is best accomplished by having one parent drop off the children at school in the morning and the other parent pick them up at the end of the day. Another option, particularly for younger children who do not attend school, is to leave the children with a relative or friend and have the other parent pick them up ten minutes after the first parent has left. Your community may also have a special facility that monitors child exchanges for a small fee. Ask your local family court services for a referral.

Thy Parent's Keeper

Occasionally a depressed or emotionally unstable parent depends on her child to take care of her. The child becomes worried about leaving this parent alone. When it is time to be with the other parent, the child protests. This is not a case of alienation: The child still loves the other parent, and actually thrives in that parent's care. But the child's fear of something bad happening to the emotionally distraught parent keeps her by that parent's side.

One mother was so bereft when her husband left her that she remained in bed for days and neglected most of her responsibilities. She told her eight-year-old daughter that she didn't know how she could live without her during the extended weekend the girl was scheduled to spend with her father. As a result, the girl told her father that she didn't want to see him that weekend. This mother was despondent and not deliberately manipulating her daughter. But some parents do express a desperate need for the children in order to discourage them from spending time with their other parent.

TAKE ACTION

If you are depressed, get the adult help and companionship you need. Spare your child the role of caretaker. Most children cannot care for a parent's emotional needs without sacrificing their own healthy development.

Situation-Specific Reactions

Owen, sixteen years old, was not emotionally prepared for his father's remarriage shortly after the divorce was final. The boy felt very uncomfortable in his stepmother's presence and decided to avoid her. As a result, he refused to spend the night in his father's apartment. Though this was a problem, and probably was influenced by his mother's contempt for the new wife, it was not alienation. Owen regularly met with his dad in restaurants and played tennis with him, but he insisted that his stepmother not be included. Although this was a problem that needed to be solved rather than catered to forever, it was not alienation.

TAKE ACTION

A child's discomfort around a new stepparent may be eased by spending a vacation together away from home. Sharing new experiences in novel surroundings, apart from normal routines, can help jump-start the stepparent-child bond.

Fourteen-year-old Philip asked to move out of his mother's home. He said he would spend time with her during the day, but wanted to sleep at his father's house. The boy was unable to articulate the reasons for his decision, which made the mother think her ex-husband had poisoned the boy against her. Philip was not a victim of divorce poison, though, and he would not be described as alienated from his mother. He still loved her and wanted to see her. But he was bothered by his mother's numerous boyfriends spending the night with her. He wanted to remove himself from the situation, though he was not fully aware of what made him uncomfortable.

The examples of Owen and Philip illustrate "situation-specific" reactions: resistance to seeing a parent under particular circumstances without being alienated from that parent.

Sharing a Wavelength

When parents are embroiled in a custody dispute, or compete for a child's affections, they may become concerned that their child's closer connection to the other parent signals alienation. Many times this concern is unwarranted. Even in intact families, children will often feel closer to, or more comfortable with, one parent than the other. And the parent they feel closest to may be different at various points in the child's life.

A child's greater compatibility with one parent has several possible roots. The parent and child may share similar biological rhythms, activity levels, interests, or temperament. The child may identify with the parent of the same sex. Children who exhibit this kind of preference are distinguished from alienated children because they continue to express positive regard for both parents and seek contact with both. Being less preferred is a far cry from being hated.

TAKE ACTION

If your child seems to occupy the same wavelength as your ex, don't confuse this with alienation. As long as your child loves you and spends time with you, this is not something to worry about. Concentrate on the positive aspects of your relationship rather than compete with the other parent. Parent-child compatibilities are normal and may shift in time. Accepting your child's natural inclinations will strengthen your bond. Protesting these inclinations will introduce unnecessary tension in the relationship.

Parent-Child Partnerships

At times a child's closeness to one parent goes beyond the "same wavelength" phenomenon described above. Fifteen-year-old Rolanda's father divorced his wife in order to marry his secretary, with whom he had been having a long-standing affair. The girl was hurt and angered by her father's actions. She sympathized with her mother's position as the spurned woman and felt that her mother deserved and needed her loyal support. She expressed a strong preference to live with her mother and took her mother's side in financial disputes with her father. Nevertheless, Rolanda was not alienated from her father. She continued to express love and positive regard for him. After the divorce was final, over time Rolanda showed increasing interest in spending time with her father and his new wife, although she continued to feel closer to her mother. Noted divorce authorities Dr. Joan Kelly and Dr. Janet Johnston label this type of mother-daughter partnership an "alignment."

Sam was a preschool boy who would be described as aligned with his father. He divided his time evenly between both parents' homes, although he clearly preferred being with his dad. Sam's father exercised a quiet yet firm authority over his son. The father was able to give Sam more latitude in his play, confident that he could assert control when necessary and that the boy would comply with the limits. This allowed Sam a feeling of greater freedom combined with the security of his father's control. Father and son shared a close bond, expressed with frequent hugs and verbal affection.

By contrast, Sam's mother was made anxious by her son's high activity level. She resorted to ineffectual yelling and set limits that were too frequent and too rigid for her young son. To complicate matters, Sam looked very much like his father, and they shared the same facial expressions and mannerisms. This resemblance became an obstacle to the mother's affection. In a subtle way she rejected Sam whenever his demeanor evoked memories of her hated ex-husband. As a result, much of their time together was marred by mutually frustrating interchanges.

When Sam was with his father and it came time to return to his mother, he would get visibly upset. Either he protested vigorously, clinging to his dad while sobbing and screaming, or he became melancholy and rested his head limply on his dad's shoulder. This was not just a manifestation of normal separation anxiety, because, without fail, Sam eagerly left his mother to be with his father.

Sam's mother accused her ex-husband of alienating the boy. She suspected that, prior to the exchanges, the father involved Sam in exciting activities and then abruptly ended them by telling Sam that he had to go be with his mother. In reality, the father hated seeing his son so upset and did everything possible to prepare Sam to have a good time with his mother. Sam clearly preferred his father's care and was, in this sense, aligned with his dad. But he was not alienated from his mom. He certainly loved her and felt a bond with her, and once the difficult exchanges were accomplished, he eagerly sought her attention.

TAKE ACTION

If transitions between parents are very difficult, arrange to do something out of the home for a while, such as having dinner or running an errand, before returning home with your child. An out-of-home activity can serve as a buffer and dilute the emotional impact of transferring from one residence to the other.

The line between extreme alignment and mild alienation is very thin. In Rolanda's case, the mother's handling of the situation was a key factor that protected Rolanda from becoming alienated. Rolanda's mother let her know that, although she did not condone the father's affair, there had been problems in the marriage for many years, and the divorce was probably the best thing in the long run. In Sam's case, the father continued to support his son's love for his mother, and made sure the boy spoke to his mother every day.

Other parents exploit their child's allegiance by actively promoting a completely negative view of the other parent or passively condoning the child's rejection of the parent without doing anything to promote or encourage a healthier adjustment. The children in these families are particularly vulnerable to becoming alienated.

TAKE ACTION

If your child displays hostile or rejecting attitudes toward you, don't assume the child is alienated and don't assume she has been poisoned against you. Take an honest look at your own behavior and circumstances that may have contributed to the alienation. Ask the other parent for assistance in improving the situation. If he willingly cooperates, there is a good chance that the child is not alienated. If the other parent refuses to help, there is a good chance that he feels gratified by the children's rejection of you and is contributing to alienation—if not actively, then passively, by condoning the children's negative behavior toward you.

The conditions discussed above can be distinguished from alienation. But they can also be the forerunners of alienation if handled improperly. Rejected parents must follow the seven rules presented on page 38. Favored parents must keep their child's welfare uppermost in their minds as they work to support their children's healthy relationships with both parents.

Whether a child is alienated and, if so, whether divorce poison has contributed to the alienation, are central and controversial issues for courts, therapists, and parents who must decide how to respond to the problem.

FALSE ACCUSATIONS OF PARENTAL ALIENATION

In chapter 2 we met Tina, whose husband, Wesley, accused her of brainwashing their son, Vince. Tina's case really had nothing to do with pathological alienation. In the first place, Vince did not reject his father. He wanted a better relationship with him. Wesley was so possessive of his time with Vince that he would not allow the boy to attend any friend's birthday party that occurred during their regularly scheduled weekends together. Wesley felt that, since they saw so little of each other, Vince should want to spend all his time alone with his father. As a result, Vince did not look forward to weekends with his father. But he was not alienated. And his mother did not brainwash him.

When the court-appointed psychologist examined the family, he concluded that Vince had none of the symptoms of pathological alienation. He recommended that Wesley consult with a therapist who could help him better understand his son's needs and use their time together to build a stronger relationship.

Parents who make accusations of irrational alienation need to be sure that they are reading the situation accurately. If they mistakenly blame their children's difficult behavior on the other parent, they may lose the opportunity to make changes in themselves that could improve their relationship with their children. Indeed, their denial of responsibility may push the children further away.

Parents who are falsely accused of brainwashing, like Tina, need information about alienated children to defend themselves. Tina's attorney needed to show the judge that Vince's behavior was not symptomatic of a child who has been poisoned against his father. All parents involved in litigation where alienation is alleged must insist that their attorneys be familiar with the issue and able to cope with relevant testimony in court. To ignore this information is to risk losing custody.

MISDIAGNOSIS OF PATHOLOGICALLY ALIENATED CHILDREN

If you have been falsely accused of alienating your child, check the following list of situations that may result in misdiagnosis of the problem. If any of these fit your family, bring them to the attention of your attorney and any mental health professionals involved in your case.

- ☐ Your child occasionally criticizes your ex but does not engage in a campaign of denigration and does not refuse to spend time with the other parent.

- ☐ Your child is antagonistic to both you and your ex.

- ☐ You occasionally criticize your ex but do not engage in a severe campaign of denigration. Some experts fail to distinguish adequately between mild occasional bad-mouthing and systematic efforts to turn children against loved ones.

- ☐ Although you may be guilty of trying to turn your child against the other parent, your child does not partici-pate in the denigration and does not exhibit the other symptoms of irrational alienation described in chapter 3. According to Dr. Gardner, "The diagnosis of PAS is not made on the basis of the programmer's efforts but the degree of 'success' in each child."

- ☐ Your child's alienation is a realistic and appropriate response to severe maltreatment at the hands of the other parent.

☐ You have neither overtly nor covertly contributed to, influenced, or supported your child's alienation at any point in time and have made considerable efforts to foster a healthy relationship between your ex and your child.

☐ Your child exhibits only temporary or occasional resistance or reluctance to be with the other parent or make the transition between parental homes.

☐ Your child refuses to spend time with the other parent only in certain circumstances, such as in the presence of the parent's new partner.

So now we know the effects of divorce poison on children. But how do children get this way? How, why, and when is the poison administered? We take up these questions next, starting with the most difficult: "How could parents do this to their own offspring?"

CHAPTER 4
MALIGNANT MOTIVES

The Court has no doubt that the cause of the blind, brainwashed, bigoted belligerence of the children toward the father grew from the soil nurtured, watered and tilled by the mother. The Court is thoroughly convinced that the mother breached every duty she owed as the custodial parent to the noncustodial parent of instilling love, respect and feeling in the children for their father. Worse, she slowly dripped poison into the minds of these children, maybe even beyond the power of this Court to find the antidote.

—FLORIDA JUDGE RICHARD YALE FEDER

From the time of your baby's birth, even during the pregnancy, you dedicated yourself to ensuring your child's safety and well-being. You provided food, clothing, pediatric visits, diapers, car seats, vegetables and vitamins, lullabies and bedtime stories. You willingly contributed your time, energy, and money to the care of your child. Your former spouse probably did the same.

So how could a loving parent deliberately poison his own child's affections? The anger and disappointment that accompany divorce may explain occasional bad-mouthing. But to understand more malignant behavior, bashing and brainwashing, we need to look further. How could loving parents do something that so obviously violates their children's trust, which so clearly damages their emotional well-being? What kinds of people do this to their children? Why do they do it? And how can we respond effectively?

POOR BOUNDARIES

As we search for the motives behind divorce poison, we should keep one thing in mind. A motive explains only the *impulse* to tamper with children's affections. But an impulse is not an action. Parents often inhibit behavior toward their children rather than succumb to impulse. For example, we don't spank every time we feel like doing so. Most divorcing parents go through a period when they feel chronic impulses to bad-mouth their ex-spouse, but they often suppress these when their children are present.

What is it that allows some loving parents to suspend their role as their children's protector—to renege on their basic parental responsibility—rather than inhibit their behavior as they do other behavior they regard as destructive to their children? In many cases the answer is simple: They do not regard it as destructive to their children. Many parents who bad-mouth are so preoccupied with hurting their ex-spouses that they choose not to think about the impact on their children. Other parents appear incapable of recognizing that their own thoughts and feelings and their children's needs may not be identical. Such parents will often refer to themselves and the children as a single unit. At the onset of the separation one mother told her husband, "We don't want to see you. We don't need you. Why don't you just stay out of our lives?" When this woman thought of her family, she drew no distinction between her feelings and those of her children.

The blurring of parent-child boundaries allows parents to pursue, with single-minded determination, their goal of demeaning the ex, even when this means embarrassing the children; even when this means confusing them, depriving them, or scaring them.

I remember one particularly cruel example. An accountant who had successfully alienated his children from their mother became enraged when his wife refused to postpone a custody hearing for which he felt unprepared. While driving his children to a court-appointed therapy session, he vilified their mother, as he had done many times before. This time, though, he told them that their mother's refusal to postpone the hearing would cause his cancer cells to spread all over his body and kill him. The father actually did have cancer, but his oncologist testified that the father's condition had a cure rate of over 90 percent. Furthermore, the idea that the man was currently facing death was totally fabricated and without any medical basis. The father knew this. But his children did not.

This man's rage at his wife, his wish to have the children align with him against her, and his unwillingness to modulate his outbursts led him to behave sadistically toward his own children. He made them think that he was near death's door and that it was their own mother who was pushing him through it. To make the scenario even worse, he tied his impending death to the struggle over custody. The children knew that they were the subject of the legal battle, so it was no surprise that they felt some degree of responsibility themselves for his "impending death." Unfortunately, after many years these children still have not recovered their love for their mother.

In their determination to undermine the relationship between the children and the target, parents act as though nothing is more important to their children than the parent's own concerns. An example occurred in a telephone conversation between a mother and her son. I use the word *conversation* loosely because it was mainly a one-sided diatribe in which the boy struggled unsuccessfully to be heard. This mother expected her boy to be her "comrade in arms" in a custody battle. She told him that Daddy suffered from a mental illness and could become violent at any moment (this was not true). She told him that she knew he was scared of his father, even though the boy showed no such inclination. She ordered him to tell everyone he saw that he was afraid of his father. She also told him to call 911 and tell them to send out the police because he was afraid. And then when the police arrive, she said, tell them that you are afraid of your father and that you need to live with your mother.

Throughout the call the boy kept trying to change the subject rather than agree that his father was a horrible person. He tried to tell his mother about a project he was working on for school and about fun things that were occurring in his father's home. The mother ignored his comments. She pursued her agenda until her son finally gave up. The rest of the conversation consisted of the mother repeating her warnings about the father and the son repeating "Yes, Mom" in a flat, monotone voice. When she was convinced of her success, the mother hung up. Her son did, in fact, call 911 and repeat verbatim what he had been coached to say. After many years this boy still refuses to speak to his father.

By treating her son as an accomplice in the custody dispute—a peer—and demanding his support, this woman was obliterating the usual psychological boundary that exists between adults and children. Kids should be able to look to their parents for support and guidance, not the other way around. When they are required to devote themselves to their parents' emotional needs, they must prematurely surrender a part of childhood.

TAKE ACTION

If parent-child boundaries are blurred or in danger of becoming blurred, begin a dialogue with your child about similarities and differences between people. First, talk about relatively neutral topics, such as similarities and differences in appearance and in preferences for food, color, music, TV shows, and so on. How is your child like, but also different from, his two parents? Enlist your child's interest in the conversation by challenging him to think of three ways in which he is like his mother and his father, and three ways in which he is different from them.

Next, move the discussion into the area of feelings. Parents and children don't always feel the same. Begin with feelings other than anger. How is your child like and different in the things that make him happy? Scared? For example, your son loves cartoons; you love romantic movies. He may be afraid of the dark, but you aren't. You may be afraid of snakes, while he enjoys handling them. Again, challenge him to think of his own examples.

Once the principle of different feelings has been taught, use an example that involves anger: Your boy may be furious with his sister and say he hates her, but you continue to love both. Examples like this can be used to show your child that he does not have to share the hatred of the alienating parent. "Because Daddy is very angry with Mommy, he wants you to be angry with me too. But you don't have to be. You don't have to feel everything the same as Daddy. You can have your own independent feelings."

Helping children insulate themselves from a parent's malignant influence is important. But it is usually not enough. To stop divorce poison, we must identify the specific motives, feelings, personality traits, and situations that drive the perpetrator. Different motives call for different responses. A strategy that ends bad-mouthing in one parent may intensify it in another.

REVENGE

Parents who bad-mouth and bash are angry people. Some may feel rejected. Some may feel betrayed. Some may believe they have been treated unfairly. Many want to get even. One way to retaliate is to deprive the ex of the children's love.

A man whose wife initiates the divorce tells her, "If you want to leave me for another man, our children are going to know what kind of woman you are. Leave me and you can say good-bye to your children." Since the court will not generally agree that this is a good reason for children to lose their mother, his next step is to undermine the children's regard for her so that they will not want to see her.

When divorce poison is driven by revenge, the most effective antidote is to eliminate the provocation. Ask yourself, "Why is he or she so angry? Is there anything I can do about it?"

Sam knew exactly why his ex-wife was bad-mouthing him to their children. When Trish decided to leave him after twenty years of marriage, he punished her by being dishonest during the divorce negotiations. He hid much of their financial assets from her. As a result, Trish received a very unfair settlement, and they both knew it. She retaliated by running him down in front of the children, telling them that he was a liar and a cheat. As his children suffered from the bad-mouthing, and his own initial anger about the divorce subsided with time, Sam did something very unusual. He instructed his lawyer to revise the original divorce settlement. This move surprised Trish. Though she didn't thank Sam (she was getting what she should have had all along), she did feel less angry and restrained her bad-mouthing. It was the beginning of a more trusting co-parenting relationship. Everyone benefited.

In most cases the anger behind divorce poison is a response to real or perceived offenses that cannot be undone. All you may be able to do is reduce the rage. A common example is marital infidelity. If you were unfaithful in your marriage, and your ex-spouse is retaliating by turning the children against you, you cannot eliminate the provocation. But you can acknowledge your wrongdoing. You can apologize for the pain you have caused. You can express regret, and ask that the children not be made to pay for your sins. By conveying that the rage is understandable and a valid response to betrayal, you may accelerate the process of healing.

You should also consider joint therapy. It offers a safe, neutral environment in which to express rage and disappointment. And it provides a forum for civil communication. A bad-mouthing parent, blinded by his anger, is more likely to accept advice when it comes from an impartial mental health professional (or a pastor or rabbi) than from the target of his anger.

Some couples who agree to get therapy have so much animosity and distrust that they cannot agree on a therapist. If you find yourself in this situation, don't give up. Ask your attorneys to consult with each other and select a therapist they both respect. Or one party can make a list of three recommended therapists and the other selects one from the list. It is in everyone's interest that the therapist be experienced, competent, and unbiased. Consult chapter 8, "Getting Professional Help," for more tips on choosing a therapist and getting the most out of your therapy sessions.

TAKE ACTION

When divorce poison is driven by revenge, the most effective antidote is to eliminate the provocation. Ask yourself, Why is he or she so angry? Is there anything I can do about it?

- Eliminate the provocation, if possible.
- Reduce the rage by taking responsibility for your part in provoking it.
- Send a "peace offering" letter, apologizing for the hurt you have caused and asking that the children not be punished for your mistakes.
- Get joint therapy.

NARCISSISM

Bad-mouthing parents act superior. But many actually feel inferior as parents. They put down the other parent in order to convince themselves, the children, and the world that they are the better parent and more deserving of love.

Such parents fail to appreciate that the bad-mouthing and bashing they use to bolster their image as parents accomplishes the exact opposite. It demonstrates, for all to see, a severe parental deficiency: the willingness to sacrifice their children's needs in order to feed their own weak egos.

In *The Custody Revolution* I described how excessive narcissism leads some parents to fight for custody. Readers let me know that it also leads to divorce poison. How can you tell when narcissism is behind efforts to turn your children against you? Look for some of the following traits:

- an overly inflated view of the person's own importance (not to be confused with genuine positive self-regard—a narcissistic man is "a legend in his own mind")
- a tendency to exaggerate accomplishments
- an excessive need for admiration
- a noticeable lack of empathy (He does not put himself in other's shoes.)
- excessive envy
- a constant belief that others envy him
- an imperious, condescending manner
- a sense of entitlement that pervades interpersonal relationships

I consulted on a case in New York City in which a man clearly fit the above profile. Vincent was well known in his community as a father who sought positions of authority in nearly every extracurricular activity that involved children. He was the scout leader, the soccer and baseball head coach, the Sunday school teacher, the safety chairman of the Homeowners Association, and so on. He did everything possible to build his résumé as a parent.

Initially Vincent impressed his neighbors. Then one by one they became disillusioned with him. They described him as someone who acted as if he were entitled to their favors. He took advantage of them. They also said Vincent always drew attention to himself. He would tell anyone who was willing to listen about how much prestige and influence he had in the community, about how much he did for his son, about how pious he was.

After his divorce Vincent married a woman with custody of her daughter. He quickly became embroiled in two separate custody disputes. First, he tried to erase his stepdaughter's father from the girl's life. Second, he tried to diminish the role of his son's mother in the boy's life. In both cases he seemed on a mission to persuade the children (and the courts) to accept him and his wife as their only legitimate parents. And in both cases the judge ruled against Vincent and expressed concern about his inability to recognize the damage he was causing.

Excessive narcissism is not restricted to men. Wanda continuously ran down her husband in front of their two boys, with little regard for the children's feelings. She craved attention from other men and dreamed of a better life, and finally she decided she deserved more. She told her husband that she was leaving and agreed that the boys would alternate weeks with each parent.

While the children were on a trip with their church youth group, Wanda moved into an apartment in another school district, closer to the friends with whom she liked to party. She took with her nearly all of the children's clothes (except old clothes that no longer fit) and most of the furniture. Her apartment was too small to accommodate everything, so Wanda rented a storage unit. In an incredible display of disregard for her family, she also took the refrigerator, which her mother had given them, and moved it into storage since her apartment was already equipped with one. Wanda told her husband that the children would have to stay with him the first week because she needed time to get settled. So the children returned from their vacation to an empty house.

The teenage son was furious with his mother. He had no clean clothes to wear to school and none of his familiar possessions. When he came to her apartment the next week, he discovered that his "bedroom" was the den, with no privacy. He saw that the refrigerator, which she took, was not there. And he had to wake up earlier than usual in order to take the city bus to his school, which was three blocks from his father's house. The boy complained and asked to spend more nights in his father's home. Wanda responded by accusing her husband of brainwashing. She failed to appreciate that her self-centered behavior angered her son. The boy's younger brother was also upset by the move, but he tried to please both parents by keeping his complaints to himself.

Parents who make false accusations of parental alienation often have narcissistic traits. Their self-centered behavior antagonizes their children, but such parents blame the resulting problems on the other parent. Narcissists rarely take responsibility for the havoc they create in their relationships.

TAKE ACTION

To protect against false charges of divorce poison made by a narcissistic ex, keep a list of your ex-spouse's behavior that creates problems in his or her relationship with the children. Include behaviors such as repeated broken promises, bad-mouthing you to the children, and ignoring the children's legitimate needs.

Continue to support your children's love and respect for your ex. Help them appreciate his or her positive qualities in addition to empathizing with their dislike of the narcissistic behavior. If you are accused of alienating the children, it is important to demonstrate that: (1) although the children have a strong preference for you, they have a balanced view of their other parent and are not alienated, (2) their difficulties with the other parent are a direct and realistic reaction to the treatment they have received from that parent, and (3) rather than exploit their complaints to turn the children against your ex, you have done the opposite by encouraging the continuation of the relationship. In most cases, even when a parent has significant psychological problems, children are better off maintaining ties in some form. In the long run your children will be grateful that you helped them achieve this.

Some narcissistic parents successfully manipulate their children to side with them against the other parent. Children may join in a campaign of denigration in order to curry favor with the parent whose capacity for genuine reciprocal attachment is more limited. The children sense the shallow emotional investment of the self-absorbed parent, and do what they can to preserve their tenuous tie to this parent. Particularly when narcissism is combined with aggression, children may fearfully endorse the parent's campaign of hatred rather than risk becoming targets themselves. I will have more to say about this in the next chapter.

Paradoxically, self-absorbed people can be charismatic and charming to others when their needs for adulation are gratified. Some of the rich and famous fall into this category. They may successfully seduce children's allegiance through an aura of excitement and special treatment and the trappings of success that surround them.

Then there are the unlucky children who have two highly narcissistic parents. Such parents blithely fight each other and accuse each other of divorce poison, all the while being oblivious to or complacent about the impact of their battles on their children.

Narcissistic parents like Vincent and Wanda generally make poor candidates for therapy or mediation. Because they are deficient in understanding other's feelings, they do not understand the necessity of compromise or how their behavior affects their children. Although you should try therapy as a first option, unfortunately it often takes the threat of legal sanctions, such as losing custody, to make an impact on such parents.

Because narcissists use divorce poison to compensate for feeling inferior as parents, anything you can do to support their egos in a reasonable manner may lessen their need to put you down. For example, encourage them to make unique contributions to their children's lives, contributions they can brag about. This might be participating in scouts or assisting with special school projects. Narcissists are exquisitely sensitive to appearances. It can be helpful for them to retain the legal title of joint custodian even if the children spend relatively little time in their care and the other parent retains the authority to make most decisions. If, instead, the court strips them of this title, the resulting loss of face could exacerbate the brainwashing.

TAKE ACTION

To respond to narcissism:

- Bolster their self-respect by providing opportunities for narcissists to contribute meaningfully to their children's lives.

- Attempt counseling.

- If divorce poison continues, consider legal action.

GUILT

All parents regret some things they did or did not do for their children. Some divorced parents have so little tolerance for guilt that they try to deflect attention from their own failings by focusing on how much worse the other parent is. A man who spent too little time with his children, for example, decides to make up for this by rescuing them from a mother whom he now regards as the incarnation of everything rotten in a parent.

Guilt can also lead a parent to make a false accusation of brainwashing. I once received a call from a woman whose ex-husband had abandoned their daughter for seven years. After the failure of his second marriage, he decided to renew contact with his child. He expected that she would be thrilled to be reunited with her father. The reality was markedly different. His daughter was reluctant to spend time with him. To her he was a stranger. She resisted going on visits with him and she was reserved in his presence. Rather than accept responsibility for causing the situation and proceed in a more reasonable manner to gradually build a relationship with his child, this father accused the girl's mother of fostering the child's estrangement. His solution was to seek immediate full custody. Fortunately, he was unsuccessful.

TAKE ACTION

Therapy is often effective when guilt is the main motive behind bad-mouthing or false accusations of brainwashing. The guilty parent must be helped to appreciate that the best way to atone for past misdeeds is to focus on the child's current needs. Bad-mouthing, bashing, and brainwashing only compound the child's problems, and will in turn increase the perpetrator's guilt.

INSECURITY

Some parents doubt their ability to maintain their children's love and affection. They regard the other parent as a competitor for the children's love and are afraid that they will eventually lose the competition. To cope with their insecurity they try to drive a wedge between the children and the other parent. Their hope is that this will cement the children's relationship with them.

From the time of the divorce Frances rejected every request made by her ex-husband to spend more time with his young son. In the face of growing hostilities, Frances's father called a meeting to try to make peace. At the meeting Frances revealed that she left her little boy with a babysitter nearly every Saturday and Sunday, in addition to the full-time day care she used during the week. Her father gently suggested that she could allow the boy's father and grandparents to care for the child some of these times. Frances was infuriated. Half screaming and half crying, she asked, "Why should I allow that? I don't want my boy to become more bonded to his dad than to me." At a deeper level Frances knew that her ex-husband had more warmth and affection to give a child and that her son probably would feel closer to his father in the long run. What she did not realize was that children have enough room in their hearts to love both parents, despite the limitations of each. You will find this type of insecurity in many instances of bad-mouthing and bashing.

TAKE ACTION

Reassure your ex of his or her importance to your children. Refrain from behavior that can appear to be a competition for the children's favor. If the children enjoy a special activity with their other parent, don't duplicate the activity in your home. Let them have unique pleasures with each parent.

SEEKING VALIDATION

Some parents denigrate ex-spouses merely because it feels good. They seek an outlet for their anger by expressing it to other people, and they hope that their audience will agree with their assessments. The audience is anyone who will listen: coworkers, relatives, friends, and at times, but not always, the children. Even when the children are not the intended audience, they will be hurt if their parents make no special effort to censor their comments when the children are within earshot.

When alienation occurs in these cases it may be an unintended consequence of the children's overhearing repeated put-downs of their other parent. But often it is no accident that the children have been exposed to the criticisms. The parent (whether consciously or not) wants the children to share the same negative opinion of the target.

TAKE ACTION

If the children overhear bad comments about you, don't assume that your ex is deliberately poisoning them. Tell the bad-mouthing parent that you thought he or she would want to know what the children have heard and repeated. Say this in a noncritical tone. If your ex will be unreceptive to anything you have to say, ask someone else in the family to bring up the subject. Parents sometimes need reminders to take care in what they say around their children. This is particularly true in the early stages of separation, when anger and distress are at a peak. Parents who have inadvertently allowed the children to overhear destructive criticisms of their other parent may be willing to alter their behavior with feedback about it if they do not feel attacked for their mistakes.

HOLDING ON WITH HATE

When a recently divorced man goes on his first date and spends most of the time complaining about his ex-wife, his date knows that this man is not yet emotionally ready for a new relationship. He is preoccupied with thoughts and feelings about his marriage and divorce. And this reveals that he is still—in some way—connected to his ex.

This is not surprising. Two people meet, fall in love, marry, conceive and raise children together, vacation together, and share life's joys and tragedies, ups and downs. Through years of shared experiences they form strong emotional ties. When the marriage fails, a judge's signature on a divorce decree may sever their legal tie. But we should not expect their emotional connection to evaporate immediately or completely.

In time most people put the marriage and divorce behind them. They gradually withdraw their emotional investment in the former spouse.

They form new relationships. They think about their ex-spouse less often and with less intense emotion. They find better things to do with their time than obsess about the faults of their former partner. And they neither seek nor want extensive contact.

Some people, though, are unwilling to let go, and they are not necessarily the rejected spouses. It is surprising and ironic that often the ones who initiated the divorce have more difficulty accepting the end of the relationship. They become determined to maintain a passionate relationship any way they can. When they are unable to arouse romantic passion, they will settle for rage. Like children starved for attention who misbehave to get it, they prefer highly charged negative involvement to none at all.

A relentless, virulent campaign of denigration guarantees ongoing contact. The goal is not to end the children's relationship with the other parent, it is to remain entangled with the ex. As long as they attack and accuse, they can look forward to some response. It is as if they are saying "I refuse to give you up. If I cannot have your love, I'll hold on with hate. I will keep you involved whether you like it or not. We will continue to dominate each other's thoughts. We will continue to stir strong feelings in each other."

These parents act as if their main goal in life is to make their ex miserable. Often they succeed. They may be so successful that they drive the alienated parent away: The target parent gives up trying to foster a relationship with the children. But the denigrating parent does not stop pursuing a relationship with the target. He or she merely finds another way to assure contact. A favorite forum is the courtroom.

Litigation provides ample opportunities to provoke hostile engagement. Most of these actually occur before trial, in the form of *discovery, interrogatories,* and *depositions.* These legal tactics give bashing and brainwashing parents a front-row center seat from which to observe intimate details of their ex-spouse's life.

Requests for discovery are formal demands that require a person involved in a lawsuit to turn over to the other side specified documents. These can include highly personal material such as diaries and bank statements. *Interrogatories* are pretrial questions put by one side to the other which, by law, require written responses. The requests can be quite intrusive. These often include, for example, questions about the frequency of sexual intercourse with a boyfriend. *Depositions* are pretrial examinations of a witness conducted by an attorney with no judge pres-

ent. The witness is sworn to tell the truth, just as in a courtroom, and a
court reporter records the proceedings. Although the opposing attorney
can raise objections, because no judge is present to rule on the objections, the witness may be asked irrelevant, provocative, and intrusive
questions. In a Connecticut deposition I recently attended as a trial consultant, a man was asked about his masturbation practices. Despite his
embarrassment (of the eight people in the room, three were women), he
answered the question. If the case goes to trial, and the judge sustains the
objection, the answer will not be part of the official testimony. But by this
point the damage is often done.

One survivor of brutal litigation felt as if she had been run through
"a psychological meat grinder." Most people feel the same. They experience it as a vicious crisis which dominates their life for months, sometimes years. But the crisis is welcome to ex-spouses who refuse to let go. It
allows the relationship with the ex-spouse to take center stage. One man
harassed his ex-wife by filing repeated suits to modify custody. Even
when the judge ordered a two-year moratorium on any such suits, the
man violated the court ruling within six months. He simply could not
resist embroiling his ex in the turmoil of a lawsuit.

Friends and relatives of such parents eventually withdraw their support and admonish them, in effect, to get a life. This is precisely what may
help the situation. When I suspect that the wish to hold on is behind a
campaign of hate, I will usually tell alienated parents that their best hope
for relief is for their former spouse to find a new love. Only then will they
be willing to close the book on their marriage.

IS YOUR EX-SPOUSE HOLDING ON WITH HATE?

The distinguishing feature of an ex who holds on is the high frequency of contact with you. By contrast, the brainwashing parent
who truly wants to end the relationship minimizes contact; all
his actions are consistent with the goal of erasing you from his
life and the lives of your children.

If you think you are the target of bashing and brainwashing
by an ex who refuses to let go, look for the following behaviors:

□ Constantly pumps neighbors and friends for information about you and your activities

□ Frequently initiates contact with you: This may take the form of stalking, calling often, leaving long voice-mail messages, or threatening lawsuits.

□ Tries to draw you into arguments that rehash old marital grievances

□ Is preoccupied with expressing hatred for you even when you are not around

□ Constantly shows up at places where you are sure to be

□ Makes no attempt to inhibit hostile exchanges in public; provokes embarrassing scenes at children's school and athletic events

□ Seems to take pleasure in the hostile encounters: for example, when talking about the turmoil he creates, is unable to suppress a gleeful smile

□ Though denouncing you as evil and worthless, periodically raises the possibility of reconciliation. Or, gives you the distinct impression that he wants to reconcile.

PARANOIA

People who suffer from paranoia have a pervasive tendency to categorize others as either "for" them or "against" them. Any life stress heightens this tendency. When going through divorce, parents with this trait worry about the allegiance of relatives, friends, and even their own children. No one they know can be neutral. Those who are not unconditionally with them are against them. As a result, their children feel pressured into joining in a campaign of denigration against the other parent.

Paranoid people are exquisitely sensitive to slights. It takes very little to arouse their suspicions. One father panicked and thought that his phone contact with his daughter was being permanently cut off simply because one scheduled call was missed. As it turned out, his daughter did try to call, but his line was busy and she went to sleep early. If the children are belligerent, whiny, or disobedient, such parents leap to the conclusion that the children are becoming alienated, and they blame the other parent. Of course all children act this way at times. Children are especially likely to be negativistic and oppositional when they have been exposed to marital turmoil. Such considerations will be overlooked by paranoid parents. They will generally dismiss the most probable and benign explanations for behavior in favor of far-fetched and malevolent interpretations. To defend against imagined alienation, these parents may engage in preemptive strikes: They try to turn the children against the parent they falsely accuse of brainwashing.

Shortly after his ex-wife remarried, Gene became increasingly worried that she might try to reduce his time with their four-year-old son. The more he worried about it, the more he convinced himself that she was in fact planning a lawsuit against him. His anxiety heightened when his son spoke positively about his new stepfather. Gene channeled his anxiety into what eventually became a brainwashing campaign. He began to inspect his son for bruises upon every return from the mother's home. The boy got the message that his father did not think the mother's home was safe for a child. Everyday childhood bumps and scrapes became evidence, in Gene's mind, of abuse. The boy tried to explain the innocuous source of the injuries, like falling off a bike or tripping over a shoelace. But Gene dismissed the explanations as cover-ups, excuses made by a child who was too scared to reveal that his stepfather hurt him. In fact, the more the child defended his stepfather, the more Gene became convinced that the boy was afraid of the man. Over time, much of the boy's behavior became signs to Gene of abuse. When the boy had a couple of nightmares, rather than accept these as normal for children this age, Gene assumed that these were traumatic symptoms.

Gene made numerous complaints to child welfare. Each complaint was dutifully investigated. The outcome was always the same. There was no rational basis to suspect abuse in the mother's home. Eventually, Gene's alienating behavior became too much for his ex to ignore and she did just what he originally feared. She filed a lawsuit to modify their custody agreement in order to protect her son from his father's paranoid behavior.

As Gene's case illustrates, when paranoid people act on their suspicions, they often bring about the very situation they feared in the first place. It is crucial that courts realize that the parent who first raises an accusation of divorce poison may well be the perpetrator rather than the victim. Otherwise the court might deprive the healthier parent of custody. In this manner, the paranoid parent's efforts are sometimes successful.

More often than not, however, their efforts backfire. They confuse and scare the children and ultimately alienate them. When this occurs the parents almost never recognize their own contributions to the problem. Instead they feel vindicated in their initial paranoid beliefs. They tell themselves, and anyone who will listen, "I knew they were against me all the time."

Paranoid parents gravitate to the courts to seek justice. So you may have no choice but to use legal remedies to respond to their destructive behavior. This is unfortunate. Courtroom battles are inevitably embarrassing and frustrating. They exacerbate rather than relieve a paranoid person's concerns about persecution. Some therapists have reported success when courts have ordered paranoid parents to participate in treatment with groups of families.

TAKE ACTION

If paranoia is fueling divorce poison, you must exercise great care in how you treat the perpetrator. Paranoid people become more anxious when they sense that important information is being withheld, or when things are uncertain. Their anxiety leads to indignation and rage. Like scared dogs, paranoid people can become dangerous when they feel threatened. The less uncertainty they face, the less they will fill in the gaps of their knowledge with suspicions and distortions.

- Try to keep a paranoid ex informed of relevant matters.
- Communicate clearly in a calm and respectful tone of voice. Avoid any appearance of concealing things.
- Give the paranoid parent time to think about any proposals before expecting a response.
- Set clear and reasonable limits and then stick to them.
- As much as possible, follow through on your agreements and act in a predictable manner.

REENACTMENTS

A few years ago I made a discovery. In reviewing the backgrounds of parents who foster alienation, I noticed that a very high percentage had a poor or absent relationship with at least one of their own parents. I think there is a connection.

Sigmund Freud wrote about our "compulsion to repeat" past unpleasant experiences and modern psychological research has confirmed this tendency. Sometimes the replay occurs in our minds, as in the case of "flashbacks" or dreams, and sometimes in reality, as in the case of child abuse victims who inflict similar abuse on their own children.

The psychological purpose of reenactment is not clear. One theory suggests that a sense of mastery is gained by inflicting the trauma on someone else so that the formerly helpless victim becomes the powerful perpetrator. This may explain why some parents mistreat their children in the same way the parents were mistreated in childhood, and why some divorced parents who have suffered the absence of a parent will try to inflict the same deprivation on their children rather than protect them from a similar fate. If we recognize when this dynamic lies behind brainwashing, we can use this information to help persuade a parent to stop the destructive behavior.

One woman in San Francisco had not talked to her own father for the nine years prior to his death. She had been programmed to believe that he was a criminal unworthy of her love. Somehow she managed to marry a man whose moral character was above reproach. He was an involved, devoted father, with a patient, good-hearted, optimistic nature. One afternoon this woman came home after having had a few drinks with lunch. She became volatile and enraged over an imagined slight on his part. Despite her sons' presence in the house, she began screaming vile epithets at her husband and clawing at his face. Then she bashed him over the head with a metal garbage can, which left a nine-inch dent (in the can, not his head). After she ripped his shirt and began choking him, he tried to restrain her by grabbing her upper arms. When she still would not stop, he called the police. They came and calmed things down.

A few days later the husband was shocked to be served with papers indicating that his wife had filed criminal charges against him. She told her sons (and everyone else who would listen) that their father was a violent man. She started calling herself a battered wife, and made it her mission to have her husband declared a felon and thrown in jail. Unlike most truly battered women, she showed no fear of her husband. Quite the opposite: She repeatedly harassed him with taunting and threatening phone calls. None of the domestic violence experts she consulted (all women) agreed that she was a battered woman. Instead they thought that *she* had trouble controlling her own violent impulses. The woman went from one therapist to another until she finally found one, selected by her lawyer, who responded to her persuasive presentation, believed her tales of victimhood, and was willing to testify on her behalf.

The mother filed for divorce and tried to keep the father from having any access to his sons. When the court did not agree, she began programming the boys to fear their father. She told them that she hoped they did not grow up to be like their father because he was evil. She tried to get the boys to regard him as a criminal and reject him, just as she rejected her own father. The court warned her that if she continued her attempts at brainwashing she would lose custody. But the impulse to re-create in her children the alienation she suffered toward her own father was strong and she continued to give in to it. Eventually she lost custody.

It is well known that some children who are abused by their parents grow up to be abusing parents themselves. Custody evaluators see a related phenomenon. Divorced parents who were victims of child abuse, eager to protect their own children from such a fate, and angry and distrustful toward their ex-spouse, may be too quick to conclude that the ex has abused the children. Normal childhood events, such as nightmares, minor bruises, touching the crotch, all become the basis for suspicions of abuse. Parents on the lookout for abuse dismiss the more probable benign explanations for such events. When these parents convince themselves that their ex has abused the children, they have less incentive to inhibit bad-mouthing and bashing because they believe their children should hate their other parent. The added danger is that, through repeated questioning, the children may eventually develop false beliefs that they have been abused. As discussed in chapter 3, such false beliefs create serious psychological problems in addition to the alienation from the alleged abuser.

TAKE ACTION

If your ex seems to be reenacting a childhood deprivation or trauma, ask one of his or her close relatives, such as a sibling, to speak with your ex about the situation. They should help your ex recall the unpleasant feelings associated with the deprivation, and encourage him or her to spare the children a similar fate. People who reenact earlier traumas may not be fully aware of what drives their behavior. They will be more receptive to hearing this type of analysis from a trusted relative than from the target of their divorce poison. It is likely that your ex will be angry if he or she learns that you spoke to the relatives. This is a risk you will need to consider before taking this action.

HOSTILITY TOWARD THE CHILDREN

Parents with weak psychological boundaries are not fully aware of the damage they are doing to their children. If they were, presumably they would stop acting so destructively. But some brainwashing parents actually harbor substantial hostility toward their children. In some cases they are jealous of the attention the children receive from the ex. To cover up such feelings, they point to their exaggerated efforts to "protect" the children from the other parent as evidence of how much they love the children. *Under the guise of protection, these parents induce unnecessary anxiety while attempting to drive a wedge between the children and the target parent. Loving parents promote their children's emotional security. Cruel and emotionally abusive parents intensify their children's fears and insecurities.*

I participated in one case in which a mother with custody protested the father's desire to spend longer weekends with his daughter, even though the four-year-old pleaded for more time with her father. The mother claimed that spending an extra night would be more than the child could handle. And she found two psychologists to support her claim. (Incidentally, it is a sad commentary on the state of forensic psychology that parents can usually locate a mental health "expert" who is willing to offer, in testimony under oath, biased opinions or opinions with no scientific foundation. Chapter 8, "Getting Professional Help," provides guidelines for evaluating those from whom you seek help.)

My review of the case revealed that this woman had a harsh and rigid approach to child-rearing. She admitting to using spanking as a regular form of discipline and seemed to take pride in this. Although the father was available to care for his daughter every afternoon and wanted very much to do so, the mother insisted on leaving the child in a ten-hour day care program five days per week. On weekends she usually left her daughter with baby-sitters while she went out to bars. And her psychological test profile showed several signs of an immature and self-centered personality with severe limitations in being able to empathize with her daughter's feelings. My conclusion: Although she presented herself as obsessively concerned with protecting her daughter, odds were that this woman had far less love for her child than she pretended.

Subsequent events confirmed my impressions. The judge decided that the girl could benefit from having more time with her father and expanded her weekend time to begin Thursday at noon and extend to Monday morning. The judge also awarded the father thirty days of contact in the summer. On my advice the father offered a plan in which the thirty days would not be taken consecutively. I thought one whole month was too long for a four-year-old child to be away from either parent. Remember, the mother originally complained that just three consecutive weekend days were too much for her daughter to be apart from her. If her complaint about three days was sincere (however misguided), she should have jumped at the chance to reduce thirty days to several shorter periods. Instead, she revealed her true colors when she rejected the father's offer and insisted that the entire thirty days be taken consecutively.

TAKE ACTION

When your ex tries to undermine your child's sense of security with you, invite the child to judge for himself whether the other parent's fears are justified. For example, if the allegation is made that you do not allow the child to call his father when he is with you, point out how this allegation conflicts with the numerous times in which such calls were facilitated. Help your child understand that the other parent sometimes has fears and worries that are exaggerated, and that the child does not have to share these worries. When divorce poison masks a lot of hostility toward the children, you will have a better chance of being effective if you concentrate on helping the children rationally evaluate the alienating parent's overprotective behavior. This should be done in a gentle manner, with sensitivity to your child's anxiety. Consider having a third party implement this suggestion. This may help the children avoid the sense that they are being asked to take sides.

Usually several factors combine to bring about bashing and brainwashing. Two situations, though, are the most likely to provoke a parent into malicious criticism: custody disputes and remarriage. These bring out the worst in parents. I estimate that more than half of all cases of parental brainwashing occur in the context of a custody battle. And an ex-spouse's remarriage may reignite the high degree of rage and hostility that can lead to divorce poison. Often the two situations combine. Remarriage, with its accompanying changes, triggers a renewed battle over where the children will live.

Let us examine how custody disputes and remarriage place your family at higher risk for divorce poison, and what you can do to protect yourself and your children.

CUSTODY LITIGATION

When Jennifer told Karl that she wanted a divorce, he was infuriated. She added insult to injury when she said she was moving to another state and taking the kids with her. Karl was beside himself with rage. He retained an attorney known for his brutal, "take no prisoners" tactics and immediately sued for sole custody. While the suit was pending, Karl took every opportunity to tell the children what a bad, selfish mother they had. He told them secrets that she had confided to him during the early stage of their marriage, such as her confession of a brief lesbian encounter in college. Blinded by his anger, Karl was committed to destroying Jennifer's reputation with her own children. Jennifer countered with some mild bad-mouthing of her own.

Custody litigation is a hostile process. Hostility generates the dispute in the first place. And the dispute itself—the stress, frustration, and legal maneuvering—breeds additional hostility. One way to express all this hostility is to destroy the other parent's relationship with the children. So if you are involved in a custody dispute, and your children are being exposed to bad-mouthing, bashing and brainwashing may come next.

Divorce poison in a custody battle, however, has a more specific purpose than the mere expression of hostility. Karl's bashing of Jennifer began as a diffuse outlet for his rage. But as the litigation heated up, he began a more systematic and focused campaign to turn the children against their mother. He began brainwashing them. Now he was not merely punishing Jennifer. He was trying to gain a strategic advantage in court. Like many parents, Karl believed that he could win the custody battle if he could successfully manipulate his children's affections. In some cases this works.

Creating False Impressions

If your children turn against you, the burden is on you to prove your innocence. You will need to present evidence of your previous good relationship with the children. And you will need to show that you have done nothing to warrant their rejection. This will be difficult if you are unlucky enough to encounter a certain type of judge or mental health professional appointed by the judge to make custody recommendations. Such professionals understand that parents influence children's affections. But they fail to realize how completely a child can be manipulated to turn against a good parent. They believe that "where there's smoke, there's fire." They assume that if your child hates or fears you, you must have done something to deserve it. And you will lose custody.

You have a better chance of defending yourself with a judge who believes that children can be brainwashed. But even then, many times the manipulations are so subtle that they go undetected. If the judge mistakenly believes that your child's alienation is reality based and not the result of programming, she will deprive you of custody. To hold on to your children, you will need to expose your ex's motives and manipulations. Review the malignant motives discussed earlier and the material in the next two chapters, which explain exactly how irrational alienation is promulgated.

Alienated parents must not only prove that their children have been manipulated, they must convince the judge that the manipulation caused the alienation. Judges are often unclear about exactly what caused the alienation. All parents occasionally act in irrational ways that frighten and anger children. This is particularly true around the time of the breakup, when parents are most stressed. A parent intent on poisoning his children's affections will use such behavior as the foundation for an alienation campaign. A few incidents, which were not at all typical of a parent's usual behavior, are cited as justification for the children's rejection of a formerly loved parent.

I was called in to one case by a distraught mother. Her son had convinced the court-appointed counselor that he should have no more than brief contacts with his mother. The boy complained that his mother expected him to spend too much time with her and not enough with his friends. He also accused her of losing her temper and spanking him. He said he was afraid to be alone with her. And when it came time to be with her, he did act frightened.

The mother admitted to the counselor that she had spanked her son on three separate occasions. She also said that she probably restricted his freedom more than most mothers and that she could stand to improve in this regard. Nevertheless, she maintained that her son's current attitude was not a realistic response to her parenting: It was the result of his father's programming.

The counselor agreed that the father was actively trying to turn the boy against his mother. Nevertheless, he concluded that the mother was equally responsible for her son's alienation. For this reason he recommended that the boy's wish to avoid his mother be honored by the court. Although the phrase is overused, I thought this clearly was a case of "blaming the victim."

I also thought this counselor's conclusion showed poor common sense. He failed to appreciate that every parent has faults. We all do or say things to our children that we regret. There will usually be some elements of truth to an alienated child's complaints about the target's behavior. Without systematic programming, however, this behavior would never result in the child's alienation from the parent. And it would never justify depriving a mother of access to her child.

This counselor did not fully comprehend the power of mental coercion, so he found it hard to believe that the boy's alienation lacked any firm basis in reality. His sympathies rested with the scared child. His first priority was to shield the boy from what appeared to be a frightening situation—spending time with his own mother!

What should you do if you are in a custody dispute and are blamed for your child's estrangement from you? Two things: You must expose the nature of the programming, a topic we take up in chapters 5 and 6; and you must present evidence of the good relationship you enjoyed with your child prior to the bashing and brainwashing.

TAKE ACTION

To show that you have previously enjoyed a good relationship with your children, provide the court-appointed evaluator with objective evidence. Bring in videotapes, photographs, gifts, and greeting cards that demonstrate your children's affection toward you. Give the evaluator a list of names and phone numbers of adults who have observed you and your children together. Make sure the list includes people who would not be expected to be biased in your favor. Your mother may give you a glowing endorsement as a parent, but the court is not likely to view her as an impartial reporter. The list should include teachers, coaches, and parents who have seen you at extracurricular activities. Ask the evaluator to contact these people. *Why?* The evaluator will hear vastly conflicting accounts of reality. If your children are alienated, their fears and complaints may appear very convincing. You will have a better chance of proving that their negative attitudes are a response to divorce poison if you can provide the evaluator and the court with evidence that your past involvement with the children was generally positive.

One father had his former mother-in-law describe the close relationship that used to exist between him and his son. This was most convincing because, if anything, the court would have expected her to be biased in favor of her own daughter. One mother, whose children claimed that she was never any fun to be with, brought in videotapes of her and the children playing happily together throughout their earlier years. This showed the court-appointed evaluator that her children's complaints were the product of recent attitude changes and were not characteristic of their relationship.

Before you convince a judge to force your child to face the object of his fear—you—the judge will need to be convinced that the fear is not a realistic response to any mistreatment on your part. Your attorney's job, with your help, will be to educate the court about the specific means by which your child has been turned against you. Sometimes a child's fear is so great, and the child so emphatic, that clear evidence of brainwashing is not enough to erase a measure of doubt about the target's parenting abilities. Particularly when allegations are raised of gross mistreatment or abuse, the judge may decide it is better to err on the side of caution and restrict the child's contact with the estranged parent. The problem with this approach is that it further entrenches alienation. In the interests of protecting the child from harm, the court inadvertently joins in emotional abuse by depriving the child of a loving relationship with the target.

> You can lose custody of your children if the judge fails to recognize that their denigration and discomfort with you are signs of bashing and brainwashing. This can occur for three reasons:
>
> 1. The judge may not believe that children can be programmed to turn against a parent.
> 2. The signs of manipulation may be subtle and elude detection.
> 3. In spite of detecting manipulation, the judge may hold your behavior accountable for your children's rejection.

The Child Preference Factor

We have discussed how divorce poison can cost you custody if the judge believes that your behavior is responsible for your children's rejection. In some cases, however, a manipulative parent can gain the upper hand in custody litigation merely by convincing the child to express a preference to live with him or her. A majority of states allow the judge to give weight to your child's preference, depending on the age of the child. In Texas, for example, a child ten years of age or older may designate the custodial parent. The child's choice is not followed automatically; it is subject to the judge's approval. But the law was enacted because the legislature wanted judges to give strong consideration to the wishes of children who had reached their tenth birthday.

When a child's custody preference is decisive, parents have a strong incentive to mold that preference. Some will resort to brainwashing to accomplish this goal. If the child can be coerced into choosing one parent over the other, it could spare a parent the necessity of a costly custody trial. Moreover, since courts generally prefer to keep siblings together, the parent who persuades the oldest child to take sides may win custody of all the children.

Here is the general scenario. The parent engages in a campaign to turn the child against the other parent. Once the child has been successfully programmed, the parent takes the child to an attorney. After hearing the child's litany of complaints against the target, the attorney draws up an affidavit, which the child signs. The child may then sheepishly avoid telling the nonpreferred parent about the trip to the lawyer's office or about the affidavit. That parent may first learn about the affidavit only upon being served with legal papers.

TAKE ACTION

If you have reason to believe that your ex is bad-mouthing you to the children, and he or she threatens to pressure the children to express a custody preference, you must take steps to protect yourself. Find out what the laws are in your state regarding children's custody preferences. Ask a family lawyer or a legal aid society. You may also locate this information on the Internet. If your children are old enough to sign an affidavit of preference, you will need to prepare them for the possibility that their other parent will ask them to do so. Tell the children that you know they love both their parents and that they do not have to take sides in the dispute. If anyone asks them to do so, they can simply say that they don't want to be put in the middle. If you wait until your children have expressed a preference, it may be too late to reverse the damage. The very act of publicly declaring their allegiance to one parent can further entrench their alienation from the other.

Lynn did a good job of helping her sons prepare for the possibility that their father might ask them to sign an affidavit of preference. She explained, "Dad wants you to live with him during the school week. I want you to live with me. If we don't agree on a solution, then we will go to court and ask a judge to decide what is best. But the decision is made by grown-ups. You don't have to choose. I know you love me and you love Dad. That's why I'm not going to ask you to decide and I hope Dad won't either. Children don't like having to choose which parent to live with."

"I know Dad has been saying bad things about me," Lynn added. "And, just in case he asks you to sign something saying you want to live with him, I'm letting you know that you don't have to do that if you don't want to. Just tell Dad that you love both of us and you don't want to get in the middle of this. Tell him to work it out with me or with a judge, but to leave you out of it. Do you think you can do that?"

I cannot emphasize enough the importance of taking action as soon as you suspect that your child might be pressured to express a preference to live apart from you. If you wait until your child makes this decision, it could be too late. Many parents are shocked to learn that their child's preference influenced the outcome of the custody battle *even when the court agreed that the preference was solely the result of programming.* This occurred in a Missouri case. An eleven-year-old girl, Marsha, said she no longer wanted to see her father. Despite years of a good relationship, she claimed that she hated him. Her mother supported her and refused the father any access to his daughter. She also filed a motion in court to take away the father's right to see Marsha.

When the judge ordered the mother to let Marsha spend time with her father, Marsha and her mother responded by telling authorities that the father sexually abused his daughter. The accusation was determined to be completely unfounded and the judge again ordered the mother to facilitate Marsha's contact with her father. Also, because Marsha was exposed to so much turmoil, the judge appointed an attorney to act on Marsha's behalf in the litigation. This attorney is known as a G.A.L., which stands for *guardian ad litem.*

The G.A.L. has the authority to initiate investigations, and in this case she did so. She learned that Marsha's negative attitude toward her father was entirely the result of her mother's insistent programming, combined with Marsha's wish to be her mother's ally. The father was relieved. He expected that this nightmare would soon be over.

At the next court hearing, the G.A.L. told the judge that she was convinced that Marsha would be perfectly safe with her father. But her next statement devastated the father. Because of the intensity of Marsha's fears, the G.A.L. did not think the court should "force the issue." Instead, she recommended that Marsha be required to see her father only under strict supervision and for brief periods of time. Thus Marsha's preference determined the outcome of this custody dispute, even though the G.A.L. and the judge both knew that this preference reflected nothing more than her mother's indoctrination. What the court needed to know is that sometimes forcing the issue is a child's only hope for normalizing relations with the target parent. Chapter 8, "Getting Professional Help," explains how courts can take a more active role in helping children like Marsha.

Wearing Down the Opposition

Marsha's father eventually gave up. He could no longer afford the toll this ordeal was taking on his physical and emotional health or on his pocketbook. Too many custody cases end up this way. Manipulation is successful not because the court is convinced that the target is a bad parent, and not because the court automatically accepts an older child's custodial preference. The manipulation is successful in helping a parent win custody merely by wearing down the opposition.

Parents who are the target of an effective campaign of bashing and brainwashing often feel powerless to reverse the process. Their initial attempts to reason with their children fail. They don't know how else to defend themselves. They see their resources dwindling. Rather than continue the battle, they decide that it is best for them and their children to accept the inevitable, cut their losses, and avoid the ordeal of a trial.

This may mean giving up hope of seeing the children, at least for a while. The estrangement, though, is not always permanent. Particularly when the chief aim of the parent doing the brainwashing is to win custody, the target's resignation may have a paradoxical effect. Once the threat of losing custody is eliminated, the brainwashing parent may reduce the intensity of the programming. The children may be allowed to resurrect positive feelings for the parent they were taught to hate.

No one can tell you when you have reached your limit, or when to call it quits. If this is what you decide, nothing will erase the heartache of losing your child. But I suggest you read chapter 9, "Letting Go," carefully for tips on how to announce your decision to the children, how to cope with the loss, and how to prepare for a future reconciliation.

Hoisted with Their Own Petards

Parents who try to poison their children's affections in order to win custody expect the courts to sympathize with their position. Some of these parents are relatively unaware that they are guilty of fostering alienation. Others know exactly what they are doing and are counting on the court's naïveté about such matters. They think they can pull the wool over the judge's eyes.

In the past, this may have been a safe assumption. But I hope books such as this will turn the tide. *As mental health professionals and family courts become more familiar with the phenomena of bad-mouthing, bashing, and brainwashing, and their harmful impact on children, parents who engage in such practices should beware: You run a greater chance of losing custody.*

First, experts and judges will discount children's attitudes and preferences when these are understood as the result of programming. So no advantage will be gained. But there will be a further disadvantage incurred by parents engaged in destructive criticism. They are apt to be judged more negatively because they are jeopardizing their child's emotional welfare. Courts do not look kindly on parents who try to deprive their children of a loving relationship with the other parent. So what is intended to bolster a case for custody will not only fail to help, it will backfire. Rather than accept a child's alienation as proof of the target's deficiency, the court will view the alienation as evidence of the manipulative parent's inadequacy.

But a wise parent does not rely on faith in the court's ability to detect manipulation. You must help the court. You must learn all you can about how your children are being programmed. You must convey this information to any mental health professionals involved in your case. And your attorney must convey this information effectively to the judge.

PREVENTING ALIENATION DURING CUSTODY LITIGATION

There are several things you can do to reduce the incidence of bashing and brainwashing in a custody battle. The most important would be to remove the incentive: Use every means to avoid custody litigation in the first place. When the custody outcome is not hanging in the balance, parents have less need to sway their children's affections, and thus you face less risk of divorce poison.

First, examine your reasons for seeking custody. If they are inadequate, you may be able to prevent or reverse an alienation campaign by dropping the threat to seek custody. Custody should not be a means to punish your spouse, avoid child support, alleviate guilt, or prove your worth to the world. I discuss these and other wrong reasons for seeking custody in greater detail in *The Custody Revolution*.

If you and your spouse have a genuine disagreement about what custody arrangement would be best for your children, before taking it to court, take it to a custody consultant for an independent opinion. A custody consultant is a mental health professional with expertise in child development and custody matters. When I serve in this capacity, I help parents understand their children's needs and the extent to which different custody plans meet these needs. Once both parents grasp the relevant issues, the optimal custody arrangement may become self-evident. Or I may think of a reasonable alternative that did not occur to either parent. I also try to impress upon parents how their custody dispute, and related efforts to poison the children's affections, will hurt the children. With such professional input, many parents are able to reduce their hostility, drop their adversarial stance, and reach an agreement. Also, the consultant's findings and recommendations can play a role in mediating or negotiating a solution that minimizes either parent's feelings of having lost the battle.

If your spouse refuses to seek custody consultation, or the effort fails, try other means to limit and reduce the hostility of your divorce. If you have wronged your spouse, recognize the damage you have caused, take responsibility for it and offer a genuine apology, and make amends when possible. If you have been unfair about the financial settlement, for example, reconsider your stance. Anything you can do to reduce anger lessens the motive for bad-mouthing.

If you must dispute custody, retain attorneys who are committed to amicable resolutions. Some lawyers subscribe to a model of practice known as "collaborative family law." These lawyers pledge to do everything possible to reach a settlement without going to court. In fact, they agree beforehand to withdraw from the case if their efforts are unsuccessful. They believe that when both attorneys make this agreement, a structure is created from the outset that encourages more constructive and creative negotiations. See the Resources section at the end of the book for more information about the collaborative law option.

Some lawyers who do not work formally in the collaborative law model nevertheless are known for their practice of encouraging and supporting efforts to settle out of court and reduce animosity. Try to find a lawyer with this reputation. When negotiations between such attorneys are unsuccessful, they will recommend mediation. Other lawyers oppose mediation. Particularly avoid attorneys who have reputations for "demolishing the opposition." Such attorneys may win you some battles, but their tactics invite retaliation, which means a greater risk of badmouthing. One prominent New York attorney told his clients that the way to win custody battles is to outspend the opposition. His cases were known for the huge expenses generated by a maddening flood of paperwork and multiple court hearings that eventually drove the opposition into submission. This left his clients facing a postdivorce atmosphere riddled with hostility.

TAKE ACTION

To prevent alienation in custody disputes:

- Consider dropping the threat to sue for custody. Don't seek custody for the wrong reasons.

- Take responsibility for your contributions to your spouse's anger and do what you can to reduce hostility.

- Seek an independent opinion from a custody consultant.

- Choose an attorney with a reputation for amicable resolutions out of court.

- Avoid attorneys who generate unnecessary conflict and hostility.

REMARRIAGE

After custody litigation, you are most at risk for bad-mouthing, bashing, and brainwashing when either you or your ex-spouse remarries. Even former spouses who got along reasonably well face new tension in their relationship when one of them finds love again.

Jealousy

People are often surprised at the intensity of their reaction to the news that an ex-spouse plans to remarry. They may not have expected to be affected by such an event. But instead they find themselves reexperiencing much of the hurt and anger that accompanied the divorce. Those who are least aware of lingering feelings for their ex, or least in touch with fantasies of reconciliation, are most susceptible to destructive reactions. They have the most difficulty coping with the jealousy and blow to their pride triggered by the remarriage. Rather than acknowledge the true source of feelings that they regard as unwanted or inappropriate, they hide behind a variety of defenses.

A common maneuver is to deny being personally bothered by the remarriage while expressing great concern about its impact on the children. Psychoanalyst Wilhelm Reich called this a "pretended" motive. Upon learning of his ex-wife's engagement a man said, "I don't care what you want to do with your life. But the children are very upset about it." At the time he said this, the children were showing no signs of distress.

Another rationalization is to claim that one is not upset by the idea of remarriage itself, but by the specific character of the stepparent, or the new partner's manner of relating to the children. Divorce poison comes into play when your ex channels unwanted and unpleasant feelings triggered by your remarriage into unwarranted denigration of you and your new partner.

TAKE ACTION

To respond to an ex who is jealous of your remarriage:

- Reaffirm the connection that will always exist between the two of you as a result of having children together.

- Emphasize that your remarriage does not diminish the importance of cooperation in raising the children.

- Acknowledge that the remarriage is an adjustment for everyone; the children deserve both parents' support in coping with this transition, just as they would expect with other transitions in their lives, such as a change of schools.

- Ask your ex to put himself in your place and imagine how he or she would like you to handle it with the children if he or she announced plans to remarry.

Jealousy on the part of the parent who learns of his ex's plans to remarry is not the only motive for divorce poison in this situation. Destructive criticism is just as likely, maybe more likely, to come from the remarried spouse and the new partner. In my work with remarried families I have identified three key factors that often trigger attempts to alienate children: (1) the wish to erase the ex from the child's life in order to "make room" for the stepparent; (2) competitive feelings between the ex-spouse and stepparent; and (3) the new couple's attempt to unite around a common enemy.

I Wish He Would Just Disappear

Parents who remarry often believe that they now have the perfect family setting in which to raise their children. But one thing mars this image: the former spouse. Many remarried couples harbor the fantasy, "If only the ex would disappear from the scene . . ." One way to fulfill this fantasy is by driving a wedge between the children and the other parent.

A parent is most likely to regard the other parent as dispensable when the child was very young at the time of the divorce, or the parents were never married, and the new marriage occurs soon after. In these cases, each parent has had little opportunity to observe the child around the other parent. A mother may believe, in the abstract, that children deserve to know their real father. But she has not seen, with her own eyes, how her child benefits from spending time with the man. Certainly a one-year-old child cannot tell her how much he looks forward to seeing his dad.

Without a history of family interaction involving mother, father, and child, it is harder for the mother to appreciate the father's role in the child's life. When she remarries, she would rather such family history be centered around her and her current husband. The father is seen as an interloper. His involvement complicates the picture. Essentially, the mother would like to pretend that her relationship with the child's father never happened. When he won't bow out gracefully, he is seen as thwarting her second chance for a happy family. As one remarried woman told her ex-husband, "My daughter has a mother and a father in her home. She doesn't need you." (Brainwashing parents tend to refer to the children as "mine" rather than "ours.") The wish to erase the ex is more likely to come from a remarried mother than father. Perhaps this is because it was not too long ago that society assumed that children should be cared for by their mothers after divorce and have only occasional contact with Dad. Despite years of research documenting a father's importance to his children, and changing custody laws that reflect this understanding, many people continue to regard fathers as marginally significant parents.

Some people believe that the less time the child has been with the father, the less is lost if the stepfather replaces the father. To a certain extent this is correct. Generally speaking, younger children find it easier to develop a relationship with a stepparent that approximates a parent-child bond, and to benefit from that relationship. However, there is no reason why children should have to choose. They are capable of having strong ties both to their father and stepfather.

Even when her child is so young that the stepfather could adequately replace the father, a mother still has reasons to promote the father's involvement. When the child is older, he or she may want to know the father. Many children suffer intense feelings of rejection when a divorced parent has not remained involved. In *The Custody Revolution* I discuss the impact of the absent parent on boys and girls. I show how children who have lost contact with a parent following divorce are more likely to have problems with interpersonal relationships and lower self-esteem. The children's problems may, in turn, diminish the quality of their relationship with the remarried parent and the stepparent.

It is worth considering, too, what would happen if the mother's second marriage failed (not an unlikely event since second marriages have a higher divorce rate than first marriages). In most such cases children lose all contact with their former stepfather even when he has been a central figure in their development. Maintaining a close tie to the father is good insurance against such a loss. Much less likely, but also possible, is the death or incapacitation of the mother. In these cases, custody is usually transferred to the father. A good strong relationship with their father can help children through such hard times. A history of alienation from the father would compound the tragedy.

TAKE ACTION

To respond to a mother who wants you out of your child's life:

- Reassure the mother that your involvement will not interfere with her new husband's forming a close relationship with the children. In fact, you intend to actively promote the children's love and respect of their stepfather.

- Point out that as the biological (or adoptive) and legal father, your commitment is a lifelong one. Few stepfathers could offer the same assurance.

- Help the mother understand what she would be destroying if she succeeded in alienating the child from you. Describe your life with the child: your routines, play, mutual expressions of affection, serious talks, and your dreams for your child's future.

- If your child is still an infant, allow the mother to observe you with the baby several times to help her become comfortable with the idea that you can provide good care.

- Set a firm limit. Insist that you will never abandon your child. That is not an option. You do not want your child ever to question whether or not he was loved by his father.

Competition

The stepparent often instigates, or at least actively supports, destructive criticism of the other parent. Competitive feelings toward one's predecessor in love, sex, and marriage are natural. In mild form such feelings do

not become a problem. They may, in fact, benefit the children by motivating a stepparent to do the very best job possible in raising the stepchildren. The children then gain an additional adult who protects and
advances their interests.

When competitive feelings are very strong, the stepparent may resent
having to share the children's affection with their other parent. He or she
may have low self-esteem and be excessively competitive in most situations. Or the stepparent may feel especially deficient as a parent and feel
a need to prove superiority over the other parent. The two leading authorities on stepfamilies, Dr. Emily Visher and Dr. John Visher, described how
a man who feels that he failed as a father in his first marriage may regard
the second marriage as a chance to compensate for his earlier shortcomings. The sense of failure may be particularly acute if the stepfather has
not maintained regular and meaningful involvement with his biological
children. Some stepparents deal with this sense of failure by trying to
replace the other parent in the children's heart. They do so through bad-
mouthing, bashing, and brainwashing.

Some stepfathers act as if they are rescuing their new family from the
father. Particularly when this is the first marriage for the stepfather, he
will usually have different expectations about how a family should work
and may be excessively critical of his predecessor.

Competitive feelings are likely to occur when stepparents have no
children of their own and, for reasons of choice or infertility, do not
expect to have their own children. This situation is seen with stepmothers
as well as stepfathers.

Nelda and Ophelia were best friends. Then Nelda had an affair with
Ophelia's husband and married him soon after his divorce. Nelda had no
children from her previous marriage, was unable to become pregnant,
and did not want to adopt any children. Ophelia's daughter was Nelda's
one chance to be a mother.

Feeling intense rivalry with her now "ex–best friend," Nelda pressured
her husband to move to a new town four hours away by car with no airport nearby. At the same time, through a variety of tactics (discussed in
chapter 6, "The Corruption of Reality"), including overindulgence, extravagant promises, and excessive bad-mouthing of the mother, along with
the father's cooperation, Nelda manipulated her stepdaughter to ask to
move with them. Ophelia initially resisted. But her daughter insisted that
she really wanted to move and was angry that her mother was making it

difficult. Against her better judgment, and without legal counsel, Ophelia caved in to pressure and agreed to the move.

Shortly before Christmas vacation, Ophelia received a letter from her daughter. The girl wrote that she did not want to be forced to see her mother during the Christmas vacation. Her dad and Nelda had scheduled a trip to Disneyland, and she would have to miss it if she spent the vacation with her mother. The vocabulary and sentence structure of the letter made it clear that, although it was in her daughter's handwriting, it was composed by adults. A note from Nelda accompanied the letter. In her note, Nelda self-righteously exhorted Ophelia to place her daughter's interest before her own. Nelda pleaded with Ophelia to allow them to establish themselves as a family before pressing for contact with her daughter. Ophelia took what she thought was the high road, and allowed her daughter to go on the trip to Disneyland instead of seeing her.

When Ophelia was next scheduled to see her daughter, on the girl's birthday, she received another letter. In this letter, her daughter expressed her resentment of what was now being called "forced visitation" and added that, instead of seeing her mother, she wanted to spend her birthday with her family. Nelda and her husband had succeeded in twisting this girl's mind so that she no longer thought of her own mother as part of her family! When I first became acquainted with Ophelia, she had been waiting two years and had still not seen her daughter.

Ophelia's error, as I have emphasized repeatedly, was to wait too long before taking action. Passivity is common among parents who are the target of divorce poison, but it is costly. For reasons that will become clearer in the next chapter, it is crucial to maintain contact with your children when they are exposed to divorce poison.

TAKE ACTION

To deal with a competitive stepparent:

- When you learn of new things that your children have done with their stepparent, or new places where they have gone, let some of these activities be ones that you do not share with the children. The more stepparents feel they have a special place in the lives of the children, the less they feel the need to compete with you.

- Express your appreciation for the stepparent's contributions to your children's welfare and your hope that you can mutually support each other's role with the children.

- If problems persist, suggest that all three parents consult a therapist to help them work together better. In sessions with the remarried couple, the therapist can address some of the underlying factors that fuel the excessive competition.

Competition works both ways. After the remarriage, your ex can support the children's relationship with their stepparent. Or he or she may try to drive a wedge between the children and your new spouse. Ex-spouses who are still single may fear that the children will prefer the two-parent household because it more closely approximates the intact family that was lost with the divorce. Driven by such fear, your ex may attempt to compete by undermining the children's sense of love and security in the remarried household.

Often the ex fears that the children will come to love their stepparent more. This fear is exacerbated if the children begin using terms similar to Mom or Dad when referring to their stepparent. Because younger children are more apt to seek and accept a quasi parent-child relationship with the stepparent, they are particularly at risk for exposure to bashing and brainwashing of the stepparent by your ex. Also, they are more likely to be influenced by your ex's negative programming, because young children are generally more suggestible. Recall the little girl whose father told her that her stepfather was sent by the devil. Even if she did not fully believe this, she did begin to feel uneasy in her stepfather's presence.

Older children may feel more initial reserve and resentment toward a stepparent. Instead of helping the children adjust to the transition, competitive ex-spouses sometimes welcome their children's nascent negative feelings about the stepparent and use these transitional feelings as a foundation for a campaign of alienation. When confronted about their manipulations, such parents will usually reply with some variant of "I can't help the way my child feels about her stepparent, but I'm not going to stop her from expressing her true feelings."

One mother with whom I worked demonstrated how parents can put their children's interests above their competitive feelings. Patty worked hard to resist strong impulses to disparage her daughter Rachel's stepmother. Through a combination of inadequate legal representation, convincing lies told by her ex-husband, and a bad court verdict, Patty's involvement with Rachel was drastically curtailed. When her ex-husband remarried a week after the divorce became final, he delegated most of the responsibility for raising Rachel to his new wife. Patty naturally resented the fact that another woman was raising the child that she had carried in her womb for nine months and taken care of for five years. Her resentment acted as a filter when it came to evaluating the stepmother's parenting skills. Criticisms came easily; positive thoughts about her rival took decided effort. When Rachel complained to her mother about the stepmother's treatment, Patty felt some secret pleasure—which she kept secret. Though her rivalrous feelings were gratified, she knew that the stepmother was doing a lot for Rachel. And she knew it would not benefit Rachel to develop a bad relationship with her stepmother. So Patty listened to Rachel's complaints but did not respond eagerly. As far as the girl was concerned, bad-mouthing her stepmother was not the way to her mother's heart. Patty set an inspiring example of a woman whose love for her child outweighed strong impulses to engage in destructive criticism.

TAKE ACTION

If your ex is trying to undermine the children's relationship with their stepparent:

- Reassure your ex of the deep attachment that the children feel for him or her, based on the many experiences that formed the foundation of their relationship.

- Ask mutual acquaintances who have themselves navigated the challenges of remarriage to share their experiences with your ex, particularly how the children maintained their strong love for their parents while still getting along well with the stepparent.

- Help the children use different terms of endearment for their stepparent and your ex. Don't threaten your ex's status as the children's "daddy" or "mommy."

The Common Enemy

Remarried families are fragile. Children do not choose their stepparents. And adults do not marry in order to acquire stepchildren. The children merely go along with the deal. It takes time for the new family to get used to each other. It takes time to feel like a family. It is even more of a challenge when each adult brings children from a prior marriage. Small wonder that these types of "blended" families suffer a high rate of divorce.

One way to strengthen family cohesiveness is to unite around a common goal. Unfortunately, bad-mouthing and bashing you may become that goal. It may be the glue that holds the new family together, that gives them the sense of being on the same team.

Even more significant, while everyone is trashing you, they are avoiding all the negative feelings that would inevitably arise among them. As their anger gets channeled into criticisms of the other parent, they distract themselves from problems within their newly constituted family. The underlying motive is to deny the presence of conflict in the new relationship. This protects the couple from the anxiety generated by the prospect of another divorce. In some families, the new partner joins in a campaign of hate as a means of ingratiating himself or herself to the spouse. The basic message is, "Your battles are my battles." Particularly in the early stages of remarriage, the new spouse may find it difficult to take a different position with respect to the ex's character and the type of treatment he or she deserves.

Hal and his second wife, Annette, spent much of their time trashing Hal's first wife, Melinda. The more they did so, the closer they felt. Annette's children joined the chorus of denigration. Hal's son, Josh, couldn't resist participating. At first he felt disloyal to his mother, but he wanted to be accepted by the family, and complaining about his mother seemed to be the price of admission.

Josh had another motive. In a contest between his father and mother, Josh sensed that his father had more power. Although he was not consciously aware of it, Josh feared that the family's criticism could turn on him if he defended his mother. Like most people, Josh wanted to side with the winner. He wasn't in a position to stem the tide of denunciation. So he chose to affiliate with it. Psychologists refer to this strategy as "identifying with the aggressor." It is more popularly known as, "If you can't beat 'em, join 'em."

Uniting against a common enemy has one fatal weakness. When the enemy is vanquished, conflicts usually arise among the former allies. This is what happened in this family. Melinda finally gave up her efforts to counter the trashing and moved to another state. The family had virtually no contact with her. They lost their common enemy. Soon after, conflicts in their own family relationships began to surface. These had been present all along, but they were able to avoid them by making Melinda the target of all their hostility.

Josh's behavior is a good example of a point Dr. Gardner has emphasized in his work on parental alienation syndrome. When a child succumbs to divorce poison, the alienation results from a combination of the parental brainwashing and the child's own contributions. A child in a situation like Josh may join in the campaign of hatred for several reasons. The child may be capitulating to group pressure in order to be accepted within the new family. The child may also be attempting to reduce loyalty conflicts or his discomfort with the remarriage.

TAKE ACTION

Emphasize to your children that it takes courage to withstand group pressure. Let them know that it is healthier to maintain love and respect for all their parents, rather than participate in a campaign of hatred.

A child who feels caught between two homes may feel that the solution to the conflict is to declare a clear allegiance to one household. This motive can result in alienation from either parent. A child who is anxious or angry about the remarriage may channel these feelings into unwarranted hatred of the remarried parent and stepparent. Or the child's alienation may express the disappointment of reconciliation wishes that have been dashed by the remarriage. Regardless of the child's underlying motivation, if the favored parent welcomes the child's allegiance and fails to actively promote the child's affection for the other parent, the child may cling to this maladaptive solution.

CHECKLIST OF MALIGNANT MOTIVES

Just as a proper diagnosis must precede the treatment of an illness, correctly determining motives is the first step in coping with bashing and brainwashing. If you have been the target of vilification, you should be able to identify the perpetrator's motives from the following list. If none of the circumstances, feelings, and personality traits below apply to your situation, then you are probably dealing with something other than bashing and brainwashing. Also, if you have been falsely accused of brainwashing, proving the absence of these motives should improve your chances of establishing your innocence.

- Poor boundaries—failure to recognize the distinction between the parent's thoughts and feelings and the children's needs

- Desire for revenge

- Narcissism—the drive to magnify one's own importance while diminishing the value of the other parent

- Guilt—the attempt to deflect attention from one's own failings as a parent by denigrating the other parent

- Insecurity—the fear that the children will prefer the other parent

- Desire to vent anger about the ex-spouse and have feelings validated by friends without taking steps to protect children from exposure to criticisms of the other parent

- Unwillingness to accept the end of the marital relationship

- Paranoia—unwarranted belief that the other parent is fostering alienation

- History of a poor or absent relationship with at least one parent

- Hostility toward the children—exaggerated efforts to protect the children cover deep-seated antagonism
- Involvement in custody litigation
- Remarriage of one or both ex-spouses

When a prosecutor tries to establish a defendant's guilt, she must show that the accused had the motive and the means to commit the crime. We have finished uncovering the various motives behind the crimes we call bad-mouthing, bashing, and brainwashing. Next we expose the means by which parents manipulate their children's psyches.

CHAPTER 5

THE ALIENATING ENVIRONMENT

Even when your ex-spouse is not consciously trying to turn the children against you, certain conditions, when paired with bad-mouthing and bashing, heighten the risk of this occurring. These are the same conditions that foster indoctrination in cults: isolation, psychological dependence, and fear. These factors may not be essential. But in most cases of unjustified alienation, at least one of these factors is present. They are the soil and nutrients that increase the probability that poisoned messages will take root and crowd out loving memories. In order to maintain or reestablish loving contact with your children, you must protect them from this environment.

Let us take a closer look at how these conditions lay the groundwork for manipulating children's affections. Then, in chapter 6, we will examine the strategies and tactics used by parents within this habitat to twist their children's minds. Chapters 7 and 8 expand on the advice introduced here.

ISOLATION

A precondition of all brainwashing is some degree of isolation of the subject from other sources of support. Sometimes the isolation is complete.

For example, before Patty Hearst's formal indoctrination into the Symbionese Liberation Army, she was kept in a locked closet for several days. She was deprived of contact with any person, including her captors. This disoriented her. It made her more malleable. It made her more receptive to her captors' view of reality. Some religious cults require members to undergo a "disconnecting" process of enforced separation from friends and relatives.

How does this apply to parents intent on poisoning their children's relationship with a target parent? *Isolation makes children more vulnerable to divorce poison.* It does so for two reasons. First, isolation breeds dependence. Second, it prevents exposure to competing views of reality. Isolation removes the child from the influence of people who would counteract the effects of bad-mouthing and bashing.

One common means of achieving isolation is to keep the target from seeing the children. When the parent arrives to pick up the children for a scheduled period of possession, no one is home. Or a parent schedules the children for activities that coincide exactly with the time they are supposed to be with the target. One father scheduled elaborate vacations every time his daughters were to spend extended time with their mother. When the mother objected, the girls became angry with her because she was interfering with their chance to go skiing or to Disney World.

Manipulative parents will also try to restrict children's communication with the other parent and the other parent's relatives. A father who is poisoning his children against their mother, for example, cannot risk allowing them to talk to their maternal grandmother. During such a conversation the children would be apt to repeat the negative messages programmed by the father. Their grandmother would then surely contradict these messages. She would remind the children of how much their mother loved them and provide evidence to support her position.

Alienating parents usually screen telephone calls and let the answering machine take all calls placed by the target. Of course, these calls are never returned. In many cases the children are not even informed of the calls. This can be very effective in promoting alienation. A sixteen-year-old girl told me that her main reason for wanting no contact with her father was that he made no effort to talk with her for a ten-month period following the separation. Although she refused to see him throughout this time, she expected to hear from him. When he did not call, she assumed that he was not genuinely interested in a relationship. This was exactly what her mother had programmed her to believe. The father, on the other hand, told me that he made numerous attempts to reach his daughter by phone and that his ex had intercepted each of these calls.

Any attempt by the target parent to have contact with the children is generally thwarted. Letters are concealed from the children or returned unopened. Information is withheld about children's illnesses, academic problems and achievements, and important school and extracurricular activities. Basically, the children never learn of the other parent's interest and love. This sets them up to feel rejected by the target and makes them more dependent on the parent doing the bad-mouthing and bashing. As birthdays and holidays pass with no cards or gifts, the children feel unwanted and angry toward the parent who has disappointed them.

As with most psychological problems, alienation is most likely to be alleviated if you do something about it right away. Some therapists routinely advise parents to wait patiently until the child is ready to see them; in most cases this is bad advice. Except in rare circumstances, you should not permit your children to be totally isolated from you. You must act decisively. This does not mean using physical force or creating frightening confrontations. If peaceful means do not work, including therapy, it is time to consult a family law attorney experienced in representing parents in similar situations. When your ex is intent on keeping the children from you, it may take a court order to reunite with your children. As one psychologist, Dr. Mary Lund, put it, "Court orders for continued contact are the cornerstone for treatment" in these cases.

The importance of taking an active stance in the face of isolation tactics has been noted in several studies. In his study of ninety-nine alienated children, Dr. Gardner found that every case in which the court decreased the child's time with the programming parent, resulted in a reduction or elimination of the alienation. By contrast, when the court did not reduce the child's time with the programming, parent, nine out of ten children remained alienated.

The largest study of brainwashed children was published by the American Bar Association. A husband-and-wife research team, Dr. Stanley Clawar and Dr. Brynne Rivlin, found that increasing the child's contact with the alienated parent was the most effective way to reverse alienation. Here is what they reported: "Of the approximately four hundred cases we have seen where the courts have increased the contact with the target parent (and in half of these, over the objection of the children), there has been positive change in 90 percent of the relationships between the child and the target parent, including the elimination or reduction of many social-psychological, educational, and physical problems that the child presented prior to the modification."

In chapter 7, "Poison Control," you will learn many tactics to counteract divorce poison. But most of these strategies require contact with your children. Some severe cases of alienation may call for another approach. In some families, children reject the parent with whom they spend the most time. In most families, though, the solution to alienation caused by divorce poison begins with renewing contact between the children and the rejected parent.

TAKE ACTION

When your ex is isolating your children, or the children are consistently refusing to see you, be firm about maintaining regular contact and communication with the children; if your efforts to have contact are unsuccessful, propose therapy for the family with a professional who is experienced in helping alienated children; if your ex or the children refuse to participate in therapy, your last resort is to take legal action. See chapter 8 for tips on how to proceed.

RELOCATION

A more extreme tactic is to move with the children to another city, state, or country. Living far apart from your child is bound to strain your tie to each other, even if your ex earnestly supports the relationship. If your ex wants to thwart the relationship, geographical distance will make this much easier to accomplish. When your child moves, you may be saying your final good-byes. Remember Ophelia, whose plight we learned about in the previous chapter? Her daughter moved away with her father and stepmother, Ophelia's former best friend. Following the move, the girl kept making excuses to avoid being with her mother.

With divorce poison at work, absence does not make the heart grow fonder, it makes alienation grow more profound.

Your ex can keep your child apart from you even when you live in close proximity, but relocation magnifies the power to obstruct contact. A parent can simply fail to take the child to the airport, or arrive late and miss the flight, or not have the children at home when the other parent arrives from out of town.

Relocation is not always part of an alienation scheme. The urge to move may be triggered by remarriage, valuable educational and occupational opportunities, the wish to be closer to extended family, or an attempt to get away from a violent, intrusive, or overly controlling ex-spouse. But in many cases the move is clearly designed to separate the children from their other parent. Even when a compelling reason is given, it may not be genuine. The new job that is touted as a justification for moving may be secondary to the parent's true intent of diluting the strength of the child's relationship with the long-distant parent.

TAKE ACTION

If your ex lacks strong roots in your geographical area (most family, friends, or job opportunities are elsewhere) or has expressed a strong desire to move away, you must act before the divorce is final. Ask your attorney to set in place whatever safeguards are possible to prevent your children from being moved away from you. This may mean a geographical restriction on how far either parent could move with the children, or at least the requirement that you be given ample notice before such a move can take place, so that you can take steps to prevent it. You may have to be a joint custodian in order to reduce the risk of relocation. It is usually easier to prevent a move than to reverse it once the children are already situated in a new home and school.

Some moves are not specifically orchestrated to rupture the child's relationship with the other parent. These parents really do prefer to live somewhere else. But their reasons are not compelling. They do not welcome separating the child from the other parent, but they also are not particularly bothered by it. Essentially, these moving parents fail to appreciate the value of their children's relationship with the other parent.

Thus, when they want to move, they see no drawback to doing so. They don't program their children to hate the other parent, but their words and deeds program the children to regard regular contact with that parent as expendable.

Phyllis dreamed for years of living in Paris. She was so eager to fulfill her ambition that she dismissed all reservations expressed by Peter, her nine-year-old son. While Phyllis rhapsodized about France's fabulous cultural opportunities, Peter despaired at the thought of leaving his father, relatives, friends, school, baseball team, and neighborhood. Contemplating the *Mona Lisa* was a poor substitute for his weekly dinners with his grandmother. His father, who coached the baseball team, would be unable to attend games in Paris, if they even had Little League.

Phyllis denied that she was trying to alienate Peter from his dad. She thought that he should still love and admire his father. But she also wanted to convince him that his father's presence was not an important value when compared to something as exciting as living abroad. Not surprisingly, the father did not agree.

In court Phyllis testified, honestly, that she was not trying to disrupt Peter's relationship with his father. Her goal was not to keep them apart. The proposed separation was merely a by-product of her wish to pursue her own happiness and fulfillment. And that, her lawyer argued, was enough reason to place five thousand miles between father and son. Because a happy mother makes for a happy child.

The judge might have rejected such an obvious rationalization were it not for the testimony of a psychologist. This expert witness, brought in by the mother's lawyer, claimed that research studies proved that a mother's happiness was more important to a child's emotional well-being than such factors as the type of contact he had with his father, the stability of his living arrangements, and the familiarity of his environment. If Phyllis's desire to move to France were frustrated, the expert testified, she might become depressed and this would create more problems for Peter. Although the studies he cited did exist, a careful reading of them would not support the conclusions he reached. Unfortunately, the judge was not made aware of the errors in the psychologist's interpretation of the research. In the end the judge allowed Phyllis to move with Peter out of the country. I never learned what happened to Peter's relationship with his father after the move.

Some courts allow a custodial parent to move a child out of the country even if the court determines that the move conflicts with the child's best interests. Instead of the traditional focus on the child's needs, judges in these courts believe the proper test should focus on the custodial parent's motives. When the court is not convinced that the motives are vindictive, the parent is allowed to move the child away from the noncustodial parent. If Phyllis's case had been heard in one of these courts, she would have prevailed without having to argue that the move was good for Peter.

Relocation means that, at least when school is in session, you will not be an active participant in raising your children. You will be absent from the rhythm and flow of daily routines, negotiations, and accommodations that provide a sense of living together, as opposed to "just visiting." You will miss sharing meals with your children, helping with homework, quizzing them on spelling words, signing report cards, driving them to soccer games, working on science fair projects, reminding them to do chores, enforcing rules, reading them bedtime stories. You will not kiss them good night.

Even if you see your child during the school year, you will try to squeeze two months of living into a three-day weekend. Your child will be entertained. You might have a good time, but it will be mutually frustrating, and it will be heart-wrenching, at the end, to say good-bye, knowing that at least another month will pass before you see each other again.

As one father told me, "The little pleasures of friendship and affection with a child pop up at any time—they don't follow a schedule. Sarah talks about her delights, her worries, her dreams when they cross her mind—when she's in the middle of playing, or doing chores, or having breakfast—and if a father isn't there, involved in this, he doesn't really know what's going on."

The loss of yearlong contact with your child certainly changes the complexion of the relationship. If you have the misfortune to face this loss in your child's early years, the damage is more fundamental. Child development experts agree that frequent, face-to-face contacts with your infant are the building blocks of a healthy relationship. When it comes to being a parent, there is no substitute for on-the-job training. It helps you learn how to recognize and respond sensitively to your baby's moods and rhythms. And it helps your baby learn to associate your presence with comfort and pleasure.

In previous work I have emphasized the importance of allowing infants and toddlers to spend overnights with each parent after divorce. Bedtime rituals, lullabies, stories, snuggling, nighttime comforting, and morning routines all serve to bond parent and child to each other. These experiences form the bedrock of a lifelong relationship. This was brought home by a Stanford University study. The researchers found that divorced parents who cared for infants during the night were much less likely to drop out of their children's lives. I am pleased to report that the consensus of divorce experts is now shifting in the direction of appreciating the unique value of such regular contact.

Young children who move away from a parent lose the opportunity to experience the day-to-day contact that experts regard as the sine qua non of a solidly grounded parent-child relationship. A parent who truly supports the child's relationship with the long-distance parent can help bridge the gap. Women whose husbands are away in the military do this routinely. They talk about Daddy constantly. "When Daddy gets home, he'll take you to the park. That's the doll that Daddy gave you. Let's watch the videotape of Daddy reading you a bedtime story. Here's a picture of Daddy riding you on his shoulders." In this manner they help their children maintain a positive connection to the absent parent. Without such efforts, you have little hope of occupying the space in your child's mind reserved for a parent.

As a virtual stranger to your baby, you will not be able to make up for lost time by spending long periods of time together. A prolonged separation from your ex will stress your infant and make it less likely that your child will associate time with you as a pleasurable experience. Until your child is older, if you don't have regular contact, you may get to see each other only when you travel to your ex's city.

When children are older, living in separate cities creates other complications. Even if your ex accepts your involvement with the children, the logistics of maintaining a long-distance relationship can be formidable. The task calls for much creativity and flexibility. Check the Resources section for books that offer valuable advice for parents in this situation.

If you travel to your children's hometown and stay at a hotel, you will be better able to fit into the fabric of their lives—attend soccer games, drive them to and from recreational and social activities, attend school events, and visit with teachers. But the experience is a mixed blessing. As you observe the children in their home territory, you will become painfully aware of how much you are missing by living apart from them.

As Miriam Galper Cohen describes in her excellent guide, *Long-Distance Parenting*, "Being in a child's home surroundings gives you a very different experience of your own child. It can be a very sad, touching time for a long-distance parent, yet rewarding in its own way." The drawback is that the children will not be part of your everyday life. If you remarry, the children will miss opportunities to form close relationships with your spouse and their stepsiblings and half-siblings.

TAKE ACTION

When you travel to see your children, bring the certified legal documents that spell out your rights to access. You may need to show these to legal authorities if your ex denies you contact.

If the children travel to your home, contacts will generally be limited to school vacation periods. The children will be out of their usual element. As they become more involved with local friends, they may resent having to travel far from their neighborhood. They may regard trips to your home as unwelcome intrusions in their social and recreational activities. They miss out on athletic events, parties, and other opportunities for socializing and strengthening friendships. Relocation creates a conflict for children between seeing the absent parent and maintaining normal peer activities, a conflict that is usually avoided when the parent lives in close proximity. Vindictive ex-spouses exploit this conflict by reminding the children of how much they are missing when they travel away from home. With older children, it is sometimes difficult to determine how much of their resistance to spending time with a parent is driven by divorce poison and how much is due to the children's genuine preferences.

When the children do make the trip to your home, your relationship will take on a different tone. You won't be involved in their daily life and routines. You won't be supervising homework and chores, setting and enforcing limits, arranging and supervising interactions with peers, and dealing with conflicts. As one divorce study put it, you won't be a "full-service" parent.

Your lack of attendance at school activities may take a toll on your children's school performance. A large U.S. Department of Education study found that the children in grades one through twelve who get mostly As, enjoy school, and participate in extracurricular events are more likely to have fathers who attended typical school events, such as parent-teacher conferences and concerts. In addition to these benefits, children in grades six through twelve with school-involved fathers were less likely to be suspended, get expelled, or repeat a grade.

Even without such consequences, relocation usually results in a decline in the depth and richness of parent-child relationships. We symbolize this decline by labeling the contacts children have with their nonresidential parent after divorce as "visits," a term that connotes that a person is set apart, in some fundamental way, from others at the same location. A visitor is a guest in the home. The term reflects the reality that, for many children, divorce transforms their relationship with one parent into something less than a normal parent-child relationship. As the children become guests, the visited parent becomes a host who entertains. So many divorced fathers fall into this pattern that the phrase "Disneyland dad" is commonly used to describe the altered relationship.

Whether or not your ex intends it, moving your children far away from you communicates a powerful message. It tells the children that their relationship with you ranks lower than their relationship with the parent who moves. If the intent is to turn the children against you, living far apart brings your ex closer to the goal. It moves you to the periphery of your children's existence. And it isolates the children from benevolent contact with you that could interfere with brainwashing. Remember, with divorce poison at work, absence does not make the heart grow fonder, it makes alienation grow more profound.

TAKE ACTION

If you are powerless to prevent a relocation, and you think your ex will try to obstruct contact with your children, try to get court orders that ensure open lines of communication between you and the children. The local parent may be required to maintain a separate phone line for the children to receive your calls, or maintain (perhaps at your expense) a computer with Internet access for E-mail and video phone calls.

KIDNAPPING

The ultimate exclusionary maneuver is to hide the child from the other parent. More than 350,000 of our nation's children are living with a parent who has abducted them. The National Center for Missing and Exploited Children receives over three million visitors per day at their website (see Resources section).

Brainwashing almost always accompanies kidnapping. As the mother desperately searches for her son, the boy is told that the reason Mom doesn't call is that she no longer cares about him. Sometimes the abducting parent tells the child that they are going on a vacation. The vacation just keeps getting extended. In one headline-grabbing case, a mother located her two daughters eighteen years after their father abducted them. The girls had been told that their mother was dead. When they were finally found, the by then adult children refused to have anything to do with their mother.

TAKE ACTION

Recovering kidnapped children is not for amateurs. The moment of recovery must be handled with care and skill, as must the reunification process. If your ex is concealing your children from you, contact the National Center for Missing and Exploited Children (see Resources section for this and other contacts). There is reason to be optimistic: The agency recovers ninety-three out of one hundred missing children.

Often an abducted child is programmed to believe that her father is dangerous and that she and her mother must hide from him for their own safety. Some parents in this category genuinely believe that their children risk physical or sexual abuse at the hands of the other parent. If they are unsuccessful in convincing the court of the danger, they decide to take the law into their own hands, kidnap their children, and go underground. One study found that mothers were more likely to abduct their children after the court had issued a custody ruling, whereas fathers were more likely to steal children in the absence of a custody order.

Unfortunately, groups exist that encourage, sanction, and facilitate such drastic practices. They help manufacture new identities and provide places to hide. Usually the parents are so focused on their own view of reality that they fail to see how much they are damaging their children. As I discussed in *The Custody Revolution*, it invariably results in trauma. Even when parents have a legitimate concern about their children's welfare, kidnapping is such a terror-filled ordeal that parents must search for a less drastic solution.

I receive many calls from distraught parents, both mothers and fathers, whose children are obviously the victims of very poor custody decisions. No matter how bad off the children were—in one case both children were expressing serious suicidal thoughts—it was never advisable for the parent to abduct the children. That would have merely added to the children's burdens. Fortunately, the parent was able to work through the legal system to make the necessary changes.

If you think your ex might try to steal your children, you must take preventive measures. But first determine whether your fears are realistic. In research sponsored by the U.S. Department of Justice, Dr. Janet Johnston and Dr. Linda Girdner have identified a list of factors associated with a high risk for abduction. Do any of these describe your ex?

- Has hidden your child in the past
- Has made one or more serious threats to abduct your child
- Had a brief, unmarried relationship with you
- Comes from a different country
- Has no strong emotional or financial ties to your community
- Has recently converted all assets to cash or borrowed large sums
- Has the financial resources to remain in hiding
- Is convinced that you have abused your child
- Is afraid of you because of past violent episodes
- Distrusts and feels victimized by the legal system
- Suffers from psychotic delusions of persecution coupled with a history of violence, substance abuse, or severe mental illness

- Feels betrayed and is preoccupied with getting even

- Is obsessed with the need to reconcile

- Is extremely self-centered, with a strong contempt for authority and the law

- Has relatives and friends who will give physical, emotional, and moral support for an abduction

- Can rely on your children not to reveal the abduction, either because they are too young to tell anyone or are sufficiently brainwashed to collude in the abduction

If none of these factors describe your ex, a kidnapping is unlikely. The presence of one or more factors heightens the risk, but certainly does not mean that an abduction is inevitable. Nevertheless, it makes sense to take precautions.

If you have good reasons for believing there is a high risk of abduction, you will want the court to issue very clear orders that specify exactly when each parent has authority over the child, and include firm penalties for violation of the orders, such as fines and jail time. It will be important to keep a certified copy of the orders with you at all times. Provide copies to school, day care, and medical personnel, and have one available for baby-sitters. If your ex refuses to return the child, the court orders need to be on hand and easy for law enforcement authorities to interpret.

The child's contact with your ex may need to take place under supervised, tightly restricted conditions when there have been prior abductions or other violations of court orders, or when the consequences of abduction are likely to be most severe, as with an ex who suffers from a serious mental disorder or has a history of violence or substance abuse, or who is a virtual stranger to the child because of lack of prior contact. If the contacts are unsupervised, your ex may be required to report in periodically, or wear the type of electronic transmitter used in cases of house arrest. If consistent with the court order, give teachers, day care attendants, and baby-sitters instructions not to release your child or your child's school records to your ex. Also, you may want the court to order your ex to post a large bond that would be released to you in the event of a kidnapping.

You may also want your attorney to write a letter explaining the criminal penalties for aiding and abetting a felony. You could send this letter to anyone who might support your ex in hiding your child.

If your ex genuinely believes that you are a danger to your child, or that you have abused your child, cooperating with a full investigation of the allegations may be your best hope of allaying such concerns and reducing the likelihood that your ex would think that kidnapping is the only recourse.

If there is a strong risk of your child being removed to another country, special travel restrictions and controls need to be in place. These might include some of the following:

- Getting court orders that require your certified written consent or permission of the court before your child can be taken out of state

- Giving copies of the orders to agencies issuing passports and birth certificates, along with a request that they notify you if your ex applies for such documents

- Having the Office of Passport Services of the U.S. Department of State block your child's passport from being issued, or let you know if a passport has already been issued (see Resources section for contact information)

- Flagging your child's passport with a restriction on any travel that does not have certified written authorization from you or the court

- Placing the passports of your child and your ex with a neutral party

- Having your ex post a large bond prior to traveling with your child

- Requiring a foreign ex to get written assurances of passport control from his or her embassy before granting unsupervised visitation

- Monitoring airline schedules to your ex's country of origin to allow interception prior to departure from the U.S. or during a scheduled stopover in a country that is a party to the Hague Convention (see Resources)

- Retaining an attorney in your ex's country of origin to petition the foreign court to issue orders that parallel the provisions of the U.S. court orders

STRIPPING

Isolation achieves physical separation. But brainwashing also requires breaking symbolic and emotional connections. This is accomplished through a process that cult scholars call "stripping." People in cultlike religious sects, for example, are often required to dress and wear their hair in a manner that clearly sets them apart from society. (Think of the Moonies.) Books, music, and art that provide exposure to the wider culture are banned.

Parents intent on alienating their children from their ex-partner also engage in a stripping process. They do so by purging their home of any reminders of the other parent. They remove all photographs of the absent parent. Some even go as far as cutting their ex-spouse out of family photos. They avoid mentioning the other parent at times when this would be natural. And they discourage their children from speaking positively about the other parent. This is usually done in a subtle manner. A child begins talking about his father, and the mother withdraws her attention or changes the subject. Before long the child understands, "Mom doesn't want to know that I am thinking about Dad."

When I am evaluating a parent suspected of brainwashing, say a father, I ask, "What do the children tell you about their mother?" If he answers, "They never talk about her," this alerts me to the possibility that such talk is discouraged. It could be that their mother has instructed the children not to talk about what goes on in her home. But if the father believes that the children just aren't interested in talking about what they do with their mother, I become suspicious.

Parents generally want to know about their children's activities. They ask, "What did you do at school, at camp, at the birthday party, at your friend's house?" No part of the children's lives is beyond inquiry. If the one exception is the time they spend with their mother, children quickly learn that their father does not want to hear about it.

When a father genuinely respects the importance of his children's relationship with their mother, he expresses interest in what they do with her. By his attitude he lets his children know that talk about Mom is welcome around him. They are not made to feel that they have to park their thoughts about her at the door before entering Dad's home.

TAKE ACTION

Set a good example for your children by leaving photographs of your ex on display and showing an interest in their life with their other parent. If your ex has stripped the home of reminders of you, give the children a photograph of you and your ex together to take home with them. If your ex destroys the picture, give the children a small picture that they can keep in their possession. It is easier for children to appreciate the irrationality of stripping when they see the other parent acting differently. By taking the high road you let your children know that you accept them as they are without requiring them to conceal their positive feelings for the other parent.

Sometimes the stripping process is quite literal. One mother met her little boy on the doorstep whenever he returned from his father. Each time she went through the same ritual. She took off all of his clothes. Then she placed them in a green plastic garbage sack, which she left on the front porch. When there were leftovers from the lunch his father packed, these too would go in the sack with the clothes. By the time the father received the bag several days later, the food was rotten and the clothes stank. Through this ritual, her son learned that anything associated with his father was unwelcome in his mother's house.

FEAR

This mother's behavior was so extreme that it frightened her son. This, in turn, made him more receptive to her distortions about his father. Fear is usually a precondition to brainwashing. Like isolation, *fear increases psychological dependence on the bad-mouthing and bashing parent.*

When a child observes his mother vent her anger in an irrational, uncontrolled manner, his main concern is to avoid becoming her next target. With the hope that she follows the dictum "The enemy of my enemy is my friend," he will turn on his father as the price he has to pay to stay in her good graces. Not to do so is to risk having her wrath fall on him.

Jill picked up her son from preschool one afternoon. She was still fuming about an incident that had occurred earlier in the day with the boy's paternal grandmother. Jill had demanded that her ex-mother-in-law give her household objects to which Jill was clearly not entitled. The mother-in-law, who had already been extremely generous with her time and money on behalf of her grandchildren, refused to comply with Jill's latest demands. On the way home from the preschool Jill called her ex-mother-in-law on her car phone. With her little boy sitting beside her, she began ranting. She called his grandmother a "greedy cunt" and screamed into the phone, "I hope you die a lonely old woman." After the tirade Jill turned to her son and said, "Grandma is a mean old witch. Right?"

How was he to respond? He correctly perceived that his mother was out of control. He had just witnessed her verbal assault on a grown-up who refused to see things her way. Although he adored his grandma, he certainly was not going to contradict his mother while she was in this state. His safest option was to join in his mother's hatred.

Jill lacked the maturity or the commitment to her children's welfare to consider what effect her tantrums were having on them. Although she did not see the connection, most people would have no trouble under-standing why, shortly after this incident, her son began misbehaving and having tantrums of his own. Or why her daughter faced a dilemma when completing a routine school assignment. She was given a sentence com-pletion exercise in which one of the sentence stems was, "The person I most admire is . . ." She automatically began to complete the sentence with, "Grandma." But then she changed her mind and wrote "Mom and Dad" over the "Gra—." One can imagine the mental gymnastics she went through responding to this one simple task. She could not afford to alienate her mother by revealing positive feelings for the hated ex-mother-in-law. But she also did not want to show a preference for her mother over her father. Her response was the safest she could think of at the moment. This is just one example of how parents' attempts to alien-ate children's affection for others permeate the children's lives.

A five-year-old girl faced the same dilemma. She figured out a unique solution to the conflict between her wish to be loyal to her mother and her love for her grandmother, whom she knew her mother hated. She told her grandmother "I hate you," and then added that whatever she said was the opposite of the truth. With this clever device, the girl could simultaneously gratify the need to align with her mother and express her love to her grandmother.

TAKE ACTION

Consider encouraging the children to ask their other parent to stop bad-mouthing you in front of them. This is best done when the other parent is calm and in a good mood. If your children tend to be overly anxious and fearful, you might not want to do this. If your ex is liable to punish the children for even this mild act of self-assertion, let the children know that you understand and accept why they want to remain silent in the face of their parent's anger toward you. Some bad-mouthing parents will inhibit destructive criticism when they hear directly from their children about how uncomfortable this makes them. Expressing feelings forthrightly will also enhance your children's self-esteem.

If your children are physically isolated from you and psychologically dependent on a vindictive ex, the chances of preventing or reversing alienation are slim. Any plan to counteract the bashing and brainwashing must place a priority on physically reuniting the children with the estranged parent. This must be done in a thoughtful manner, carefully safeguarding the children's welfare. But as long as the children are exclusively dependent on the parent doing the bad-mouthing and bashing, there is little hope that they will be able to resist the mental manipulation maneuvers that we are now ready to examine.

CHAPTER 6

THE CORRUPTION
OF REALITY

You've got to be taught to hate and fear.
—OSCAR HAMMERSTEIN II, *SOUTH PACIFIC*

Isolation, psychological dependence, and fear set the stage on which psychological manipulation occurs. Within this setting, parents use specific strategies and techniques to warp the child's mind against a loved one. Understanding these maneuvers is the key to designing an effective response to bad-mouthing, bashing, and brainwashing. This chapter exposes the most common ploys used to coerce children into rejecting parents and grandparents.

THE NAME GAME

Parents will frequently manipulate names in a particular manner in order to disrupt children's identification with the target. I have seen three different tactics used. What all three have in common is that, when successful, they change the way children relate to the target.

Pejorative Labeling

Cult leaders understand the power of language. They refer to the wider culture in pejorative terms, such as "infidels," and thus reinforce the sense of "us" versus "them." Racial hatred is propagated by the same method. Epithets are spoken in a derisive tone and context, conveying the message that "those people" are bad, inferior, to be avoided. Use a racial slur enough times and children will soon follow the example. The offensive word becomes part of their vocabulary. And without thinking, they absorb the hatred tied to the label. This is how we convert innocent children into racists. It is also how we turn them against formerly loved parents and their families.

Vindictive parents begin this process by letting the children overhear them refer to the target parent or grandparent only in derogatory terms. A parent may, for example, refer to the former mother-in-law, the children's grandmother, as a "witch." Next, the children are manipulated into using the term themselves. The parent shows approval when the children follow the example. This will result in more frequent use of the term because children strive for their parents' acceptance. Over time the derision will come to seem natural and justified. When children hear their grandmother referred to disrespectfully, and are encouraged to do the same, or are not discouraged from speaking disrespectfully themselves, they will lose respect for her. Contemptuousness replaces love. After associating Granny with the label "witch," their minds are tricked into thinking that somewhere along the line they decided for themselves that their grandmother was bad. The children lose sight of the origin of the derogation. They forget that it was not based on a realistic assessment of Granny but was merely their mother's expression of her own irrational anger.

For about a year Jill, whom we met in the last chapter, was successful in undermining the strength of her children's love for their grandmother. They became more reserved and less affectionate around Granny. They never actually believed she was a witch. They just thought she was greedy, difficult, and someone to be avoided.

In some cases, though, children are convinced that a formerly loved relative has become the incarnation of evil. This occurred in an American family living in the Middle East. A fanatically religious father successfully brainwashed his four children into sharing his belief that their mother was the devil. This was how the father rationalized his brutal battering of his wife. For this disturbed man it was literally the defense of "the devil made me do it." After his wife finally fled from him, he refused to permit her any contact with the children. (Unfortunately, that country's law was on his side in this matter.) Without her presence to counteract their father's views, the children succumbed to the brainwashing and regarded their mother as the devil. After monumental efforts the mother succeeded in reuniting with three of her children. Over time they relinquished their belief that she was the devil, but a legacy of distrust lasted a good portion of their childhood.

TAKE ACTION

If you are the victim of pejorative labeling, let the children know right away that you disapprove of such behavior. Help them understand the name-calling, and remind them that they have always been taught to be polite to others and that this certainly applies to their parents and other relatives. One mother told her children, "Daddy is very angry with me and that is why he is calling me names. But you know, deep down in your heart, that it is wrong to call people names, even when you're angry with them. We can't stop Daddy from doing this, but I want you to be clear in your mind that when he does this, he is making a big mistake. Remember that Daddy and I always taught you not to call people names and to respect your elders."

The children know that the alienating parent's behavior is wrong. By addressing name-calling directly, you validate the children's judgment, help them cope with it, and neutralize its destructive potential. Instead of being brainwashed by pejorative labels, the children will dismiss name-calling as an attempt to manipulate their feelings.

On a First-Name Basis

Using pejorative terms is an obvious, heavy-handed way to undermine children's respect for a parent. Many divorced parents find a more subtle way to accomplish the same result. When talking to their children they simply refer to the other parent by his or her first name. Instead of telling the children, "Your mother is on the phone," a father says, "*Gloria* wants to talk to you." Or "Is *Amy* coming to your basketball game?"

At first when parents use this ploy children are puzzled. In most families, children are encouraged to use some variation of "Mommy" and "Daddy." They go through a brief period in early childhood when they become aware that others address their parents by first name and they experiment by doing so themselves, usually in a playful manner. But they quickly revert to the familiar terms reserved for parents. (I recognize that in some families children routinely refer to their parents by first name. I believe this represents a misguided attempt at egalitarianism, but obviously the following discussion does not apply to such families.)

The way we address people reflects something about the type of relationship we have with them, or at least would like to have. She is Susie to her cousins, Susan to her employees, and Ms. Rosenberg to the telephone solicitor.

So what is accomplished when a father begins referring to the mother by her first name when talking to their children? First, this practice suggests to the children that, in Dad's mind, their mother no longer has the status of a parent. The relationship has changed in some significant manner. In essence the message is "Since my relationship with Mom has changed, so must yours." This is directly opposite to what mental health experts usually advise: Divorcing parents are told to emphasize to the children that divorce is between the grown-ups and not between parent and child.

Second, the father is also encouraging a change in the children's relationship with him. He is attempting to obscure the normal psychological boundaries between a parent and child. He talks to them about their mother the way he would talk to an adult friend. The implication is that they are his peers when it comes to discussing his ex-wife. Though his children might enjoy such camaraderie and the implied elevation of their status, they pay a heavy price for this promotion.

Third, addressing Mom by her first name implies that she no longer commands the respect implicit in the title "Mommy." With this loss of respect comes a loss of authority. Somehow it is easier to talk back to Amy than to Mom. Again, though some children are eager to sign on with the new "first name" policy, they lose a lot by doing so.

Some parents are not as subtle in their attempts to manipulate the children into discarding the label "Mom" or "Dad." Rather than merely encourage the practice, they insist on it. These parents are usually remarried. They require the children to refer to their other parent by first name because they want the more familiar title, Mom or Dad, to be reserved for the stepparent. One little girl said that her mother would not serve her dinner unless she called her stepfather Daddy and referred to her father by his first name. A boy told his mother that when he forgot to call his stepmother Mom, she simply ignored him. His father confirmed that this was the family policy. He thought this was reasonable because, he said, it was awkward for his new wife's son to call her Mom while his own son did not do the same. While this explanation has a certain surface plausibility, millions of remarried fathers face the same issue and are able to find a solution that does not require children to repudiate their relationship with their mother.

TAKE ACTION

If your children begin addressing you by your first name, put a stop to it immediately. If you tolerate an occasional use of your first name by children who are subjected to divorce poison, the practice will become habitual. Tell them that you expect to be called Mom or Dad just as they have always done and just as every other boy and girl they know does with their parents. Reminding them about what is normal among their friends will help them appreciate the inappropriateness of calling you by your first name. Also, it may help motivate them to comply, because most children want to fit in with their peers. If your ex persists in undermining your status in this manner, try to involve your ex in joint therapy, either voluntarily or by order of the court.

Child Aliases

If it is puzzling to children to begin calling a parent by another name, imagine their confusion when they are required to begin calling themselves by a different name. This happens surprisingly often in cases of parental alienation.

Kidnapping parents often create aliases for their children in order to elude capture. But even when they are not hiding, some divorced parents change children's names. In most of these cases, the mother wants the children to share her last name. If she is remarried, she wants them to take the name of their stepfather; if she is not remarried, she wants them to use her maiden name.

In all the cases I have seen, the mother has never explained to the children that she is changing their name or why she is doing so. She merely begins using the name she prefers in all situations. Doctors' receptionists are told to cross out the old name and substitute the new one. School registrations are made in the new name. Older children may learn of the change on the first day of school when the teacher calls the roll for the first time or confronts the child with the discrepancy between the name as the child wrote it and the way it appears on the teacher's records.

Parents who engage in this practice are usually oblivious to the impact on the children. Their main intent is to eradicate traces of their own former connection to the ex-spouse. The name change also expresses a depreciation of the child's tie to the other parent. These parents fail to consider the children's feelings about being different from all their friends who do share their father's last name.

Child aliases also extend to first names. Fathers as well as mothers play this version of the name game. I have seen fathers who resented the association of a child's first name with the mother or her family. In one case the mother was a graduate of St. Anne's Academy, an exclusive prep school. The girls at St. Anne's were affectionately known as "Annies." Because the father and mother first met each other at the annual "Annie" ball, when they had their first child they named her Annie. Three years later, when the marriage was over, and the father wanted nothing to do with his ex-wife, he stopped referring to his daughter as Annie and instead began using her middle name. Although under oath the father denied doing so, the mother's attorney introduced pictures the little girl had drawn, on which the father wrote only her middle and last names. Even more conclusive were the copies of the father's income tax returns, where he omitted his child's legal first name.

I know of a few families in which young children suffer the confusion of having each parent refer to them with a different name. When these children leave one home and return to the other, it takes them a while to get used to the alternate name. Some parents are so caught up in their battle with their ex that they lose patience when their children fail to respond to the preferred name.

TAKE ACTION

If you object to your child using a different name, register your objections as soon as possible. Your attorney may need to write letters to your child's school and doctors explaining the necessity of using the correct legal name. The longer an alias is used, the more likely a court is to allow it to continue. Since it is not usually a child's idea to use a different name, it is best for the adults to handle the dispute without pressuring the child to take sides in the dispute. In most cases, the conflict over the child's name is more destructive than any particular outcome of the conflict. The real issue is not the name but what it symbolizes to each parent. To spare your child distress, consider a compromise, such as allowing your child to use two last names.

Stephanie, an alienated Canadian teen, expressed her hatred for her father by severing all ties with him. She and her mother stripped the home of any reminders of the father. She changed her last name to her mother's maiden name. When her mother told her that the name Stephanie was originally her father's preference, she invented a new first name. She began calling herself Rainbow.

The girl's therapist, who zealously championed her patient's right to disown her father, supported this charade. She congratulated the girl for asserting her independence. She used the new first and last names in her official notes and reports. And, at the depth of offensive thoughtlessness, she insulted the father by using Stephanie's alias in correspondence with him, knowing full well that the name change was designed to repudiate him. This is an example of how bystanders can contribute to alienation, even therapists, if they undertake treatment with an inadequate understanding of divorce poison.

In Stephanie's case, as her therapy continued, her hold on reality slipped. She began to suffer from hallucinations directly related to her irrational alienation, and she eventually required psychiatric hospitalization. In the end, Stephanie's alienation not only cost her mentally and emotionally, it cost her financially: When it was clear that his daughter would have nothing to do with him, her wealthy grieving father wrote the girl out of his will.

REPETITION

Jill's children did not start calling their grandmother a witch the very first time their mother used this put-down. But when they heard the word used many times, it began to seem natural.

Repetition of desired messages is common to all forms of indoctrination. The more we hear an idea or a word, the more familiar it becomes. When children have heard their grandmother referred to as a witch for several months, it is a shorter mental leap to begin thinking of her as basically bad and undesirable. We come to assume that there must be some truth behind an idea, merely because it is repeated so often. This is a common tactic of politicians and propagandists. In fact, *parental brainwashing can be thought of as propaganda in the home.*

Repetition also helps embed messages in memory. This is the principle behind rote drill. Repeat the multiplication tables enough times and they become second nature. If a false impression—an unjustified denigration of a parent or grandparent—is repeated enough times, it too can become second nature. And ultimately it becomes indistinguishable from beliefs based in reality.

Recall the research discussed in chapter 3 in which Cornell University researchers demonstrated how easy it is to implant false memories in young children. What they found is that repetition is a key element in convincing children that they have experienced bad events that never actually occurred. If children can be led to believe that a parent has grossly mistreated them, alienation of affection is a predictable outcome.

TAKE ACTION

If your ex repeats false negative messages about you, take action before the negative messages take root. Help your children protect themselves against brainwashing by explicitly identifying how repetition works to create false perceptions. Repetition is a potent manipulation tactic. If your children are alerted to its use, they will be better able to resist its influence. A father told his son, "Sometimes when children hear the same bad thing about a parent over and over, they make the mistake of thinking that the bad thing is true, even though they knew from the start that it wasn't true. I know Mommy keeps saying that I'm mean and that I don't care about you, but just because she says it a lot doesn't make it true. Don't you be fooled."

SELECTIVE ATTENTION

At first glance it seems a formidable task to transform a child's love for a parent into hatred and derision. After all, what greater love is there than the love between child and parent? What is it that allows such a drastic transformation to occur? In a word: ambivalence. Parents intent on fostering alienation of affection rely on their children's ambivalence as their most powerful ally.

All child-parent relationships are fraught with ambivalence, mixed feelings, conflict. Even the most nurturing and gratifying parents frequently disappoint their children. Consider how often we tell children that they may not have what they want or do what they want. In the eyes of our children we comfort and satisfy, but we also frustrate, deprive, and at times frighten.

Parents who promote alienation capitalize on this ambivalence. It makes their job easier. Rather than topple an idealized parent off a pedestal, they merely need to highlight the cracks in the pedestal—cracks formed by the accumulation of past disappointments. They take every opportunity to focus their child's attention on traits and behaviors of the other parent that the child dislikes. Little if anything positive is ever said about the target. Eventually negative perceptions, feelings, and memories crowd out the positive. The child reacts to the target parent as if he or she is all, or mainly, bad. Without favorable memories and perceptions to balance the ledger, the child succumbs to alienation. The parent who formerly was ambivalently loved is now hated.

> Selective attention is a potent image-shaping tool. If a child attends only to things that make a parent look bad, eventually negative perceptions, feelings, and memories will crowd out the positive.

The movie *Hook* provides a good example of this process. The evil pirate Captain Hook reminds the little boy that his father missed his most important baseball game because he was working at the office. Hook taps into all the child's resentments and disillusionments to persuade the boy that his father doesn't truly love him.

Psychologists call this technique "selective attention." It is the stock-in-trade of skilled magicians, salesmen, politicians, and lawyers. The magician directs our attention to his left hand while he reaches in his pocket with his right hand. We see only what he wants us to see. The salesman extols the virtues of his product while overlooking its drawbacks. The politician focuses the spotlight on the opposing candidate's worst mistakes, hoping that these low points will define the opponent's image in the public eye.

As a participant in custody trials I have held a ringside seat watching attorneys practice the art of selective attention. They introduce only the facts that support their client's position. They don't pursue the "whole truth" but only that portion of the truth which will further their case. When I am being cross-examined, the lawyer wants to control my testimony so that I say only things that support the position the lawyer is arguing. To do so, she or he attempts to restrict my answers to yes or no. If I try to explain myself or elaborate an answer, the lawyer interrupts: "Objection, the witness is being nonresponsive." In fact, trial lawyers are taught to refrain from asking any question whose answer they cannot anticipate. The reason for this practice is to avoid the possibility that testimony will be elicited that directs the court's attention to facts that the attorney would prefer that the court overlook.

Selective attention is a potent image-shaping tool. It helps racists maintain their bigotry. They listen to the evening news, for example, and selectively attend to crimes committed by members of the hated race. They pay no attention to announcements that do not support their preconceived opinions. Significant accomplishments by members of the hated race go unnoticed, as do crimes committed by people of the same race as the racist. The result is a self-perpetuating prejudice that filters out information that might correct distortions.

Indeed, selective attention is a gatekeeper that allows only material that conforms to the program to enter consciousness. If the program is "Don't love your other parent," everything that makes that parent look bad is welcomed; everything that opposes the program is rejected.

TAKE ACTION

Teach your children about how selective attention is used to manipulate thoughts.

- Begin with familiar situations that are far removed from divorce poison. Television commercials for toys suit this purpose. Point out how the commercial presents the toy in the best possible light. It uses special effects and additional props to make the toy appear more elaborate than it is, while the fine print at the bottom of the screen discloses that the toy's movements are simulated. Or the announcer discloses in rapid-fire speech that assembly is required, or batteries are not included. You might tell the children about a time when you bought something that subsequently disappointed you because you failed to pay attention to the drawbacks. Make a game of challenging the children to find examples of selective attention in advertisements.

- Next show how selective attention can be used to devalue a person. Again, use examples that are familiar to your children, such as sports: If we judged a baseball player only by his errors, we would have a distorted picture of his abilities.

- After laying the previous groundwork, relate selective attention personally to your children. Ask them how they would feel if their teacher judged their ability based only on their lowest test grade. Remind them of a time when they did something bad, mean, or cruel. Explain that if you judged them only on the basis of those behaviors, you would have a negative view of them that ignored all their good points. My oldest grandson, Aaron, was ready to label himself "clumsy" after he broke two glasses in two days. I reminded him of all the years he did not break things in our home when, as an infant and toddler, more accidents would have been expected. He actually had a great record—only two broken glasses in three years. If he attended only to the recent mishaps, he would develop a warped view of himself. The underlying message is "No one is perfect," a good principle for all children to learn.

- Finally, relate the child's understanding of selective attention to your ex's bad-mouthing and bashing. Explain your concern that if they only hear about and think about your bad points and mistakes, they will forget all the good things about you.

- It is important to use good timing in following these steps. It is usually best to spread out this process over several conversations rather than do it all at once. Try to strike a balance between this type of conversation and interaction with your children that is enjoyable and gratifying.

Along with the focus on negative qualities is the total absence of attention to the target's positive attributes. Every time his child mentions something Mommy has done for her that exhibits good and loving parenting, a father changes the subject. A woman who was trying to alienate her children from their paternal grandparents had to downplay their significant contributions to the children's welfare. When she did not actively disparage their efforts, she simply ignored them. For example, the grandparents took the initiative to inculcate a love of music in the children. They rented and bought musical instruments, located good

SPORTS

teachers, and scheduled, paid for, and transported the children to and from their lessons. Not only did the mother fail to express any appreciation for all of this, she never asked the children about their lessons, and never even discussed the fact that they were learning how to play music. When the children played in school concerts, the mother deprived the grandparents of the joy of seeing the fruits of their efforts by neglecting to inform them about the events. Through such omissions she hoped that her children's feelings about their grandparents would fail to reflect their numerous acts of kindness and caring. Fortunately, using some of the strategies discussed in this book, the grandparents were able to help the children understand and resist the divorce poison. In the end the children were more perceptive than their mother anticipated, and her efforts backfired.

Some parents will use selective attention in a subtle way that makes it harder for children to realize what is happening. Instead of saying negative things about the other parent, they merely ask questions that are calculated to draw attention to the other parent's lapses. While braiding her daughter's hair, a mother asked, "Does Daddy do this for you?" This and similar questions repeatedly drew the girl's attention to all the things her father did not do for her. After a while she came to believe that Daddy did not care about her as much as Mommy. Of course, her mother never asked what her father did do for her or with her. Another example is the father who knew his ex-wife was struggling financially. While doling out allowance to his children this father asked, in an innocent tone, "Do you get allowance from Mom too?"

Such comparisons are constantly being made by bad-mouthing and bashing parents. It is the flip side of selective attention. The target parent is seen through a negative lens, while the children's attention is directed to only positive aspects of the bad-mouthing parent. During interviews these children embrace a polarized view of their parents: they find it difficult to think of anything bad to say about one parent, and have equal difficulty saying anything good about the other. Lack of ambivalence is a hallmark of alienation. I often wonder how parents engaged in bashing explain the fact that they fell in love with, married, and had children with people who are so utterly lacking in any redeeming qualities. They seem unaware of the common observation that the mates we choose reveal much about our own personalities and emotional needs.

TAKE ACTION

If your children view your ex as all good and you as all bad, try to help them understand that ambivalence in relationships is normal. Explain that everyone has good and bad points, and that parents and children don't stop loving each other just because they are not perfectly good all the time. Gently remind them of some of the negative things their other parent has done and explain that these do not wipe out all the good that parent has done. Don't let your anger keep you from thinking of your ex's good points; in most cases the alienating parent has done many things over the years on behalf of the children. If your children grasp the concepts that no one is perfect and that it is okay to have mixed feelings about people you love, they will be less apt to view you in an entirely negative light.

Incidentally, mental health experts, even those appointed by the courts, are not immune to selective attention. When a custody evaluator writes a report, lawyers look to see if the criticisms of each parent are balanced by a discussion of each parent's assets. A report that fails to say anything good about a parent (other than that they love their children) is strongly suspected of being biased. Very often when I am asked to give a second opinion on a custody evaluation I detect more subtle signs of selective attention. For example, the examiner may cite only the psychological test results that support his or her conclusions and ignore test results that are incompatible with the conclusions.

JUDGING BEHAVIOR OUT OF CONTEXT

We can thank Sigmund Freud for helping us appreciate that things are not always as they seem. This is especially true when we judge someone's behavior without knowing the full context in which the behavior occurred. It is easy to draw wrong conclusions. A brainwashing parent takes advantage of this to persuade the children that their other parent has acted without regard for their welfare.

A common maneuver is to put an ex on the spot by asking for money or other favors in front of the children. The parent looks bad if he or she turns down the request. The children are told, "Sorry, I can't buy you that because Daddy wouldn't give me the money" or "We can't go to the circus because Mommy won't let you stay an extra day." If the children appreciated the full context of the request, they would understand why it was refused. The mother may be getting a sizable child support check to cover expenses. The father may have told the children he would take them to the circus on a day he knew would interfere with the mother's plans. But, taken out of context, a parent's behavior can appear unnecessarily neglectful or depriving.

Judy and Kent agreed that they would move their family to allow Kent to pursue his education and then relocate again to allow Judy to continue her graduate education. When Judy's turn came she moved to the new city first to begin her studies and locate a home for the family. The understanding was that the rest of the family would soon join her. During this time Kent engaged in a series of behaviors that convinced Judy that their marriage had to end. When she filed for divorce, he filed for sole custody of their three children.

While the suit was pending, Kent began a campaign to alienate the children. He programmed the children to believe that their mother had abandoned them and that her education was more important to her than her children. He did this by discussing Judy's behavior without giving the context or the reasons for her actions. First the setup: "Didn't Mommy move away?" And "She didn't take you with her, did she?" The children agreed. Then the dropping of context: "That means that Mommy cares more about going to school than she does about us. I'm sorry for you kids, but your Mom just moved away on her own and abandoned her family." Without more information the children were unable to provide an alternative to their father's explanation.

By the time Judy heard these accusations and tried to defend herself, the children were not receptive. It was too late. They had already been successfully programmed. They blamed her for the divorce and their anger fueled their alienation. Their refusal to consider her point of view was in part their way of punishing her for the divorce. As Dr. Gardner observed, children's motivations often contribute to the alienation.

After a while, Kent came to believe his own misrepresentations. Like many in his position, he was surprised when his elaborate stories, which worked on his vulnerable children, failed to impress the judge. After realizing that he could not prevail in court, Kent offered to settle the custody dispute. The two younger children ended up spending enough time with their mother that she was able to use some of the ideas presented in the next chapter to reverse their alienation. Unfortunately, her older son was so identified with his father and his alienation was so entrenched that he has yet to recover affectionate feelings for his mother.

One fairly common scenario of context-dropping does often mislead courts and professional evaluators. In this situation the target parent, standing by helplessly as the breach with the children widens, and feeling powerless to stop the process, loses his or her temper in a moment of utter frustration. The target may yell at the children, or curse the other parent in front of the children, or act in some other frightening and uncharacteristic manner. The brainwashing parent then claims that this incident is representative of the target's usual behavior and accounts for the children's alienation. He or she ignores the fact that the alienation preceded the incident and contributed to, rather than resulted from, the target's behavior.

When dealing with physical brutality directed against children, sexual abuse, or repeated acts of domestic violence, legal and mental health professionals are clear that the perpetrator owns primary responsibility for the problem. The spouse may need to learn to be more assertive and protect the children, but we would not hold the spouse equally responsible for the abuse. Similarly, we should not be too quick to blame the rejected parent for his or her ineffective reactions to divorce poison. And we should certainly not confuse these *responses* to alienation with the initial *causes* of the disturbance. This type of confusion, unfortunately, is common among legal and mental health professionals.

Johanna's nine-year-old son and eleven-year-old daughter began acting belligerently and saying they didn't want to be forced to see her. The children's father enlisted their allegiance by taking a lax attitude toward homework and chores and sympathizing with their complaints about Johanna's more structured, authoritative approach. This devoted mother now found herself the target of malicious accusations. As her relationship with her children deteriorated, Johanna became depressed. She sought advice from a therapist who did not understand parent-child alienation. The therapist assumed from the outset that there must be a rational basis for the children's rejection. He prescribed a parenting skills class. Johanna's ex-husband poured salt on the wound by asking the court to suspend her contact with her children pending the results of a family evaluation. He also wanted Johanna to pay child support for the children she was not allowed to see.

By the time Johanna had her first interview with the court-appointed social worker, she was desperate and distraught. Her patience taxed beyond its limit, Johanna came across as angry, hysterical, and unstable. She reviled her ex-husband and the judicial system that threatened to deprive her of her children. She did not make a good impression on the evaluator. Failing to put herself in Johanna's shoes, the social worker thought, "No wonder these children don't want to be with her." The final report recommended that Johanna seek treatment to improve her parenting skills before the court allow her to spend time with the children.

Johanna's experience is all too common. To protect yourself from a similar fate you must learn all that you can about the behavior of alienated children and about how you can best respond to it.

TAKE ACTION

Target parents must exercise self-restraint. When you know that your ex wants to make you look bad, don't make it easier. Expect no mercy when you are the target of a hate campaign. When you give in to anger and frustration, your behavior will be taken out of context, and will provide ammunition for a campaign of hatred. Your ex will put a spotlight on your mistakes, claim that this is typical of your behavior, and cite this as the reason for your children's alienation. Your ex's contributions to alienation may then be overlooked or minimized.

To help avoid losing your temper in response to your child's rejection, remind yourself that this would be playing into the hands of your ex. Instead, channel your anger into devising an effective response to brainwashing. If you must blow off steam, find a friend to listen, not your ex or your children. Remember, *no parent ever softened a child's heart by treating her harshly.*

Sometimes a parent deliberately provokes a scene in order to produce evidence that can be used during custody litigation. The stage is set ahead of time with witnesses on hand and a video camera in place.

Dan was a victim of such a plot. His ex-wife, Marsha, moved across the country primarily to limit Dan's contact with their two sons, ages eight and ten. The court granted Dan access to his children, making him responsible for scheduling and paying for flights and Marsha responsible for getting the boys to the airport and on the plane.

Twice Dan arranged flights and scheduled days off from work in anticipation of spending time with his sons. And both times Marsha sabotaged his plans by failing to take the boys to the airport. Rather than inform him ahead of time, she let Dan drive to the airport and wait expectantly at the gate, only to be crestfallen as the last passenger exited, with no sign of the boys. Dan worked for a company that required employees to schedule vacation time in advance with no last-minute changes allowed. So both times Dan used up vacation days without being able to spend the time with his sons. He also had to pay fees to the airlines to change the tickets.

When he called Marsha to rearrange the trip, she told him that in her opinion the boys were too young to fly unaccompanied by an adult and that if he wanted to see them he would have to come get them himself. Dan weighed his options. He could file a motion for contempt of the court orders. But this would cost a lot of money and take a lot of time. In the meantime he would not see his children. And there was no guarantee that he would prevail in court. Instead he decided that it would be easier and less expensive to comply with Marsha's demand. With his money tight, and confident that the boys would make their flights now that he was escorting them, he purchased nonrefundable, nonexchangeable tickets.

He took off from work and traveled across the country. When he arrived at Marsha's house she came to the door and said, "I'm sorry. The boys are not feeling well and can't travel. You'll have to visit them some other time." Then she slammed the door in his face.

Dan was outraged. He pounded on the front door demanding to see his sons. In the process a small glass pane in the door cracked. Marsha began screaming, which could be heard from outside the house by way of a side window she conveniently left open.

Earlier in the day Marsha told an unsuspecting neighbor that her violent ex-husband had threatened to snatch the children that afternoon. She asked her neighbor to please be alert to any disturbances and call 911 if necessary. The neighbor did so. The police arrived and filed charges against Dan.

Marsha used this episode to convince her children that their father had become dangerous. She also used it as ammunition in a court battle to further restrict Dan's parental rights. Dan thought the court would sympathize with his side of the story. What he did not know was that Marsha had someone videotape the incident. The tape showed a fist-clenched Dan banging on the door and yelling, "I want my children. You can't keep them from me!" Even Dan had to admit that he looked scary.

You may have watched trials on television and heard an attorney object to a picture being entered into evidence on the grounds that it is "prejudicial." Now you know why. The concern is that a picture does not present the full context of the event it depicts; thus it may stir up strong emotions that interfere with a more objective appraisal of the defendant.

The neighbor appeared in court on Marsha's behalf. Knowing nothing about Dan other than the scene she had witnessed, she testified honestly that she would never leave her own children alone with a man like Dan.

Marsha also brought into the courtroom not a photograph of a cracked glass pane but a plastic bowl filled with broken pieces of glass, which she claimed resulted from Dan punching his fist through the glass. Thank God, she testified, the flying pieces of glass missed her children's eyes.

Dan's attempt to defend himself backfired because it made him appear to be minimizing his outburst. He explained that he was normally a patient and gentle man with no history of violence. The incident was a singular and momentary lapse of good judgment in response to over-whelming provocation. And the glass pane cracked accidentally from the vibrations caused by the banging on the door; he was not so out of con-trol that he would have punched the glass.

Nevertheless, the tape, the neighbor's eyewitness testimony, the pieces of shattered glass, Marsha's testimony, and the criminal charges all combined to make a powerful case against Dan. The judge feared for the children's welfare and preferred to err on the side of safety. In a ruling that played right into Marsha's hands, he ordered that Dan could only see his sons under strict supervision. The supervisor's presence was a con-stant message to the boys that the judge agreed with Mom that Dad was too dangerous to be entrusted with their care. Unfortunately, I don't know the long-term outcome of this case. When I last spoke with Dan he despaired of ever repairing his relationship with his sons.

Often a target parent reacts to a campaign of vilification by indulging the children. Wanting to avoid their rejection, he tries to make their time with him as rewarding as possible. He will relax the usual limits, perhaps giving in to a child's demand to watch an R-rated movie, stay up too late, or engage in a marginally dangerous activity. The other parent then cites the excessive permissiveness as proof of poor parenting ability. I have seen many cases in which mental health professionals failed to recognize the bind in which the target parent finds himself. When the target's context is taken into account, often his indulgent behavior appears more understandable and less pathological.

Before rushing to the judgment that a rejected parent's behavior is directly responsible for the children's estrangement, we should place it in the following context. Making mistakes as a parent or grandparent (absent a pattern of gross negligence or abuse) does not normally result in children's hatred and does not mean we are unworthy of their love or companionship. If all parents who ever lost their tempers or overindulged their children were to be judged as unfit parents, every child would become a ward of the state.

EXAGGERATION

Selective attention and context dropping both involve focusing on certain aspects of reality while excluding others. Many times parents will actually depart from reality by exaggerating the target's behavior. A shove becomes a violent attack. A parent who is three days late on a child support payment is a "deadbeat." A father whose work schedule does not allow him to coach his son's teams is labeled "uninvolved" despite all the other activities he shares with the boy. A mother who occasionally dates is said to be preoccupied with men.

When combined with repetition and selective attention, this strategy can be difficult to counter. Repetition increases the likelihood that the exaggerations will be accepted as true accounts. Selective attention keeps the child from recognizing positive traits that would modify the impression created through exaggeration. Because there is a kernel of truth, it is often difficult for the target to defend herself. Both parents may have experimented with marijuana. But on this basis the target is labeled a drug addict. If the exaggeration is repeated enough times, it becomes incorporated into the child's view of the target. The child has heard so often that his mother is a drug addict, that he assumes it is true. It is used by the brainwasher regularly and casually, as in, "Well, you know, she was probably stoned again and that's why she was late to get you." The brainwasher speaks of it as fact, and eventually the child comes to share this distortion.

TAKE ACTION

If you are the victim of a hate campaign, expect your past deficiencies as a parent to be taken out of context, attended to selectively, and exaggerated. Though these past errors do not justify your children's total rejection, the sensible response is to do everything possible to improve your skills as a parent. For example, you may have been relatively uninvolved, or frequently delegated responsibility for your children's care to baby-sitters, or treated your children with little interest or patience. Correct these deficiencies. When the children are finally reunited with you, let them experience you not as you were before, but better. *Why?* The more your behavior differs from what the children have been programmed to expect, the easier it will be for them to recognize that they have judged you wrongly. Also, by using unfair and harsh criticism as a stimulus to self-improvement, you remove yourself from the passive victim role and are less likely to feel despondent. Your self-respect and your confidence as a parent will grow and you will find that any such improvements will make you more effective in your other relationships.

LIES

Selective attention, context dropping, and exaggeration are generally sufficient to smear a target parent or grandparent. When more is needed, the next step is a further departure from reality: outright lying. Sometimes the lies are gross distortions of actual events. Other times they are manufactured totally out of thin air. Though such behavior is common among psychotic parents who have lost touch with reality, it also occurs among less disturbed people.

Louise and Gary were recently separated. They met in a restaurant to begin negotiations on the terms of their divorce. Louise announced her intention to move with their nine-year-old son, Jeffrey, to another city. Gary objected. Jeffrey was enrolled in a superior elementary school. He had lived in the same neighborhood all his life and had many friends within a few blocks of his house. He participated in several team sports. Living in another city would drastically reduce Gary's contact with his son. And Gary's parents were available to baby-sit every day after school while both parents worked. Ever since he was born, Jeffrey spent at least one night a week with his grandparents, and he enjoyed these contacts. In fact, he was at their house while his parents were meeting.

Louise countered that she would either enroll Jeffrey in a day care center before and after school, or leave him home alone. Gary said he could not accept that arrangement. Louise had not expected any resistance from Gary; she was furious that he intended to thwart her plans. She stormed out of the restaurant, sped over to her in-laws', and when she was let in the door yelled, "Come on, Jeffrey. We're out of here!" His grandfather asked if Jeffrey could finish his dinner. Louise said she didn't want him spending another second in the house. Jeffrey burst into tears. He was scared and quickly gathered his things. His grandfather helped him into his jacket and then gave the boy a hug and kiss. Louise jerked Jeffrey out of his grandfather's arms and charged out of the house.

Later the grandparents were shocked to hear Louise's account of the incident. According to her, the grandfather had forcibly detained Jeffrey and was not going to let him leave the house. She repeated her version of the incident so many times on the return home that she actually had Jeffrey believing that this is what happened. The episode was then used as the kernel of a campaign to program Jeffrey to believe that his grandparents were volatile and could not be trusted. Though Jeffrey had always experienced them as more patient than either of his parents, he also learned that the way to please his mother and ward off her anger was to tell her that he didn't want to see his grandparents anymore.

One father distorted an actual event when he successfully convinced his children that their mother kidnapped them. In reality she had been granted temporary custody and took the children on a vacation. At the time the children loved their vacation at the seashore. But afterward their father programmed them to regard the experience as a frightening ordeal in which they were kept incommunicado from him. Periodically he reinforced the program with reminders such as, "Remember the time when

Mommy kidnapped you and you didn't know if you would ever see me again?" The children not only "remembered," they embellished the incident with their own details. This is a dramatic example of how a parent can alter children's perceptions and memories.

When parents cannot find enough incidents that lend themselves to distortion, they are not deterred. They simply make things up. Dr. Gardner wrote about a mother who answered the father's telephone call while her son was nearby. She greeted the father's innocuous statements with a long, stony silence, after which she said, "That's *your* opinion. In *my* opinion he's a *very fine* boy." In this manner she created the impression that the father was attacking the boy's character and that she was defending her son. These types of maneuvers can be so effective that the child believes that he actually heard the offensive conversation. If so, the innocent parent's subsequent denials fall on deaf ears.

TAKE ACTION

Lies should be challenged as soon as possible because the repetition of lies creates false memories in children that are difficult to erase. When your children have been told lies about you, invite them to think for themselves. Are the allegations consistent with what they know about how you behave? It may be best to have another trusted person correct the distortions rather than attempt to do it yourself. The children are apt to dismiss your denials. Another person may have more success in convincing the children that they are mistaken.

REVISIONIST HISTORY

> *Who controls the past controls the future.*
> —GEORGE ORWELL

Communist rulers in the Soviet Union were masters at propaganda. When it came time to convince the populace that a formerly revered leader was really a scoundrel, they knew the job required more than implanting false beliefs about the target. Their corruption of reality had to reach back in time. They had to erase benevolent memories of the person—memories that conflicted with the new party line. They had to silence potential critics who would object: "How could this person [Stalin, for example] be so bad when for years we were told that he was great and worthy of adulation?"

So they simply rewrote history. One strategy was to say, in effect, "Our previous judgment was mistaken." The other tactic was an outright denial that the leader was ever held in high esteem. Textbooks were revised to conform to the new doctrine. Institutions and places named in the person's honor were renamed. Portraits were removed from public areas. Heads were airbrushed out of official group photographs.

Editing the past to deflate a person's reputation is also common in certain intellectual movements and in divorced families. In 1968 the famous novelist-philosopher Ayn Rand broke off all relations with her closest associate, psychologist Nathaniel Branden. Before the break Rand praised Branden as brilliant, heroic, intellectually creative, a genius. She dedicated her magnum opus, *Atlas Shrugged*, to him, and in a statement at the end of the novel called Branden her intellectual heir. Many of Rand's followers developed a cultlike worship of Rand and Branden. So when Branden fell from grace, the past had to be rewritten to conform with Rand's new position.

She and her close disciples began claiming that Branden was a hack. His contributions were unoriginal. He merely passed off Rand's ideas as his own. (At the time Branden was completing his pathbreaking work, *The Psychology of Self-Esteem;* the book is currently in its thirty-fifth printing, still selling briskly after three decades, and Branden has since written more than twenty books that present his innovative psychological theories and therapeutic techniques.) Rand removed Branden's name from the dedication of all subsequent printings of her novel. And in a move reminiscent of the missing heads in the Soviet photographs, her followers erased Branden's voice from taped lectures and dubbed in others reading the words originally spoken by him.

Brainwashing parents follow the same principle: They revise history to obliterate positive memories of the target. A father tells his children that their mother was always more interested in her work than in them, even though she only began working outside the home after the divorce. A mother transforms a past vacation planned and enjoyed by both parents into the time that "Daddy insisted we leave you for a week." The target's former involvement with the children is minimized or denied; photographic evidence to the contrary is destroyed or hidden. A husband wrote numerous notes to his wife during their marriage that praised her patience and attention to the children; he seized and destroyed these notes in the midst of a custody battle in which he claimed that she neglected her children. The basic message is that nothing about the target is any good, or ever has been.

It is not unusual for spouses to devalue each other as they go through a divorce. It is easier to tolerate the break-up when you focus on negative aspects of the relationship that you will be escaping, rather than positive aspects that you will be losing. Parents intent on divorce poison, though, carry this process to an extreme, and they encourage or manipulate their children to do the same. According to Dr. Stanley Clawar and Dr. Brynne Rivlin, "It is fairly easy to confuse children into doubting their own perception of reality due to the high regard and awesome power most parents hold in their children's eyes."

When I interview child victims of divorce poison, they usually give me a revised history of their relationship with the rejected parent. Children who were close to a parent now insist that they never enjoyed being with that parent. When I ask about photographs and videotapes of family holidays and vacations that show them being very loving toward the alienated parent, they dismiss these with a variety of excuses. The most popular excuses are: "I was just pretending to have a good time," "She made me act like that, but I didn't really feel it," "I was only happy because [the favored parent] was there," "What do you expect, everybody is happy on a vacation, but it doesn't mean I enjoyed being with her," or "The times in those videos were the only times I ever enjoyed being with her. All the rest of my life was miserable."

Alienated children similarly dismiss the significance of cards and gifts they gave the target parent in the past. Often they insist that their other parent made them give the card and write on it, "To the best daddy in the world. I love you very much." One boy claimed that the only reason he gave his mother a gift on Mother's Day was that the entire class made something and he didn't want to be different from his classmates. This did not explain why he signed the accompanying handmade card, "Love and kisses."

In one of the worst cases of divorce poison I have seen, a girl named

Mindy claimed to have total amnesia for a music box that her mother had used to wake her up every morning of her life. The mother brought the music box to a meeting with her alienated daughter. "Remember this?" asked the mother. She wound it up and lifted the lid to release the tune, "You Are the Sunshine of My Life." The mother choked back tears evoked by memories of better times, but Mindy sat stone-faced. "Sure," she said, "I've heard that song. But I've never seen that music box before." Her mother was astounded. How could her daughter not remember the morning ritual that had been a fixture in their lives for eight years? Mindy could have been lying. Or she could have blocked out these memories in the service of maintaining her cold rejection of her mom.

Mindy's mother expected to correct her daughter's misperception of their past relationship by presenting clear evidence to the contrary. She did not count on the tenacity of a brainwashed child's corrupted view of reality. In a clash between reality and an alienating parent's distortions, the distortions usually win out, unless groundwork has been carefully laid. One cannot reason with an alienated child until the child's mind is open to reason.

TAKE ACTION

Don't squander valuable opportunities by naively assuming that brainwashing will be reversed by the simple presentation of reality. When you have strong evidence that a child's view of the past is distorted, withhold the evidence until there is a good chance that your child will be open to considering it, rather than reject it out of hand. It is best to use a therapist's assistance with this process. With correct timing, the evidence can be a potent antidote to divorce poison. With poor timing, you will encounter the brick-wall resistance of a mind closed to reality and reason, and you will have wasted an important weapon in the battle against alienation.

THE TOTAL CHANGE THEORY

Sometimes a child's past relationship to the target parent was so positive, so filled with gratification and memorable moments, that any attempt to obliterate the good memories would be futile. In that case, what is revised is not the past assessment but the current one.

A woman adamantly refuses to encourage her daughter to maintain ties with her dad. This mother admits to the therapist that her ex used to be a very kind and loving father. But, she claims, since the divorce he has totally changed. He is no longer the same man. His change is so complete that he no longer has anything positive to contribute to his daughter's life.

Alienating parents often support this maneuver by emphasizing their ex's superficial changes, the type that are common in the recently divorced. The ex-husband begins to wear his hair longer. He changes his wardrobe, listens to different music, drives a sports car. He compensates for the loss of his marriage by trying to recapture a sense of his youth and of his opportunities for a new beginning. Nevertheless, his commitment to his children remains intact, and his underlying character is unchanged.

As with most forms of divorce poison, children are most susceptible when they have no meaningful contact with the target and thus little chance to test the reality of what they have been taught.

TAKE ACTION

If your ex is complaining to your children that you have changed, tell the children:

- Changes are a fact of life.
- The important thing is that your love for them is unchanged.
- Despite any changes, your commitment to their welfare will never change.
- They too have changed over the years and you have certainly not rejected them.

SUGGESTIONS AND INNUENDOS

Parents can communicate negative messages about the target without telling a single lie, even without lodging a single criticism. Consider the following very common scenario. The children are at their father's home, watching cartoons or playing, and their mother calls and asks to speak with them.

In one home the father says, "Mommy is on the phone. Come and talk to her. Who wants to go first?" If the children respond, "Not now. We're busy," he says, "I know you're busy, but now it's time to talk to Mom. Let's go." The father essentially handles the call the way he would have before the divorce. His attitude conveys his belief that talking to Mom is a priority and is nonnegotiable. The underlying message is that their mother deserves their respect.

In another home the father announces, in a disdainful tone, "Your mother is on the phone. Do you want to speak with her?" His attitude suggests that he does not welcome her call and they don't have to either. The underlying message, communicated solely by implication but not lost on the children, is that their mother is not worthy of respect. They sense that it would be perfectly fine with Dad if they snubbed Mom. In fact, even though he has not explicitly said so, he would probably be pleased with them if they did reject their mother's call.

Often the most potent divorce poison takes this form. It relies on suggestion, innuendo, and implication. It is more difficult to expose because it is sneakier and more subtle than outright lies and misrepresentations.

A mother phoned her children while they were with their paternal grandparents. Her daughter enthusiastically described a variation of tag that she and her brother invented and were playing. The mother's only response was to express concern: "I hope you're not getting hurt." This conveyed the impression that the grandparents could not be trusted to prevent the children from playing a dangerous game. The other hidden message was that the mother was not interested in hearing that her daughter was having a good time with her grandparents. When her son got on the phone, also sharing his excitement about the game, his mother asked, "Are you having fun or is it kind of silly?" Her inflection made clear what answer she wanted to hear. Although her son had been having a great time, he muted his expression of enjoyment and instead said, "It's okay."

This boy was very troubled by his mother's negative attitude about his dad and his dad's family. He tried to cope by pleasing her. He would rather tell his mom what she wanted to hear than forthrightly state his own opinion. But in the process of doing so, his own feelings changed.

His mother's small dose of divorce poison, administered in her brief suggestion that he was not having fun with his grandparents, achieved its purpose. Following the phone call, the boy had mixed feelings about what had been a very gratifying activity.

An example of the power of suggestion to alter a child's view of reality occurred in my own home while I was writing this book. My grandsons were spending the night and the youngest boy, Shaun, talked us into ordering pizzas from a certain heavily advertised franchise rather than from our favorite local pizzeria. The pizza arrived burnt on top, with a crust that was too soft, and with too little of a bland sauce that had lived in a can too long.

My wife and I could not restrain our disappointment with the product. As we openly expressed our opinion, hoping to instill better taste in a nine-year-old, we unwittingly programmed Shaun to dislike the pizza. He went from loving it to passing up seconds. All he could say, in his defense, was that this franchise outlet did a worse job than the one in his neighborhood. His father later verified that the pizza we had was perfectly consistent with what they usually get and with what his son loves. We had inadvertently changed our grandson's normal taste preference merely by repetitively expressing our very negative opinion of the food.

One of the most common complaints of divorced parents is shabby treatment during the transfer of the children. A mother arrives a few minutes early to pick up her son. It is raining outside. She rings the doorbell, but there is no response. The boy has his coat on and is ready to leave. He watches his mother from the window. But his stepmother makes him stay in the house until the very last second. After repeated experiences like this the mother learns that she will be kept waiting, regardless of the weather, until the exact time that her official period of possession begins.

What is the effect on children of witnessing such treatment? The boy in the above example received two messages through his stepmother's behavior. First, his mother's wish to be with him is seen as an unwelcome nuisance. She is excluded as long as possible, as though spending time with her has no value. Second, she is not worthy of being treated with compassion or common decency. She is given less consideration than a door-to-door salesman.

Children will usually feel very uncomfortable when a parent is treated so disrespectfully. This is especially true when the mistreatment is at the hands of someone else they love. To relieve themselves of loyalty conflicts, they may join in devaluing the parent. By convincing themselves that the parent deserves poor treatment, they avoid conscious feelings of guilt.

Younger children are most susceptible to suggestion. Treat them as though you expect them to be scared of the target, and they will respond with fear. Shortly after the marital separation a mother tells her daughter: "Daddy is coming to take you for a visit, but you don't have to be afraid." Prior to this the girl had no reason to fear being with her father. She generally was excited to see him. But now her mother has introduced the idea of fear as an expected response to her father. A small seed of insecurity has been planted. When the father arrives, the programming continues. In front of the girl the mother says, "She seems to be a little uneasy about going with you." The mother then turns to the child and says, "Now remember. I told you there is nothing to be afraid of. Don't be scared." With this repetition the seed has taken root. The girl is reluctant to leave her mother's side. The mother feels triumphant. The father feels bewildered.

Suggestions can be just as powerful when conveyed without words. Behavior and gestures do the job. A father and his new wife constantly roll their eyes and smirk when the children speak about their activities with their mother. The disapproval is obvious. Over time, the children either adopt the same critical attitude toward their mother or learn to avoid speaking about her in their father's home.

Infants and toddlers can learn to fear someone merely by seeing how their parents act in the person's presence. When a mother begins to cry and cling tightly to her daughter as the paternal grandmother reaches out to take the child for a visit, she "infects" her daughter with her anxiety. Predictably, the little girl will respond with her own tears and clinging behavior.

Older children are generally less suggestible but not immune. A father cautions his twelve-year-old daughter, "Don't get too close to your stepfather in the swimming pool." After a few such warnings it is difficult for the girl not to look at her stepfather in a different light. A fleeting physical contact becomes a possible cause for concern. The girl has succumbed to her father's suggestion that the stepfather could be a sexual predator.

TAKE ACTION

Identify the unstated implications of suggestions and innuendos, and clarify reality, to help neutralize the harmful impact of this form of divorce poison. For example, "Mommy worries that you won't have a good time with me, but we know that we have a good time together, don't we?" Or "I've seen how Daddy frowns when you tell him what we did together. That must make you very uncomfortable. I guess he disapproves of almost everything that goes on here. Even when we were married, your daddy and I had different ideas about how to do things. In fact, that's one of the reasons we got a divorce. But you know in your heart that there is absolutely nothing wrong with how we live in this house." As with most discussions of divorce poison, it is best to choose a time when you and the children are relating well. With younger children, simply identify the underlying message conveyed by the suggestion and clarify reality. Suggestions and innuendos lose their potency when they are openly confronted.

EXPLOITATION

It is bad enough when a parent acts as though the other parent's participation in the child's life is unwelcome. Even worse is when a parent suggests to the child that it is permissible, even desirable, to exploit the other parent.

It is very common for parents to support their children's rejection of the other parent while encouraging the children to ask for money and favors from the hated parent. The children are taught to feel entitled to money and services from the parent they otherwise shun.

At times the sense of entitlement stretches credulity. A teenager expected her father to buy her a new car even though she admitted that she would never allow him even to sit in the car with her. A college student expected his father to send extra money to cover additional expenses, but the father was not welcome at the graduation exercises. A high school senior demanded that his mother select, pay for, and deliver to him a corsage for his prom date. This mother was unwelcome at her son's basketball games and was excluded from every other aspect of her son's life. She was not even to have the pleasure of getting a photograph of her son and his date in their prom clothes. Perhaps the height of audacity was a young lady's expectation that her father would contribute substantially to her wedding expenses, even though she refused to invite him or any of his family to the wedding.

For the child, exploitation is another expression of alienation. For the parent who encourages or sanctions this behavior, it is a form of divorce poison, another means of corrupting the child's view of the formerly loved target. By not expressing disapproval of the exploitation, the alienating parent contributes to the notion that the target parent is so worthy of contempt that the usual rules of civility and decency do not apply.

This tactic is especially pernicious. The sense of entitlement corrupts not only a child's relationship with a parent but the child's character. Alienating parents teach their children to suspend the usual rules of morality when dealing with the target. What these parents may not appreciate is that a child can become accustomed to treating others as objects to be used. Exploitation can become a permanent mode of dealing with people and handicap the child's ability to form and maintain emotionally gratifying relationships. When this occurs, the alienating parent is guilty of contributing not only to the loss of love but to the perversion of the child's soul.

PROJECTION

When a person makes several accusations about another person that have no basis in reality, very often the accusations turn out to be self-descriptive. This was true of Louise, who accused her father-in-law of being volatile when she herself was prone to fits of rage.

The practice of falsely attributing to others one's own unacknowledged feelings, impulses, or thoughts is known as "projection." It happens so much in custody disputes that I often advise parents to begin keeping a list of possible projections. It is uncanny how often a parent will be guilty of the very things he or she accuses the ex-spouse of doing.

Sometimes projections provide clues to behaviors and intentions that the parent attempts to conceal. I remember one woman who told me that her ex-husband repeatedly accused her of tape-recording their phone conversations. I advised her that it was a good bet that he was taping. This proved to be true. As I discussed in chapter 4, very often the first parent to raise an accusation of brainwashing is the one who has already begun such a campaign.

To detect the possibility of projection, follow this procedure. First you must be sure that you are not guilty of whatever is being attributed to you. Then ask yourself: Why would he be saying that? Where did that idea come from? Since it isn't true for me, perhaps it is on his mind because it is something he thought, felt, or did, or is contemplating doing. Is there any evidence for this?

Not every false accusation is the result of projection. It is only one possible explanation. But when projection is present, you need to know about it. It alerts you to potential and actual destructive behavior on the part of your accuser. It helps you explain the situation to your children when appropriate. And it is essential in defending against allegations in court.

PROJECTION: NOT I, YOU!

Following are some examples of the use of projection in custody litigation. In each case, the person attributes his or her own thoughts, feelings, or behavior to another.

- A man attributes his ex-wife's effort to gain more time with the children as retribution for the divorce that he initiated. In reality she is happily remarried and grateful to be free of her first husband. He, on the other hand, has gone through a series of unsuccessful relationships and regrets the divorce. His envy of her newfound happiness fuels his refusal of her request. *He projects his unhappy preoccupation with the divorce and his ulterior motives in the dispute onto his ex-spouse.*

- A man wants joint custody of his daughter. His ex-wife accuses him of merely trying to avoid child support payments. In reality the father has no intention of reducing his support even if his girl spends more time in his home and his expenses increase. But the mother has sued for more child support, despite currently receiving more money than she actually spends on her daughter. *She projects her preoccupation with finances onto her ex-spouse.*

- A girl in the custody of her father asks to live with her mother. She is uncomfortable with her father's ongoing criticisms of her mother and the parade of girlfriends who spend the night with Dad. The father is unable to recognize or admit that his daughter's preference is a result of his behavior. Instead he attributes her request to "the grass is greener" phenomenon. In reality *his* behavior is constantly motivated by the expectation that the key to happiness lies elsewhere. It is what resulted in his divorce and in his inability to settle down with one woman. *He projects his belief that "the grass is greener" onto his daughter.*

- In her previous marriage a mother relinquished custody of her three boys to their father. When she is going through her second divorce, her husband tells their daughter that her mother abandoned her other children. In truth she reached her previous decision after agonizing over it. She stayed in close touch with her boys and had a good relationship with them. However, her current husband did threaten to move to Ireland and never see their daughter again. *He is projecting his thought about abandonment onto his wife.*

- A woman accuses her husband of being cruel. In reality she has falsely accused him of child sexual abuse, thereby subjecting their son to numerous unnecessary examinations and smearing the father's reputation. She disrupted his family reunion by sending the police to investigate a frivolous complaint that the children were being mistreated. She spread a rumor throughout the community that her husband was violent toward her and the children. And she called his employer in an effort to get him fired. *She projects her cruel behavior onto her spouse.*

People are usually unaware that they are projecting. Projections are not only self-descriptive, they are self-deceptive. In fact, psychologists regard projection as a defense that people use to protect themselves from facing their own unpleasant thoughts or feelings.

The woman in the last example who accused her husband of being cruel was not just trying to win a custody battle. She actually convinced herself that her husband was a monster. This corruption of reality was the price she paid to avoid the disturbing truth that the cruelty she sensed was her own. Because of its protective function, confronting the woman with her projection was futile. When the court-appointed psychologist suggested that she was trying to brainwash her children, she was indignant. She was convinced that she was a victim of a terrible injustice. In her mind all she was doing was trying to protect her children from their cruel father.

RATIONALIZATION

While working on this chapter I came upon a news item that illustrated, in another context, a form of reality corruption favored by bad-mouthing and bashing parents. In an entire Alabama school system of 2,600 students, the only Jewish high school student complained of ongoing harassment. Some examples he cited were the assistant principal ordering him to write an essay on "Why Jesus loves me," and a teacher ordering him to remove a Star of David lapel pin. The superintendent confirmed the allegations but explained that the teacher thought the Jewish Star was a gang symbol.

This sort of excuse is known as a rationalization. It is a lie that is intended to seem plausible. In this case the school superintendent apparently thought it sounded reasonable enough to repeat to the national media.

Men who beat and intimidate their wives rationalize their disgraceful behavior. A man testified that he did not verbally abuse his wife. During his cross-examination he admitted that he frequently called her a whore, a liar, a slut, a horrible mother, and worse epithets, usually modified with curse words. When asked how he reconciled such behavior with his prior testimony that he did not verbally abuse her, he said that his insulting and name-calling was not abusive because it was true. The judge was not convinced by such twisted logic.

A woman told her husband that if he didn't agree to all her demands in the divorce, she would call his employer and get him fired. During her deposition, she denied making such threats. On further questioning she admitted that she "may have alluded to getting him fired," but she did not regard this as a threat. Quibbling about the exact meaning of words is a common form of rationalization used even by presidents of the United States.

When confronted with evidence of wrongdoing, a popular rationalization is to dismiss the behavior as a joke. The woman who ignored her stepson unless he addressed her as Mom told the court that she was only kidding. The judge dismissed this rationalization because the behavior occurred over a long period of time and was consistent with other versions of the name game played by this woman: She referred to the boy's mother by her first name in conversation with him and she required her own son to call his stepfather Dad.

Parents dispensing divorce poison use rationalizations in two ways. Most frequently they rationalize in order to defend their behavior, as did the Alabama schoolteacher. They attempt to convince themselves and others that they are doing nothing wrong. The rationalization is a cover-up to hide their real motives. Second, rationalizations can be used to make the target's behavior look bad.

A noncustodial mother complained that despite repeated requests she was never shown anything her six-year-old daughter brought home from school, including report cards. The father and stepmother responded that they were not deliberately withholding the material. They were merely respecting the girl's own choice. If the girl wanted her mother to see her schoolwork, she would have taken it with her when she saw her mother every other weekend.

This explanation sounded reasonable to them. But of course it was a rationalization to justify their lack of support for the girl's relationship with her mother. We don't ordinarily expect a six-year-old to be responsible for keeping track of her school papers. And we don't ordinarily assume that if the child neglected to pack her schoolwork then she did not want her mom to see it. Finally, we would not leave such a decision to the child. Everything else that went with her on weekends spent with her mother was packed by her stepmother. If the father and stepmother wanted the mother to see the schoolwork, it would have happened.

This couple used the rationalization about the girl's failure to show her mother her work not only to excuse their own behavior. They also cited it as evidence that the girl must not feel close to her mom.

Like many rationalizations, this one was easy to expose, especially because it was part of a wider campaign to exclude the mother from her daughter's life. This couple also played the name game by requiring the girl to call her stepmother Mommy and her mother by her first name.

The "respect for the child's choice" shown by this couple is another popular rationalization used by most parents in the latter stages of brainwashing. Once a child has been successfully alienated from the target, the programming parent sits back and disavows any role in the conflict. When the child protests seeing her mother, the father says, "That is her choice." As an enlightened parent he "respects her autonomy"; he fails to facilitate the contact.

But curiously his permissiveness seems to operate only in this sphere. He sends his daughter to school even when she feels like staying home. He would never allow her to avoid a checkup because she was afraid of the doctor. And before the divorce, when she protested going somewhere with her mother, he insisted she do as she was told. But now, after months of programming, when his daughter resists spending a weekend with her mother, her choice is elevated to the status of a sacred precept not, under any circumstance, to be violated.

Parents who use the "I respect my child's autonomy" defense pour salt on the wound by blaming the target for the child's alienation. This is always some variant of "My child does not want to see you because you mistreat her." The perpetrator never acknowledges responsibility for masterminding the schism between the child and the target.

Norma testified that, despite her best efforts, she was unable to overcome her five-year-old daughter Megan's refusal to go to her father's home. She claimed that Megan was afraid of her father and her paternal grandparents. Norma blamed this on the father's yelling and not keeping all his promises to Megan and the grandparents' ignoring and teasing her. The court-appointed psychiatrist found no evidence to suggest that Megan feared her father, but did conclude that she avoided her father because of subtle pressure from her mother, combined with a wish to please her mother and avoid her anger. Like many alienated children, Megan insisted that it was her own choice to avoid her father and that her mother had nothing to do with it. In fact, her mother wanted her to see her dad. The following conversation exposed the flimsy rationalization:

Doctor:	What does Mommy do when you don't want to take your bath?
Megan:	She makes me.
Doctor:	What does Mommy do when you don't want to go to bed?
Megan:	She makes me.
Doctor:	What does Mommy do when you don't want to see your Daddy?
Megan:	She says I don't have to if I don't want to and Daddy should respect my feelings.

During cross-examination, the lawyer accused Norma of actively inducing the alienation. She was indignant. Here she had been doing everything possible to persuade Megan to visit her scary father, and instead of being commended for her valiant efforts she was portrayed as the villain. Norma failed to consider that she was asking the judge to give her custody of a child whom she admitted she was unable to control. If the judge were to believe her testimony, he could conclude that Norma was a weak parent who lacked appropriate authority over a five-year-old girl.

TAKE ACTION

To show your children how their rejection of you fulfills the desires of their other parent, despite your ex's rationalizations, initiate a conversation similar to the one that took place between the psychiatrist and Megan. Most children know that if one parent really wanted them to see the other parent, they would insist on it and back it up with the threat of punishment. Exposing this rationalization provides a relatively strong demonstration of how a parent can indirectly influence a child, and it paves the way for other efforts to reverse alienation.

HOLIER THAN THOU

Indignance, such as Norma's, is common among brainwashers. In her case it was a reaction to being accused of brainwashing. Beyond its defensive use, self-righteousness helps foster indoctrination. By combining moral outrage with certainty of conviction, the aim is to ward off careful scrutiny of the programmer's reality distortions. The strident tone is the argument.

Trial attorneys favor this tactic. In deliberations before the judge, who is not likely to be taken in by such maneuvers, lawyers show emotional restraint while advocating their position. But let the jury enter the courtroom, and the emoting begins. Haughty, reproachful, disdainful, lawyers attempt to bypass the jurors' critical faculties. They want the jury to believe, in effect, "The lawyer feels so strongly about his position: It must be justified."

Jurors may not always be swayed by such tactics, especially since they get it from both sides. But children are much more suggestible. The tone of their parent's voice carries weight, even more that the words being spoken. And the self-righteous tone of a bad-mouthing parent communicates that the target deserves contempt.

The particulars of the condemnation are limitless. A man accuses his ex-spouse of neglecting her children because she cares passionately about her career and relies on baby-sitters too much. A wife accuses her husband of being a lousy father because he lets them do things she views as dangerous. A man tells his children that their mother and her new husband are "liars and morally bankrupt" because they began dating before the divorce was final. The "holier than thou" attitude is expressed with comments such as "That's just what I would expect from her" or "I can't believe he did that!" Whatever "that" is, the child gets the idea that it is very bad.

TAKE ACTION

If your breakup is accompanied by your ex using self-righteous tones to denounce you to your children, take this as an early warning signal that your children may be pressured to turn against you. Children are easily impressed by self-righteousness. Therefore, as soon as possible arm your children with a defense by teaching them that a strident tone is no index of the reasonableness of an idea. Children should learn to judge ideas by their merit and not by the emotion surrounding their delivery. They need to learn to recognize a parent's strong denunciations of the other parent as expressions of hostility, not representations of truth.

WITH GOD ON OUR SIDE

Self-righteousness is most powerful when paired with religiosity. "Your mother," decries Dad, "is not just a bad parent. She's a sinner." Why? Usually one of three reasons. Most often because she slept with another man. In some cases just because she initiated the divorce. And in other cases merely because she has not embraced the father's new religious beliefs.

Children hear a bitter refrain that their mother is evil and worthy of contempt because she has violated God's law. She has Satan in her heart. She will be destroyed at Armageddon for her lack of love for God.

This strategy is particularly effective because it capitalizes on years of religious training. From the beginning children are taught to accept religious doctrines on faith. The Ten Commandments are—just that. Commandments. Not proposals to be carefully evaluated before accepting. Religion enjoys a mantle of legitimacy and absolute authority. *So, when a father's denunciation of a mother is cloaked in religious dogma, the children are primed to accept it without question, as they would any other religious teaching. Even if it clashes with common sense.*

When a wife—before, during, or after divorce—sleeps with another man, her ex-husband's religious indignation is almost always a cover-up for more personal feelings. The real issue is not her fall from grace. It is his hurt, anger, jealousy, and humiliation. Certainly we can understand how he would feel this way. But if he acted on these feelings by lobbying his children to reject their mother, it would be obvious that he was sacrificing his children to pursue personal revenge. Instead the children get the message that Dad wants them to condemn Mom, not because she offended him, but because she offended God. The children are pressed into alienation as a demonstration of their faith. Many times the father is not fully aware that his pious stance is a front.

But make no mistake about it. The father is not simply expressing his religious beliefs. Nor is he sincerely attempting to give his children a moral education. This he could accomplish without mentioning the mother's behavior. The father is clearly trying to turn the children against their mother. And he is using selective attention and context dropping to do it. No matter how he rationalizes his behavior, he is brainwashing.

The strategy is to equate the mother's value as a person and as a parent with one moral transgression, and then to persuade the children to do the same. Ask these children to describe their mother and they say,

"She's a sinner," as though this were all one needed to know about her. It overshadows the entire history of their relationship with her. It obliterates everything she has done for them. They have been programmed to believe that their mother's sin defines her character and renders her unworthy of love.

Children are particularly vulnerable to thinking in global terms about a person's character. People are either good or bad. It requires a certain level of psychological maturity to maintain a balanced image of others, to feel positive about them while simultaneously recognizing their flaws. Some adults never reach this level of maturity. When a father encourages his children to hate their mother because she has done something wrong, he is fostering an attitude that will limit their capacity for healthy, rewarding interpersonal relations. By extension, he is also implying that he is free from any wrongdoing. Selective attention operates to magnify the mother's flaws while overlooking those of the father.

TAKE ACTION

Under the sway of guilt, a spouse who has had an affair may passively accept her children's total condemnation as punishment for her wrongdoing. To avoid this mistake, keep in mind that our souls are not defined merely by our worst sins. It is unfair for your ex and your children to select one aspect of you and respond to you as if that were all there is. Allowing your children to lose their relationship with you multiplies the harmful impact of your behavior on your children. A far better way to atone is to take whatever steps are necessary to heal the relationship.

Some fathers label the mother a sinner merely because she chose to divorce him. He maintains, and persuades the children, that the divorce is all her fault. In failing to take responsibility for his contributions to the failure of the marriage, he ignores the full context of the divorce. In almost every case the husband shares culpability for the marital problems. Indeed, what type of man rigidly espouses extreme religious views that require the children's total repudiation of their mother? Most likely one who has character traits that made him hard to live with in the first place.

The third category of "sinful" mothers are those who do not share the father's religious affiliation. In this situation either the father has converted to a religion or sect that preaches intolerance of outsiders. Or, less often, both spouses had observed this faith until the mother decided to leave the fold.

When a father embraces new religious practices after the breakup, his children are less likely to ally with him. In these cases the father is usually preoccupied with his new beliefs. In a heavy-handed way he tries to convert the children, but his proselytizing backfires. The pressure to adopt unfamiliar beliefs meets with contempt on the part of older children and confusion and fear on the part of their younger siblings. Their father is different, and they do not like the change.

When the father undergoes a religious conversion before the breakup, which is often the case, the children are usually more susceptible to his influence. In a typical scenario, the father joins a fanatic sect or cult that devalues outsiders. He feels that he has finally found meaning in life and wants to share this with his family. His wife resists indoctrination; his children may not.

The father zealously devotes himself to the new cause, learning its teachings and becoming, himself, brainwashed. Then the father-brainwash-victim becomes the father-brainwash-perpetrator. He begins taking his children to services and they are gradually brought into the fold. They get a weekly dose of doctrine that is antagonistic toward established churches and synagogues, including the one their mother still attends.

By the time the mother realizes the seriousness of this, the children may be beyond her reach. They have been taught that nonbelievers are their "spiritual enemies." That people who try to dissuade them from "the truth" are pawns of the devil. They may also have been taught that the father is the spiritual head of the household; such a belief reinforces the pressure to accept his pronouncements. If the mother had once shared the same religious affiliation, but then defected, she is regarded as a heretic who merits scorn.

When divorce occurs in these families, religious conflict is very often the trigger. The wife cannot tolerate the personality change in her husband. He becomes emotionally withdrawn from her. And in some cases, bolstered by a newfound sense of self-righteousness, he becomes abusive. Certainly she does not want her children influenced by his beliefs.

Under these circumstances it is easy to see how a custody battle would erupt. In fact, it is so predictable that cults develop well-organized approaches to help their members prevail in custody litigation. They produce and distribute booklets that instruct followers on how to respond to questions from psychologists and lawyers. Parents are taught to coach their children to give misleading testimony in court. When the children are asked about their religion, they give answers that conceal the radical and intolerant nature of the cult.

You may have noticed that I have repeatedly referred to the behavior of men in my discussion of religious-based attacks. Women also use this maneuver, but in my consultations and studies I have encountered far more men who justify their brainwashing on religious grounds. Brainwashing mothers, in my experience, are more likely to express moral indignation without religious rhetoric. For example, a mother may rationalize her attempt to keep the children from their father by objecting to their exposure to his girlfriend. But she does not label the father and his girlfriend "pawns of Satan." Instead she expresses concern over the impact of the father-girlfriend relationship on the children's moral or emotional development.

It is possible that the differences I have observed between men and women in this regard are not representative of brainwashing parents in general. Perhaps religiosity is equally prevalent among brainwashing mothers. If so, I hope readers will set me straight.

Parents of many different faiths draw on religion to foster alienation. But regardless of their sex or their particular religion, every parent who resorts to this tactic to promote parental alienation is caught in a curious contradiction. While ostensibly upholding religious ideals, they are coercing their children to violate one of the most sacred religious tenets, the Fifth Commandment: "Honor thy father and thy mother."

TAKE ACTION

Meet with your minister, rabbi, or priest, explain your situation, and ask about your religion's position on the sanctity of parent-child relationships. If he supports the importance of your children's contact with you, ask him to intervene with your ex and with your children. This can be especially helpful if you choose a religious leader with training in family therapy. Despite moral transgressions of parents, noncult religions usually encourage children to honor their parents. If your ex is using religion to turn the children against you, the children are more likely to accept contrary advice from a respected religious leader than from you.

"THE TRUTH"

Members of religious cults always feel that they possess the truth. The truth, of course, is defined as their particular set of beliefs. Dr. Gardner discovered that when children suffer from parental alienation syndrome, the phrase *the truth* takes on special significance.

During indoctrination, programmers repeatedly label their distorted version of reality as "the truth." Over time, "the truth" becomes associated with the programmer's implanted scenarios. "The truth," instructs the father, "is that Mamma's boyfriend showed you his pee-pee, right? That's the truth." After several repetitions, "the truth" becomes a shorthand code term for the father's program. When he wants his daughter to repeat the false allegations, he merely needs to ask her to tell the truth.

This pays dividends during subsequent investigations by courts and mental health professionals. When asked if she has been coached by her parent to say anything in particular, the child responds that she was only told to tell the truth. In her mind the truth has come to mean "all the bad things I have been told about the target." But the unwary examiner may believe the child is giving an accurate account of the target's behavior.

TAKE ACTION

Make sure that your attorney and any mental health professionals involved with your children understand that "the truth" has become associated with your ex's programming. When questioning your children, professionals will want to ask, "How did you come to learn that this was the truth?" Or "Is that what really happened?" When examiners probe for the meaning of "the truth," they may learn that it stands for the misrepresentations of the alienating parent, not for reality.

Alienating parents also use "the truth" as an excuse for divorce poison. They defend their bad-mouthing and bashing with the claim that they are only being honest with the child and that it is always better to be honest. Of course, their commitment to honesty does not extend to letting the child know about their own flaws or about your virtues.

Jerome insisted that he was right to tell his son the truth about his mother and stepfather. Jerome suspected that they began their affair prior to the divorce, and he repeatedly told his son that his mother and stepfather were morally bankrupt because they lied about their relationship. When the boy asked his stepfather if he thought his daddy was a good father, the stepfather said, "Yes, and he loves you very much." Jerome then accused the stepfather of lying to the boy. The stepfather didn't really like the father, therefore he was obviously showing what a pathological liar he was. According to Jerome, a person who was committed to the truth would have told the boy honestly that he thought he had a bad father. Jerome failed to understand how a commitment to a child's emotional welfare and need to hold a positive image of his parent could take precedence over an opportunity to express negative feelings. Parents who bad-mouth often assume that everyone else operates as they do. If they freely vent destructive criticism without regard for the impact on their child, they believe their ex does the same.

TAKE ACTION

Never get in a battle with your children about what "really" happened. Accusing your children of lying will only drive them further away. Instead, when an impasse is reached, bypass the controversy by "agreeing to disagree." Your children's agreement that their rejection of you is irrational is not a precondition of healing your relationship. It is more effective to focus on creating a rewarding, affectionate relationship in the present.

OVERINDULGENCE

Earlier I discussed the target parent's indulgence of the children as a means of avoiding their rejection and counteracting the malevolent asso-

ciations built up by the programmer. Alienating parents also indulge children. Their goal is to cement the children's alliance to them while fur-
thering their alienation from the target.

One form of indulgence is to seduce the children with age-inappro-
priate privileges and material things. A parent allows her adolescent to
have parties in the home without supervision. By comparison the other
parent appears overly restrictive. Another parent offers extravagant gifts,
such as a new sports car and season tickets to pro-football games, if his
teenage son will move in with him. The parent with fewer resources is
unable to compete. To her children she appears less generous and less
gratifying.

Indulgence can take the form of having lower expectations for
responsible behavior. A lax attitude is taken toward chores, homework,
and junk-food snacks. When a homework assignment is challenging, or
requires a lot of time and effort, the parent does it for the child. If your ex
caters to your children's wishes for immediate gratification and avoid-
ance of frustration, the children may regard your demands for more
mature behavior and frustration tolerance as overly strict and odious. You
make them brush their teeth and do their homework; their other parent
lets them avoid these chores. Your ex may exploit the situation by being
very receptive to your children's complaints about you. Instead of reinforcing the need for good nutrition, for example, your ex sides with the
children and agrees that you are being unfair to insist that they eat their
vegetables. By suspending ordinary expectations of the children, your ex
panders to their immaturity and encourages them to reject you as unreasonably demanding.

Children who have reached a certain level of development will sense
that the permissive parent is shirking the responsibility to provide more
structure and authoritative guidance. But their wish for freedom and possessions can undermine their better judgment. The pleasure of immediate
gratification can seduce them into an unhealthy alliance with the programming parent.

Overindulgence can backfire. When children learn that their allegiance is being bought, the price may rise. They may threaten to defect to
the enemy (i.e., move in with the other parent) if their increasing
demands are not met. In this way the victims of manipulation become
the manipulators. The exploited become the exploiters.

TAKE ACTION

Confront overindulgence directly by reminding your children that a parent's job is to set and enforce limits, and that this is one way to show love and caring. Explain that even though you and your ex do things differently, you both love the children and they need to have a good relationship with both of you. Children understand that responsible adults set limits. It is relatively easy for them to understand that it is unfair to reject you merely because you do not indulge them as much as their other parent.

Look for ways in which you could "lighten up" or compromise with the children without excessively indulging them. Alienated children need to have enjoyable times with the rejected parent to rebuild bonds of affection and respect and offset divorce poison. Parental authority is best exercised when it is grounded in a loving relationship. You may have to temporarily relax some of your expectations while you concentrate on reestablishing affectionate bonds.

ENCROACHMENT

Overindulgence works as an alienating tactic only if the child is kept from enjoying time with the target. When efforts to eliminate contact between the target and child are unsuccessful, one option remains. The parent tries to sabotage the child's enjoyment of the contact. There are many ways to accomplish this goal. All involve some form of encroachment on the child's time with the target or on their relationship.

A common ploy is to involve the child in frequent and lengthy telephone calls while the child is in the target parent's home. This serves several purposes. It reduces the time the target parent and child can interact; it keeps the child focused on the brainwashing parent; and it provides an opportunity to reinforce the programming.

When parents call they will ask, regardless of how happy the children sound, "What's wrong? Are you okay?" This reminds the children that the parent fostering the alienation expects them to have problems when in the company of the enemy. Children who have not fully succumbed to the brainwashing may regard such inquiries as a nuisance; they will answer in an annoyed tone, "Nothing." Often, however, the children will oblige the parent by thinking of some complaint about the target. "Mommy is making me eat food I don't like." "Daddy won't let me watch TV." This is music to the brainwasher's ears. He or she is very receptive to such complaints and commiserates with the children's terrible fate of having to be with the target. When the children get off the phone, their mood has soured. The brainwashing parent has successfully diminished their enjoyment of the target.

Often the purpose of the phone call is to generate homesickness or guilt. The parent tells the child how much she misses him. She cannot wait until he returns home. One mother carried this ploy to extremes. She told her son, Ward, not only that she missed him, but his dog, guinea pig, plants, teddy bear, goldfish, grandparents, the house, and the swing set missed him. At the end of the conversation Ward felt that somehow it was wrong for him to be enjoying himself with his father. His proper place was with his mother.

Like many parents who promote alienation, Ward's mother worried when her son was out of her orbit of influence for very long. Her frequent calls to Ward when he was with his father carried the underlying messages, "You must think about me at all times. If you spend time away from me you might forget me. I can't bear the thought of being without you."

Another ploy to detract from the child's enjoyment of the target is to manipulate the child with the promise of rewards for returning home soon. One father called his son at the mother's home to tell him that there was a great surprise waiting for him when he returned. Naturally, the boy could not wait. What parent could possibly compete with such an enticement?

Even without phone calls parents can intrude into the time children spend with the target. One mother devised a creative strategy for monopolizing her son's attention during his one-week vacation with his father. She sent seven gift-wrapped packages in his suitcase. The boy was instructed to open one package a day. Each package contained one module of a toy; when the modules were joined they formed a whole. The catch was that each module took hours to assemble. And the one condition of the gift was that the boy assemble it himself without any outside help. Thus the mother gave her son a vehicle for avoiding meaningful contact with his father throughout the week. I have seen several variations of this maneuver. All serve the purpose of keeping the child focused on the brainwashing parent while encroaching on the relationship with the target.

A common strategy for undercutting children's pleasure with a parent is to refuse to let the children take important possessions with them when they spend time with their other parent. A father would not allow his son to take his baseball glove with him when he returned to his mother's home. This was a problem for the mother because sometimes she had to take her son to his practices. For those readers who never played baseball, let me tell you what a problem this is for the boy. Over time, with proper preparation and care, a baseball glove conforms to its owner's hand. It becomes indispensable to the enjoyment of the game. To a child who loves baseball, his own glove is as important as the teddy bear was in earlier years.

What does it mean when a child cannot bring his glove, or other important possessions, with him to the other parent's home? If he is allowed to bring it anywhere else, such as friends' homes and to school, the message conveyed is that either the object will become tainted at Mom's home, or not returned, or that Dad is so angry with Mom that he does not want her to benefit from anything he bought his son. As with all such vindictive behavior, the child suffers.

The other message to the child is that he does not really own the glove. Ownership means the right to use and dispose of the possession. If he can't decide where he takes it, is it really his? Or is it Dad's? Of course parents place restrictions on children's use of their toys. Sometimes children are not permitted to bring a toy in the car. But the only reason for not allowing the boy to take his baseball glove to Mom's is to gratify Dad's own wish to hurt his ex. Many parents who apply such restrictions rationalize their behavior by expressing concern that the object would not be returned. The child is old enough, though, to take responsibility for his possessions. And if he forgets it, his mother can always return it for him. Without divorce poison in operation, the situation could be handled the same way it would if the child left the glove at school or on the baseball field.

One of the ways children experience a bond with a parent or other relative is by sharing special interests and activities. Parents who wish to break such a tie, or prevent its development, must find a way to dilute the significance of the shared pursuits. They can do so by duplicating the activities in their own home. In this way they undermine the child's association of the pleasurable activity exclusively with the target.

For example, Sammy's grandparents introduced him to the hobby of collecting seashells. They kept the shells for Sammy in a shoe box in their home and the boy looked forward to handling the shells every time he visited them. Sammy's dad, intent on promoting his son's alienation from the grandparents, began buying bigger and better shells for Sammy and a beautiful glass case in which to store and display them.

Another time the grandparents discovered a television comedy that appealed equally to children and adults. Because the shows aired way past their grandson's bedtime, they videotaped the shows. Each time Sammy visited, they played the episode from the previous week. Watching these shows and laughing out loud together became a highlight of the visits and a potent antidote to the father's negative programming. When Sammy's dad learned about this, he simply allowed Sammy to stay up late and watch the shows when they originally aired. This effectively extinguished Sammy's excitement at viewing the programs with his grandparents.

When confronted with his obstructive behavior the father pleaded innocent: "What is wrong with supporting my son's interests?" What's wrong is that his selection of which particular interests to support was dictated by what he feared would foster a unique bond between Sammy and his grandparents.

A common maneuver is to arrange a very enjoyable activity for the children that encroaches on the time they are scheduled to be with the target. The target must then choose between forgoing the time with the children or interrupting their fun. The children come to associate contact with the target with disappointments such as prematurely ending a game, leaving in the middle of a movie, or missing the chance to go ice-skating. The effectiveness of this tactic is enhanced when the programming parent expresses indignation, as in "I can't believe your mother insists that you go home right now when we are in the middle of this great video!" The self-righteous tone makes it difficult for the child to see through the father's manipulation.

Dr. Clawar and Dr. Rivlin described a mother who upstaged a father's birthday celebration plans for their ten-year-old son. She hosted a lavish party for the boy's entire class and then told him that it was silly to have two parties and that the father would never provide the big celebration that he deserved. Initially the boy was unenthusiastic and withdrawn at his father's small gathering with relatives and a few neighborhood friends. Later, though, he recognized that his mother attempted to sabotage his enjoyment of his father's party.

A mother who sought my assistance with her custody case was excited about taking her young children to an afternoon Christmas show at Radio City Music Hall. She told her husband about the show weeks in advance in order to make sure that he would return the children in time. Her husband upstaged her by taking the children to the midmorning performance of the same show on the same day they were scheduled to see it with their mother. As if that were not spiteful enough, the children arrived at their mother's apartment late and in inappropriately casual clothing, which meant that the father first took them home to change out of their good clothes. The mother and children were unavoidably late to the performance. Fortunately, despite the father's attempts to ruin the mother's good time with the children, they were excited about seeing the show again and enjoyed being able to predict what would happen next.

Although encroachment, by itself, is probably not enough to induce alienation, it does contribute to an ongoing process of estrangement by reducing the child's enjoyment of the relationship with the target parent or grandparent.

TAKE ACTION

If your ex attempts to sabotage your child's enjoyment of time spent with you, and is to some extent successful, you should try to help your child understand what has happened rather than remain silent. If you remain passive in the face of encroachments, you give your child no help in resisting divorce poison. Children are more likely to resist alienation if they perceive the target parent as willing to confront and expose the manipulations of the other parent. First, ask your child for his ideas. If he is unable to identify how his negative behavior was influenced by your ex, give your explanation. For example, "Mommy wanted you to think your party couldn't be much fun if we only had eight guests." Reminder: Most discussions of divorce poison are best conducted at a time when you and your child are relating well.

CLOAK AND DAGGER

As alienation becomes more entrenched, some parents enlist their children as accomplices in clandestine operations against the enemy target. They instruct the children to keep secrets, to spy, and to report back to the other parent. Often they require the children to tell lies. An element of excitement accompanies such collusion and appeals to children of all ages.

Children are told to hide the fact that Daddy had his girlfriend spend the night at the house. They keep secret Mommy's plans to baptize them without the father's knowledge or attendance. They tell the other parent that they had a baby-sitter when in fact they were left in the home alone. When in the target's home the children call the other parent and in hushed tones report on the alleged misdeeds occurring in the home. When a boy told his father, "Mommy's being mean," the father replied, "Don't let Mom hear you. When you get home you can tell me all about it." In essence the father told his son to hide his feelings from his mother, with the innuendo that she was so irrational that it would be dangerous to discuss grievances with her.

During custody battles these parents give their children assignments to steal documents from the other parent's home. A man told his daughter to rifle through her mother's desk and take her check register, a diary, and letters. One mother, whose divorcing husband had not yet moved out of the home, asked her adolescent daughter to intercept the mail to keep the father from seeing the mother's exorbitant credit card bill. Some of the purchases were for the girl, and she willingly colluded with her mother. Two years later she still regarded her father as the enemy and refused to have any contact with him. She even refused to invite him to her high school graduation despite the fact that he had been the parent most involved in helping her with homework.

Parents will even coach their children to lie in court under oath. An alienated father accused his wife of fostering an unhealthy dependent relationship with their twelve-year-old son. One of his examples was that she slept regularly with the boy. To counter this accusation, the mother had her son testify on the witness stand that he had never slept with her. Eventually the truth came out during a psychological evaluation in which the younger siblings all confirmed the father's allegations. After being confronted with this evidence the boy admitted that he lied in court. He said that his mother told him that if he did not lie he would have to go live with his father.

It is easy to see how covert operations corrupt children's characters. The alienating parent encourages and sanctions dishonest and even cruel behavior. Also, as we see next, the more children behave in this manner, the more alienated they become. Their role as pawns for the brainwashing parent further entrenches their estrangement.

TAKE ACTION

Set a firm limit on dishonest behavior. Try to arouse your children's underlying guilt and discomfort with covert operations by telling them that it must not feel very good being dishonest. Remind them that they were always taught not to keep secrets from their parents, and that this rule doesn't change just because parents don't get along with each other. Children know that dishonesty is wrong. Despite their overt behavior, they often welcome external control when their behavior is out of bounds. Particularly when an authority figure sanctions immoral behavior, children need someone to uphold proper standards and provide a moral compass.

Explain that experts on divorce tell parents not to put their children in the middle, and that you follow that advice. Help them decide how to assert themselves appropriately with your ex in order to resist colluding. For example, "Tell Mom that you love both parents and don't want to take sides." Or "Tell Dad that you don't want to keep secrets from either of your parents." Children need permission to stand up to a parent when that parent is asking them to do something wrong. If your ex persists in involving the children in covert operations, legal intervention may be necessary.

COGNITIVE DISSONANCE

Think back to the last time you purchased a car. If you are like most people, chances are you were even more convinced that your choice was correct after the purchase than before. Psychologists explain this process as reducing "cognitive dissonance." It is the tendency to bring our beliefs in line with our behavior. This helps reduce uncertainty, inconsistency, and conflict. Thus, if we act in a manner inconsistent with our beliefs, we may change what we believe.

This is one reason it is so important to interrupt your children's hateful behavior toward you as soon as possible. The more they mistreat you, the more they must convince themselves that you deserve to be mistreated. The more they reject you, the more they convince themselves that you are bad and worthy of rejection. This reduces the dissonance caused by acting so hateful to a person who was loved for so long. It spares children inner turmoil about their behavior. In this manner, alienation feeds on itself and becomes entrenched.

TAKE ACTION

If your children's alienation is not too severe, and your ex plans to call them as witnesses in a custody trial, consider asking your attorney if there is a way to prevent their participation. *Why?* After publicly denouncing a parent, a child may intensify negative feelings in order to reconcile his beliefs with his disloyal behavior.

CONSPIRACY

Parents intent on promoting alienation often get assistance from others who serve as co-programmers. For example, a father's extended family might join in the denigration of the mother and her family. This increases the pressure on the children to conform or else risk being rejected by grandparents, aunts, and uncles. Bad-mouthing the target becomes the family pastime, uniting them with a common enemy.

Sometimes the co-programmer is an older sibling who has already been brainwashed. This is particularly effective when the children visit the target away from the alienating parent. The older sibling carries on the brainwashing campaign by proxy, making sure that the younger ones remain loyal to the brainwashing parent.

One boy had been abducted by his father and brainwashed against his mother. The court reunited the mother and son and eventually the boy began calling her Mom again. However, when his severely alienated sister had to spend the day in the mother's home, he reverted to calling his mother Sharon. Although he had recovered his good feelings for his mom, he felt that he could not afford to show this to his sister or he would appear disloyal to her and the father. Victims who are rescued from cults also feel such disloyalty when they turn their backs on the cult. It is as if there is an aspect of themselves that continues to think and feel as they did in the cult, although this is kept apart from their usual functioning.

TAKE ACTION

It is often best to arrange to spend time alone with each child, rather than have siblings together as a group. This "divide and conquer" approach is discussed in the next chapter. There is strength in numbers. It is easier for a child to act hateful toward a parent when his siblings are doing the same. Even a mildly alienated child may succumb to peer pressure. By contrast, it is more difficult for a child to sustain a rejecting attitude when no one is supporting him. Also, separating a child from his siblings makes him more dependent on you, and thus increases your influence over his behavior.

TAMPER-RESISTANT PACKAGING

Brainwashing is not complete until the children are programmed to resist any attempts to undo their indoctrination. This is accomplished by implanting messages similar to posthypnotic suggestions. For example, a father teaches his children that people who ask you what Daddy has said about Mommy are themselves trying to brainwash you. He instructs the children to refuse to participate in any such discussions, even when initiated by relatives or court-appointed evaluators. Dr. Clawar and Dr. Rivlin call these "shutdown" messages because, when they are triggered, the children shut down communication.

Do you recall the couple Kent and Judy from our discussion of context dropping? Kent had convinced their three children that Judy had abandoned them, when in fact she relocated to pursue graduate education, with every intention of having the children join her. One reason that Judy's efforts to defend herself fell on deaf ears was that Kent had anticipated Judy's efforts to set the record straight. So he told his children that their mother would probably come up with some lame excuses for her behavior. She might tell them that she thought they were all going to move with her. Or that Daddy had done some things wrong. "If she does try to tell you this, you'll know I'm right about things and you should just tell her that you don't want to hear her excuses." Of course, when their mother responded exactly as their father predicted, the children discounted her version of events and took her defense as proof of her guilt.

TAKE ACTION

Shutdown messages are effective in keeping a child's mind closed to evidence that would assist in rebuilding bonds. It is easier to reverse alienation if tamper-resistant packaging is exposed and neutralized. If you detect the presence of shutdown messages, tell your child that you think you touched on something that she is not supposed to talk about. Ask her if she has decided she can't talk about something or if someone has told her not to talk about it. If the answer is yes, remind her that children are not supposed to keep secrets from their parents. Explain that you think she is not supposed to talk about certain things because her other parent is afraid that when she hears your side of the story, she will start liking you again.

The presence of shutdown messages usually signals the need for professional intervention to reverse brainwashing.

CORRUPTING REALITY

To intervene effectively in a campaign of denigration, we must understand exactly how the child's view of reality is being manipulated. Following is a summary of some of the most common strategies for distorting the child's perceptions, beliefs, and memories of the target.

- Manipulating names to disrupt children's identification with the target
- Repeating false ideas until they are assumed to be true and are embedded in memory
- Selectively directing the children's attention to negative aspects of the target while ignoring positive aspects
- Dropping the context of a target's behavior
- Exaggerating the target's negative behavior
- Telling lies about the target
- Revising history to erase positive memories of the target
- Claiming that the target has totally changed
- Suggestions that convey in a covert manner negative messages about the target
- Encouraging the children to exploit the target
- Projection of the brainwasher's own thoughts, feelings, or behavior onto the target
- Rationalizations that hide the perpetrator's real motives and make the target look bad
- Self-righteous tones intended to ward off careful scrutiny of the programmer's reality distortions
- Denunciations cloaked in religious dogma
- Associating the label "the truth" with the programmer's implanted scenarios
- Overindulging the children with excessive privileges, material possessions, and low expectations for responsible behavior to buy their allegiance
- Encroaching on the children's time with the target and sabotaging their enjoyment of special activities
- Instructing children to keep secrets from, spy on, and lie to the target
- Conspiring with others to reinforce the programming
- Programming the children to resist attempts to undo their indoctrination

CHAPTER 7

POISON CONTROL

Love must be supplemented by deliberate efforts on the part of the parent.

—Bruno Bettelheim

Love is not enough. It is not enough to protect children from divorce poison. And it is not enough to reverse its pernicious effects.

Every brainwashed child once expressed love for the now rejected parent. Given the conditions and treatment discussed in the preceding chapters, most children will succumb to divorce poison. They may escape the complete rupture of their relationship with the target, but they will suffer in other ways.

One of the emerging and disturbing conclusions from recent divorce research, documented by experts such as Dr. Robert Emery, Dr. Joan Kelly, and Dr. Judith Wallerstein, is that children who receive clean bills of health when examined by gross measures, such as behavior checklists and report cards, may be suffering great emotional distress that goes undetected. Sometimes a parent uses a child's apparent good adjustment to keep the other parent at arm's length. The argument goes like this: If the child gets along well with teachers, friends, and one parent; earns good grades; stays out of major trouble; and claims to be happy, why rock the boat? Why require the child to relate to the other parent? This is often punctuated with a warning that this "well-behaved" child has threatened to run away if forced to have contact with the hated parent.

Too many therapists endorse this misguided thinking. They fail to recognize the devaluation of the parent-child relationship that is inherent in ranking school and friends above family. They take an astonishingly casual attitude toward the child's loss of a parent, and the parent's loss of a child. These therapists advise courts to allow children to suspend contact with alienated parents, essentially to disown their parents. And they admonish alienated parents to cease and desist efforts to reconnect with their offspring. By now I am sure it is clear that I oppose such a hands-off policy.

This book grew out of the conviction that children deserve protection from divorce poison. It won't help merely to blame your ex, bemoan your sorry situation, and sink slowly into the passivity of victimhood.

If you fail to take responsibility for responding effectively, how can you expect your children to do otherwise? If you fail to take a firm stand in support of your relationship with them, how can you expect them to withstand your ex's manipulations? If you fail to uphold the reality of your value to them, how can you expect them to remain in touch with this reality when assaulted with a campaign to corrupt their positive vision and memories? By your actions, you must demonstrate your conviction that your relationship with your children is worth fighting for, is worth preserving.

Taking responsibility does not mean that you should blame yourself for the problem. And it does not mean that your efforts will always pay off. At some point the sensible thing to do may be to back off and postpone the project. Chapter 9, "Letting Go," can help you with this tormenting decision. If you decide to let go, at least let it be with pride in the knowledge that you did everything in your power to help your children, rather than with regret that you passively allowed your children to slip away.

In this chapter I revisit and expand on the coping tips found throughout the book and give additional antidotes to divorce poison. Before doing so, I want to suggest some general guidelines for increasing your child's receptivity to your communications.

EMPATHY

The late great child psychologist Dr. Haim Ginott taught parents how to speak to their children's hearts. To connect emotionally, he advised, parents must learn to communicate genuine empathy. Dr. Ginott's seminal books are filled with practical suggestions and examples of how to do this. Though he wrote the books many years ago, his advice is timeless. And if ever a parent needed good communication skills, it is a parent whose children's hearts are determinedly and tightly shut. See the Resources section for books by Dr. Ginott and others that will help you improve your parenting skills.

When your children express contempt or fear of you, regardless of whether these feelings were implanted by your ex, the feelings are real for your children at that moment. If you too quickly attempt to dispute their words, or defend your view of reality, the result is likely to be a communications impasse. Your children will feel that you have not taken them seriously, that you fail to recognize the extent of their unhappiness. Instead of dismissing your children's negative feelings, identify them with words and let your children know that you understand exactly how they are feeling. Dr. Ginott showed how strong feelings can "lose their sharp edges when a sympathetic listener accepts them with understanding." It may seem a paradox, but the way to get rid of your children's hatred is first to show them that you acknowledge the reality of their feelings and that you treat their feelings with respect. This does not mean that you approve of your children's rudeness or misbehavior. Nor does it mean that you tolerate repetitive expressions of hatred. But it does mean that you face the reality of the negative feelings before attempting to change them.

THE POWER OF INDIRECT COMMUNICATION

Children know how to frustrate adults. When we want to help them, they make it difficult. They clam up. They evade communication. They erect a simple three-word barricade that many parents find impenetrable. In response to questions about feelings, they shrug their shoulders and say, in an innocent voice, "I don't know." And they keep repeating it until we give up. Breaking through this requires special techniques that child psychotherapists have developed to communicate with reluctant children.

First, we must appreciate that children do not necessarily want to foil our efforts at communication. Most younger children are simply not able to identify and put into words their exact feelings. Even if they could, children and teenagers (and most adults) find it difficult to discuss their worries and fears openly. And they resist lectures and advice. When we talk about their feelings, children feel as though they are under a bright spotlight and they want only to escape the glare. So we have to find ways to make the process more comfortable.

We have all heard of the patient who brings up an embarrassing concern by talking about his "friend's" problem. When a child does this, a sensitive therapist does not rush to expose the ruse. He knows that confronting the child too soon may abruptly end the dialogue. Under the guise of talking about the "friend," the therapist is able to get more details about the child's deepest concerns and then communicate therapeutic messages.

I often advise parents to read a book with their child, such as Dr. Richard Gardner's *The Boys and Girls Book About Divorce*. When you do this you will come across many passages that seem to have been written especially with your child in mind. Your child can profit from these passages even without acknowledging that they apply to her. Sometimes this activity does lead to a more direct discussion of the child's feelings. After reading each section of the book, ask your child if she ever feels the way the child in the book feels. A book can often serve as a springboard for heartfelt discussions. Children will more readily acknowledge uncomfortable feelings when they know they are not the only ones who feel that way. By the way, if your child has older siblings who might not be too receptive to the idea of reading a book on divorce, it is a good idea to read the book within their earshot. Though they may pretend a casual indifference, parents report that the older children stay in the room and, after a while, may even join in the discussions.

With older children and teenagers you can talk about other boys or girls "their age" or about what you "heard somewhere" or "read somewhere" about how children their age feel about things. It is also helpful to begin conversations by talking about your own thoughts and feelings.

One mother began a conversation with her fourteen-year-old daughter like this: "I've been thinking about how I've been yelling at you for the bad grades you've been making lately. I know it doesn't help for me to lose my temper. You always used to care about your grades, so something must be bothering you." The girl remained silent. Her mother continued: "I read an article that said when girls your age start making bad grades it often means that some things about their parents' divorce really bug them. The article also said that most girls feel bad that they aren't doing

as well as they used to." With older children such indirect communication may result in more candid discussions. But this girl said, "Yeah, well,
I don't really care." Her mother responded, "Well, I can understand if you
did feel that way," and then dropped the conversation.

The next day the mother took the conversation one step further by
identifying the feeling she thought was tied to her child's problem behavior. She said, "I've been thinking about what we talked about yesterday.
Many girls feel really mad at their parents for getting a divorce." This time
the girl said, "What difference does it make? You're not going to get back
together." Her mother said, "I know that sometimes girls will try to get
back at their parents by doing poorly in school, especially when they
know that good grades are important to the parents. I've been thinking
that maybe you are angry with me. I don't blame you if you are. I know
you didn't want this divorce. But it would be better if we could talk about
your feelings, or maybe you could write me a letter about how angry you
really feel. Why should you take your anger out on yourself and have to
feel bad about screwing up in school when it's really your father and me
that you're angry at?" In this way, the mother was suggesting a healthier
way for her child to cope with angry feelings. The girl did not acknowledge that her mom was correct, but later that night the mother saw the
girl in her room doing schoolwork.

An excellent book for learning more about effective communication
is *Growing Up with Divorce* by Dr. Neil Kalter. He describes a six-step strategy for using indirect communication and illustrates it with numerous
examples. If you are tempted to dismiss indirect communication as ineffective, or only second-best, consider this: Throughout the ages fables
have been used to teach moral principles. If you want your child to
appreciate the value of persistence, you'll get much further with Aesop's
"The Tortoise and the Hare" than with a lecture.

FLY ON THE WALL

Another way to get a message across is to let the children "accidentally"
overhear you speaking to someone else. All children eavesdrop on private
conversations, and alienated children are no exception. In fact, children
in advanced stages of alienation may try to monitor everything the target
says in order to report back to the favored parent. Take advantage of this

to say to someone else what you want your children to hear. As flies on the wall they will get the message.

An alienated parent who tries to correct her children's distortions directly will find them resisting the conversation. Many children cover their ears as soon as the hated parent begins talking to them. But these same children will listen intently as the object of their scorn speaks openly with a friend or relative over the phone. This is a good opportunity to give your version of what is happening between you and the children.

In these conversations, it is best to emphasize what you and the children have lost, how sad you feel for the children, and how different things used to be. Talk about all the past signs of the loving relationship. Speak of your confusion and puzzlement about the dramatic change in attitudes. Tie the alienation to the divorce and to your ex's anger at you. But be careful not to focus on your anger at your ex for maligning you. The children are primed to believe bad things about you. If they overhear you discussing your anger at their other parent, they will interpret this as an act of bad-mouthing and will use it to justify their criticisms of you.

Repeated conversations that the children overhear lay a foundation for a more explicit and direct discussion at some later point in time. By then, the children have heard your side of the story expressed in a manner that might garner their sympathy for you and their willingness to begin healing the ruptured relationship.

TWO STEPS REMOVED

Even when using the fly-on-the-wall technique, it is usually more effective to introduce emotionally laden topics by discussing a situation two steps removed from the children's personal experience. Alienated children, like brainwashed cult members, are unaware that their feelings are the result of manipulation. If you try to explain that they have been brainwashed by their other parent, they will probably resist listening to anything you have to say about it. Instead, approach the topic by first talking about another means of manipulation, and one not involving the children. For example, you can discuss how advertisements induce people to focus selectively on certain attributes and overlook others. This introduces the general idea of mental influence. Then move one step closer by talking about someone else you know using mental influence to persuade someone to dislike another person. Or you might discuss how politicians smear opponents. Finally, when you think your children will be receptive, you can relate these ideas to your family situation by introducing the topic of your children's negative feelings resulting from manipulation.

An advantage of discussing a topic, like brainwashing, two steps removed from your children's situation is that they will be less likely to resist the communication. They will be more likely to consider that they have been programmed when they have already accepted the idea that people, in general, are susceptible to such influence. If you were to begin by confronting them with the idea that they have been brainwashed, without laying the groundwork, they would experience this as an assault on their view of reality and would be more likely to dismiss what you say without any consideration.

The two-steps-removed technique can be used when speaking directly with your children, as well as when communicating indirectly.

USING THIRD PARTIES

Several times throughout this book I mentioned the desirability of having someone else implement the coping tips with your children. If you have no contact with your children, this will be your only way of reaching them. Even if you do have contact with your children, you should consider enlisting help from other people. If your children are alienated from you, they will dismiss anything you have to say as worthless. It helps to designate others who do enjoy your children's respect to intervene on your behalf. These can be trusted relatives, members of the clergy, teachers, coaches, scoutmasters, anyone respected by your children.

Third parties can use any of the principles and techniques discussed in this chapter to try to open your children's closed minds. Because they may be pivotal in reversing alienation, it is best to give them plenty of preparation before they begin. You may want to have them read portions of this book. They need to have a clear understanding of how children can be programmed to turn against a parent. They also need to have a clear sense that a parent's minor flaws and errors do not justify losing contact with her children. Without this sense, they may inadvertently be taken in by your children's complaints and become one more person supporting the alienation. If you are working with a therapist who understands these situations, the therapist may want to meet with the third party to offer guidance and support.

The third party has a difficult assignment. He or she must maintain your children's respect and affection while attempting to engage them in reconsidering their negative attitudes toward you. The role calls for someone who can maintain a curious yet concerned posture, showing patience, warmth, and caring. The more important this person becomes to your children, the less dependent they will be on your ex.

I must emphasize the importance of patience. The third party must be willing and able to listen to the children's complaints, however trivial or false, without prematurely confronting or criticizing the children. Moving too quickly to confront alienation can end all hope that this person will be able to reach your children. This is particularly true if the children are wrapped in the tamper-resistant programming described at the end of chapter 6. This will lead them to clam up as soon as their alienation is mentioned. With sensitivity and finesse, though, the third party may help rescue your children from divorce poison and heal family relationships, thereby earning your eternal gratitude.

STRIKE WHILE THE IRON IS COLD

Experienced psychotherapists know that the best intervention can fall flat if not timed properly. The film *Analyze This* portrayed this with humor. Mobster Paul Vitti (Robert De Niro) consults with psychiatrist Dr. Ben Sobol (Billy Crystal). Vitti disguises his need for help by describing a problem suffered by a "friend." He takes offense when Dr. Sobol too quickly assumes that the "friend" is himself. Yet less than a minute later the same assumption earns high praise from Vitti, who concludes that since this shrink is clever enough to see through the ruse, he is the best therapist for the job.

The same principle applies to conversations with your children. In chapter 3 I described the technique of striking while the iron is cold. If you have something to say that your children are going to argue with, or at least resist hearing, it is often best to wait until the children are in a receptive mood. If you and the children are enjoying yourselves, they will be less likely to automatically reject what you say. Striking while the iron is cold means avoiding "hot" topics when the children are already upset. If your children are acting disrespectfully toward you, they are probably not going to place any value on what you say about their situation. And the more they ignore or disparage what you say, the more they will feel that you are worthy of such mistreatment. When things are going well between you and them, they will be more likely to value you and what you have to say.

"Strike while the iron is cold" is a good principle to keep in mind, especially when you feel like lashing out in anger after being provoked by your child's hostility. But it is not always the best course. Sometimes it is best to do the opposite. Sometimes it is best to initiate a difficult conversation at the time of your child's emotional outburst.

Earlier in my career I worked as a counselor in a residential treatment center for children with severe emotional disturbances. Many of these children had frequent emotional storms in which they abandoned self-control. Sometimes the counselors could best help a child by calming him down and postponing any discussion of the event that triggered the rage. Other times we learned that we could use the crisis of the moment to help a child gain insight into his behavior and find better ways to cope. Psychoanalyst Dr. Fritz Redl called this technique a "life space interview." He believed that a child is most receptive to change when in a crisis.

Using this approach, an alienated mother might respond to her child's belligerence by first acknowledging how upset her child is and pointing out that it must not feel very good to be that angry with your own mother. The mother might then assert her belief that the child's rejection is unreasonable. She may even mention some of the factors that could be influencing the child, such as fear of the father, or feeling sorry for the father. The mother's communications have a greater chance of being effective if she remains calm and concerned. Sometimes emotional breakthroughs occur during a heated conversation. But this approach is risky. It could result in the child's feeling that his view of reality has been dismissed. The result would be an increase in alienation. For this reason, it may be best to allow a third party to conduct the life space interview.

CREATING BRIDGES

Third parties can help in two very important additional ways. I have already covered their role in trying to persuade your children to reach a more realistic view of their parents. Third parties can also serve as a bridge between you and your children. And by their positive treatment of you, they set a good example that will help offset the exclusively negative image held by your children.

The sister of an alienated father invited his children (her niece and nephew) to her home for Thanksgiving. When she told them that their father would be present, they said they did not want to come. She was not dissuaded. She exploited her status as their favorite aunt to convince them to come.

No pressure was placed on the children to interact directly with their father. But their aunt provided a relaxed setting that reduced the intensity of the children's first contact with their father in over two years. Over the course of the afternoon, they did respond to their father's efforts at casual conversation. They talked about the food, the football games, the usual sort of banter that goes on at holiday gatherings. No one spoke of the prolonged absence of contact. But the ice had been broken. The aunt bridged the gap between the children and their father. It took a few more events like that to bring them closer together.

In addition to serving as a bridge, the aunt provided another corrective experience. The children had been brainwashed to regard their dad as an angry, rigid man with no redeeming features. Yet here they saw other people they respected treating their father with value. This clashed with their perception of reality. Perhaps this introduced a small measure of doubt about their judgment. The other relatives' treatment of the father also introduced an element of social pressure. If the children wanted to "fit in" they would have to be cordial. Such positive behavior, in turn, can awaken positive attitudes. Certainly it would have been more difficult for the children to be rude to their dad in this setting. At home, people fit in by bad-mouthing the father. Here, such behavior would be seen as odd.

As much as possible, arrange for your children to see other people treating you with high regard. Let them see that their opinion of you, and the opinion of their other parent, is not shared by the rest of the world. This type of experience will leave a stronger impression than anything you can say on your own behalf.

Several years ago a judge appointed me to try to help an eleven-year-old alienated girl and her mother reconnect. They had not seen each other for four years, and Amanda had been programmed to believe that her mother was a violent and disturbed woman. In an early session with the mother I learned that she was an avid collector of antique lace. She even knew how to make lace. Now, my wife loves lace and has her own collection. Despite years of being around the stuff, though, I have a hard time distinguishing one pattern from the other. To tell the truth, I was never very much interested. It would have been better for me if the woman collected old jazz records. But it was lace.

I knew that the mother and her daughter would be very anxious during their first session together. My job was to make the experience tolerable for both. At the same time, I wanted to begin the project of correcting Amanda's distorted perception of her mother. I asked the mother to bring in some of her lace pieces and her lace-making equipment. We were going to have show-and-tell.

During the joint session I asked the mother many questions about lace. I gave her an opportunity to show her knowledge and her competence. She herself did not seem to appreciate the range of talent that went into her creations, and the qualities of personality that it took to persevere from start to finish. Amanda sat stone-faced and mute.

The mother offered to demonstrate how to make bobbin lace. This seemed to stir Amanda's interest. I drew Amanda into the conversation by asking about her own hobbies and interests. When she answered that she likes to draw, I knew her angry veil was lifting. Her mother asked about Amanda's artwork. Amanda gave brief, terse answers.

I asked the mother if I could hold a delicate antique baby bonnet. I cradled it in my hands and then asked if Amanda could hold it. The mother said, "Of course," and, without giving Amanda a chance to refuse, I passed it to her. She acted uninterested, but she held the bonnet. A fragile tie between mother and child.

I wove in questions that gently alluded to the unique bond between them. "Did you make any lace when you were getting ready to give birth to Amanda?" The mother answered and then added casually, "You know, Amanda, that used to be your bonnet. I'm saving it for your children, my grandchildren." The underlying message was that Amanda's relationship with her mother had significance beyond the present.

I turned to Amanda. "Can you believe your head was ever that small?" The bonnet provided an easy segue to questions about their early relationship. "What did you do to prepare for Amanda's birth?" "What was she like as a baby?" "What was her first day in kindergarten like?" "What were her favorite things to do when she was six years old?"

Again, I drew Amanda into the conversation. "Is your memory good enough to recall any of the things Mom is talking about?" "Do your remember Mom taking you to kindergarten?" Throughout the session I referred to the mother as "Mom." I wanted Amanda to hear it enough that it would become natural to a girl who currently referred to her mother only by her first name or as "that woman."

As the session drew to a close, the mother said that next time she could bring some lace she made when Amanda was a baby. I asked Amanda if she would like to see it and she said, without much enthusiasm, "Sure." For a girl who didn't want to see her mother, this was progress.

The session went better than expected. It would have been valuable even if Amanda did and said nothing. It had to make an impression that her mother was the learned authority teaching the doctor, and that the doctor treated her mother with obvious great respect and dignity. Her mother could not be as worthless as she had been programmed to believe.

The lesson was not about lace. It was about a mother's value. And about her place in her child's life. The session was a bridge, a bridge made of fragile lace strong enough to support an estranged mother and daughter as they took their first steps back toward one another.

HEALING EXPERIENCES

Your goals are to regain an affectionate relationship with your children and help them have a more realistic and balanced view of you and your ex. If they are severely alienated, and the alienation has been entrenched over a long time, it is not likely that you will be able to accomplish your goals without educating the children about brainwashing and probably seeking professionl help. In many cases, though, alienation can be reversed merely by allowing your children to experience you as you really are and to have some warm, relaxed times together.

In 2000, in the aftermath of his mother's drowning, a young Cuban boy named Elián Gonzáles was isolated from his father by relatives in Miami, Florida. The relatives wanted to give Elián the chance to grow up in a free country. In the service of this goal, the relatives released a video-tape showing the boy pointing his finger at the camera and insisting that he did not want to return home. Despite the strength of the negative feelings, and the prolonged separation from his father, after only a brief time in his father's presence Elián's loving feelings returned.

Before addressing the issue of divorce poison with your child, either indirectly or directly, concentrate on creating pleasant experiences together. Many parents find that their alienated child's hostility or fear recedes as the child becomes involved in activities with the parent. Choose activities that are inherently fun for both of you and require direct interaction. Cooking is one.

If your child is withdrawn, don't ask if she would enjoy helping you. The answer is likely to be no. You should not expect an alienated child to volunteer to do anything with you. Merely state that you need her help or participation. Your tone should be warm and matter-of-fact, suggesting that, despite your child's negative attitude, you expect her cooperation. Do what you can to coax her. During the activity, focus on having a good time. Neatness, precision, and final product don't count. Allow the child to make many decisions. Encourage her spontaneity and creativity. Remember, the object of the project is to have fun. Do your best to lighten up. If your child follows suit, if she allows herself to relax and have a good time in your presence, you have accomplished your goal, whether or not the cake rises or the cookies burn.

Playing in a swimming pool together is another great healing activity. There is something about being in the water that encourages children to seek physical contact, even with a parent who is otherwise shunned.

Humor is a powerful antidote to hostility, as long as it is not at the expense of the child. One little boy had been kept apart from his father for more than two months. The boy refused to speak with his dad on the phone, and said he never wanted to see him again. When the father arrived to pick up his son for a scheduled day together, the boy cried and screamed for a half hour, insisting on returning to his mother. The fit ended when the father accidentally dropped his keys in the swimming pool. The boy laughed involuntarily, and so did the father. Sharing this humorous moment was enough to break the ice. The boy dropped his angry facade. The rest of the day, father and son played together normally. Watching them together, no one would ever have guessed at the prior problems in their relationship.

I have seen this type of rapid transformation repeatedly in my practice. Generally speaking, the younger the child, the more easily the alienation will dissipate with benevolent experiences. Divorce experts Dr. Joan Kelly and Dr. Janet Johnston attribute this to a young child's immaturity.

Caught up in the moment, the child forgets that she is supposed to reject the parent.

Rapid transformations can also occur with older children. I consulted to a distraught mother whose ex refused to return their nine-year-old daughter at the end of a weekend and would not return the woman's phone calls. After three weeks of isolation, the girl said that she did not want to see her mother or her older sister. The court ordered the father to return the girl. The mother contacted me because she was concerned that her daughter was programmed by the father and would be alienated upon her return. I thought that there was a strong enough bond between mother and child that most likely, by bedtime, the girl would warm up to her mother. As it turned out, I was right in principle but wrong with my time estimation. The mother reported that, after the daughter's initial discomfort in the car, she was fine and literally within minutes was back to normal. To assist the girl with any future such episodes, I suggested some mild debriefing about how her dad tried to trick her into not liking her mom and sister.

The lesson to be taken from this is that, rather than try to correct your child's distortions by addressing them directly, show them by your actions that you are not the bad person they have been led to believe. If this works, then discussions about the alienation should follow the "strike while the iron is cold" principle. Wait until you have built a reservoir of good feeling between you and your child. Then you can provide age-appropriate education about bad-mouthing, bashing, and brainwashing in order to inoculate your child against future exposure to divorce poison.

Children who are more severely alienated may stubbornly refuse to allow themselves to enjoy any time spent with the hated parent. In that case, you may have no choice but to confront, either directly or indirectly, the programming to which the children have been exposed. The principles and strategies presented in this chapter will help. But you should consider enlisting the aid of a therapist experienced in helping alienated children.

MEMORIALIZING THE POSITIVE

If you are effective in breaking through your child's animosity, if you able to create good times together, capitalize on this success. You want to use this experience to heal your positive bond. But it can also help inoculate your child against future efforts to turn her against you.

The way to do this is to make sure that the experience becomes embedded in your child's memory. Begin by directing her attention to the fun you are having together. Say something simple, such as, "Isn't this fun?" In a casual way try to get your child to elaborate on how she is feeling. "What do you like best about what we are doing?" Repeatedly call attention to, and label, the emotions that each of you are experiencing. "Isn't it nice how much we are laughing together?" "It feels so good to see you having fun over here." "You've really got the giggles now." By repeatedly focusing attention on the positive interaction, you are strengthening the reality of the moment. This helps offset the idea that being with you is a negative experience. Even more important, though, is that it makes it less likely that your ex will be able to eradicate the memory.

A very common frustration for rejected parents and grandparents is the retrenchment of alienation that follows early signs of progress. During the prior contact, Timmy shed his cold demeanor and allowed himself to have a good time with his mother. Her hopes were raised that they could return to a normal relationship. But the hopes were dashed. To the mother's dismay, the next time Timmy was scheduled to be with her he protested going. Once with her, he acted as if the prior good experience never occurred.

There is a way to decrease the likelihood of such setbacks. After directing your child's attention to the good time you are having, focus more directly on strengthening the memory. Then, help your child anticipate the possibility of the return of alienated feelings, and arm him with a way to cope.

Timmy's mother could have said in a low-key, gentle manner, "I want you to remember how good you feel right now, and how much we love each other. If you start thinking that you don't want to see me again, remember the good time we had today. Will you do that?" Asking the child to respond verbally (not just with a nod of the head) ensures that the message was received and helps to further embed it in memory. To motivate your child to retain and acknowledge the memory, you can issue a mild challenge, such as, "I think you have a strong memory. Strong memories make people smarter and do well in school. Do you think your memory is good enough to remember what we did today, and how much fun we had?" It is a rare child who will deny recalling the experience when his intellectual competence is at issue.

Other effective ways to memorialize a good experience with your child are to take pictures and videos of both of you during the activity. Let the child snap a few of the photos or hold the video camera for a while. Keep a journal together that records the date, the activity, and each person's thoughts and feelings about the activity. Young children can draw a picture of the activity in the journal. The very act of recording in the journal will help embed the experiences in memory. The journal will also serve as objective proof of better times, in the event that history is rewritten.

A few caveats. If your child seems uncomfortable reflecting on the experience, don't insist on it. Just concentrate on creating the experience. Later, you can use the fly-on-the-wall maneuver to get the point across. Perhaps you will arrange for her to overhear you talking to someone on the phone about how much fun you had together.

Also, you must be careful not to be too heavy-handed or insistent with your communications. Your tone should be casual and conversational, not preachy. Don't exaggerate. Your goal is to foster an accurate perception of reality, not to fool your child. And don't repeat yourself too much. Remember, the primary achievement is the experience. Don't let your talking about it detract from the positive atmosphere. If your child becomes exasperated when you talk about the good time you are having, then you will know that you are overdoing it.

The advice I am giving may seem unduly manipulative, perhaps even reminiscent of some of the strategies described in the previous chapter that parents use to alienate children. After all, I am advocating that you actively direct your child's attention in a certain direction, and work to entrench the memories of your positive interactions. Is this merely brainwashing in reverse? Definitely not. There are three crucial differences. (1) You are trying to correct distortions of reality rather than induce them. (2) Your goal is to foster your child's positive relationship with you, not a negative relationship with your ex. (3) If successful, these techniques will result in your child having a balanced, realistic view of you and your ex, rather than polarized views in which one parent is hero and the other villain.

THE WAY WE WERE

While you are in the process of memorializing the good times in the present, remember that you probably have many reminders of good times in the past. In fact, one of the best activities in which to engage your child is looking at visual evidence of your past positive relationship. Photographs, videotapes, souvenirs, gifts, favorite storybooks all serve this purpose. Reminiscing not only counteracts the distortions of revisionist history. Enjoying memories of old times together is a powerful bonding experience.

If you can successfully coax your children to enjoy watching videotapes of "the good old days," you will have gone a long way toward repairing your relationship. This is such a valuable resource that you must be careful not to squander it by introducing it prematurely, or in a way that arouses your children's resistance. Remember, alienated children resist obvious efforts to change their feelings. If you have to force them to look through photos, you have lost the benefits of the experience. Instead, you should initiate the activity in a casual manner, and at a time when you sense that they might be receptive. You want to pique their interest. In this sense, coping with alienated children is like playing poker. For the sake of your ultimate goal, you must learn to conceal the strength of your hand. Otherwise the children may just walk away.

A third party can be useful here. Bring out the photos or videos to show to another person while your children are in the room. Arrange for the third party to engage the children in looking at the pictures. The conversation should feature recollections about the activity captured in the mementos, emphasizing the close parent-child bond that existed in the past. "We had a great time on that vacation. Do you remember when we were so proud of ourselves for reaching the top of the trail? You were so tired that I carried you half the way down." If you think your child will listen, you might add, "Love like that doesn't disappear. I'll be glad when you are able to show it to me again and let me show it to you."

Children younger than about ten years old usually enjoy hearing about the day of their birth, or the day of their adoption. The story of the blessed event, and the preparations for and reactions to it, can captivate children, and remind them of your lifelong investment in their welfare. Tell them about your excitement that day. Discuss all the preparations you made at home and for the hospital. The childbirth classes; the baby-furniture purchases; all your thoughts and worries about the birth; your initial reactions; your recollections of the day they first said Mama and Dada.

One very creative grandmother was the target of a vicious alienation campaign to which her two grandchildren were beginning to succumb. For Valentine's Day she painted a two-foot-high valentine and wrote an original poem on it. In evocative language the poem poignantly recalled the attachment and love of the past, expressed empathy for the blow dealt by their parents' divorce, reassured them of their grandparents' love, and inspired them to surmount the crisis and live life to the fullest.

Here is an excerpt from the poem:

> We care and we want you and want you to know
> We see, know and feel for the really hard blow
> Torn between parent and grandparents, your backs to the wall
> With all of life's challenges, this may be the hardest of all
> Torn from your friends, neighborhood, routines all the rest
> It takes courage to stand tall and still do your best.

All around the valentine, in small letters and at different angles, she wrote every special activity, unique game, and bonding experience between the grandparents and the children that she could remember— about a hundred. This generated the most interest from her grandchildren. They read each of these and then enjoyed thinking of those she had omitted, which of course she then added. The entire experience was enormously healing.

If your children are severely alienated, be prepared for the type of dismissals discussed in the section on revisionist history in chapter 6. The children may resent your efforts to "prove" that they loved you in the past. They will claim that you made them smile in the photograph. Or that the only reason they were having a good time on the videotape is because their other parent was present. Don't let this deter you. Although the children may not acknowledge the reality of the past at this moment, you are planting seeds that remind them of what they have lost and of how much of the past is not what they have come to believe. Ultimately, such seeds may bear fruit. Certainly if the children remain in the room while you are showing the videotapes, they are giving at least some attention to them.

SOWING SEEDS IN THE PSYCHE

In his book for psychotherapists on treating parental alienation syndrome, Dr. Gardner underscores the importance of planting seeds in the minds of these children. It is often difficult to know whether or not our messages are getting through to our children. The lack of immediate results does not necessarily mean that the effort has been wasted. You should not expect to dissolve alienation overnight. The process may take many weeks or months. And you may have to settle for a relationship that is somewhat less than you previously enjoyed.

Even when neutralized, divorce poison can leave traces. It is often difficult to know how much of the residual reduction in affection is due to divorce poison, how much is due to the divorce in general, and how much is due to your child's natural development. Keep in mind that many children, as they enter their teen years, naturally reduce the intensity of their affection and respect for their parents. They tend to be moody, and they certainly want to spend less time with parents. It is important not to mistake normal adolescent behavior for alienation.

VACATIONS

If you can afford the time and expense, consider taking your alienated child on a nice vacation. There is a risk that the child's negative attitudes will spoil the trip. But there is a greater possibility that the circumstances of the trip will contribute positively to your relationship.

I can think of three reasons why vacations work in this way. First, there is the element of fun and relaxation that contributes to a better mood. People on vacation are more predisposed to treat others with benevolence. Second, there is the separation from the other parent, a separation magnified by geographical distance. Being apart from the alienating parent and being in a novel environment increase your children's dependency on you. It gives you a chance to be experienced as someone who is gratifying their needs. There is no one else who will do it. Third, it is easier to change attitudes when people are cut off from their usual circumstances. Recall the discussion in chapter 5 about how isolation makes a child more susceptible to the alienating parent's manipulations. Well, it works for the target parent as well.

A twelve-year-old boy refused to come to his father's home on weekends because he did not want to be around his new stepmother. The boy identified with his mother's resentment of the remarriage. She made it clear to him that she would regard it as an act of disloyalty to her if he accepted his father's wife. Though the boy was not alienated from his father, he was moving in that direction.

In the summer, the father announced his plans to take his wife and his son to Hawaii. The boy protested. The father was firm. The boy was going with them. (Having to be *forced* to go to Hawaii is just about the clearest indication of how irrational these children can be.)

While packing, on the way to the airport, and while waiting in the airport lounge, the boy was grumpy and noncommunicative. Once on the plane, though, the excitement of the trip overcame his resolve to be unhappy. As his mood improved, he began to take part in planning activities for the vacation. He wanted to rent a jet-ski. His dad said it was too dangerous. His stepmom came to his defense, "Let him try it. I'm sure he will be careful on it. He doesn't want to ruin his vacation." It became increasingly clear to the boy that he had a lot to gain by abandoning his angry facade. When they were laughing at a joke his dad told, the stepmother decided to strike while the iron was cold. She told her stepson, "I know it is not easy getting used to having me around. But I love your dad very much and that's how it is. I'd like us to be friends. At least let's do our best to have a great time on this trip."

Being forced to live with his dad and stepmom, in a setting where it was difficult to withdraw from them, was just what this child needed. Discovering new things together, making decisions together, having his stepmother attend to a cut he received on the beach—these types of experiences cemented their comfort with each other. The vacation proved to be a great way to begin their relationship. Following the Hawaii trip, the boy had no objection to being around his stepmother. In fact, she became very important to him and he was as likely as not to be disappointed when she was not around.

DIVIDE AND CONQUER: THE VALUE OF SEPARATING SIBLINGS

There is strength in numbers. It is easier for a child to act hateful toward a parent when his siblings are doing the same. Even a mildly alienated child may succumb to peer pressure. By contrast, it is more difficult for a child to sustain a rejecting attitude when no one is supporting him.

Very often, reversing alienation is easier when you spend time alone with each child, rather than have siblings together as a group. As mentioned in the preceding chapter, an older child sometimes serves as a stand-in for your ex, reinforcing the negative attitudes about you. One teenager told me directly that he would not allow his younger sister to develop loving feelings toward her mother. If he saw this happening, the boy said, he would tell his sister she was stupid and tell her that she had to choose between Dad and Mom.

I recommend focusing first on rekindling your bond with the child who is least alienated. Success with this child will give you more confidence and hope in repairing the other relationships. Also, when your other children see their brother or sister enjoying the benefits of a happy relationship with you, it may remind them of what they are missing and motivate them to reconnect with you.

The drawback of the divide-and-conquer approach is that it may create conflict among your siblings. When the child returns to your ex's home, she will probably be subjected to a great deal of pressure to renew negative feelings toward you. She may be teased or rejected when she reveals any positive feelings toward you. Ironically, her other parent or siblings may accuse her of being brainwashed.

If your bond is strong with your child, you can help her prepare for the return to her other home. Discuss the possibility of her other parent and siblings disapproving of her love for you. Help your child think of alternative ways of dealing with such pressure. You can teach her to stand up for her right to love whomever she wants. You can teach her to assert her desire to have her own opinions about her parents.

One child asked his father, "Are you going to stop loving me if I love Mommy?"

The father had to say no.

"Well, then I'm going to love both of you, and that's that," said the child.

Not only did the father back off, but the child's older brother was impressed with this assertiveness and asked to go with his brother the next time they were scheduled to see their mother.

The divide-and-conquer approach can also be effective with the child who is more alienated. When a child is separated from his siblings, he is more dependent on you. This increases your influence and makes it harder for the child to sustain the alienation. Even if this approach is not successful with all your children, it may at least help you open the heart of one child. Sometimes we have to settle for what we can get.

CONTAGION CONTROL: HELPING CHILDREN STAY NEUTRAL

Divorce poison engenders a sort of tribal warfare in which each family member is expected to takes sides. When you use the divide-and-conquer method, make sure that you do not contribute to this warfare. The goal of divide and conquer is to overcome alienation. It is not to promote conflict among siblings, or turn your children against your ex. But you do want to give nonalienated children the support they need to resist pressure to turn against you.

Children who refuse to join in a campaign of denigration risk disapproval. *The alienating parent and alienated siblings expect them to be loyal to the cause. Your job is to teach your children how to disappoint this expectation while continuing to treat their other parent with love and respect.* In doing so, you may find it useful to compare your family situation to a war. Countries form alliances with one side or the other. But some countries stay neutral throughout the conflict. They continue friendly relations with both sides, without participating in the hostilities. Depending on the circumstances, this may or may not be the best or most moral foreign policy. But it is the best way for a child of divorce to retain a relationship with both parents.

Stress the values that your children were taught during the marriage. Reinforce the obvious position that it is healthier to maintain love and respect for all their parents rather than participate in a campaign of hatred. Emphasize the virtue of showing courage in the face of group pressure.

Children need to learn to tell both their parents that they do not want to be placed in the middle of conflicts. They do not want to hear each parent say bad things about the other. They do not want to spy on a parent. They do not want to carry messages back and forth.

When a child learns to assert himself in this manner, it has been my experience that the alienating parent and alienated siblings eventually accept the child's neutrality. They continue to bad-mouth the target. But they exhibit a curious contradictory stance. On the one hand, they think the target is despicable and unworthy of respect. On the other hand, they tolerate the child who holds a different opinion and maintains a positive relationship with the target. Harmony exists as long as the target is not the topic of conversation. I have wondered whether this tolerance allows alienated siblings to gratify vicariously the aspect of themselves that longs for a reunion with the formerly loved parent.

I must add that, although children should attempt to maintain cordial relations with both parents, this does not mean that they must refrain from expressing their opinion about what each parent says about the other. Children who express their true thoughts and feelings, however unpopular, will reap the benefits of higher self-esteem.

A parent who has been successful in preventing or reversing alienation in one child may expect help from this child in persuading the others to follow suit. In general, I think this is a mistake. It is a major achievement for a child to resist divorce poison, particularly when her siblings have succumbed. This should be enough. I do not recommend burdening a child with the additional assignment of converting siblings to her way of thinking. The effort is likely to meet with failure, and the result may well be a rupture of the sibling relationship. This serves no one any good. Exceptions might be made in the case of older adolescents or young adults who might have more influence over younger siblings.

WITH GOD ON OUR SIDE—REVISITED

In the preceding chapter, I showed how appeals to religious authority can be used in the service of brainwashing. Religion can also be used to undo brainwashing.

If you have taught your children a set of religious beliefs, and the children recognize this belief system as a valid guide to moral conduct, you should not hesitate to use the teachings of your religion to counteract alienation. The religious precept most obviously relevant to alienated children is the Fifth Commandment, "Honor thy father and thy mother." The major Western religions teach other practices that may prove useful.

Judaism has specific and strong prohibitions against disparaging speech, known as *Lashon Hara* (literally "the evil tongue"). Jewish law regards the harm done by malicious speech as worse than the harm done by stealing. Stolen objects can be returned. But words, once said, cannot be unspoken. There is a Hasidic tale of a man who told malicious lies about the rabbi. Feeling remorse, he went to the rabbi and asked how he could make amends. The rabbi told him to cut open a pillow and scatter the feathers to the wind. The man followed the rabbi's unusual instruction and then returned. The rabbi told him, "Now, go and gather the feathers. Because you can no more make amends for the damage your words have done than you can re-collect the feathers."

Christianity repeatedly emphasizes the virtue of forgiveness. And dishonesty is prohibited by most, if not all, major religions. Confronting your children with the discrepancy between their religious values and their treatment of you may help open them up to the desirability of reconciliation.

Consider asking the clergy in your place of worship to assist you. If they support the sanctity of parent-child relationships, and believe that your children should be loyal to both parents, perhaps they can assist by talking with your children.

Dr. Gardner wrote about a case in which the religious beliefs of an alienated child played a pivotal role in keeping her father from being unjustly imprisoned. The girl had falsely accused her father of repeatedly fondling her genitals.

Before his daughter testified in his criminal trial, the father helped the attorney prepare a series of questions designed to remind the girl of the religious implications of her behavior. When she was on the witness stand, the attorney elicited from the girl her beliefs that lying is a sin, that one should honor thy father and thy mother, that God punishes people who violate these precepts, and that God sees and knows everything that happens in the universe, including the courtroom. With this preparation, the lawyer asked her to tell, while God watched and listened, the truth about whether her father touched her private places. After a long pause, the girl recanted her previous allegations. She admitted that she had been lying. She felt that God would be happy with her now.

When asked why she told the lie, she said that when her mother first asked her whether her dad ever touched her private place, she said no. But when her mother kept repeating the question, she finally said yes just to put an end to the questions. After she said yes, her mother was happy and kept asking her to repeat it. After a while she thought maybe it really happened. But she knew it really didn't.

Some people might object to this lawyer's tactic because it relies on inducing guilt. My response: A child who makes false abuse accusations needs to feel more guilt. The alternative is to live for the rest of her life with the knowledge that she is responsible for sending her father to prison. Eventually she would feel much greater remorse or, worse, she could have such a corrupted character that she would be apathetic about causing this much damage to her father and the people who love him.

AGREE TO DISAGREE

Craig had not seen his son and daughter for four years. The court awarded him custody at the time of the divorce, but his ex abducted the two children and fled the country. By the time the children returned, they were programmed to believe that Craig was a child molester and a wife beater.

For the time being, the court left the children with their mother and appointed a therapist to work with the family. Craig eagerly awaited his first joint session with the children. This would be his first face-to-face contact with them in four years.

The therapist warned Craig that the children were angry with him. He advised Craig not to argue with the children. Craig was optimistic. He assumed that his bond with the children would overcome any initial problems. Craig sat on the couch. The therapist brought in the two children. Craig could barely restrain himself from hugging the children and crying. Instead, he asked, voice choked with suppressed tears, "How are you two doing?"

The older child said, "Horrible. Why do we have to be here? You sexually abused us and we don't want to have anything to do with you. We despise you. You're a dirty child molester, a pervert, and you belong in jail." The words fail to capture the venomous tone in which they were delivered.

Craig's lower jaw dropped. He was unprepared for the rage directed at him from his own children. Without thinking, Craig blurted out, "That's a dirty lie. I never did anything like that. You've been brainwashed."

The older child screamed, "You're calling me a liar. I don't have to stand for that. I'm out of here." Whereupon both children fled from the office. They never returned.

Five months following this aborted treatment effort, another therapist was brought in to assist. This therapist spent several sessions with Craig before scheduling a joint session with the children. Craig explained that he felt compelled to defend himself against the horrible, gross distortions of his character. The new therapist understood Craig's sense of outrage and injustice. But she told him that it was best to wait before trying to respond to the accusations. This was excellent advice. She helped him rehearse how to bypass a confrontation over the abuse allegations. The therapist then proceeded to use the divide-and-conquer approach combined with other techniques to successfully facilitate the reunion.

One of the biggest impediments to reconciliation occurs when a child is convinced that a parent is guilty of a major transgression, such as child abuse, domestic violence, or alcoholism, and the parent adamantly denies guilt. Both sides insist that they are telling the truth. And each expects the other's agreement before they can have a relationship.

Professional negotiators table the most difficult issues until the end of the negotiations. The idea is achieve success with more modest goals, and then build on those successes. The same goes for reconciling with your children.

As much as possible, avoid arguments about whether or not you did the horrible things you are being accused of. Do not demand a resolution of this dispute when you are first trying to reunite with your child. I am not suggesting that you capitulate to your child's version of reality. Just table the discussion. Agree to disagree.

I cannot emphasize this enough. A premature attempt to resolve an explosive issue, particularly without the assistance of an experienced therapist, will not only meet with failure, it will blow up in your face, leaving a trail of destruction that makes the prospect of reconciliation even more remote.

I suggest telling your child something like this: "I know you and I have a big disagreement about what really happened. We both know we are not going to settle that today, so let's not even talk about it. Let's just try to have the best time we can. This is called 'agreeing to disagree.' It means that we are not going to waste our time trying to convince each other of who's right. Sometimes in life you have a disagreement that you can't settle right away. It doesn't mean we can't enjoy each other's company. Now, what would you like to do today?"

You will find it a lot easier to address the major allegations after you have built other bridges to your child's heart. In fact, you may find that the allegations need hardly be addressed once a reconciliation has been achieved. Naturally, none of this applies to parents who actually are guilty of the misdeeds attributed to them. In such case, you and your children will probably need professional guidance to build a healthy relationship. Part of the work will involve facing up to what you have done, understanding its impact on your children, preventing any recurrence, and finding a way to atone.

NO ONE'S PERFECT

One of the hallmarks of children whose alienation is irrational is that they come to see one parent as a villain and the other as a hero. They need to be helped to appreciate that both parents have their good qualities and their bad qualities. Even the most virtuous parent falls short of perfection. Your children will be less likely to see you as all bad if they grasp this concept and if they learn that it is normal to have mixed feelings about people you love.

Review the section on selective attention in the preceding chapter. Show the children how easy it would be to form a negative opinion of anyone based only on their mistakes and worst performances. Remind them of a past time when they misbehaved. Point out that neither parent stopped loving them just because they did something bad, mean, or cruel. Explain your concern that if they only hear and think bad things about you, they will forget all the good things. Tell them that their other parent, like every parent, also makes mistakes, but that this does not and should not keep them from seeing the good in him or her.

A father taught this lesson using the indirect technique described earlier. He told his son, "I read in a book about this boy whose mom was very angry with his dad. Every time this mother talked about his dad, all she could think of were bad things to say. She was constantly criticizing him. Pretty soon this boy forgot that his dad, like everyone, was a mixture of good things and bad things. He forgot how his dad used to throw him up in the air and catch him. He forgot how his dad used to coach his baseball team. He was too young to remember how excited his dad was when the boy was born. But this boy's father loved him very much."

THINK FOR YOURSELF

"Mommy says all you care about is your girlfriend, that we're not important to you anymore, and that's why you left us."

The best response to this sort of comment is not, "She's wrong." It is "What do *you* think?"

The problem with the first approach is that it assumes that the children will accept your assertion, uncritically, in place of their mother's assertion. It teaches them to accept what you say because you said it. It does not teach them to think critically, to judge the facts for themselves. It leaves them in no better position to deal with all the other allegations about you that they might hear.

If the children are not taken in by the allegation, you can simply say something like, "I can see that you are too smart to be fooled into thinking I don't love you." But you should say something. Many well-meaning parents work so hard to keep children out of the middle of divorce conflict that they say nothing. They may act as if they didn't hear the children, or they may change the subject. But they fail to help their children cope with bad-mouthing. Think about it this way: The children would not have mentioned the bad-mouthing to you in the first place if they weren't looking for a response.

"Daddy says you don't feed us healthy food." (Differences in attitudes about nutrition are a familiar battleground for divorced parents in conflict.) Instead of saying "That's nonsense," or something worse, ask the children what they think about it. "What have you learned in school about nutrition? Do you get sick a lot? Did the doctor ever say you weren't eating right? Did Daddy ever complain about this when we were married? Am I feeding you any differently now than I used to?"

After helping them think through the issue, you may want to help the children understand why their father would say something like this.

"I know Daddy and I don't make the same kind of meals. When you are older, you can decide for yourself what kind of food you think is best to eat. But why do you think Daddy says these things about me? Do you think he is really worried about your health, or do you think maybe he says these things because he is still mad at Mom?"

When your children repeat something critical about you that they heard from your ex, resist the temptation to immediately correct the distortion. Instead, invite the children to judge for themselves. If necessary, help them consider the evidence for and against the statement. And then help them figure out what might have motivated their other parent to say these things about you. By engaging your children in this way, you encourage the virtue of rationality and strengthen their ability to resist mental manipulation.

BRAINWASHING 101

Whether or not the procedures presented above are successful in preventing or reversing alienation, an important aspect of helping children caught in the middle of their parents' battles is to educate them about divorce poison. This can help children who have already recovered their affectionate feelings cope with future exposures to divorce poison. And it can help open the minds and hearts of children who are still alienated.

A reminder: Any of the following strategies for educating children about brainwashing may be more effectively introduced through third parties and through the indirect means described earlier. Also, it is best to implement these strategies under the guidance of a therapist.

Victims of brainwashing—whether prisoners of war, members of cults, or alienated children—do not recognize that they are brainwashed. If you tell an alienated child that he is brainwashed, he will resent the implication that his attitudes are not his own. He does not recognize that he is a puppet controlled by the alienating parent. Indeed, a common feature of these children is their insistence that they have arrived at their negative attitudes about the target solely through their own independent judgment.

The process of helping children recover loving feelings for a parent has a lot in common with deprogramming cult victims. The key to recovering from divorce poison is to gain the insight that one has been influenced by it. It will be easier to demonstrate to a child that he has been brainwashed if he at least accepts the possibility of such an occurrence.

The first step, therefore, is to provide general information about how people can influence our thoughts and feelings. I recommend doing this in a graduated fashion. Begin with situations that are most removed from divorce poison. Choose something familiar to your children, such as television commercials and sales tactics. Show how these try to convince you that a product is worth buying. You will be more effective if you can coax the children to take an active part in the conversation. For example, challenge them to identify the particular strategies a commercial uses to influence consumers.

One day I took my two youngest grandchildren to a discount department store. A manufacturer's representative had set up a demonstration booth to pitch sales of a new type of sponge. He promised free gifts to people in the audience. My grandchildren begged me to stop shopping so that we could attend the demonstration. Instead of telling them why I thought this was a bad idea, I decided to let experience be their teacher.

So we stayed. And stayed. And stayed. The sales pitch and demonstration were well crafted. The longer it went on, the more it seemed it was just about to end. With all the time we had already invested, why leave just before the free gifts were distributed? The audience was captivated.

Finally, the eagerly anticipated end came, and the gifts were given out. Each person received a five-by-seven-inch blue synthetic cloth, reputed to have near magic absorbency. Naturally the children were disappointed. They desperately wanted me to buy the sponge mop that was the ultimate subject of the demonstration. They were convinced that it was the greatest thing since sliced bread. But I wasn't buying it. I patiently explained why.

Afterward, when the glow of the sales pitch wore off, we discussed the experience. The children were shocked to learn how much time they had given up to watch the show. I called their attention to some of the gimmicks used to maintain our attention: the promise of a gift; involving the audience by challenging them to guess the outcome of a particular part of the demonstration; not allowing questions until the very end; avoiding any mention of the product's drawbacks; keeping the price a secret until the end; claiming an artificially high list price in order to make the actual purchase price look like an incredible bargain. Typical sales tactics.

I was even able to get in a discussion of cognitive dissonance. After spending so much time watching the demonstration, I explained, people wanted to believe that it was a worthwhile venture. Instead of telling themselves that they wasted their time, they preferred to tell themselves that they were lucky to get such a wonderful bargain. What really convinced my grandchildren was when I asked them, "If the salesman told you at the beginning how long the demonstration would last, and he showed you the gift you were going to get, would you have watched the show?" The little blue rag is a constant reminder of a lesson learned. To assuage their regret, I reassured them that, in a way, their time was well spent. They learned something that would probably save them a lot of time and money in the future.

Once the principle of persuasion has been established, work your way closer to direct discussions of the situation in your family. This should be done over time, and spread out over several discussions. Introduce the idea of people trying to convince others to think about another person in a certain way. Politician's speeches, propaganda, and ads are good examples. Before discussing your ex's behavior, try talking about divorce poison in general. Talk about something you read in a book, perhaps about how divorced parents sometimes bad-mouth each other. Better still, involve your children in reading a book that discusses such problems. Dr. Gardner's *The Boys and Girls Book About Divorce* has advice for children "when your mother talks about your father" and "when your father talks about your mother." Reading these sections together can provide a point of departure for conversations about the children's own family situation.

It is important to tailor the conversations to your children's age and maturity. Young children understand the concept of people "tricking" others. Eventually they can understand that sometimes one parent can trick them into being angry with the other parent in order to punish the target parent.

A mother told her son, "Sometimes children get mad at a mother because their father is angry and tricks the children into thinking that the mother is a bad person. Sometimes a child will forget all the fun things his mom did with him. After all, if the mom was so bad, why did the daddy marry her in the first place? She must have had many nice things about her for the father to fall in love with her and have children with her. But once parents get divorced, they may start thinking mainly about the bad things about each other. If the children keep hearing only about the bad things, they may forget about all the good things."

If the children are old enough, try discussing mind control that occurs in other contexts. Hypnosis is a good vehicle for such discussions. People are always fascinated with this topic. Since children like to show how smart they are, invite them to tell you what they know about hypnosis. Where have they seen it demonstrated? Do they think it is really possible to hypnotize someone into doing something without the person being aware of the external influence? It is very important that the children understand that a hypnosis subject will follow the hypnotist's suggestions while denying the hypnotist's influence. If your children can accept this idea—that people under the influence of posthypnotic suggestions act without awareness that they are hypnotized—it will be easier to convince them that they could be rejecting you because of your ex's influence.

Older children can also take part in discussions about brainwashing of prisoners of war, and enticement of people into religious cults. Such discussions are far enough removed from their own situation that they are less likely to shut you out.

Of all the advice in this book, the one that may be the most contro-versial is the recommendation to teach your children about how they are being manipulated by your ex. I can understand people's concern. In many divorces, parents mutually bad-mouth each other. Some of these parents will misuse my advice to avoid taking responsibility for their own behavior. They will use it as a license to continue bad-mouthing their ex. This is why I began the book with an entire chapter defining the delicate balance between constructive and destructive criticism.

Helping children understand how a parent has tried to poison their relationships is no more an example of bad-mouthing than is helping children understand a parent's physically or sexually abusive behavior. Authorities may disagree about what term best describes children who irrationally reject a parent. But most agree that these children have suf-fered a type of emotional abuse at the hands of the other parent.

Do alienated parents contribute to the problem? In many cases they certainly do. But this fact does not absolve the perpetrator from primary responsibility. The analogy with other forms of abuse holds. A mother may fail to prevent her husband from physically brutalizing their child. Any treatment program will certainly need to address her passivity. But we would never hold her equally responsible for the abuse.

Psychotherapists do not like to place blame. Effective treatment usu-ally rests on the therapist's ability to accept a client's problems in a non-judgmental manner. But therapists who are unaware of the dynamics of brainwashing will fail to recognize the importance of educating children about it. They may be too quick to advise alienated parents to wait pas-sively, hoping that someday the children will change their minds.

Chapter 3 described the most common errors that alienated parents commit. I will remind you of them shortly. A key mistake is being too passive about responding to divorce poison. In recommending that you teach your children about what is being done to them, I am advocating an active approach. This is consistent with my conviction that children deserve help in navigating the difficult terrain of a high-conflict divorce.

FILMS AND TELEVISION

One of the best projective forms of communication with alienated chil-dren is the type that comes out of a movie projector. Stories, fairy tales, and fables are the age-old ways of communicating life's important lessons to children. Movies and television shows are two modern ways. Fortunately, both the big screen and the little screen have produced shows that relate directly to many of the ideas that alienated children need to learn. Watching such shows with your children is an entertaining, low-anxiety strategy for introducing important themes. Certain shows will allow you to introduce the topics of mind control, hypnosis, brainwashing, parent-child relationships, even difficult divorces, in a relaxed atmosphere. The same children who would immediately shut down if you attempted to discuss their alienation will actively take part in a conversation about a hypnotized child or a brainwashed assassin.

I will present a brief list of shows to give some idea of the wide range of possibilities, and the potential of this strategy to help open communication between you and your children. I encourage you to be alert for others. In fact, I maintain a list of such "alienation busters" at the Divorce Poison Control Center on my website, www.warshak.com. I welcome additional suggestions from my readers. These shows can have value merely if your children watch them. (If you watch them together, at least you and they are sharing an enjoyable activity.) But the shows will have their biggest payoff if you can initiate a conversation about them and successfully engage your children in the discussion. The principles of indirect communication and graduated exposure are applicable here. Don't be too quick to relate the movie to your child's own situation. You do not want to arouse your child's resistance. Learning about related situations lays a foundation that you can draw on in future conversations. The temptation will be to move too quickly. Given the frustration of rejected parents, this is understandable. Try to resist the temptation. Opening a closed mind is a delicate operation. Take your time and you will more likely meet with success.

Here are some shows to get you started:

- *Hook*—for its clear portrayal of Captain Hook enticing a boy to renounce his father

- *The Manchurian Candidate*—for older children, a gripping film illustrating the frightening extent to which a person can be brainwashed

- *The Wave*—this hard-to-find video depicts a teacher's experiment to demonstrate how easily people can be manipulated to hate

- *The Stepford Wives*—a classic portrayal of women whose husbands have stripped them of their own will

- *The Invasion of the Body Snatchers*—can stimulate a discussion of people acting without volitional control

- *Jack Frost*—a movie about a boy whose father dies and comes back to life as a snowman. The film speaks volumes about the importance of a father to a child.

- *Terms of Endearment*—shows the importance of a mother to her daughter despite conflicts in their relationship

- *Mrs. Doubtfire*—portrays the pain of a parent being kept apart from his children

- *Table for Five*—shows that even a parent with many flaws occupies a unique space in the hearts of his children

- *The Honeymooners*—"The Hypnotist" and "The Sleepwalker," episodes in which Ralph Kramden and Ed Norton are hypnotized

I hope you get the idea. Now, bring out the popcorn, pop in a video, and begin your journey back to your child's heart.

BECOME A BETTER PARENT

Some of the parents reading this book will be too quick to blame their ex-spouses for their children's alienation rather than take responsibility for their own substantial contributions.

An eleven-year-old girl hated going to her father's house every other weekend. Every weekend was the same. The father stayed at his computer the entire time, while the girl watched television. The father was extremely isolated socially and had no contact with friends or family. The girl was not allowed to attend parties on these weekends, nor participate in soccer games, because the father was afraid that the girl would see her mother at these events. The father was adamant that the mother not have any more time with their daughter than she was entitled to by the terms of their divorce decree.

The girl did not complain to her father because when she did, the father called the mother, and the parents got in terrible arguments.

Month after month the girl complied with the schedule. She grew increasingly estranged from her father. When the mother learned of her daughter's unhappiness, she tried to modify the custody arrangements. She did not want to eliminate the father-daughter contact, but she did want to give her daughter more control over when it would occur. In response, the father accused the mother of brainwashing the daughter. By blaming her for the problem, he was missing the chance to learn what he could do to improve the situation.

Parents who are excessively self-centered or rigid may have a hard time creating an environment in which their children feel comfortable and welcome. These parents need to learn more about their children's needs and interests and about how to build a closer relationship. Blaming the ex-spouse, without doing anything to improve themselves, will merely drive their children farther away.

If you have been accused of poor parenting, instead of automatically defending yourself, consider the possibility that there is some basis for the accusations. Get an objective appraisal of your parenting practices. If trusted friends and relatives tell you that you are too harsh with your children, or too lenient, or expect too much, or give too little attention, or show too little patience, it is likely that you have a blind spot when it comes to evaluating yourself as a parent. If a psychotherapist tries to explain how you have contributed to the problems in your relationship with your children, pay careful attention. Demonstrate the intelligence and the courage to admit when you are at fault. Read books on parenting. (I list my favorites in the Resources section.) Attend parenting classes. Learn more about your child's unique interests and personality. Build bridges with your child by engaging in activities that are mutually enjoyable.

One father whose son was beginning to turn against him exploited their common interest in collecting stamps. This gave them a comfortable way to relate without having to focus on their problems. Rather than tell his son that he was a rewarding parent to be with, he showed him. They went to stamp shows together, looked up stamps in a catalog, and compared collections. This was enough to reinforce their bond.

The days and weeks surrounding a marital breakup are a particularly volatile time in a family's life. Parents often say and do things they later regret. If you haven't already done so, apologize to the children for mistakes such as things said in anger about the other parent, revelations that would have been better left unsaid, acts of violence, intimidation, harshness, or rejection.

Even if your ex-spouse takes your parenting deficiencies out of context, exaggerates them, and ignores your parenting strengths, it still makes sense to make yourself the best parent you can be. The more your behavior differs from what the children have been programmed to expect, the easier it will be for them to recognize that they have judged you wrongly. By using your ex-spouse's criticisms as a stimulus to self-improvement, you are acting more responsibly and removing yourself from the passive victim role. The result will be greater self-respect and confidence as a parent.

Being a good parent doesn't guarantee your children's love, respect, and trust. But it certainly doesn't hurt.

AVOID COMMON ERRORS

The suggestions in this chapter focus on what to do to protect your bond with your child. But there are also things you should try to avoid doing.

Targets of divorce poison usually respond in ways that make the problem worse. I have already emphasized the mistake of being too passive. You cannot watch idly as your children drift away from you. You cannot wait until they feel ready to see you. You may be waiting the rest of your life.

However, being with your children is not enough. How you treat them is what has the most impact. While you work to implement the strategies already discussed, do your best to follow the rules below. I am aware that these rules set a high standard that parents with the best intentions cannot always meet, but the more closely you follow them, the greater your chance of successfully helping your children cope with divorce poison.

Don't Lose Your Temper

Alienated children can be rude, obnoxious, hateful. They express, and provoke, great hostility. No one would blame the target of mistreatment for responding in kind. But it just makes things worse.

If your children are succumbing to divorce poison, they will be unfazed by your criticisms. They act with the blessings and encouragement of your ex, and they no longer respect you enough to want your approval. Besides, you won't win your children's affection by fighting with them or frightening them. Any aggression that you show, either verbal or physical, will merely play into the hands of your ex. It will be taken out of context and blown out of proportion and used to justify the children's rejection.

Don't Reject Your Children

In the early stages of alienation some target parents counterreject their children. They rebuke the children for their negative attitudes, and tell them, in effect, "Shape up or ship out." They expect, of course, the children to shape up. This might have worked prior to the onset of the alienation. But it no longer works when the children have lost respect for the parent or lost sight of their need for the parent.

Parents use this ploy before they appreciate the nature and seriousness of the problem. They never consider the possibility that the children will choose to sever contact permanently. By the time they realize their mistake, it is often too late.

Counterrejecting your children is the wrong move for several reasons:

- It breaks contact with your children, which is so crucial to resisting and reversing alienation. If the children become solely dependent on your ex, they may not be able to resist divorce poison on their own. Losing contact with them means losing the opportunity to help them escape or withstand the noxious environment.

- It stings the children who, despite their overt belligerence, at some level continue to need your love and acceptance. They will feel hurt and abandoned and express their pain with more anger and alienation.

- It sets you up to be seen by the children, and possibly by the court, as the bad guy who caused the alienation.

Pushing the children away will not bring them closer. Even if your push seems gentle to you, it could strike the mortal blow to your relationship.

Don't Try to End Alienation with Lectures

Lectures are rarely a useful response to negative feelings even with non-alienated children. Not only is your attempt likely to fall on deaf ears, it detracts from the quality of your time together. Instead, concentrate on creating conflict-free, pleasurable experiences. Good times together will do more to promote your bond than the most carefully crafted words.

Don't Dismiss the Children's Feelings

"You don't really hate Daddy." As with lectures, denying the reality of children's feelings won't make them go away. Even though you know their newly developed anger or fear are products of divorce poison, the feelings are real. Dismissing them will further entrench your children's estrangement. They will take this as evidence that you are not listening to them, or that you don't understand them, or that you don't care about their feelings. For the same reason, it is best to avoid arguing with your children about the origin of their negative attitudes. They may be using the exact same words as your ex, but if you deny the autonomy of their feelings, whether or not they realize what they are doing (and many times they do not), they will feel dismissed and insist that no one told them what to say.

This does not mean you have to dwell on negative feelings. In fact, other than acknowledging the feelings when first expressed, it is best not to become preoccupied with them. "I can see that you don't want to be here, but what can we do today that will be fun for both of us?"

Don't Overreact

If your children repeat a bad thing your ex has said about you, don't automatically conclude that the children are on their way to becoming alienated. They may be repeating the comment because they are troubled by it. They may be wanting help from you. As calmly as possible, ask them how they feel about what your ex said. Express empathy for how uncomfortable it must be for them to have to hear such things. You want to make sure that your response to their revelation is not so angry that they will regret having told you.

Don't Bad-mouth Your Ex

You will accomplish nothing by bad-mouthing your ex except to give your children a genuine reason to feel uncomfortable around you. Before criticizing your ex to your children, review the test in chapter 1 (page 16). This will help ensure that what you are about to say is truly for the children's benefit, and not merely to indulge your wish to retaliate. If your ex is trying to poison the children against you, find a constructive way to address the problem. Gratuitous insults will only make it harder for your children to benefit from your legitimate criticisms.

If your children are victims of divorce poison, they already have one home in which they have to listen to a parent being run down. Let them experience your home as a demilitarized zone, a respite from the hostilities. In time they may notice the difference and appreciate your stance. In fact, at an appropriate moment, you can draw their attention to the contrast: "Have you ever noticed how, when you are here, you don't hear me bad-mouthing your dad? This is how it should be for children whose parents are divorced. I read somewhere that children really wish their parents would stop putting each other down."

A grandfather was taken aback when his granddaughter asked him if he loved her mother, his former daughter-in-law. The girl's mother had been extremely destructive during the divorce. She threatened to kidnap her children, and she had attempted, with only partial success, to poison her children's relationship with her ex and his entire family. The grandfather wanted to answer honestly. But he also sensed that his grandchild was looking for reassurance, and for a way out of the tribal warfare to which she had been subjected. After a few seconds, he gathered his thoughts and responded: "You know that your mother says some very mean things about me, Nanna, and your daddy. She is still very angry with us. I'm sorry she feels that way. I know it is hard for you and your sister when you hear Mommy talk like that. It makes it harder for me to feel friendly toward her when she acts that way. But I do love her. I love her because she and your daddy had you. There will always be a special place in my heart for the mother of my grandchild. I hope Mommy will get over her anger so that you can enjoy seeing us be friendly with each other. But even if she doesn't, you can love all the grown-ups who love you. And they will always love you."

DAMAGE CONTROL

Up to this point I have described how to deal with alienated children. But there may also be things you can do to encourage your ex to reduce the hostilities, which, in turn, will remove some of the impetus for divorce poison.

Right the Wrong

To whatever extent your ex's anger at you is partially a reaction to your misdeeds or mistreatment, you must face up to your responsibility and do what you can to set things right. If you were dishonest in your financial settlement, have your attorney propose a modification of the divorce decree. If your affair triggered the end of the marriage, apologize. It is important to show regret not just for your behavior but for the entire chain of events that resulted from the deed. Psychologist-attorney Dr. John Zervopoulos uses the analogy of a pebble dropped into a pond. The affair is the pebble. The concentric rings that emanate from the pebble in the water are the aftereffects of the affair—the sense of betrayal, the breakup of the family, your spouse's depression, your children's embarrassment, the financial cost of the divorce, your children's anxiety. Your apology will have more meaning if you show that you understand the full ramifications of your actions.

Be More Cooperative

In general, think about what changes you can make to lessen the hostilities. Perhaps there is something you do that is particularly troublesome to your ex. You may be too rigid when it comes to last-minute changes in the residential schedule of the children. Try to accommodate your ex when this would benefit the children. Avoid unnecessary harsh words. If you want the tone of your coparenting relationship to improve, take responsibility for initiating the improvement.

Reassure

A personal problem, such as alcoholism, substance abuse, depression, or impulsivity may have contributed to the failure of the marriage and your children's discomfort around you. Even if your ex exploits the situation to turn the children against you, provide the level of reassurance that your ex and the children have the right to expect regarding your state of recovery. Let them know that you recognize that you have a problem and that you are getting help for it. This will set a good example for your children about how to handle a difficult personal problem with honesty and dignity. Devise an explicit relapse prevention program and share this with your ex and with your children if appropriate. Because your communications may someday have legal ramifications, you may want to have your attorney review these before delivering them. You should be honestly apologetic, but you should not admit to things you didn't do merely to try to make peace.

Reassurance is particularly important if you are planning to remarry. As I discussed in chapter 4, remarriage, and the anxiety it stirs, often serves as a trigger for divorce poison. If you remarry, reaffirm to your ex-spouse your awareness of his or her central importance to your child. Emphasize your wish to cooperate in bringing up the children. If your ex remarries, communicate your intention to actively promote the children's relationship with their stepparent.

Send a Letter of Peace

In her excellent book *Between Love and Hate,* Lois Gold advises parents to write letters of goodwill to each other. The advantage of a letter is that it gives you a chance to organize your thoughts and express yourself without getting drawn into a nonproductive argument. Ms. Gold believes, "If you are able to speak from the heart of your desire to move beyond the anger and destructiveness, you can often cut through your spouse's animosity and touch his or her deeper concerns also."

The letter should express your concern about how the children are being harmed by being caught in the middle of their parents' battles. It should affirm your desire to improve cooperation and shield the children from further damage. Your ex may dismiss your letter as self-serving and manipulative. But it won't hurt to go on record offering the olive branch.

Learn How to Negotiate

Unresolved conflicts between ex-spouses often sow the seeds for the discontent and animosity that drive divorce poison. The conflicts remain unresolved because one or both parents are poor negotiators. They may each take a firm stand using highly inflammatory, blaming language that sinks negotiations before they get under way. Neither one may understand the importance of recognizing the underlying needs and concerns that may be satisfied by positions other than the ones they rigidly advance and defend.

Good negotiation skills are indispensable if you continue to relate to a difficult ex. In the Resources section I list some books that can get you started on learning these skills.

ANN LANDERS'S RECONCILIATION DAY

Since 1989, Ann Landers has designated April 2 as Reconciliation Day. On this day, she urges everyone to make an effort to mend a strained or broken relationship. She also advises everyone to "accept the olive branch" extended to them. As Miss Landers explains, "Life is too short to hold grudges. To be able to forgive can be enormously healing and life-enhancing."

Each year the April 2 column includes letters from readers who took advantage of Reconciliation Day to reach out to someone with whom they had lost touch because of hurt feelings. Some letters describe success. Others describe failure.

I suggest sending this column to your children every year, and a copy to your ex. With it, send a note requesting contact, or better still, a follow-up phone call. It is a small effort that may yield a huge return. You never know when the words of Ann Landers and her readers will break through the wall of alienation. I would be very interested to hear from any readers who find success with this tactic.

With the exception of the Ann Landers column, all of the advice in this chapter assumes that you have some contact with your children. If you are denied any contact with them, then you must first work to reestablish this. If your ex will not cooperate with you, then it is time to get outside help.

CHAPTER 8

GETTING PROFESSIONAL HELP

Your best chance of helping children survive divorce poison is to work with a good psychotherapist and, if necessary, a good attorney. In some cases, professional assistance is essential. This chapter will help you decide when and how to seek professional help, and how to make the most of any help you receive.

WHEN TO CALL THE THERAPIST

Although technically "psychotherapy" is a different form of treatment from "counseling," in popular discussion the terms have come to be used synonymously. To avoid confusion I will use only the terms *psychotherapy* and *therapy and* not the term *counseling*. These terms refer to services provided by mental health professionals whose aim is to alleviate psychological disturbances.

In the immediate aftermath of their parents' separation, most children show some signs of distress. Don't overreact to these signs by rushing to the therapist. And don't assume that your children's difficult behavior means they are being poisoned against you. They may be just as difficult with their other parent. As long as you and the children have regular contact, and their attitude is not consistently negative over a long

period of time, the children may settle down after the divorce is final and
everyone begins to feel more grounded.

If your children are brought into the middle of conflicts between you
and your ex on a regular basis—if they are repeatedly exposed to bad-
mouthing, or are asked to carry angry messages from one parent to the
other, or are pressured or manipulated to devalue or distrust a parent—it
is a good idea to consult a therapist. Even if the children show no out-
ward signs of disturbance, the chances are that divorce poison is taking its
toll or will do so in the future. A mental health checkup could not hurt.
Children whose parents are locked in battle often hide their feelings from
both parents. A therapist's office can be a safe harbor in which to express
feelings and learn how to maintain love for both parents despite pres-
sures to align with one against the other. If the therapist learns that your
child is suffering as a result of the conflict between homes, the therapist
may be able to use this information to motivate you and your ex to
improve the situation.

Certainly if your child seems chronically disturbed, it is best to call a
therapist. Symptoms of disturbance include excessive worries and fears,
sadness, decline in school performance, irritability, sleep problems,
behavior problems, and physical problems for which no medical basis is
found, such as frequent aches and pains. Or your child may show the disrespect, rejection, and declining affection characteristic of children who
are, or are becoming, alienated. If your best efforts to help the situation
result in no improvement, it is time to call in the experts. When children
consistently refuse to see you, you should not allow the situation to continue without getting help. The risk is too great that the lack of contact
will entrench the alienation and make it all the more difficult to alleviate.

HOW THERAPY CAN HELP

When divorce poison reaches a moderate or severe level, family members see
reality differently. Each parent blames the other for problems, while overlooking his or her own contributions. The children are pressured to take
sides. Often the children see one parent as a saint and the other as a sinner.

A good therapist can bring a needed neutral perspective to the family
conflicts. He or she challenges distortions of reality and encourages more
realistic thinking. The therapist helps each member of the family under-

stand the needs and feelings being expressed through problematic behavior and find healthier ways to adapt. He or she teaches parents and children how to communicate clearly and directly. A breakdown in communication between parents allows the children to play one off against the other. Parents who are eager to hear bad things about the ex will uncritically believe their children's negative reports or be too quick to conclude that the ex is brainwashing the children. Sometimes, though, the children give each parent a different story. They may try to ingratiate themselves with the parents, get material advantages, or stir up conflict in order to release their own tension and anger. These types of manipulations are interrupted when the parents have reestablished effective lines of communication, and the therapist is the person who can facilitate this. The therapist also teaches everyone in the family how to negotiate with one another, rather than stubbornly hold to a single position that results in unresolvable conflicts.

A therapist's involvement with the child can assuage a parent's concern that the child is being abused in the home of the other parent; at the same time, therapeutic oversight protects a parent against false allegations of abuse. This type of oversight is usually preferable to on-site supervision of parent-child contacts; the supervisor's presence is apt to reinforce the child's sense that the rejected parent is dangerous to be around.

Alienating Parents

Therapy with alienating parents helps identify the fears, hurt, and shame that often lie beneath the anger that drives divorce poison. It provides a forum for the safe release of hostilities. It helps parents resolve the anger rather than use the children to express it. It helps the parent who is holding on with hate to let go of the ex-spouse and move past the divorce. Therapy helps parents find other outlets for narcissism that do not involve putting down the ex-spouse. It provides the validation that a brainwashing parent often seeks for the disappointments and sense of betrayal he or she has endured, while restraining the expression of these disappointments through the children. It helps parents define clearer boundaries between their feelings and those of the children.

Therapy helps parents find more benign interpretations of the target parent's behavior. It provides a nonjudgmental atmosphere in which parents can safely admit that they have dispensed divorce poison; this is the first step toward resolving the problem. It helps parents find ways to apologize for their destructive behavior and to help mend the sabotaged relationships. When an alienating parent has decided to cease fire, the therapist will stress the importance of convincing the children of the change in attitude, of letting the children know that the parent now welcomes hearing good things about the other parent.

The therapist will educate alienating parents about the long-term damage caused by divorce poison. Parents will learn how their behavior undermines their children's self-esteem. (In *The Custody Revolution* I explain how and why a child's self-esteem suffers when the child turns against a parent.) They will also learn about how a child's problems in relating to a parent can generalize to other people and thus handicap the child's pursuit of gratifying relationships in the future. Even when an alienating parent continues to regard the ex as severely flawed, he or she may understand the need for children to learn how to deal with difficult people assertively, rather than passively avoid them.

Brainwashing parents will learn that continuing their destructive behavior may cost them custody of the children, and that ultimately it may cost them their children's affection. This may result from having taught their children to end relationships that become uncomfortable, rather than work on improving them. When conflict arises between the brainwashing parent and children, particularly when the children reach adolescence and young adulthood, the children may apply this lesson and end that relationship as well. Or the children may ultimately reject the brainwashing parent because they come to realize and resent their exploitation as soldiers in a war they had no business fighting.

Alienated Parents

Therapy with alienated parents helps them understand how and why divorce poison works, and what they need to do to counteract it. It provides needed validation of their worth as parents when they are under attack from the ex and the children. It supports their continued commitment to the children when they may be tempted to withdraw in defeat. It helps them avoid the common errors of target parents. It helps them strengthen their parenting skills. And it helps them exercise the damage control discussed in the preceding chapter.

In much of the work with alienated parents, the therapist offers specific guidance on how to relate to the children and deal with their hateful or fearful behavior. I think of this type of treatment more as coaching than therapy. Its aim is not to promote insight into personal motivations as much as it is to provide direct, concrete advice and strategies for managing a difficult situation.

In *very rare* cases a child's alienation is so severe that it resists all attempts to reverse it, and all possible remedies have been exhausted, including legal recourse. If the point of no return is reached, the therapist will assist the parent to prepare a letter or videotape formalizing the interruption of efforts to reunite, expressing the parent's lifelong love and commitment to the child, and leaving the welcome mat out for a future reconciliation. Because this communication is apt to be the child's only remaining tie to you, it is very important to have help in its preparation. See chapter 9, "Letting Go," for a detailed discussion.

Alienated Children

Therapy gives alienated children a neutral territory in which to air grievances. The therapist tries to help children extricate themselves from their parents' battles. Alienated children need to achieve a more balanced view of each parent rather than a polarized view of one parent as saint and the other as sinner.

The competent therapist is a voice of reason and balance. He listens carefully to the children and shows them that he understands. But he also gently confronts their corrupted view of reality. He encourages the children to judge for themselves the accuracy of each parent's allegations. Therapists are often in a better position to do this than target parents are. If your children are moderately to severely alienated from you, they may refuse to listen to what you say. Or, if you challenge them to think about whether they have been told the truth about you, they may feel that you are putting them in the middle. They may mistake your attempt to clarify reality as pressure to side with you against your ex.

In therapy alienated children learn how to stand up to parents who dispense divorce poison. They learn that they do not have to please one parent by hating the other. In some cases, they learn to recognize how they have been influenced and hurt by the battle between their parents.

In other cases, they reunite with a parent without ever explicitly acknowledging the manipulations to which they have been exposed.

The therapist oversees reunions between children and their alienated parent and structures these in a manner that creates the least anxiety for all participants. He tries to help children regain their moral compass by pointing out the cruelty of their rejection of the target parent and reminding them that their abusive behavior would never have been tolerated when the parents were together. Even when children seem unreceptive to the therapist's words, the discussions plant seeds that may later bear the fruit of insight.

HOW YOU CAN HELP YOUR THERAPIST

The best patients take an active responsibility for their treatment. This is especially the case when it comes to psychotherapy. In addition to working hard to discover what you can do to contribute to the resolution of family problems, here are some things to do to make your therapist's job a little easier.

- Feel free to ask the therapist about his or her education, training, and thoughts about working with alienated children. A competent therapist will respond to such requests in a nondefensive manner, viewing them as an opportunity to build the trust that is a cornerstone of the therapeutic relationship.

- If you have read a book that you find helpful in understanding your situation, recommend it to your therapist, but don't insist that the therapist read it. And don't inundate the therapist with mountains of information downloaded from the Internet. Much of this is of limited value to therapists and they can get it themselves if they need it. A therapist's time is his livelihood. Unless he requests additional reading material, you should not impose on his time by providing it.

- Share with the therapist any reservations you have about the conduct of the treatment. Therapists welcome such discussions. Worries and criticisms that are expressed are less likely to sabotage treatment progress.

- Help the therapist understand the history of your relationship with your child. What special games and activities did you do together? (If you have trouble thinking of any special bonding activities, this might be a good clue about why your child has chosen to align herself with your ex.) If the therapist is unsure about the nature of your predivorce relationship with your child, offer to bring in greeting cards, photographs, videotapes, and other memorabilia that demonstrate the loving relationship that used to exist between you and your child.

- If your therapist criticizes your behavior, don't automatically dismiss him or her as biased against you. Take time to consider the feedback. If you don't agree with the therapist's appraisal, seek an opinion from someone else whom you can trust to be objective. It won't help to ask only the people who automatically take your side against your ex.

- In joint sessions with your ex or your children, be sensitive to the therapist's efforts to steer the conversation in the most productive direction. If you insist on "having your say," you may be trading long-term gains for short-term satisfaction.

- In joint sessions with your children, don't insist on analyzing the accuracy of every allegation made against you unless the therapist invites this. The time together is usually better spent working on the positive aspects of your relationship rather than rehashing old grievances.

- Keep all appointments promptly.

- Respect your therapist's personal life. Refrain from calling outside of normal business hours unless the matter truly cannot wait.

- Be patient. Therapy usually takes longer than you expect to produce solid gains.

It is important that you embark on a course of psychotherapy with hope but with reasonable expectations. Psychotherapy is not magic. Even the best therapists cannot help all families. All they can do is try to help you alleviate the problems. Their efforts may fail because you, or your ex, or your children, choose to ignore painful realities. The importance of people's choices is perhaps the most overlooked aspect of psychological development. We are not merely products of our environment and our genes. For better or worse, each of us plays an active role in the development of our own personality.

SELECTING THERAPISTS

Locating the right therapist can be frustrating. Therapists come with different educational backgrounds and different training experiences. They come with different degrees and different certificates and licenses.

Psychotherapists can be clinical psychologists, psychiatrists, social workers, or counselors. Each discipline has its share of excellent, good, fair, and bad therapists. In the United States the use of the title psychologist is regulated by law. Most clinical psychologists have earned a doctoral degree (Ph.D. or Psy.D.) and completed an internship, although some may have a master's degree (M.A.), which takes fewer years in graduate school. Psychiatrists are medical doctors (M.D.), most of whom continued their training in a residency program following medical school. However, a physician may use the title psychiatrist without having completed a psychiatric residency. Most social workers and counselors have a master's degree, although some have a Ph.D. and others have only a bachelor's degree.

Look for a therapist with credentials and experience beyond the minimum required to hang a shingle. For a psychologist this could be a listing in the National Register of Health Service Providers in Psychology (see Resources at the end of this book). For a psychiatrist it could be the completion of a psychiatric residency. For a social worker it could be certification through the Academy of Certified Social Workers (ACSW) or status as an Advanced Clinical Practitioner (ACP). For counselors it could be a doctoral degree or status as a licensed professional counselor (LPC) in states where a license is not necessary to call oneself a counselor.

You should not choose a therapist, though, based solely on degrees, certifications, and licenses. Paper credentials are no guarantee of competence or expertise. Doing therapy with alienated children and their parents is a difficult professional challenge that requires specialized skills, knowledge, and experience. Select a therapist the way you would a surgeon. If you would not pick your surgeon from the telephone directory, don't choose a therapist this way. It is no exaggeration to say that your contact with your children may depend on getting the best help. Get recommendations from people you trust who are in a position to know which therapists work best with families such as yours.

Family law attorneys usually have enough experience with local professionals to make a referral. Your child's pediatrician may have some suggestions. Other parents who have been through similar situations may have located therapists with expertise in this area. Check with some of the organizations listed in the Resources section. If you have trouble locating a therapist in your geographical area, write to me and I will do my best to help you find someone competent.

Working with people who intentionally or unintentionally poison their children's affections is one of the most difficult challenges for a therapist. It requires the willingness to temporarily suspend judgment while searching for the keys to understanding how parents could visit such abuse on their own offspring. This understanding must then be used to help parents channel their pain and personality deficits in another direction, one that protects their children. There are some truly gifted therapists—I'm married to one—who combine the exact amount of empathy and confrontation to promote understanding and change without chasing the patient away. They are able to gently yet firmly encourage better behavior. It is a delicate dance and as difficult to learn as it is to become a ballroom dancer by reading a book.

The right therapist may use terms such as *parental alienation* or *PAS*. Or the therapist may characterize her work as helping high-conflict families after divorce or alienated children. The term used is not important. What is important is that the therapist understand the roots of alienation and how to differentiate alienation that is primarily a result of divorce poison from other conditions. You also want a therapist who knows that children can be manipulated to hate a parent and that contact between the alienated children and rejected parent is usually essential to repairing the relationship. When allegations of abuse accompany the alienation, the therapist should have experience in working with children who have made such allegations.

It is very important to select a therapist who understands the unique importance of the parent-child bond. The therapist should regard the loss of this bond as tragic. Regardless of how well your child is functioning in other areas of life, the therapist should be extremely reluctant to throw in the towel and conclude that your child would be better off if you gave up your efforts to reunite.

If you live in an area where no therapist is known for expertise in working with alienated children, choose someone who has general experience in treating parent-child conflicts and who is willing to learn about effective interventions with victims of divorce poison. Show the therapist the list of resources at the end of this book.

Therapists to Avoid

It is well known in the professional community that some therapists do their clients more harm than good. When treating families in which divorce poison is rampant, too many therapists take sides in the tribal warfare and lose their objectivity. They meet with only one parent and the alienated child, conclude that the child's alienation is reasonable, and never speak with the rejected parent to get the other side of the story. Often these therapists have a poor understanding of the dynamics of brainwashing and thus have a hard time believing that a child's hatred could be the result of manipulation. They will recklessly offer opinions to the court about a parent they have never seen. They may write letters to the judge recommending that a parent have no contact or only supervised contact with the child. In some cases they go so far as to diagnose a parent they have never even met as a pedophile.

The best therapists judge their clients on the facts and not on preconceived biases. It is usually a mistake to choose a therapist who has worked extensively with your ex and your child without asking to meet with you. The very fact that you were excluded from the work must raise a suspicion of bias. How can a therapist expect to repair your child's relationship with you without seeing you or at least collaborating with your therapist?

Some therapists believe that children who reject a parent should be allowed to withdraw from contact until they change their attitude. These therapists hope that time and therapy alone will heal wounded relationships. In most cases they will be disappointed. And so will you if you put your hopes in such a therapist. Although research on treating alienated children is still at an early stage, every published study to date has reached the same conclusion: If a child's alienation is unjustified, the most reliable path to recovery is to get the child together with the target parent. Unless there are compelling circumstances that require postponing contact, one aspect of the treatment plan should be to have the child spend time with the rejected parent. If the therapist opposes this on principle, he or she is not the best therapist for the job.

Another type of therapist to avoid is one who is biased against either women or men. Even if the bias favors you, this type of bias compromises the quality of the treatment. But be aware that sometimes a therapist's reputation for bias is undeserved. It is important to investigate the source of the accusation, speak to the therapist about it, and give him or her a chance to explain. You may learn that the therapist has helped many mothers and many fathers. The allegations of bias may have originated from one disgruntled parent who blames his problems on the therapist's alleged prejudice rather than accepting personal responsibility.

If allegations of abuse accompany alienation, avoid therapists who believe that all such allegations must be true. You can recognize such therapists by their opinions that "children never lie" or "where there's smoke, there's fire." Either they are unaware of the professional literature in this area, or they have a personal ax to grind. Also, avoid any therapist who tends to deny the reality of child abuse and assumes that all such allegations are false.

The Selection Process

If you and your ex agree to seek professional help for the family, it is important that both of you have a say in choosing the therapist. Recommendations can come from your child's pediatrician, school, a former or current therapist, an attorney, friends, the local university or medical school, or a professional organization such as one listed in the Resources section at the end of this book.

When ex-spouses have a high level of mutual distrust, it is common for each to automatically reject any therapist proposed by the other. A good way around this problem is for both of you to write down the names of three to five therapists who have come recommended. Then agree to select the first therapist whose name appears on both lists. Another way to resolve disagreements is for each of you to designate one therapist and then have the designated therapists select a therapist they can both agree upon. If the animosity between you and your ex is too strong to allow even this level of cooperation, you can ask your attorneys to select a therapist through the same processes. Attorneys who are oriented toward helping their clients resolve conflicts amicably will usually know several competent therapists whose work they respect.

If your ex will not agree to participate or allow your child to participate in receiving professional help, you may have no alternative but to ask your attorney for help. Your attorney may file a motion to ask the court to appoint a therapist and order both parents to cooperate with the treatment. A disadvantage of this approach is that it puts such an important decision in the hands of someone who knows little about your family. Often, the judge will ask the two attorneys to suggest a therapist they can agree upon, or to provide a list of therapists from which the judge will choose.

Even when both parents agree to consult a therapist, it is very often a good idea to secure a court order for treatment. This is particularly true when one parent actively opposes the child's having contact with the other. A court order at the outset ensures the continuity of treatment. Without such an order in place, as soon as the therapist expresses an unfavorable opinion or recommendation, a parent can drop out of treatment and prevent the child from getting help. Another advantage of a court order is that it can specify certain conditions of therapy that will maximize the chances of a successful outcome.

CONDITIONS OF TREATMENT

Suppose a ten-year-old child got fed up with writing book reports and decided to quit school. Let us further suppose that our fifth-grade dropout lives with her divorced father, a man who has never valued education and has often expressed this opinion to his impressionable daughter. The girl's mother seeks my help to get her child back in school. What can I accomplish?

If I have access only to the mother, I can coach her about how to speak with her daughter and ex-husband about the issue. I might also suggest that she enlist a third party to try to reason with the child, such as an older cousin whom the girl admires. But if the father does not respect the mother's opinion, and actively encourages his daughter to stay home from school, my coaching is not likely to be helpful.

Suppose this mother gets a court order that requires the father to see me in therapy and bring his daughter as well. Even then, if the man stead-fastly opposes education, continues to undermine his child's respect for school, and stubbornly refuses to make her attend, my efforts would most likely fail.

This situation is analogous to a pathologically alienated child, a child who irrationally rejects one parent primarily as a result of the other parent's influence. But there is one essential ingredient missing from our scenario of the fifth-grade dropout: the truant officer. In real life the mother and therapist would not have to change the father's attitude before getting the girl back to school. They would have the law on their side to enforce the child's attendance. The therapist could then work with the father and daughter to help them accept the circumstances imposed by the law. Over time, the therapist might help them appreciate the value of an education. (To home schoolers: I am not suggesting that a child's education must take place in a schoolhouse. In our scenario the father has no respect for any type of education.)

The point of this exercise is that a psychotherapist is relatively impo-tent to effect change in a child when the parent in authority adamantly refuses to recognize the problem or do anything about it. For therapy to have the best chance of success with alienated children, we must have the equivalent of a truant officer. The force of the law must make itself felt in the consultation room. This is usually accomplished with court orders.

The Role of the Court

Effective court orders do more than merely appoint a therapist and require the child and parents to participate in treatment. The best court orders establish:

- Prohibitions against either parent's taking the child to see a ther-apist not mutually agreed upon or appointed by the court

- An exact schedule of contact between the child and each parent that gives the child sufficient time with the alienated parent

- Prohibitions against encroaching on the child's time with the other parent by arranging special activities that conflict with this time

- Clear procedures for how and where the parent-child contacts will take place

- Neutral transfer sites, such as the school, when open hostility between the parents is expected

- Low-conflict methods, such as E-mail and faxes, for the exchange of important information about the children, such as report cards and schedules of athletic games and scout meetings

- Restrictions and regulations on the alienating parent's contact with the child when the child is with the other parent

- A procedure to change the schedule as needed

- A mechanism through which the court can get information about the progress of treatment and the therapist's recommendations

- Explicit, specific, and clear penalties for failure to comply with the court's directives

This last point is crucial. The orders are effective only if they are enforced. Violations of the orders that go unpunished generally encourage the violator to continue to flout the authority of the court. Very often, court orders do not specify the consequences for failure to comply. I think this is a mistake. In most cases, it is better if both parents know ahead of time how the court will respond to violations.

The orders should include a continuum of consequences from less to more severe, with stiffer penalties for each subsequent offense. If a parent is very late in bringing a child to a scheduled transfer, the parent may have to assume more of the responsibility for driving the child to and from the other parent's home. If the child misses scheduled time with a parent, the orders can provide for makeup time.

Financial penalties can include the requirement that a parent pay fines, post a bond, or pay court costs and all attorneys' fees for extra court hearings that are needed to rule on violation of the orders. Some states grant courts the power to suspend the driver's license of people who are found in contempt of court orders or order them to perform community service. Other penalties include imprisonment or being placed under house arrest. The use of such punishments may seem harsh or excessive, but actually they are not that different from those the court would use against a parent who failed to pay court-ordered alimony or child support. In some cases the judge makes the alienating parent apologize to the children and the other parent in the courtroom and pledge not to interfere in their relationship again. Or the judge may have the parent write a letter of apology to other individuals who were involved in the campaign against the alienated parent, such as coaches and teachers who had been misled about the target.

When a parent repeatedly refuses to cooperate with the court orders and continues to obstruct the children's contact with the other parent, the court may transfer custody and severely restrict the children's contact with the alienating parent. Just the threat of this occurring may be enough to motivate the alienating parent and the children to change their behavior. The result may be the resumption of a positive relationship between the children and their other parent without a transfer of custody.

I worked with one family in which three girls refused to spend any time with their mother. After eighteen months of no contact, the mother filed a motion to obtain sole custody of the children. The judge gave her temporary custody of the children for the entire summer, ordered the family into therapy, and carefully regulated the children's access to their father. Over the next few months, as the children regained their affection for their mother, their contact with their father gradually increased until they were spending about equal amounts of time in each home. At this point, knowing that he could lose custody if the alienation returned, the father ceased his brainwashing.

Absence of Confidentiality

Usually when people consult a psychotherapist, they expect their communications to remain private. The rule of confidentiality is a cornerstone of doctor-patient trust. But therapy for divorce poison often requires a relaxation of this traditional rule. In order to effectively explore and resolve disagreements, the therapist must be free to bring up with one family member issues raised by the others. This does not mean that the therapist haphazardly reveals everything. One of the arts of conducting psychotherapy is deciding what, when, and how to reveal information. An experienced and good therapist (experience by itself is no guarantee of competence) uses discretion. Information is revealed when there is a good chance that the revelation will further the goals of therapy. Information is withheld when it is likely that the repercussions of revelation will cause more harm than good and interfere with the progress of treatment.

Everyone in the family also needs to know that, depending on the conditions of treatment set up by the court and the laws of your state, what goes on in therapy may be revealed to the attorneys and the judge. If parents are not able to resolve their dispute outside of court, the therapist's records may be subpoenaed and the therapist may be compelled to testify.

Of course, knowing that their words and behavior may be subject to the scrutiny of the court, parents are apt to be selective in what they say. They will try to appear cooperative and reasonable. They will hide behavior that would cast them in a bad light. They will present themselves as "new and improved" parents.

This type of posturing may not be entirely bad. In the process of trying to look good, people often become better parents. Everything they do to make a good impression on the judge can simultaneously benefit the children. They may be more attentive to the children than usual. They may be more patient. They may become more involved in school activities. They may be more supportive of their children's relationship with the other parent. All of these improvements, even if calculated to impress the court and gain advantage in a custody battle, can help the children.

Communication Between the Therapist and the Judge

One issue that must be decided prior to beginning treatment is how involved the therapist will be in court proceedings. Sometimes the therapist reports directly to the court if there are problems in the treatment, if a parent does not cooperate with court orders, or if the schedule of contact needs to be adjusted.

In one case, a therapist was appointed by the court to facilitate a child's relationship with his father after the child was kept from his dad for three years. The mother used the father's first name when talking with the child about him and told her son that the man was dangerous and evil. The therapist attempted to use a gradual approach to reunite the child with his father, while allaying the mother's concerns about her son's safety. When the therapy reached the point of having the child meet in a joint session with his father, the mother refused to cooperate and claimed that she would not force her son to be in the same room with such a horrible man.

The therapist informed the judge and the attorneys of the impasse. He suggested that the goal of healing the father-son relationship was feasible if the treatment plan included having the boy live with his father for a significant block of time and carefully regulating his contact with his mother. The judge went along with the therapist's recommendations. The mother, who was already upset with the therapist for even attempting to place the boy in the same room with his father, was now furious with the therapist. As a result, she did not benefit from subsequent therapeutic sessions. Her son was very upset with the judge's new order and initially withdrew from the therapist. After a very short time, though, the boy established a close bond with his dad and a warm relationship with the therapist. Eventually this boy was able to express love for both his father and his mother. And despite his mother's denigration of the therapist, the boy looked forward to his sessions and expressed regret when the treatment came to an end.

The obvious drawback to an arrangement where the therapist makes recommendations to the court is that as soon as the therapist does so she will be seen as taking sides in the dispute between the parents. If, for example, the therapist tells the court that the children are ready to spend more time with their maligned father, the children and their mother will see the therapist as an enemy. This will make it difficult for the therapist to keep them meaningfully involved in treatment. The father may also resent the therapist's testimony, believing that the therapist did not go far enough in supporting him or in criticizing the mother.

To circumvent this problem, some courts appoint another professional to oversee the progress of the case, talk with the therapist and other relevant people, such as the child's teacher, and make recommendations to the court when changes are needed. The therapist is explicitly shielded from participating directly in the litigation. Attorneys are not permitted to subpoena his records, and they cannot require him to testify in court. The "go-between" professional may be called a special master, a parenting plan coordinator, a case manager, or a guardian ad litem. Legal or mental health professionals can fill this role, depending on where the case takes place. When speaking to the court, in order to protect the therapist's relationship with the parents and children, this person attempts to conceal the exact source of information that led to the recommended changes. The hope is that the parents will continue to see the therapist as neutral in their disputes, and that the alienated children will not hold it against the therapist if the court requires them to spend more time with the hated parent.

In some cases this approach has merit, but it has at least three significant problems. First, even though an attempt is made to conceal the therapist's true opinions, the parents can usually figure out that something the therapist told the go-between led to the new court orders. Second, the legal requirement of due process may conflict with this model. In our courts a person has the right to confront the evidence that is used in a trial. If a case manager bases a recommendation on something the therapist has reported, both parents may have the right to know what that information is, and to put the therapist on the witness stand in order to verify the therapist's report. Third, this approach is more expensive, because it requires parents to pay for the services of the additional professional and to pay two fees when the go-between meets with the therapist.

There is a third option for a therapist's involvement in court proceedings that is something of a compromise between making recommendations in court versus avoiding any participation in the litigation. Under this option, the therapist testifies strictly about the current and past status of treatment, without offering any recommendations regarding such matters as the child's schedule of contact with each parent. When asked for such a recommendation, the therapist responds that she does not have all the information she would need to make a recommendation. If the therapist has worked with only one member of the family, and has had no communication with therapists of the other family members, this is probably accurate. If the therapist does have knowledge of the entire family system, though, she may not be able to testify honestly that she has no recommendations regarding the schedule.

Let us suppose that the therapist has concluded that a father is actively brainwashing his child against the mother and that the child's only hope for forming a more realistic view of his mother is to have a longer block of time with her than the every-other-weekend schedule currently in place. If the therapist is asked in court what it would take for the child to make progress toward the treatment goals, an honest answer would be to recommend a change in schedule. The only alternative is for all the attorneys in the case to agree not to require the therapist to offer a specific recommendation. Instead, another professional is appointed to make recommendations. These recommendations are based on his own investigations of the family, the therapist's account of the treatment and her opinions about the reasons for the lack of progress, and his own knowledge about how to reverse alienation. Although this third option keeps the therapist from having to endorse recommendations that one parent sees as unfavorable, the parents still hear the therapist's opinions about why the child has not made more progress. This testimony itself is likely to anger whichever parent is seen as contributing most to the lack of progress.

Models for providing treatment to high-conflict divorced families are in a very early stage of development. Different approaches are used in different parts of the country. At present there is no research that allows us to conclude which approach is best. My best guess is that each approach will work well in some situations and not as well in others. Because therapy with these families is such a delicate process, a difficult professional challenge even for the most experienced therapists, I recommend providing the additional insulation for the therapist if the family can afford it and the laws allow it. There may be a psychological advantage to having this cushion between the therapist and the court. Even when the parents know where the recommendations originate, it may sting less to hear a case manager or guardian ad litem make them than to read them in the therapist's report or hear the therapist make them from the witness stand. But I am not convinced that this insulation is essential, or even superior to the approach where the therapist is allowed to testify in court or report to the judge and attorneys on the current status of treatment and on recommendations for accelerating the progress of treatment.

Single versus Multiple Therapists

Another decision that must be made before beginning treatment is whether to have one therapist for the entire family or one therapist for each member of the family. Each approach has advantages and disadvantages.

Having one therapist instead of several saves a lot of expense. Also, it avoids problems that arise when more than one therapist is involved with a family. Twenty-five years ago Dr. Gardner wrote about the drawbacks of each parent's consulting a separate therapist. In recent years, other therapists have noted the same problems. Therapists who hear only one side of the story may lose their objectivity and adopt the distorted positions held by their patient. If they do so, they may contribute more to the problem of ruptured family relationships than to the solution. When a single therapist works with the entire family, there is less chance that the therapist will be taken in by each person's reality distortions. There is a greater chance that the therapist will have an active awareness of each person's contributions to the problems.

The major disadvantage of the single-therapist approach is that it is quite difficult to carry out successfully. The therapist must strive to understand each person's perspective, and communicate this understanding to each member of the family. At the same time, the therapist must promote changes in attitudes and healthier family functioning. This role is familiar to family therapists.

The therapy may flounder when the therapist conducts joint sessions with various family members. At least one of the participants is likely to be disappointed that the therapist was not more of an advocate for his position. If the therapist's input is seen as playing a role in court decisions, whichever parent was most unsatisfied with the court's actions will probably hold it against the therapist. It is easy to appreciate the delicate balancing act that a therapist must perform in order to simultaneously maintain the positive regard of the children and both parents over the course of treatment. If the problems in the family are too severe, if a person is too rigid and unyielding in his distortions of reality, even the most skilled therapist is likely to meet with failure.

To avoid these pitfalls, sometimes a separate therapist works with each member of the family. This approach has its own problems. In order to avoid the problems discussed above when a therapist hears only one side of a story, the therapists must remain in close contact with each other. They must schedule periodic conferences to keep each other informed of their progress and insights and to coordinate their efforts. Naturally, such conferences, in which each therapist charges for his time, add to the expense of the treatment. The logistics of coordinating the schedules of four or more professionals to locate a time for conferences often results in less than optimal communication among therapists. Even with good communication, the more therapists there are, the greater the chance that one of them will lose objectivity and accept the distortions of his patient. If this problem is not resolved early enough, it could sabotage the entire team's efforts.

I consulted on one case in which a therapist was taken in by his thir-teen-year-old patient's misrepresentations. The therapist became a strong and vociferous advocate for his patient. Despite the reservations expressed by the other therapists involved with the family, the therapist testified in court that his patient was afraid of his mother and should not be forced to spend time with her or even talk to her on the phone. The therapist recited a long list of alleged misbehavior by the mother that he thought justified his patient's alienation. In reality, the boy was extremely hostile toward his mother, openly denigrated her, and showed not the slightest fear in her presence. The allegations of her misconduct were typical distortions of an irrationally alienated child. In fact, the child was actually afraid of his father, whom he desperately tried to please by going along with the cam-paign of hatred against the mother. Not only did the therapist fail to help the boy repair his relationship with his mom, in his zeal to defend his patient's "right" not to see his mother, he overlooked the high price the boy was paying for his alienation. The longer the boy remained out of touch with his mom, the more his mental health deteriorated. Eventually, the boy became so depressed that he had to be hospitalized. Even then, the therapist insisted that the mother not be allowed to visit her son in the hospital. The boy did not begin to recover until he was assigned a new therapist, who worked toward reuniting mother and son.

If several therapists are going to be involved with the same family, it is easier if the therapists are all part of the same practice or close profes-sional associates. Communication is less of a problem because the group practice may hold regularly scheduled conferences to review their cases. When therapists have worked together for a long time, they are more receptive to each other's feedback. They are less likely to disrupt the team effort by overidentifying with their patient's distortions and becoming adversarial toward other family members and their therapists.

In our work with alienated children and their parents, my wife and I have developed a model that capitalizes on the strengths of both the sin-gle therapist and multiple therapist approaches, while minimizing the drawbacks of each. Both of us meet initially with each member of the fam-ily. We then divide up the therapeutic work. Some members of the family see my wife in therapy; the others meet with me. Usually one of us sees one parent, while the other sees the other parent and the children. When the parents meet together in a joint therapy session, both therapists are present. Both parents find it reassuring that their therapist participates in the joint session. Both parents feel that they have an ally. The odds that either one will walk away from a joint session feeling unsupported by his or her therapist are much less than with a single therapist. Yet the parents are unable to manipulate either of us to accept their distortions, because we have many opportunities to discuss between ourselves our impressions of the family. Thus, the treatment enjoys the benefits of the multiple-therapist approach, but does so without the great cost of having a separate therapist for each member of the family.

As with the issue of whether or not the therapist should have contact with the court, we don't yet have research studies that allow us to conclude whether it is better to have a single therapist, two therapists, or more. Some families will probably do best with one therapist. Other families will benefit from having the talent of several therapists at their disposal. The time to decide this issue is usually before treatment begins. The person who helps decide it is usually the mental health professional who first evaluates the entire family.

CHILD CUSTODY EVALUATIONS

If your family's problems with divorce poison reach the courthouse, the chances are that your first encounter with a court-appointed mental health professional will not be for therapy; it will be for a custody evaluation.

In order to sort out the cross-allegations that are common to disputes about child custody or child placement schedules, courts often appoint a mental health professional to conduct a thorough evaluation of the family. Depending on the provisions of the court order, the evaluator will send a report of the findings and recommendations to the judge, the attorneys, or both.

Court-ordered evaluations often play a pivotal role in the outcome of cases in which there is actual or alleged alienation. This is good if you have a competent and thorough evaluation. You can have confidence in an evaluator who

- treats you with respect and fairness
- takes enough time to get to know your family
- carefully investigates the history of family relationships

- uses more than one procedure to learn about your family, such as interviews and direct observations of you and your ex with the children

- gives you enough time to say what you need to say

- interviews other people who know your family

- administers, scores, and interprets psychological tests accurately (if tests are given) (You would not know this unless another professional reviews the evaluator's work.)

- seriously considers the possibility that your children have been subjected to divorce poison

- uses special procedures to bypass the potential effects of programming on the attitudes expressed by your children during the evaluation

- carefully investigates allegations of abuse and domestic violence

- does not automatically assume that in high-conflict divorces both parents are equally at fault

- develops a comprehensive and detailed understanding of the factors that have resulted in your child's alienation

- develops a balanced view of each parent's strengths and limitations

- understands that personality weaknesses in parents and less-than-perfect parenting skills do not ordinarily justify a child's total rejection

- clearly recognizes the importance of children's relationships with both parents

- does not allow personal, cultural, and gender biases to influence the evaluation

- does not rely on unproven psychological theories or misapplication of accepted theories (Again, you would not know this unless another professional tells you.)

- considers alternative interpretations for the findings

- pays attention to information that does not support the conclusions of the evaluation

- provides a clear explanation of the basis for conclusions and recommendations

- draws conclusions that are consistent with the information gathered in the evaluation

- makes recommendations that flow logically from the conclusions

If your evaluation meets these criteria, whether or not the findings and recommendations are what you had hoped for, I advise you to seriously consider using the evaluation to guide your resolution of your dispute.

Unfortunately, many custody evaluators appointed by a judge fail to meet these high standards. Many so-called impartial court-ordered custody and sex abuse evaluations are incomplete, incompetent, and far from impartial. They suffer from numerous and critical flaws that don't merely detract from their value but also seriously undermine the court's search for the optimal custody disposition.

What should you do if you have good reason to believe your evaluation was not fair or competent? First, discuss your concerns with your attorney. Many parents automatically dismiss conclusions and recommendations that are disappointing. Yet we all have blind spots that keep us from seeing ourselves as others see us. A good attorney will try to help you see things more objectively. If your attorney recommends that you accept the evaluator's recommendations, give this advice from your ally your most careful consideration. Your attorney may not be right, but you should certainly entertain the possibility that you are wrong.

After you first hear the examiner's findings, allow yourself time to process the information. It may help to seek the counsel of someone you trust to be objective, such as a therapist, a religious leader, or a wise relative who has stayed out of your family's conflict. You don't want to ask the opinion of friends or relatives who have joined in the tribal warfare. You already know they will take your side, and that is not what you need at this time.

Ask yourself if the examiner took all the important information into account. Were her statements factually correct? Did she discover reasons for your child's negative feelings that you had not thought of? Or did the evaluator place too much emphasis on your child's trivial excuses for the alienation, or on your child's wildest allegations about your behavior? Did the examiner attribute your child's alienation to your behavior, even though similar behavior in other divorced parents does not generally cause a child to be so totally rejecting? Did the examiner fail to consider that your child had a better relationship with you before your ex started bad-mouthing you, or before the divorce, even though you showed the same type of behavior and personality traits in the marriage that your child now sees as enough reason to reject you?

If after all this thinking and discussion you believe that your evaluator is mistaken, what should be your next step? Do what you would do in any other situation in which you were unsure of a doctor's recommendation. Get a second opinion. When I am asked for a second opinion, I will review as much information as possible to give parents, their attorneys, and the court a thorough analysis and critique of the evaluation.

As I wrote in *The Custody Revolution*, I am repeatedly chagrined at the incompetence that passes for professional work in this realm. Obvious biases are disguised as pronouncements of established scientific fact. Lawyers have a term for the serious-sounding deceptions of pseudo-science that trade on the respect accorded real science and masquerade as the real thing in court. The term is *junk science*. I am sorry to say that *junk science* is widespread in the work and testimony of court-appointed experts.

Inexperienced Evaluators

One reason it is so difficult to locate an excellent custody evaluator is that many of the professionals doing this work are inexperienced. Conducting a custody evaluation is a stimulating professional challenge. It is an opportunity for the professional to contribute meaningfully to the best interest of children caught in the crossfire of their parents' war. But the rewards of the challenge are soon outweighed by the mental anguish, the threats (of violence, malpractice suits, and complaints to licensing boards), the schedule disruptions necessitated by being on call to give testimony, and the unpaid bills that are part and parcel of this work. As a result, many seasoned veterans refuse court appointments for this work. Among those who remain in the field, a large percentage are handicapped by lack of experience.

The practice of managed care has driven many psychologists and psychiatrists into the courtroom. They are able to charge higher fees for their services, and they do not have to rely on third-party providers to approve their charges. Some of these evaluators have years of experience and finely honed skill in conducting evaluations and psychotherapy with their office patients. However, these skills do not automatically transfer to work that will influence custody dispositions.

An evaluation for court purposes requires different types of interview techniques and different approaches to interpreting the results of clinical examinations and psychological tests. One obvious difference: A psychotherapist must be concerned with building and maintaining a good relationship with the patient. This goal dictates the therapist's choices regarding the conduct of treatment, choices such as when to ask questions, when to probe for more details, when to challenge the patient, and when to allow contradictory statements to pass without comment. In gathering information for the court, however, the examiner is more concerned with getting specific details, resolving contradictions, and evaluating the credibility of the participants. The examiner can risk alienating a forensic client because the relationship will not continue past the litigation.

Another difference between purely psychotherapeutic work and work that involves legal decisions concerns the degree of confidence the expert must have in the opinions expressed. A therapist can afford to form a tentative hypothesis about a person's problems and share this with the patient. If the therapist is wrong, subsequent work will reveal this and allow the therapist to revise his or her interpretation. But when the interpretation influences a decision that will have a lifelong effect on the psychological welfare of all the participants, the expert had better have a higher degree of certainty before expressing an opinion. Usually no opportunity exists to correct errors.

Even professionals who are experienced in conducting custody evaluations and enjoy excellent reputations in their community are often weak when it comes to identifying the process of parental alienation. Special interview techniques are necessary to unmask systematic programming. Detailed knowledge of brainwashing helps the examiner know where and how to look for evidence of indoctrination. Many examiners lack this knowledge.

I hasten to add that there are many hardworking exceptional professionals whose contributions to the resolution of difficult child custody disputes are nearly priceless. But, as in any profession, there are also those whose work falls far below acceptable standards. A second opinion can help you and your attorney understand where an evaluator went wrong, and whether the errors were substantial enough to change the basic conclusions and recommendations. If so, your attorney will need to expose the flaws of the evaluation and ask for a new evaluation, or at least ask the court to give little if any weight to the evaluator's report and testimony.

But remember, don't be too quick to dismiss the evaluator's recommendations because they are not what you had hoped for. The evaluation report may be your last opportunity to avoid the spirit-sapping bitterness of a trial in the family law court, which one California judge described as "the place where they shoot the survivors." Don't let disappointment and anger lead you to irrationally cast aside the treasure of a good evaluation. In your quest for your children's love, it could be your biggest mistake.

PHASING IN VERSUS MOVING IN

Even among mental health professionals who agree that an alienated child should be forced to spend time with the rejected parent, there is disagreement about how to bring this about. Some therapists recommend beginning with brief contacts and then gradually expanding these. When alienation is not too severe, this may work. In many cases, though, I have found this not to be the best way to repair relationships.

As I have discussed several times throughout the book, divorce poison is most potent when the child is isolated from the target parent. A daylong or even weekend contact may be an insufficient antidote. Many alienated children require more time to emerge from the shadow of the alienating parent and respond positively to the target. When these children first arrive at the home of the alienated parent, if they are not loudly and rudely expressing their hatred, they are acting sullen, withdrawn, and emotionally frozen. Over time the icy barrier of their negative attitudes melts under the warmth of the parent's love and attention. Generally, the older the children the longer they maintain their angry withdrawal and the more time is needed for the thawing process.

When children have been isolated for several months or more from a parent with whom they previously enjoyed a close relationship, and they are now severely alienated, I have seen the most success when they are placed with that parent for at least one month. Rather than gradually phase in contact with the formerly loved parent, we reverse the process. The children move in at once and then gradually phase back into the life of the alienating parent. This assumes, of course, that the alienated parent can manage the responsibilities of caring for the children on a daily basis and can provide a good environment for the children. Also, this usually works best with children younger than fifteen years old.

While the children live with the target parent, I recommend carefully restricting and regulating their contact with the alienating parent. We begin with a period of no contact, followed by phone contact, then brief in-person supervised contacts, and then more extended contact. Everyone in the family is made aware that I will be constantly evaluating the progress the children make with the rejected parent and the impact of contact with the other parent on this progress. This serves as an incentive for both parents to minimize divorce poison, and it motivates the children to treat the rejected parent with greater respect. At first this better treatment may not be heartfelt. Nicer behavior toward the target, though, can awaken dormant warm feelings. Also, when the children are not outwardly rebuffing overtures of love, it makes it easier for the alienated parent to keep making those overtures.

In some cases the alienating parent continues active efforts to program the child against the target. If these efforts are successful, and retard or reverse the recovery process, the contacts are supervised, reduced, or temporarily eliminated. If the child's renewed bond with the target is strong enough to withstand efforts to poison it, the contacts with the alienating parent continue and are increased when appropriate.

Also, as mentioned in the previous chapter, the recovery of loving relationships is often easier when siblings are separated. The child who is least alienated is the first to move in with the rejected parent. When that relationship is on a strong footing, the other children are introduced into the alienated parent's home. In some cases, the other children spontaneously ask to spend time with their rejected parent when they see their sibling benefiting from the relationship.

Children who are poisoned against a formerly loved parent should not be confused with those who never had a relationship with a parent and whose other parent is not promulgating alienation. In cases, for example, when a parent who had previously abandoned an infant returns and claims the right to see the child, it is often best to expose the child to the parent in a gradual manner and allow the relationship to develop naturally. If the other parent supports the developing relationship, and the returning parent treats the child with sensitivity and understanding, this phasing-in approach will work best for everyone.

It is important to consider the individual circumstances of each case and craft a plan that fits the circumstances, rather than squeeze every family into the same treatment. Also, I remind the reader of the many conditions discussed in chapter 3 that are either not alienation or are not alienation that results from a parent's malignant influence. These conditions require different treatments from the ones prescribed in this book for victims of divorce poison.

The importance of reuniting children with the alienated parent does not necessarily mean that the children should permanently spend more time with the target parent than with the alienating parent or that legal custody should necessarily change. If efforts to reduce divorce poison are unsuccessful, the alienating parent will continue to do a poor job of supporting the children's relationship with the target. In other respects, though, the alienating parent may be better situated to manage the children. For example, a mother who influences her children to turn against their father may be more available during the school week to supervise the children. Or the father may have limited skills in dealing with the routines of the school week and easily lose his patience. The custody decision must ultimately rest on a careful consideration of all the factors that influence children's welfare and of each parent's capacity to provide a healthy growth-promoting environment. Certainly the emotional abuse I call divorce poison should weigh heavily in the decision. But it should not be the sole criterion to the exclusion of all other factors.

MOVING OUT OF ONE HOME WITHOUT MOVING INTO THE OTHER

In some families moving in with the alienated parent cannot be accomplished without incurring too great a risk of harm to the child. Yet if the child remains in the alienating parent's home he stands little chance of escaping divorce poison and renewing a bond with the other parent. In such cases courts can consider placing the child in another environment that serves simultaneously as a bridge to facilitate contact with the target parent and as a barrier to restrict and monitor contact with the alienating parent. Depending on the child's behavior and emotional status, this environment can range from the home of a relative or friend to a foster home, community shelter, boarding school, residential treatment center, or psychiatric hospital. The situation is analogous to the treatment of a truant child. If a parent is unsuccessful in getting a child to attend school on a regular basis, the child may eventually be removed from the home and placed in a foster home or more restrictive facility.

Candidates for a transitional placement are those children who threaten dire consequences if they are forced to see the alienated parent. They promise to defy the court order, run away, attempt suicide, or become violent. Some of these are idle threats, but they all must be taken seriously and properly evaluated. If the evaluator finds a substantial risk, or if a child has already successfully resisted court-ordered contact with the alienated parent, the child may be better off in a transitional facility. Also, a facility such as a hospital permits a more in-depth investigation of the risk of suicide. Other children are so filled with fear of the target parent that they are unable to subdue their panic long enough to experience the parent as benevolent. In this case, it helps them to be in the home of a relative who serves as a bridge to the irrationally feared parent. Again, let me stress that experienced mental health professionals should recommend and carry out treatment plans that are tailored to the circumstances of your family. Avoid one-size-fits-all solutions that end up fitting no one.

In his books for therapists, Dr. Gardner has described in detail how to use transitional sites to rebuild parent-child bonds. If your situation qualifies as high-risk, you will want the court to have this information. Ideally this knowledge will come to the court through the recommendations and testimony of a mental health professional.

When considering the option of a transitional site, it is important not to minimize the risks of harm to a child who is with the target parent. It is also important not to exaggerate the risks, however. Embittered parents who have lost custody often blame all their children's psychological problems on the court or the target parent. While we would expect a child caught in the maelstrom of divorce poison to carry the scars of battle, we have no reason to assume that the potential harm caused by reuniting with a parent is greater than the harm caused by losing that parent. In a study published by the American Bar Association, Dr. Stanley Clawar and Dr. Brynne Rivlin reached the same conclusion: "There are risks incumbent in any process; however, *a decision has to be made as to what is the greater risk.* It is usually more damaging socially, psychologically, educationally, and/or physically for children to maintain beliefs, values, thoughts, and behaviors that disconnect them from one of their parents . . . compared to getting rid of the distortions or false statements."

HIRING AN ATTORNEY

In most cases of severe alienation, working through the legal system is indispensable. It is equally indispensable to hire a good attorney to help you navigate the rough waters of this system. In fact, selecting the right attorney is at least as important as selecting the right therapist. It can mean the difference between success and failure in maintaining or reclaiming your bond with your child.

To save money, or simply because they do not have enough funds, some parents choose to represent themselves in custody litigation. I think this is a big mistake. Any case involving allegations of divorce poison, whether you are the accused, the accuser, or both, is not one in which to indulge Perry Mason fantasies. The difference between self-representation and attorney representation is like the difference between treating your own superficial cut and having major surgery. You can put a Band-Aid on a cut, but you do not perform surgery on yourself. Trying an alienation case is not a do-it-yourself operation.

I have sympathy for those who want to save themselves the expense of hiring a lawyer, but I much prefer to work with families in which each parent is represented by counsel. I will usually turn down a parent's request for trial assistance when he or she has no attorney. I know I am not the only custody expert who feels this way. A lawyer can help get unreasonable clients to be more reasonable. A good attorney, despite zealous advocacy for the client's position, will be better able than the client to maintain objectivity.

The best type of attorney to hire is one who believes in amicably settling family disputes. In chapter 4 I mentioned the model of practice known as "collaborative family law." Collaborative lawyers pledge to work exclusively for an out-of-court settlement. They have nothing financial to gain by going to court, because as soon as you decide to litigate rather than negotiate a settlement, collaborative lawyers by contract must withdraw from the case. The idea is to encourage an atmosphere of constructive and creative negotiations to help the family best weather the crisis of divorce. If you and your ex-partner choose at the outset to have a collaborative divorce, you will be taking a giant step in the direction of safeguarding the welfare of your children. The odds of your children's becoming alienated will be dramatically reduced.

Some lawyers who do not formally subscribe to the collaborative law model nevertheless have reputations for encouraging and supporting efforts to settle conflicts in a peaceful fashion. Find one of these to represent you. Try to avoid lawyers who generate unnecessary conflict and hostility. Your family already has enough of that.

In choosing a lawyer, find one who specializes in child custody matters. Any such attorney will have had a lot of experience with divorce poison. They may not be familiar with the term *parental alienation*, but you can educate them by showing them this book and encouraging them to refer to the Resources section.

Let your attorney know from the outset that you prefer to resolve your dispute out of court. If your child appears to be losing respect or affection for you, don't make the mistake of rushing into a legal battle before exploring other options. What you are seeing may not be alienation, and it may not be a result of divorce poison. The best thing to do is for you and your ex-spouse to consult a therapist. This would be a natural adjunct to a collaborative divorce.

If you think your ex is not committed to your active participation in the lives of your children, or your ex will not voluntarily participate in therapy, then you may have no choice but to seek help through the court. Speak to your attorney about getting the court to order an evaluation and treatment. The attorney can also help ensure the best conditions for treatment in line with the guidelines discussed earlier in this chapter. This may be your attorney's most important contribution toward resolving your child's alienation.

Psychotherapists, divorce attorneys, and family court judges agree that families with children who refuse to spend time with a parent present tough challenges. First we must determine if the child is truly alienated and, if so, why? Who is contributing to the alienation and how they are doing it? In some cases one parent is primarily responsible for the child's alienation. It may be the favored parent, who poisons the children's affections. Or it may be the rejected parent, whose treatment of the children is bad enough to push the children away. In other cases both parents, the children, and perhaps an earlier therapist have made substantial contributions to the rupture of the relationship. Either way, parents who are responsible for alienation almost always deny their role and blame the other parent. As we have seen, even if you are a relatively innocent victim of divorce poison, your mistakes can make things worse. I hope this book will help you take an active role in correcting the problem.

Even with full knowledge of the causes of alienation, the problem is extremely difficult to overcome. Some parents are so rigidly stuck on the notion that the other parent is worthless and that the children are better off without a parent, no therapist will be able to make a dent in their position. At the first sign that the therapist is not in perfect agreement with everything they say, they dismiss the therapist as biased or in collusion with the other parent. Some of these parents even accuse the judge of being in collusion with the therapist, the opposing attorney, and the target parent, or accuse the entire judicial system of being corrupt. If your ex-spouse exhibits signs of being this rigid and is unable to establish a trusting relationship with any competent therapist, you will most likely end up in court.

Make sure your attorney is experienced in trying these types of cases. If you have the misfortune to get a severely flawed custody evaluation, your attorney may want to hire a trial consultant to assist in the cross-examination of the evaluator. Also, the attorney may want to secure the services of an expert who can testify on general issues related to your case, such as the diagnosis and treatment of alienated children.

It is my hope that the advice in this book will help you maintain or reclaim your child's love and respect without the expense of professional assistance. But if your situation warrants it, you should not hesitate to avail yourself of the help good mental health professionals and good attorneys can provide. Years from now your children will thank you for your efforts.

CHAPTER 9
LETTING GO

For of all sad words of tongue and pen,
The saddest are these: "It might have been!"
—John Greenleaf Whittier, "Maud Muller"

This last chapter, the saddest in the book, is one I wish I did not have to write. If it applies to you it means that my advice has been insufficient in helping your children recover from alienation. It means that you have exhausted all efforts to reclaim your children's love. Perhaps we were too late. Their alienation is too severe and entrenched. Your ex is unable or unwilling to stop the bashing and brainwashing. Your attempts to get the court to intervene effectively have met with failure. Your ex has abducted the children and you can't locate them. Or some combination of the above. As a result, you may find yourself considering the option of giving up. And you may be encouraged in this direction by the mental health professionals who evaluate or treat your family.

I am sure it is clear by now that I am very conservative in recommending that parents throw in the towel and accept defeat. As I see it, some therapists have an astonishingly casual attitude about leaving children in the home of a brainwashing parent and terminating their contact with the other parent. These same therapists agree that the brainwashing is a form of emotional abuse. What puzzles me is why they are so willing to leave children in what is clearly an abusive environment when they would be the first to want to remove a child from a parent who is physically or sexually abusive.

I recognize that there are some families in which the children, particularly older adolescents, are thoroughly brainwashed, and all avenues of help are exhausted, so that a parent has no choice but to give up. I just urge all alienated parents and relatives, and all therapists who work with these families, not to wave the white flag of surrender too soon. Again I draw on the work of Dr. Clawar and Dr. Rivlin and their study published by the American Bar Association: "Caution must be exercised in judging that the point of no return has been reached. We have seen numerous cases where children have been successfully deprogrammed by making radical changes in their living arrangements—often with appropriate legal interventions."

WHEN TO LET GO

At some point, though, the sensible thing to do may be to withdraw your efforts, or at least postpone your efforts, to reunite with your children. Here are seven reasons why a loving parent would reach such a difficult and painful decision:

1. Your children are too alienated or emotionally unstable to return directly to your home, and a suitable transitional site is not available or affordable.

2. You have exhausted all legal channels to improve the situation.

3. The court recognizes that your children are unreasonably alienated but will not place them in your home long enough to allow them to emerge from the shadow of your ex's negative influence.

4. You have other children in your home who will suffer if you continue to expend emotional and financial resources on a battle that has little chance of success.

5. Your ex is so disturbed that a continuing battle could provoke him or her to violent action against the children or against you or other members of your family.

6. You have tried the advice given in this book and have met with repeated failure.

7. You are working with a therapist who clearly understands pathological alienation (regardless of what term is used to designate

it) and is dedicated to helping you repair your relationship with your children, but who has finally reached the point of advising you to consider letting go.

No one can make this decision for you. I have seen parents who were ready to quit when I thought they should continue to pursue reconciliation. And I have seen parents who persisted in their quest when I thought they were being unreasonably optimistic. They are your children. You must reach a decision that you can live with.

HOW TO LET GO

If you do decide to let go, here is some final advice to increase the odds that your decision will pay off in the long run. You should announce your decision in the most constructive manner possible. You want to leave the door wide open for your children's future return. If and when they eventually change their minds, you want to make sure that it is as easy as possible for them to act on the change. You don't want their anxiety or uncertainty to keep them from reaching out to you. The best way to do this is to let them know clearly and definitely that when the time comes for them to reunite, you will welcome them with open arms. You will celebrate their return, not castigate them for their absence. The reunion will be a joyous occasion, not a time for recrimination.

The announcement of your decision is best made in person. Although you may have no contact with your children, if you let them and your ex know that you want to meet just one more time in order to properly say good-bye, they may agree to the meeting. Some children will agree to attend a last meeting if it takes place in the presence of the therapist. As a last resort you can request a meeting in the attorney's office, in the judge's chambers, or in open court. If feasible, videotape the meeting and make a copy of the videotape for the children.

No template exists for the perfect parting session. But your good-bye to your children should include the following:

- Review your relationship, from conception to the present.

- Emphasize the pleasure you have received from your role as a parent.

- Describe some fond memories of the bond you used to enjoy.

- Emphasize your ongoing love for them despite their rejection of you.

- Let them know that you could continue to fight to see them, but that you think it is better for everyone if you admit defeat.

- Announce that you have decided to stop pressuring them for contact.

- Express your grief at the way things turned out (expect to cry; don't hold back your tears).

- Invite them to contact you by any means in the future when they are ready.

- Make it clear that you have not given up hope of a relationship.

- Tell them that you will keep them posted with changes in your home and E-mail addresses and phone numbers in the hope that they will some day reach out to you.

- Designate a third party, usually a relative, through whom you will communicate messages if you are unsure your communications are getting through to them.

- Let them know that you will never stop loving them and that you will be sending birthday cards every year to let them know that you are thinking of them.

Whether or not you have the opportunity to say good-bye in person, it is important to say good-bye in writing as well. Your children should have something to hold on to, to look at from time to time, rather than have to rely solely on memory. Your letter should be handwritten to emphasize its personal nature. And it should be on nice stationery, in accordance with its importance. This is a document you hope your children will retain. Be sure to save a copy of your letter. In the future your children may deny ever having received it. In fact, there is a good chance that your note will be demeaned and ridiculed by your ex. If so, the children may feel obligated to demonstrate their loyalty by similarly dismissing the letter, and even destroying it. Because of this possibility, you might want to mail a copy of the letter each year along with a card wishing your child a happy birthday.

If you do not get the chance to say good-bye in person, consider preparing a farewell video on tape or CD-ROM. In addition to including the points from your letter, the video can show photographs of better times and objects that have special significance for your bond with your children. The video can also include messages from other relatives who have been rejected.

Pay careful attention to the nuances of your communications. Sometimes words convey an impression different from the one intended. Have someone review the letter and video and make suggestions for improvement. If you or your children have been working with a therapist, ask the therapist to read the letter and make suggestions for improvement. One father wrote a letter with the phrase, "You know my number if you want to get in touch." The words suggested an indifference that was light-years apart from the father's intense pain and longing for his child. After our discussion he changed it to, "My heart aches for the day when you decide to call me."

Every year on April 2, Ann Landers's Reconciliation Day, clip her newspaper column and send it to your children with a note. The note should say that you want to follow Ann's advice and make contact, but you do not want to be seen as applying pressure. So you are sending the note with a reminder that you would be thrilled to hear from them.

The Question of Gifts

Alienated parents ask whether they should give expensive gifts to their children in an effort to maintain some tie. This is an individual matter. There is no clear-cut right or wrong answer. I generally recommend giving small thoughtful presents and greeting cards to mark an occasion and to let the children know you are thinking of them. Such signs of your ongoing love may be reassuring to the children, notwithstanding their overt rejection. It certainly reminds them that you are still waiting in the wings for their return and have not counterrejected them.

The problem with expensive gifts is that it gives the children an opportunity to exploit you. They usually will not even acknowledge receipt of the gifts and certainly will not express appreciation. By continuing to give presents to children who show no gratitude, and in fact cruelly reject you, you may be encouraging and supporting an unhealthy sense of entitlement.

Should You Pay for College?

This is another difficult question. If your children want to forgo a relationship, they ought to be prepared to forgo the financial benefits of the relationship. What does it mean if they want to have nothing to do with you, except to have their hands in your wallet? What lesson do you teach if you fund their college education, knowing that you will not even be welcome at the graduation ceremonies? On the other hand, if a child regards a college education as a necessity of life, like food on the table, withholding the funds, if you can readily afford it, may create so much more animosity that it dashes any hope of a future reconciliation. If there is a renewal of bonds in the future, it may be too late for them to attend college. So you might want to fund the college education, hoping that your children eventually will understand this as an act of love and caring. There is really no one right course of action. You will have to do what seems right. I do recommend that if you contribute to college expenses, it should be for the barest essentials—tuition, books, and lodging—and not extra frills and luxuries. After all, by this time your children will be adults and should expect to experience the reasonable consequences of unreasonably rejecting you.

STAYING IN TOUCH AFTER LETTING GO

Severely alienated children usually resent any attempt by the rejected parent to have contact with them. They regard phone calls as "harassment" and claim to be very upset if they spy their parent in the stands at a high school football game or in the audience during graduation.

Sometimes, though, after their parent has agreed to cease efforts to see them in person, the children will agree to take phone calls and read rather than tear up letters. Whether or not the children agree, I encourage parents to make periodic attempts to reach out to their children with phone calls, cards, and letters, unless the court has prohibited such contact. How often you do this depends on the response you get. If the calls are tolerated, keep them up. If you attend your child's special events, such as athletic games and school performances, send a note of congratulations with attention to specific aspects about your child's performance.

When you acknowledge specific details, this lets your child know that you really paid attention and that you are not just going through the motions of offering praise.

Also, I suggest reaching out to your children during significant milestones in their lives, such as birthdays, graduations, weddings, and the birth of their own children, your grandchildren. There is a good possibility that you won't even know when such events take place. But with luck, the benevolent emotion surrounding such events may leave your child receptive to "burying the hatchet" and renewing ties. The downside of this recommendation is that severely alienated children will resent such attempts and feel that the rejected parent is intruding and spoiling their happy occasion. If the alienation is irrational, I regard this as one price the children pay for their cruel and unreasonable rejection of their mother or father.

Consider maintaining a website on which you post photos from your current life, along with old photos of the family together. Send the address of your website to your children. They could then "visit" you without the discomfort of having direct contact. Eventually these visits may chip away at their armor.

NEW BRIDGES

In chapter 7 I discussed using another person as a bridge between alienated children and parents. If you have decided to let go, I assume your attempts to use such bridges have proved unsuccessful. I urge you to encourage any friends and relatives who still have relationships with your children to maintain them. They may be your only link to the children, keeping you informed about them and delivering your messages and gifts to them.

As your children grow up they will form new attachments. The new people in their lives may have more success facilitating a renewal of bonds. This is especially true of your adult child's new spouse and in-laws. You may find that these people have sympathy for your loss and will become your ally. They may hold the key to healing the relationship between you and your children. Certainly you should appeal to them for help.

In most cases your children have either not spoken much about you or have presented a horribly distorted image of you. Even without that image the in-laws might assume that you must be a very bad parent to have alienated your children. So your first step after making contact with them is to disabuse them of this false idea. Open their minds by educating them about the impact of divorce poison. Share this book with them to help them understand how children could come to so totally reject a parent without good reason.

Ask them to tell you what they have heard about why, for example, you were not invited to the wedding of a child. If the reasons are the trivial ones usually given by alienated children, emphasize the irrationality of disowning a parent over such trivial matters. If they have heard that you were abusive or violent, offer to provide evidence disproving the accusations. Point out that such accusations and innuendos are common weapons in a custody battle. Most important, show them how it furthers their own interests if your child overcomes the alienation.

ALIENATED CHILDREN AS ADULTS

Irrationally alienated children harbor hatred for a parent that is dissociated from their earlier love for that parent. Their internal mental state has a rift that cannot heal until it is acknowledged. Psychologists call such rifts *unresolved feelings* or *unresolved relationships* to signify their unprocessed state. Most alienated children have not come to terms with their feelings for their parents; they have merely parked their feelings on a mental shelf and tried to ignore them. Their lack of ambivalence toward the target is the tip-off.

Adults who have truly suffered at the hands of inadequate parents and subsequently resolved their feelings are able to express a wide range of feelings about their parents: love, sympathy for the parents' own early deprivation that contributed to their deficits as parents, regret for what was missed, anger for the mistreatment they suffered. This is something a pathologically alienated person is unable to do, and it handicaps them in their most important personal relationships.

Psychotherapists know that, in general, adults who are more aware of their loving feelings for their parents have more love to give their spouses and families. They make better husbands and fathers and sons-in-law, or mothers and wives and daughters-in-law.

Let me use the example of a son alienated from his father, with the understanding that the same principles apply to daughters of fathers and to sons and daughters of mothers. A man who is out of touch with his loving feelings for his father has more difficulty promoting the highest-quality loving relationship with his own children.

- A man who cannot appreciate the importance of his father in his life, and of what he loses by not having a father, has more difficulty appreciating his own importance in his children's lives.

- A man who cuts himself off from his own feelings is less sensitive to the feelings of his wife and his children.

- A man who has no contact with his father and extended family deprives his own children of a grandparent and his wife of the support available through the extended family.

The saddest consequence of divorce poison occurs when a rejected parent or grandparent dies before the child has come to his senses, given his love, apologized for his mistreatment, and expressed regret for the lost years. It is at this point that a child is most apt to resent the brainwashing parent whose efforts deprived the child of a relationship that cannot be recaptured.

When alienated children, as adults, eventually realize what they have missed out on and the immense magnitude of the hurt their behavior has caused their loved ones, they suffer an unbearable guilt and sadness. This suffering has a direct effect on their marriage and on their children. This is one more reason why the new spouse and in-laws have a personal stake in fostering a rapid reconciliation.

One of the unfortunate legacies of divorce is that the children of divorced parents are more likely to have their own marriages end in divorce. No one knows for sure why this is so, but one factor may be the example set by walking away from a problematic relationship rather than living with conflicts or resolving them.

If children of divorce are more likely to end a marriage rather than work out conflicts, this risk is multiplied for children who have totally rejected a parent. They already have experience treating someone they used to love as dispensable. Their spouses have a personal interest in impressing upon them the importance of maintaining important relationships. Adults who overcome their alienation from a parent and who learn that obstacles in a relationship are to be surmounted and not avoided will have a greater commitment to the sanctity of family and are more likely to maintain their wedding vows despite the inevitable hassles, upsets, and hurts that all couples experience.

COPING WITH THE LOSS

The death of one's child is said to be the most difficult loss to accept. Eventually, though, most bereaved parents do accept their loss and complete a healthy process of mourning. Their pain, though still present, exists in muted form. Some people believe that the bereavement of alienated parents is more complicated and drawn out and difficult to resolve. Their child is gone, but they cannot be sure the child is gone forever. Not having directly experienced either tragedy, I won't attempt to say which hurts more. But I can say that therapists who work with parents who have lost children to divorce poison note the tremendous grief they encounter in trying to help these parents accept their loss.

In his book *Father and Child Reunion*, Dr. Warren Farrell writes about the grief suffered by divorced fathers whose children reject them. He compares their situation to that of grief-stricken relatives who cannot begin their mourning process until the body of the deceased is located. The lack of finality keeps them in limbo—heartbroken yet unable to complete a mourning process. My work with alienated mothers has taught me that the pain is no less intense for them. In addition to the loss of contact with the children is the agony that comes from knowing that your children could be living three minutes away yet be no more available to you than if they lived on Mars.

Parents in this situation must grieve their loss as they would the death of their child. The parting communication—whether in person, by letter, or by video—helps in the mourning process because it forces parents to publicly acknowledge that their children are, at least for now, gone. Like a memorial service, this formal ending unleashes the expression of grief and the acceptance of loss.

Healthy mourning requires sympathetic listeners to whom the bereaved can express their pain. As a rejected parent, though, you may have trouble getting this sympathy. You are in such a unique position that those around you may not fully comprehend what you are going through. They may lose patience with your grief and urge you to get on with life. Of course they are right that you should not wallow in your pain, but the timetable of when to move on, and the manner in which you do it, is yours to determine.

Many parents ask me about support groups for people in their situation. Check with the organizations listed in the Resources section at the end of this book to locate such a group in your area. People who have traveled the same painful path will be most sympathetic to your loss and most understanding of what you are going through.

It is important that you do not let yourself become mired in anger and bitterness. Indeed, such bitterness will be mistaken by others as the reason your children avoid you. Instead find a productive outlet for your anger. Perhaps in concert with other parents you can work to get laws passed that provide sanctions to discourage parents from violating custody orders, just as there are punishments for parents who avoid child support obligations. Or you may help set up local facilities that offer transitional sites for the reunification of alienated parents and children. Or perhaps you can raise funds to provide educational, therapeutic, and legal services to needy families in these situations.

Do not let the trauma of your loss keep you from achieving gratification in other areas of life. Do not let your awareness of the fragility of relationships create barriers to close emotional investment in others. If you have a spouse, other children, or stepchildren, bask in their love as you allow them to reap the benefits of yours.

HOPE FOR THE FUTURE

Therapists who encourage alienated parents to acquiesce to their children's demands for an end to the relationship usually attempt to console parents by raising their hopes for a future reconciliation. Many, many alienated parents receive advice to back off and give their children time, with the Pollyannaish prediction that eventually the children will drop their angry stance and renew their ties. The problem is that we really don't know if this is true. No one knows the prevalence of such changes of heart. What we can say for certain is that even if a child eventually reconciles with a parent, nothing can make up for the lost years. Nothing can make up for what both parent and child missed: hugs and kisses, shared laughter and shared tears, pride and poignance of special occasions—communion, bar mitzvah, graduation—all the everyday interactions and all the milestones that form the fabric of a relationship.

Therapists are not completely wrong, though, in holding out hope to victims of divorce poison. Some children do change their minds. Some children do come to a realization that they have been brainwashed. Some children do come back. We have yet to identify the factors that can help us predict which children will eventually return and which will stay lost forever. But we can take some comfort in knowing that there is some reason for hope.

To prepare for the possibility of their children's return, some parents keep a diary or scrapbook filled with thoughts about the children and clippings of things that would interest the children. Such a project brings your absent children into your daily life. The hope is that someday when your children return and see the scrapbook, they will know that they have never been out of your heart, never been absent from your thoughts. The drawback to this project is that it could keep you focused on your loss and steal your attention from the many positive things life has to offer. If so, this exercise is not for you. But if it allows you to integrate the tragedy in your life while freeing you to affirm life's value, it could be a most elegant solution to your grief.

Victims of divorce poison who await the return of their beloved children might take comfort in the words of Rudyard Kipling from his great poem, "If":

> If you can keep your head when all about you
>   Are losing theirs and blaming it on you,
> If you can trust yourself when all men doubt you,
>   But make allowance for their doubting too;
> If you can wait and not be tired by waiting,
>   Or being lied about, don't deal in lies,
> Or being hated, don't give way to hating . . .
>
> If you can bear to hear the truth you've spoken
>   Twisted by knaves to make a trap for fools,
> Or watch the things you gave your life to, broken,
>   And stoop and build 'em up with worn-out tools . . .
>
> If you can force your heart and nerve and sinew
>   To serve your turn long after they are gone,
> And so hold on when there is nothing in you
>   Except the Will which says to them: "Hold on!"

Finally, I hope that any alienated children old enough to read this book will recognize themselves in it and exercise the wisdom and courage to reach out to the hearts that yearn for them. Nothing could be more important. Nothing could make me more thankful for the years I invested in writing this book.

RESOURCES

ORGANIZATIONS

American Academy of Matrimonial Lawyers
50 N. Michigan Avenue, Suite 2040
Chicago, IL 60601
Phone: 312-263-6477
www.aaml.org

Association of Family and Conciliation Courts
6515 Grand Teton Plaza, Suite 210
Madison, WI 53719-1048
Phone: 608-664-3750
www.afccnet.org

Bonus Families
www.bonusfamilies.com
A Web site for stepfamilies.

Children's Rights Council
300 "I" Street NE, Suite 401
Washington, DC 20002
Phone: 202-547-6227
www.gocrc.com

Creative Therapeutics
www.rgardner.com

The website is that of Richard A. Gardner, M.D., and includes a frequently updated bibliography and list of legal citations on parental alienation syndrome.

International Academy of Collaborative Professionals
163 Miller Avenue, Suite 4
Mill Valley, CA 94941
Phone: 415-383-5600
www.collabgroup.com

National Association of Non Custodial Moms, Inc.
www.noncustodialmoms.com/PAS%20Page.htm

National Center for Missing and Exploited Children
Charles B. Wang International Children's Building
699 Prince Street
Alexandria, VA 22314-3175
Phone: 703-274-3900; 800-THE-LOST (843-5678)
www.missingkids.com

A national clearinghouse of information and assistance on missing, abducted, and exploited children.

National Register of Health Service Providers in Psychology
1120 G Street NW, Suite 330
Washington, DC 20005
Phone: 202-783-7663
www.nationalregister.org

Shared Parenting Information Group
home.clara.net/spig

Stepfamily Association of America
650 J Street, Suite 205
Lincoln, NE 68508
Phone: 800-735-0329
www.stepfam.org

U.S. Department of State, Office of Passport Services
Office of Children's Issues
2401 E Street NW, Room L127
Washington, DC 20037
Phone: 202-736-7000
http://travel.state.gov/passport_assistance.html
http://travel.state.gov/int'lchildabduction.html

If you fear that your child might be abducted and taken abroad, you can place your child's name in the name-check system. If an application is received, you will be informed before the passport is issued. If you have provided a court order that forbids your child's travel without the consent of both parents or the court, the passport office may deny issuance of the passport. The second URL offers a free pamphlet for parents whose children have been internationally abducted.

RECOMMENDED READING FOR CHILDREN

Brown, Laurene Krasny, and Brown, Marc. *Dinosaurs Divorce*. Boston: Little, Brown and Company, 1986.

Gardner, Richard A. *The Boys and Girls Book About Divorce*. New York: Bantam Books, 1970.

RECOMMENDED READING FOR PARENTS

Abduction

Greif, Goeffrey, and Hegar, Rebecca L. *When Parents Kidnap*. New York: Free Press, 1993.

Custody and Divorce

Ahrons, Constance R. *The Good Divorce*. New York: HarperCollins, 1994. Sets the standard for loving parents who want to move from a failed marriage to a successful divorce.

Biller, Henry B., and Trotter, Robert J. *The Father Factor*. New York: Pocket Books, 1994.

Blau, Melinda. *Families Apart: Ten Keys to Successful Co-Parenting*. New York: Perigee, 1995.

Farrell, Warren. *Father and Child Reunion: How to Bring the Dads We Need to the Children We Love*. New York: Tarcher/Putnam, 2001.

Gold, Lois. *Between Love and Hate: A Guide to Civilized Divorce.* New York: Plenum Press, 1992.
  True to its subtitle, this practical and powerful guide helps parents communicate, cooperate, negotiate, and resolve conflicts.

Kalter, Neil. *Growing Up with Divorce: Helping Your Child Avoid Immediate and Later Emotional Problems.* New York: Free Press, 1990.

Lyster, Mimi. *Child Custody: Building Agreements that Work.* Berkeley, Calif.: Nolo Press, 1995.

Stahl, Philip M. *Parenting After Divorce.* Atascadero, Calif.: Impact Publishers, 2000.

Teyber, Edward. *Helping Your Children with Divorce.* New York: John Wiley & Sons, 2001.

Visher, Emily, and Visher, John. *How to Win as a Stepfamily.* New York: Brunner/Mazel, 1991.

Warshak, Richard A. *The Custody Revolution.* New York: Simon & Schuster, 1992.

Parenting

Faber, Adele, and Mazlish, Elaine. *How to Talk So Kids Will Listen and Listen So Kids Will Talk.* New York: Avon Books, 1999.

Ginott, Haim G. *Between Parent and Child.* New York: Macmillan, 1965.

—*Between Parent and Teenager.* New York: Macmillan, 1972.

Gordon, Thomas. *Parent Effectiveness Training.* New York: Three Rivers Press, 2000.

Gurian, Michael. *The Good Son: Shaping the Moral Development of Our Boys and Young Men.* New York: Tarcher/Putnam, 2000.

Pruett, Kyle D. *Fatherneed: Why Father Care Is as Essential as Mother Care for Your Child.* New York: Free Press, 2000.

Turecki, Stanley. *The Difficult Child.* New York: Bantam Books, 1989.

Negotiation

Stone, Douglas; Patton, Bruce; Heen, Sheila; and Fisher, Roger. *Difficult Conversations: How to Discuss What Matters Most.* New York: Penguin Press, 2000.

Uri, William. *Getting Past No: Negotiating Your Way from Confrontation to Cooperation.* New York: Bantam, 1993.

Relocation

Cohen, Miriam Galper. *Long-Distance Parenting: A Guide for Divorced Parents.* New York: Signet, 1991.

Newman, George. *101 Ways to Be a Long-Distance Super-Dad*. Mountain View, Calif.: Blossom Valley Press, 1984.

(To order, write Blossom Valley Press, PO Box 4044, Blossom Valley Station, Mountain View, CA 94040.)

Wasserman, Selma. *The Long-Distance Grandmother: How to Stay Close to Distant Grandchildren*. Point Roberts, Wash.: Hartley & Marks, 1990.

RECOMMENDED READING FOR MENTAL HEALTH PROFESSIONALS AND ATTORNEYS

Ceci, Stephen J., and Bruck, Maggie, *Jeopardy in the Courtroom: A Scientific Analysis of Children's Testimony*. Washington, D.C.: American Psychological Association, 1995.

Clawar, Stanley S., and Rivlin, Brynne V. *Children Held Hostage: Dealing with Programmed and Brainwashed Children*. Chicago: American Bar Association, 1991.

Gardner, Richard A. *Family Evaluations in Child Custody, Mediation, Arbitration, and Litigation*. Cresskill, N.J.: Creative Therapeutics, 1989.

——*The Parental Alienation Syndrome: A Guide for Mental Health and Legal Professionals* (2nd ed.). Cresskill, N.J.: Creative Therapeutics, 1998.

——*Therapeutic Interventions for Children with Parental Alienation Syndrome*. Cresskill, N.J.: Creative Therapeutics, 2001.

Garrity, Carla B., and Baris, Mitchell A. *Caught in the Middle: Protecting the Children of High-Conflict Divorce*. New York: Lexington Books, 1994.

Gould, Jonathan W. *Conducting Scientifically Crafted Child Custody Evaluations*. Thousand Oaks, Calif.: Sage Publications, 1998.

Johnston, Janet R., and Kelly, Joan B. (Eds.) "Alienated Children in Divorce." *Family Court Review*, 2001, 39 (3).

Poole, Debra A., and Lamb, Michael E. *Investigative Interviews of Children*. Washington, D.C.: American Psychological Association, 1998.

Rand, Deidre C. "The Spectrum of Parental Alienation Syndrome" (parts I and II). *American Journal of Forensic Psychology*, 15, no. 3 (1997):23–51 and no. 4 (1997):39–92.

Warshak, Richard A. "Social Science and Children's Best Interests in Relocation Cases: *Burgess* Revisited." *Family Law Quarterly*, 2000, 34(1), 83–113.

Warshak, Richard A. "Blanket Restrictions: Overnight Contact Between Parents and Young Children." *Family and Conciliation Courts Review*, 2000, 34, 396–409.

Warshak, Richard A. "Current Controversies Regarding Parental Alienation Syndrome." *American Journal of Forensic Psychology*, 2001, 19, 1–31.

Warshak, Richard A. "Misdiagnosis of Parental Alienation Syndrome." *American Journal of Forensic Psychology*, 2002, 34, 396–409.

INDEX

ABOUT THE AUTHOR

Dr. Richard A. Warshak is a clinical, consulting, and research psychologist in private practice in Dallas, Texas, clinical full professor of psychology at the University of Texas Southwestern Medical Center, and past president of the Dallas Society for Psychoanalytic Psychology. He earned his B.S. from Cornell University and his Ph.D. from the University of Texas Health Science Center in 1978.

Since 1976, Dr. Warshak has studied the impact of divorce and remarriage. His work has been published in numerous scientific and legal books and journals and he is frequently invited to lecture to professional groups. His studies, landmark work in child custody research, are cited often in courtrooms and legislatures throughout the world, and he was invited to the White House to discuss custody reform.

Dr. Warshak evaluates and treats children, adults, and families, and consults in custody disputes. In addition to his office practice, Dr. Warshak consults with attorneys, mental health professionals, and parents around the world on child custody matters and he serves as an expert witness in selected cases.

His 1992 book *The Custody Revolution* advocates fundamental reform of our custody policies and offers practical advice to parents and professionals dealing with custody decisions.

He has appeared on *Today, Weekend Today, CNN,* and the *Home Show,* and his work has been covered in *Time, Parade, Psychology Today, Parents, The London Sunday Telegraph,* the *Los Angeles Times, Washington Post, USA Today, Chicago Tribune, Boston Herald, Boston Sunday Globe, Dallas Morning News, Redbook, Men's Health, Parenting,* and *Working Mother.*

His website, www.warshak.com, offers reprints of his articles, chapters, essays, and lectures on various aspects of child custody and divorce; the Divorce Poison Control Center, which contains frequently updated suggestions for helping alienated children and their parents; announcements of upcoming appearances and articles by Dr. Warshak; instructions for arranging office and telephone consultations with Dr. Warshak; and resources for parents and legal and mental health professionals.

Dr. Warshak lives and works with his wife in Dallas, Texas. He can be reached at:

Richard A. Warshak, Ph.D.
16970 Dallas Parkway, Suite 202
Dallas, TX 75248
www.warshak.com

About the Authors

Barbara Salsbury

Best-selling author Barbara Salsbury, a nationally recognized personal-preparedness expert, is one of America's leading authorities on self-reliance. For more than twenty-five years, she has been teaching self-reliance and showing people how to get more for their money. In November 2002, *Family Circle Magazine* named her one of the "Top Five Penny-Pinchers in America."

She has produced two national newsletters and three videos. In addition, she is the author of seven books, including *Just Add Water, Just in Case*, and *Plan, not Panic.*

Active in church and community, Barbara serves as a personal preparedness consultant for Sandy, Utah, and has served as assistant director for San Francisco Key Cities-Area Public Affairs for The Church of Jesus Christ of Latter-day Saints. She and her husband, Larry, live in Sandy, Utah. They have two children, seven grandchildren, and two spoiled dogs.

Sandi Simmons

Sandi Simmons is a freelance writer. She has written numerous articles, scripts, and newsletters, including a national e-newsletter, "Preparedness Perspectives." She and her husband, Tom, live in Sandy, Utah, with their four children.

Photo of Barbara Salsbury used with permission from MarDel Photography

Beating the High Cost of Eating

Beating the High Cost of Eating
The Essential Guide to Supermarket Survival

Barbara G. Salsbury
with
Sandi Simmons

ISBN: 0-88290-786-7
v.1

Published by Horizon Publishers,
an imprint of Cedar Fort, Inc.
925 N. Main Springville, Utah, 84663
www.cedarfort.com

Distributed by:

Cover design by Nicole Williams
Cover design © 2005 by Lyle Mortimer

Printed in the United States of America
10 9 8 7 6 5 4 3 2 1

Printed on acid-free paper

Disclaimer: The names of any companies, brands, products, or periodicals mentioned or displayed herein are used as examples only, with no criticism or endorsement intended.

Contents

Introduction

If you shop at a grocery store, this book is for you! Without any games, gimmicks, or coupons, you can easily save more than the cost of this book within one month by following the simple principles presented here. *Beating the High Cost of Eating* is an all-out campaign to put buying power back in your pocket. It presents proven strategies to get the most from your grocery dollar, beginning with your very next paycheck. As you read, you will gain a new perspective that will have a significant impact on your buying power. Your shopping skills will expand, and your buying power will increase by at least 33 percent as you follow the step-by-step instructions outlined.

Beating the High Cost of Eating is based on more than 20 years of experience and research, including in-trade data, reports, advertising, and trade journals. This is not a typical how-to-shop book. It is a money-management program that deals with the core of everyone's money: the grocery budget. In essence, it is a self-help workshop.

The principles of smart shopping have been a passion with me for most of my life. While my girlfriends collected dishes, linens, and silverware in anticipation of a future marriage, my hope chest was filled with 10-pound bags of sugar and flour—purchased, of course, on sale. On my wedding day, I had an eight-month supply of groceries.

Our budget as newlyweds and the arrival of two children kept my penny-pinching skills sharpened. We managed unexpected financial dips by paying bills with grocery money and eating extra food I had on hand. But one year we suffered a string of financial disasters. Within a three-month period, my husband, my son, and I were hospitalized. A few months later, I was in the hospital again, for major surgery.

At the same time, my husband changed jobs, which required a move from southern California to northern California. We began preparing to sell our house—only to discover we had been caught in a land fraud and did not really own it. We packed our things to leave but were robbed one evening while we were out of the house. We traveled to a new city with almost nothing except the doctor bills that were still arriving weekly. My super shopping methods, which I had begun to share with friends, were severely put to the test.

Thinking such financial disaster could not strike twice, we were caught by surprise when my husband was laid off four years later. This time, we were determined not to settle for a job that was at the mercy of the economy. After careful consideration, we made the decision to return to school for a university degree.

Sending my husband to school meant the support of our family of four became my responsibility. Since I was determined to not work full time outside of the home while my children were still young, I chose to pursue lecturing and writing on the shopping concepts I had developed. During those college years, we lived on less than $5,000 a year, well below the national poverty level of $6,200. Since our paydays came from royalties from a small book I had written, we were paid only twice a year, in January and July. We never knew how much would come: 25 cents or $2,500. But whatever the amount, it had to be budgeted for the next six months for *all* expenditures. Grocery shopping and money management became my in-home business, and I spent many hours following and honing the principles I preached. Because of these principles, we were able to live without the assistance of government programs with all of our needs met and even a few of our wants.

Since those days, I have lectured across the country on the guidelines presented in this book. The advice is not based on gimmicks or fads or luck but on principles that can be applied to any budget and any situation. The solutions are not miraculous; they require effort and habit changes. But even applying part of them can stretch your grocery dollars significantly.

If you want to learn how to reduce your grocery bills without lowering your standard of living, read this book. Its principles work.

I have lived them for years. To help you implement these principles, I have included several helpful worksheets and charts in the appendix. Using these worksheets and charts is what will make this book—and its principles—yours.

Finally, the names of any companies, brands, products, or periodicals mentioned or displayed herein are used as examples only, with no criticism or endorsement intended.

Section One
Things to Know

1

Begin Your Campaign:
Beat the High Cost of Eating

Skyrocketing prices. Inflated costs. Always more month than money. Doesn't it seem as if you could spend your total food budget in half the time it took only a few years ago? And the amount of groceries that you purchase seems more likely to fill a thimble than a cupboard. Isn't there anything you can do about it? Plenty! And you've come to the right place.

There are no magic words to stretch your grocery dollars further, and I don't have a money tree in my backyard, but I am going to share the next-best thing with you: how to beat the high cost of eating!

You'll find a lot of advice these days about how to shop and save. However, when it comes to grocery shopping, most of what you'll hear is vague tips like, "Make a list," "Buy the specials," and "Don't shop on an empty stomach." These tips are not incorrect, and they may actually save you a couple of dollars here and there. But they're not enough.

> **Can you identify with this?**
>
> "I almost feel guilty. I just can't make ends meet with our budget. Prices are no longer creeping, they're leaping! A hundred dollars doesn't buy a hundred dollars worth of anything anymore."

Tips alone will not significantly impact your buying power.

Shopping for groceries is such a routine part of our lives that we rarely think about it. It is a necessary inconvenience—a high priority in terms of the budget (whether we like it or not) but a low priority in

3

the hurried, complicated business of living.

However, if you step back and look at the cost of this neces-sary inconvenience, you'll see why controlling your shopping habits is so vital. In 1999, the average family of four in the United States spent between $6,400 and $9,400 on grocer-ies.[1] Over a 10-year period, this is an investment of $94,000! Big investments deserve more than cursory attention—especially if you don't need to be spending this much!

> Does it seem that your teen-age son is eating you out of house and home? Well, he is. An average child adds $22 per week to your food bill. But an average teenage boy adds $45 per week! It's no wonder you can't keep enough food in the house!

Let's look at an example. One of the most significant indicators that all is not well with the average American grocery budget is the powerful claim from within the grocery industry that "81 percent of [consumer] buying decisions are store decisions"[2], or decisions you make once you are in the grocery store. That means over three-quarters of your purchases are influenced not by what you need but by persuasive marketing tactics. If you happen to be one of those average families of four, you'll spend up to $7,600 this year because someone else told you to. Someone, by the way, who does not have your best interests at heart!

The good news is that it doesn't have to be this way. Today's soar-ing costs require strong measures to keep your budget under control. And that's what you'll find here—not just tips and tricks but a whole program that can put you in control of your grocery budget, no matter how high prices are or how small your budget may be. Each separate section

> *81 percent of buy-ing decisions are store decisions!*

in the program allows you to save significantly, but the real power comes when you grasp the whole program and make it a way of life.

---

1. Adapted from U.S. Statistical Abstract (U.S. Census), 1999.
2. POPAI Report, Point of Purchase Advertising Institute, 1992.

After an initial period of learning new skills, you'll find shopping for food is no more complicated than what you're currently doing, but you'll have far better results, buying far more groceries with far less money expended. The concepts in this book are an all-out campaign to beat the high cost of eating.

Definition of Buying Power

You'll read a lot in this book about *buying power*. Buying power is the ability to buy more commodities for less money. This program features many concepts that help you save money. For example, in chapter 5 you'll discover you can save at least 20 percent by buying house brands instead of national brands. Let's say, arbitrarily, that this month that 20 percent equaled $20. You could use that $20 to go to a movie, or go out to eat, or buy a pair of shoes. All of these things would be nice, but they wouldn't be increasing your buying power.

> **Buying power**
> is the ability to buy more commodities for less money.

Buying power comes from consistently reinvesting your grocery savings in your grocery budget, which will cause the savings to grow exponentially. You may save $20 this month, but by reinvesting that $20 in bargains and good deals, next month you'll have a savings of $30. The following month it may be $40, and so on and so on.

It's like investing in the stock market. The financial power of the stock market comes from wise choices and continually reinvesting your earnings over the long term. It's the same with buying power. To get the most for your grocery dollar, you need to use the money you save to take advantage of additional grocery bargains.

The Pantry Principle Foundation

The foundation of this program, the concept that supports all the other savings solutions, is the Pantry Principle. The Pantry

Principle, in a nutshell, means stocking up on commodities purchased at today's best prices for use in tomorrow's situations, whatever they may be. Not only is it economical (since you extend your buying power when you stock up at bargain prices), but it provides security as well.

> The **Pantry Principle** means stocking up on commodities purchased at **today's best prices** for use in tomorrow's situations.

With the Pantry Principle, you're never caught short! When emergencies arise, whether major or minor, you can free grocery money to pay unexpected bills and still eat well out of the cupboard! Your pantry becomes a key to greater buying power—the foundation for money management.

In addition, the Pantry Principle ensures that your emergency cupboard will never be bare in times of crisis or disaster. Should the need arise, you will be prepared to "shelter in place" because your shelves are already filled with necessary supplies.

In Search of a Pantry

Stocking up when the price is right is crucial to the Pantry Principle, but you don't have to turn your home into a warehouse, rent a storage unit to stockpile supplies, or have your groceries delivered in a semitruck. Buying in bulk (or stocking up) doesn't have to mean lugging home hundred-pound bags of sugar or flour. Picking up a few extra cans of anything when the price is a bargain will stretch your budget and build up your pantry.

One shopper wrote: "After attending one of your workshops in August, we began to systematically fill our small pantry. 'The System' helped us to stay out of debt when unexpected expenses came up. Expensive and unplanned car repairs hit us in December. But with food in our pantry, our grocery budget allotment was used for that expense. We still ate well!"

You may think this program won't work for you because you don't have any space to store groceries for more than a day or so. Yet no matter how small your home or apartment, a pantry system of one or two small storage spaces is not out of reach. If you were to win $500 worth of groceries at the local supermarket, would you turn down the prize because you didn't have anywhere to put it? Not likely! You would find some way to cram those cans and boxes into unused nooks and crannies in your home. If you're interested in putting the Pantry Principle into practice, space can be found. More about that later.

The Goal:
You Don't *Have* to Go to the Store

My purpose in sharing this program is to help you reach the point where you don't *have* to go to the store. You heard me right. You want to get to the point where you don't have to go to the store. You may want to, but you won't have to.

Now, I'm not suggesting that you boycott supermarkets; in fact, I'm a regular shopper. Rather, my intention is to teach you to use stores to your best advantage. I advocate mastery over your shopping situation so that you only go to the store when you *want* to, not because you *have* to.

If prices are up on some items and down on others, you buy only the good bargains. If prices are too high, you simply don't buy that week. You choose when, where, and if you go to the store. You can do this because your pantry has become your store. It will be stocked with supplies that you've purchased at the best possible prices.

You reach this goal just like any other goal, by breaking it down into smaller, more manageable steps—and it doesn't matter how small your pantry space is. Chapter 12 will show you how to make the most of the space you've got, and the rest of the chapters will show you how to fill that space.

Important Things to Know and Do

The steps to beating the high cost of eating fall into two main categories: important things to *know* that can affect your buying power, and important things to *do* that can increase your buying power. Some of the important things to know are why you buy what you buy, what influences your choices, and the psychological snares designed to snatch your hard-earned dollars.

> Important things to **know** can affect your buying power, and important things to **do** can increase it.

Awareness, and its impact on your ability to stretch your buying power, is so important that this book is saturated with quotes, statistics, and insider insights on how the grocery industry influences your budget. Some of the important things to do will be filling out worksheets and making the right kinds of lists. Begin now to compile a notebook where you can keep all these things together in one place. An ordinary three-ring binder with pocket pages, paper, and a pencil works fine, or you may make copies of the worksheet pages in this book.

Your grocery spending is obviously influenced by things you do or don't do, but your budget is also influenced by what you know or don't know. In order to beat the high cost of eating, you need to have a little background on why you buy what you buy.

There is no question about whether or not you will eat. Nor is there a debate about whether or not you will spend money to eat. The real questions, then, are:

+ What will you buy?
+ How many of your hard-earned dollars will you spend?
+ Where will you spend them?

The power that drives most of those decisions is an incredible marketing machine.

The days of self-sufficient agricultural communities are long gone. Even if we, the consumers, had room to grow all our food at home, we lack the skills (and desire!) to harvest, preserve, and pre-

pare it. And so we depend on the grocery industry to provide us with commodities we cannot live without, and we pay whatever price is asked.

An entire industry has been designed to persuade you to part with your money; in fact, most colleges and universities offer degrees teaching people the complex art of that persuasion. It's not just marketing, it's super marketing! Every manufacturer, grower, distributor, and grocery store owner wants you buying their products. Doesn't that make you feel needed?

Target Marketing

In order to appeal directly to you and sway you in favor of their particular store/product/brand, manufacturers and grocers need to know about you. They turn to demographic information gathered from public records and other sources for this information. These sources report all about you and your neighbors, what you like and dislike, how much income you make, your culture, the size of your family, and other pertinent facts.

This key information helps super marketers identify how to

Jan B. of Salt Lake City, Utah, and her mother sat in the front row of my workshop as I discussed industry insights, displayed ads to the grocers, presented "their" side of the story, rebutted with my version, and discussed how you shop to be able to save money. They both said that they were familiar with grocery industry material. "You see," they explained, "our dad and husband was in the grocery business for years. In fact, he was the president of the State Retail Grocer's Association for a long time." They went on to explain it was interesting and exciting to hear some of the material from my point of view. They had never seen it in that light before. It had always been "how to market, how to market." And that day they were hearing the material reversed into "how to buy, how to buy." Then Jan's mom said, "I think it's marvelous. It will finally give the people who do the shopping an understanding of how to shop better. It's not negative toward anyone. In fact, it's a reeducation process."

persuade you to patronize their stores and purchase their products. This is target marketing, and you and your budget are the targets!

As a shopper, your job is to become a super buyer. Understanding target-marketing strategies directed at you could make the difference in how effectively you beat the high cost of eating. Awareness and defensive spending skills allow you to put buying power back into your pocket.

It's important to realize there is no villain here. The grocers, the manufacturers, the marketers all have a job to do, and they're doing it. We need to be grateful for the services they provide. However, just as they have a right to sell and make a profit, we have the right to buy and save money. Understanding marketing strategies is one of the first steps in controlling the budget. Remember, your goal is to beat the high cost of eating.

By the time you finish reading these chapters, you will know the steps you need to take to gain complete control of your grocery budget. In other words, you'll have a shopping plan that you can carry out at your convenience, to feed your family the foods they like, on the amount of money you want to spend. It is a detailed blueprint for success. Roll up your sleeves! You have a lot to learn!

THINGS TO KNOW

- ✦ Buying power is the ability to buy more commodities for less money. It comes from continually reinvesting your grocery savings into your grocery budget.

- ✦ The foundation of the Beating the High Cost of Eating program is the Pantry Principle. The Pantry Principle means stocking up on commodities purchased at today's best prices for use in tomorrow's situations.

- ✦ A crucial step is stocking up when the price is right.

- ✦ The marketing machine is a network of grocery industries designed to persuade you to purchase their products and to show you how to make those purchases most effectively.

✦ Manufacturers and grocers use demographic information gathered from public records and other sources for information they can use to influence you to patronize their stores and purchase their products.

THINGS TO DO

✦ Compile a notebook where you can keep your lists and worksheets together in one place.

2

Market to Market:
A New View of Comparison Shopping

Regardless of where I go, the question I'm asked most frequently is always the same: Where's the best place in town to shop? People seem to feel that their budget problems would be solved if I could simply name the store in their area that has all the best prices and bargains.

I do have the answer, but it's probably not the answer you're hoping to hear: There is no one store that is cheaper than the rest; there is no one best place to shop!

For good reason, people want to know the best place to shop for good reason. The differences in stores are vast, yet each store claims to be the one that has everything you need—from convenience and quality to the lowest prices in town. How do you determine which store really is the best place to purchase your groceries?

Some people insist that Such-and-Such Grocery Warehouse has to be the cheapest because the name says warehouse. The stuff is stacked in cardboard boxes, and the stores don't spend money on extras such as fancy lighting and decorations. That has to be cheaper than Uptown Snooty Supermarket, with its Mantovani music in the background and interior-decorated produce section.

Maybe . . . maybe not. Stores sell more than just groceries; they also sell image. You'd be surprised how little a store's décor, or lack thereof, has to do with the price of food. To make wise shopping decisions, you must be aware of three points:

✦ A store's image may have no relationship to what it charges for groceries.

✦ No one store undersells its competitors on every item in stock.

✦ Many places besides supermarkets sell groceries, and all the alternatives should be considered.

Store Image

Competition in the grocery business is intense. Grocers who want to attract a stable base of repeat customers are as concerned with marketing their stores as they are with selling the groceries inside. They accomplish this by creating a store image. And while store image may not always be an accurate indicator of what a store is, it certainly reflects what that store is perceived to be.

> No single store has the lowest prices on everything.

In other words, if a grocer feels his store is in a price-conscious neighborhood, he may try to create a low-price image. If elegant, high-priced homes surround his store, he is more likely to cultivate a high-quality image. In fact, store image may have no relationship at all to what the store charges for groceries! Fancy, upscale markets may offer great bargains, and no-frills, warehouse-type stores may charge an arm and a leg. No single store or chain of stores has the cheapest prices on all products, no matter how hard they try to position themselves in your mind.

Image filters to the public in many ways. Radio, TV, and newspaper advertising often blatantly describes the store the way the owner wants the customer to think of it: a friend to the consumer, efficient check-out, lowest prices in town. But image associations are also drawn in more subtle ways, from the use of soft colors and artistic displays that speak *quality* to a jungle of handmade signs and overflowing dump bins that yell BARGAIN.

High-Quality Image

A store with a high-quality image often avoids the issue of competitive prices by emphasizing the superiority of its services and products. The store caters to our pride and vanity with things such as crystal chandeliers and imported tile floors, valet parking, and loads of pampering services. The store's advertising and philosophy might gently insinuate that anyone who shops there is a better educated, more sophisticated consumer who is willing to pay extra to stand a little above the crowd. The focus is not on convincing you that the store has the lowest prices but on convincing you that the store is the best place in town—and you're worth every dollar you spend there!

One luxury-image store in Houston, Texas, refuses to offer promotions or specials. Instead, they concentrate on pampering their shoppers. The owner himself hands carts to customers as they walk in the door, and a clerk is available for nearly every customer. Gourmet and everyday grocery items are stocked in every conceivable brand and size, including truffles, smoked frog legs, canned eggs, 40 kinds of vinegar, and more than 250 kinds of cheeses.

Another quality-image store, this one in Minnesota, is fully carpeted and decorated, including wallpaper. The store even boasts a $50,000 chandelier above the mid-store freezer wells. Although most high-quality image supermarkets can't carry the theme as far as these stores do, they do play on the same consumer desires.

Warehouse Image

On the other end of the spectrum, we find the low-price, bargain-warehouse image. This type of store is particularly popular when the economy threatens instability to many consumers. Some authentic box stores and warehouse stores *do* undercut competitors by an impressive margin by cutting overhead costs and stocking fewer items.

However, warehouse-like stores cloud the picture somewhat by projecting the warehouse-store image through special signage or suggestive names. These supermarkets imitate the theme without actually lowering overall prices. By displaying goods in packing cartons,

lowering prices on obvious staple items, and plastering handmade posters around the store, they convince consumers they have slashed prices. They even stack and pile merchandise in free-for-all fashion on every shelf, aisle, and square foot of floor space in sight. This thrown-together, jumbled look is deliberately designed to suggest amazing clearance bargains.

Yet another popular grocery-store image is the friendly store. When we're convinced that store owners and employees genuinely care about us, we naturally assume they'll give us the best prices—because we're friends. Other stores promote convenience, or helpfulness, or concern for the environment, or even social consciousness. Grocers determine what tactics are most likely to draw local customers into the store, and they position their store in your eyes with that in mind.

As with most areas of big business, image making is more sophisticated than simply choosing a theme. Never-ending research aids the industry in analyzing its customers so grocers know which features attract which shoppers. Information from generalized groups of shoppers are analyzed and categorized, complete with demographic profiles (average age, income, and so forth).

> According to the 2000 Census Bureau report, there are 11.8 percent more people over the age of 65 than in 1990. There are 40 percent more Hispanic-Americans and 42 percent more Asian-Americans than a decade previously. Together, these two groups account for more than 15 percent of the total U.S. population. Married couples decreased by 5 percent, female heads of households increased by 20 percent, and 21 percent more heads of households are living alone.
>
> In addition to changing consumer demographics, changing consumer lifestyles impact the marketing industry. The average consumer now purchases 73 takeout meals and 64 restaurant meals each year. They make 2.2 shopping trips each week, with each transaction averaging $23.03. They spend $38 per person per week.
>
> *2003 Reports on the 2002 Coupon Trends*
> (Elmwood Park, Ill.: Santella and Associates, 2003)

Studies are conducted and summarized, detailing how many stores each type of consumer shops, the method of payment those consumers use, and their attitudes toward various aspects of shopping. This kind of information is made available to assist grocers in attracting the customers they prefer. If you find yourself drawn to a certain type of store, think of yourself as a moth drawn to a flame.

Fortunately, you aren't a moth. You need not fly helplessly into the flame and get burned. Knowing that a store's image doesn't necessarily indicate good prices, you can resist the allure of an image and make intelligent choices based on fact rather than hype.

Take a minute to fill out the chart titled "A Look at Supermarket Image" (page 182 in the appendix) to see how image has affected your shopping habits.

Variable-Price Merchandising

Grocery stores operate on what is called a variable-price merchandising system. Instead of applying a standard price markup on everything, such as a flat 10 percent above cost, each item is priced individually. The cost of any product can be marked up or down at will. (Some states do require a minimum markup by law, usually 6 percent, but retailers can charge whatever they want above this amount.)

Variable-price merchandising is noted for lowering prices on products that draw customers into the store—and advertising these price changes—while quietly raising the prices of other incidental items purchased by most shoppers once they are inside the store. A store that is successful in using variable-price merchandising may appear to have low prices when actually its overall price level is relatively high.

Studies indicate that consumers are sensitive to the price of anywhere from 300 to 500 items. A smart grocer prices these products carefully to attract local clientele. Yet the balance of items, some 10,000 to 15,000, carried by a store may be priced significantly higher.

No need to despair, however. With a little effort on your part, the variable-price system can work to your advantage. In a competitive market, you need to be a competitive buyer and purchase products wherever you find the best prices.

The Key to the Question

So back to that most frequently asked question: Where is the best place in town to shop? The answer: For the greatest buying power, shop a combination of stores rather than

> For the greatest buying power, **shop a combination of stores** rather than at one place!

just one store. Each store features certain items or categories of items priced to draw you inside the door. If you shop to take advantage of these various prices at different stores, you'll enjoy tremendous savings. Combination is the key here.

One-Stop Shopping

Stores work hard to develop store loyalty. They want you to come back every week, to feel a sense of loyalty. In fact, to earn your store loyalty, many provide innumerable other goods, services, and rewards; they call it one-stop shopping. This approach implies that, for your convenience, everything you need is available under one roof: food, flowers, videos, vitamins, even gasoline for your car.

> *One-Stop Shopping* is a **"buy word."**

One-stop shopping has become a *buy word*! As shoppers, we have allowed ourselves to be convinced that our pace of life is so hectic that one-stop shopping is a favor and a blessing we can't do without, no matter the cost.

One-stop shopping is much more than a combination of food, general merchandise, and services. It's power! And it is the focus of

attention as stores compete for your business, which translates to your budget. Therefore, super marketers will heavily promote the following:

✦ The convenience of one-stop shopping
✦ The service of one-stop shopping
✦ Your need for one-stop shopping

Granted, one-stop shopping may be convenient, but is it best for your budget? Keep the following two points in mind: there is no quick fix to better budget control, and easier and faster do not usually save money.

Nontraditional Grocery Outlets

In addition to traditional supermarkets, many other outlets sell groceries. You should consider them all on your quest for greater buying power. You'll find discount drug stores (Walgreen's, Rite Aid, Longs, Rexall), membership clubs (Sam's Club and Costco), and mass merchandisers (Target, Phar-Mor, Wal-Mart).

These stores offer traditional supermarket items, such as paper goods, health and beauty products, detergents, soaps, canned goods, and so on, at significantly lower prices than you would pay for the same items in a grocery store situation.

For example, I priced ten items at seven different stores, three grocery stores (one was a one-stop-shopping megastore) and four mass merchandisers. You can save as much as 50 percent over typical grocery store prices when you shop around. (See the "Comparison of Nonfood Items" worksheet, page 183 in the appendix.)

Outlets

On the other end of the size scale, you'll notice small specialty shops, day-old bread outlets, dollar stores, odd-job-lot companies, and others that also offer great deals for your dollars. Here's just one example of the value you can find in these small outlets: I love a certain kind of brand-name, whole-grain bread. In the grocery stores,

it costs nearly $3 per loaf. However, a day-old bread store that my husband passes on his way to work sells this bread for 75 cents per loaf. He stops in regularly to stock our freezer at a tremendous savings. At two loaves per week, that's a savings of over $200 per year on only one item!

New Meaning to Comparison Shopping

It's vital that you develop the strategy of shopping at several different stores! This means comparison shopping the stores as well as the products in them. Comparison shopping brands and labels is important, but before you do that, you need to comparison shop the kinds of stores in your area that sell those brands and labels.

> **Every** *alternative should be considered.*

There are many places where groceries are sold, and all alternatives should be considered. The following list includes types of stores or outlets that commonly carry groceries. Although you may not be familiar with some of the alternatives, they can be found in or near most cities. (Note that my comments apply only to groceries and not to other items that may also be stocked for sale.)

Superstores

More and more grocery stores are entering the one-stop shopping arena and are branching out into related and not-so-grocery-related services. Those with a large selection of nonfood merchandise plus a few services are called *combination* or *combo* stores. Some of these stores feature other customer services, such as camera bars, optical centers, and restaurants; these are called *superstores*. In some superstores, food is very competitively priced and is used to attract people into the store. Profit is then made mainly on services and nonfood products.

Supermarkets

Any medium-to-large grocery store that does an annual business of $2 million or more is defined as a *supermarket* by the industry. There are more supermarkets than any other type of grocery store. The names you see most often are probably chain stores. However, the fact that they are owned and operated by a larger parent corporation does not necessarily mean they are more expensive. Suppliers often sell products to chains at cut-rate prices to attract large-volume business. The stores can pass these lower prices on to you. Also, most chains offer some kind of house brand, which they sell at competitive prices.

Other supermarkets are individually owned and are referred to as *independents.* To compete with chain-store prices, many independents join organizations such as Associated Grocers, Inc. (AGI) or Independent Grocers Association (IGA). By pooling their orders, they create enough bulk to qualify for the same cut-rate prices offered to chain stores. They also combine efforts to produce independent house brands as well. Basically, the advantages of shopping at chain supermarkets or independents are about the same.

Corner Grocery Stores

Not large enough in dollar volume to be dubbed supermarkets, the independent *corner* grocery stores and small neighborhood Mom-and-Pop stores sometimes have a difficult time competing with large chains. They deal in much smaller volume and usually pay more for their stock. They rarely advertise and are often family owned, serving a local and loyal clientele that care more about convenience and friendship than price. However, some small markets feature a few products, perhaps local commodities, that can be purchased fresher and cheaper there than at the supermarket.

Warehouse Stores

Warehouse stores are based on a low-overhead concept. They contain most of the departments found in conventional grocery stores (including produce, meat, and other perishables) but offer a

reduced selection of brands and sizes. Stock might average between 1,000 and 7,000 thousand items, compared to the 10,000 to 20,000 items found in a standard supermarket. Most warehouse stores operate on a deal basis, offering whatever items they are able to obtain cheaply from wholesalers. For this reason, different items may be stocked from week to week. Customers usually provide their own bags and pack their own purchases.

Discount Stores

A true discount store is usually small, with a limited choice of brands in each product category. Advertising is minimal and low key, with little or no emphasis on store promotions such as coupons or trading stamps. Rather than sponsoring huge weekend specials, they feature consistent low pricing. Shopping hours may be limited compared to regular supermarkets.

Discount Drugstores

A common type of discount store, which occasionally offers bargain-priced food as a come-on, is the discount drugstore. Discount drugstore chains sometimes carry house-brand varieties of health and beauty aids, often at prices lower than you'll find in supermarkets.

Bargain Discount Stores

Stores such as Big Lots and Dollar Tree specialize in items that are factory overages, mislabeled, have had label changes, or are last year's styles. Consequently, most products are sold for less than comparable products in regular grocery stores or department stores.

Many of the items are brand-name products; some are brands from other regions or areas of the country. Some are house brands. One growing chain of discount outlet stores specializes in finding bargains. They will re-label, change packaging, or do whatever is needed to make a saleable product that they can offer to the public at substantial discounts.

This type of store does not consistently stock the same brands

or items, nor do they carry everything you need. However, you can take advantage of these prices by being familiar with the types of commodities they generally have in stock and checking there first when you need that type of item. If you have such an outlet in your area, you'll definitely find it worthwhile to take your brand worksheet (page 192 in the appendix) and visit the store, and ask the manager about the different brands. You'll find more information in chapter 5.

Specialty Stores

Any store that features a single commodity, such as health foods or imported cheeses, is a *specialty* store. The availability of such shops depends on where you live. The main advantage to shopping these options is the variety they offer in a chosen product line, often unmatched by any other stores. Generally, specialty stores are more expensive than supermarkets, although bargains can be found from time to time.

Natural, Organic, and Whole-Foods Markets

Natural foods markets are emerging as a viable alternative to regular supermarkets, with a devoted clientele. There are several national chains, such as Whole Foods Markets and Wild Oats Markets, whose store inventory is dedicated to health and well-being. These stores operate much like other supermarkets, with aisles for cereal, bread, produce, dairy products, canned goods, and so forth, as well as in-house bakeries and delis.

These stores should not be confused with traditional health food stores, whose lines of products consist mainly of vitamins, herbal remedies, and supplements. Natural foods stores are usually, though not always, more expensive than standard supermarkets due to their highly selective product line.

If their products meet with your personal health criteria, you can still use your shopping skills to get the most for your budget from them. Some national natural foods chains carry their own line of house brands. Another money-saving feature are the rows of bulk

bins for grains, beans, cereals, and dried fruit. Be sure to compare prices whenever possible, both with traditional health food stores and also standard grocery stores, which also often will have aisles and sections dedicated to health and natural foods.

Thrift Stores

Also specializing in a single commodity but at discounted prices are *thrift* stores. They deal in leftover items, or foods that have exceeded their freshness dates. A common example is the baked-goods thrift store where you can purchase day-old bread, cookies, buns, donuts, and other baked items. Savings may be as high as 20 to 40 percent on products that sat on supermarket shelves the day before. To find thrift stores, check the Yellow Pages under Thrift Stores, Food, Groceries, or the names of specific commodities.

Convenience Stores

The main product for sale in a convenience store is exactly that—convenience. Usually located in high-traffic areas in the middle of populated neighborhoods, they are open later and earlier than most grocery stores, if not around the clock. Usually, though not always, they sell gasoline as their main product, with a little store attached that is stocked with staples such as bread and milk, plus a variety of snack and high-impulse items.

Prices are often outrageously high but are paid by those who can't wait until the next day to shop. Some are as small as a tiny room at a gas station, and some are as large as one in Kermit, Texas, that houses a deli, a bakery, a dining area, a laundry area, and a game room. Generally, any major grocery shopping done in a convenience store is a drain on the budget. However, some are beginning to offer specials on staple items, such as bread and milk, in hopes of drawing in customers who will buy other merchandise on impulse.

Food plans and home delivery wagons also belong in the convenience category. Comparison shopping reveals that you almost always pay extra for the services involved.

Membership Stores

Membership stores sell exclusively to consumers who can present a membership card at the door. These cards can be purchased by anyone for a nominal fee. These chain stores are found all across the United States, and their enormous collective buying power is reflected in their low prices. They carry everything from computers and lawn mowers to milk and eggs. Many even have their own house brands.

Membership stores can keep their prices low for two reasons:

> I was standing in line at a membership store with my overflowing basket when I overheard a young man bemoaning the upcoming check he was going to have to write. He said, "I'd heard that this store was a 'Fortune 500' and now I know why. It seems like every time I come in here I spend a fortune, and most of the time it's close to $500!"

- ✦ They order in huge quantities due to the vast number of stores; they get the highest discounts from manufacturers, and then pass that savings on to you.

- ✦ Typically, they only sell in bulk or large quantities. You must buy milk in a two-gallon pack, batteries in a package of 28, and laundry detergent in a 120-load box, and so on. Because you have to buy more, they can sell for less. The main disadvantage of a membership store is that to achieve these wonderful savings, you have to buy in bulk. That might work for something like laundry detergent or printer ink cartridges, but not every family can use five pounds of cheese or four heads of lettuce before they spoil.

> **Share-and-save** with a friend to get the **benefits** of buying in bulk without dealing with spoilage.

If most of your purchase spoils before you can use it, you're wasting money rather than saving it. Also, before you can shop at a membership store, you must first purchase the membership, which costs $35 or more

annually. If you don't intend to shop there more than once or twice a year, it probably wouldn't be cost-effective. To take advantage of the great bargains available at the membership stores, you may opt to use the share-and-save concept. Two or more friends combine shopping trips and divide the bulk purchases into more manageable sizes. You get the benefit of the savings without dealing with spoilage.

While most membership store prices are excellent, they still may not beat loss-leader prices or exceptional sale prices in supermarkets. And their selection of items is still limited, despite their enormous proportions.

PX or Commissary

The armed forces of the United States run membership stores for families in military service, known as commissaries. If they were privately owned, the volume of business transacted in the nearly 400 commissary stores would rank them among the top ten grocery chains in the country.

Although the commissary can sometimes undercut local grocery stores by 20 to 30 percent, savings are generally on name-brand items that may be more expensive initially. Be sure to comparison shop. You may find better bargains elsewhere.

Groceries on the Side

Grocery stores are not the only place you can find groceries any more. Gas stations alone sell billions of dollars worth of groceries each year, and department stores, such as Macy's and Nordstrom's—whose main products have traditionally been clothing and accessories—are equally industrious. Some cater to customers who want top-quality goods by offering a bakery, a deli, a coffee shop, or all three, and may even offer expensive candies, top-of-the-line canned goods, and gourmet foods.

We are familiar with grocery stores diversifying into the field of one-stop shopping by expanding into nonfoods sales. However, a current trend has some nonfood stores aggressively experimenting with full-scale grocery departments.

For the quintessential one-stop shopping choice these days, look to the discount department store (such as Wal-Mart or Target) that has expanded into the food business. Stores like Super K-Mart and Super-Target still have enormous inventories of nonfoods and services, but they've added full-service grocery stores to the mix also. Most even stock their own house brands. (See chapter 5 for details on quality and savings with house brands.)

While it may be convenient to have everything under the sun under one roof, remember that convenience can be costly and that no single store has the cheapest prices on all products, not even a colossal discount department-grocery store combination. It's possible to find bargains in these hybrid superstores, as long as the boost to your budget isn't undermined by impulse purchases.

Direct to the Source

A price-is-right option often overlooked by shoppers, especially in cities and suburban areas, is buying food directly from the farmers who grow it. Even the largest and busiest cities have farmers' markets. Usually located in the dock or trucking districts, the produce is set up and sold in the early, early morning, between 2:00 a.m. and 6:00 a.m. Consumers who buy in bulk, and can survive the early hour, are welcome. The clamor, the aroma, and the hustle-bustle of haggling are enough to make the experience worthwhile. Add true bargain prices, and the shopping trip becomes sheer delight.

There are other ways to find farmers willing to sell their freshly picked fruits and vegetables. Scaled-down versions of the traditional farmer's market, set up once or twice a week during daytime hours in a central location, are becoming more popular. Be sure to know prices well enough to avoid tourist traps. Roadside stands and truck stands, which dot the highway in most communities during the summer months, can stretch your budget as well.

Also, don't be afraid to buy from the small farmers or avid gardeners who post signs to direct willing passersby to an abundant crop for sale at their homes. Newspapers can even serve as a guide to local sources. Check the classified ads for names and phone numbers

of growers who want to sell produce. Weekly food sections may run a seasonal article listing local produce stands or farms that allow the public to "pick your own" at excellent prices.

In some areas, such as northern California, Utah, and Virginia, maps of such farms are available at newsstands, libraries, and even at supermarkets themselves. Since some of the best savings will be found in a bushel or peck, one way to take advantage of the good prices is to go in together with a friend. You can share the ride, the work, and the savings.

Manufacturers' Outlets

Going directly to the source is not limited to fresh produce. In some areas, semitruckloads of seafood roll into town every few months to sell directly to consumers in shopping center parking lots. Legitimate sellers will have proper identification and posted licenses and will usually name their fisheries.

Similarly, products that are grown, processed, or manufactured near your hometown may be available at special outlets. Canneries, dairies, factories, mills, egg ranches—all processing plants, with the exception of slaughter houses and some firms with closed-door policies—run outlets where overruns and products with minor defects are sold. Check your Yellow Pages under each product category.

Wholesale Outlets

Many wholesalers, especially those that stock small grocery stores, restaurants, schools, and hospitals, are willing to deal directly with the public. (Smart & Final and Sysco are two examples.) A 20 to 40 percent savings can often be obtained by buying wholesale, but be prepared to buy in bulk. Many of the items sold at such outlets are packaged in much larger quantities than at the grocery store.

Also be aware that most wholesalers keep different hours than supermarkets. Sometimes goods are sold to individuals only on certain days of the week, at certain hours of the day. Call ahead to make sure you understand the way the wholesaler operates. Again, the Yellow Pages generally list all wholesale businesses.

Buying Clubs and Co-ops

An obvious way to save money on groceries is to pay fewer middlemen. Yet few consumers realize how easy it is to circumvent retail outlets and buy directly from suppliers. It takes surprisingly few families to create enough buying power to interest wholesalers in delivering groceries right to your door.

Co-ops and buying clubs are on the upswing in every part of the country. These groups are made up of families and individuals who have pooled their efforts and ingenuity. By trading work for savings, they buy goods directly from manufacturers and wholesalers and assume the workload of the middlemen they have bypassed. Members of such groups spend time telephoning, taking orders, picking up and delivering groceries, even dividing and repackaging bulk orders. In return, they average a 20 to 40 percent savings on the products they order. On certain commodities, savings even exceed 50 percent!

Existing co-ops in your area may be hard to discover. Some may be listed in the Yellow Pages or registered with the county or state as nonprofit organizations. You might check libraries, newspaper classified ads, and other sources for public notices on the subject. Sometimes small wholesalers or restaurant suppliers, listed in the Yellow Pages by commodity, maintain lists of co-ops they sell to. If you can find one co-op, leaders or members can usually lead you to others.

Most areas have co-ops of every size and organizational structure imaginable. In fact, few of the thousands of co-ops in the nation are run alike. Each group goes about accomplishing its own goals in its own way. Generally, these groups are more than willing to share their ideas and successes with others. The Cooperative League of the U.S.A. (Cooperative League of the U.S.A. 1401 New York Avenue, NW, Suite 1100, Washington, D.C., 20005-2160) maintains a library of books and pamphlets on every aspect of co-oping. Some of these materials are free or are available for a small fee.

If your community doesn't seem to have a co-op whose goals fit your needs, you might consider forming one of your own.

Salvage

Some discount stores and other food outlets sell products marked *salvaged* or *freight damaged*. Usually, these items have been damaged in shipping, salvaged from train or truck wrecks, overproduced at canneries and packing houses, or stocked too long at grocery stores and warehouses. Occasionally, salvage items include seconds or items not up to a manufacturer's standards. Certain wholesalers buy up these items, which would otherwise be discarded, and sell them at phenomenally low prices.

Although you'll find bargain-basement prices, shopping for salvaged goods involves expertise and caution. Always avoid freight-damaged canned goods, particularly crushed or dented liquid-packed food products. Dented cans may eventually split at the seams, allowing bacteria to enter the food. Even apparently undamaged cans may have been subjected to abnormal pressure and rough treatment, causing weaknesses and breakage that can't be seen.

Never purchase any cracked or broken containers, which might allow the contents to become contaminated. Even dry food products, such as gelatin or pasta, should be checked for rips, cracks, breaks, holes, or punctures. The low prices on these goods are not worth the risk to your health.

Nonfood goods such as toilet tissue, facial tissue, napkins, hand soap, and paper plates may be excellent buys. Still, compare prices before making a purchase.

Create a Store Information Worksheet

Create a store information worksheet like the one on pages 184 to 185 in the appendix. This worksheet will help you discover the different shopping options available to you. To begin, list all the possible grocery outlets within a reasonable distance that you might possibly consider going to. This will become a resource sheet, so include information you may need again such as location, address (to plan a better shopping route), and hours of business. Make quick notes that will help you recall that precise outlet, such as "membership card

required" or "cash only, no checks accepted."

Keep this information in your notebook or hand-held planner, and glance at it before you read the ads to refresh your mind as to which stores to consider. Once this information becomes old hat, you'll most likely ignore this step. But until it is, consider it homework as you gain new skills. Don't be lulled back into the habit of frequenting only a few favorite stores. Consciously look for new sources to check out and add to your list.

The Best of Two Stores

While it is true that no one store has the best prices on all items, sometimes certain stores consistently offer better deals on certain categories of food. For example, one store near my home regularly offers lower prices on canned and packaged goods than most grocery stores in the area, but their produce and meat are quite expensive. Another store a mile or so away sells produce at significantly lower prices than surrounding stores.

> A **combination** of store alternatives is the key that unlocks greater buying power than could ever be obtained by one-stop shopping.

Look at this comparison. I compared prices at the two stores near my home, for exactly the same items at each store. At Store A, the bill totaled $26.85. At Store B, the same groceries came to $24.52. However, by buying the canned goods at Store A and the meat and produce at Store B, my total was only $19.29. I saved 21–28 percent by dividing my shopping trip between only two stores (page 186 of the appendix).

As you research the options around you, you'll become familiar with which stores emphasize which products on a regular basis. If all you did was shop two or three stores for the things they normally feature lower prices on, you would significantly lower your grocery bills.

But that's just the tip of the iceberg when you shop more than one store.

Combination Is the Savings Key

You may not shop every store option every week, but you must be aware of the benefits that are there for you. Remember, a combination of store alternatives is the key that unlocks greater buying power than could ever be obtained by one-stop shopping. Shopping more than one store, even only once a month, results in significant savings.

Eliminating the Myths

Shopping at several places to find the best bargains doesn't mean that shopping has to be an arduous, exhausting, store-hopping marathon. Multiple-store shopping can easily be broken down into mini-shopping trips. Mini-shopping trips are just that: smaller, shorter shopping trips that conveniently take advantage of planned, manageable minutes. This approach combines time management with your convenience and your schedule.

You do this by paying a little more attention to your schedule. Assess the routes you regularly drive to and from employment, day care, the spa, or any other places to which you travel frequently. Plot and keep track of the store options that are located along or close to those routes. Then, with a minimum expenditure of time and effort, you can spread out your small shopping trips quickly and efficiently.

Erase the image from your mind that these are leisurely, time-wasting excursions. You are a shopper on a mission. If a drugstore has pickles and peanut butter on sale, you go in with blinders on, buy pickles and peanut butter, and get right out again. You are not there to browse—you are there to extend your buying power! If you want to browse, you can come back another time.

I've had people say to me that it just isn't worth the time to run from store to store for bargains. I beg to differ. For example, not long

The Thrill of the Hunt

As a young married mother of two small children, making my budget stretch until it screamed was a way of life. There was a group of us young mothers who took shopping seriously, and we were always on the lookout for great bargains. It became quite common when we discovered a terrific deal to call the other two and say, "Did you see this one?"

The phone rang one morning and my friend Pat said, "Wow, did you see this morning's ad?" I had, and the immediate question was, "Should we go?" "Of course. Call Carol," was her response.

Three mothers and six small children piled into my station wagon. (This was back in the old days before seat belts were widely used.) We drove several miles across town to the lure of prices that were unbeatable, even then: Cornstarch—5 cents a box; pudding—5 cents a box; Jell-O gelatin—5 cents a box; and salt—5 cents a carton. The buying power of my bargain-hunting budget went through the roof.

I moved through the store, piling my treasures on top of the kids in the cart and headed for the checkout. There I discovered each of my friends and their children at two other checkouts. As my cashier was ringing up the myriad little boxes, the clerk at the next check-out stand murmured something to him. He loudly replied, "Yeah, I know. I've got one too." That drew an additional comment from the other checkout clerk, who said, "Yeah, so do I. What's going on anyway?" We all laughed and then loaded the car and headed home, basking in the thrill of the hunt.

ago a local discount store advertised jars of seasonings and spices for a dollar a jar, as opposed to an average regular price of $2.89 per jar in the grocery store. Over the next few pay periods, I restocked my spice pantry with 25 jars of different seasonings and spices for just $25, for an immediate savings of $47. That sounds like a sensible use of time and money to me!

Cost of Gas Myth

Some people insist that gas expenses negate any savings gained by shopping several stores. Their calculations may be correct—*if* you are running from store to store trying to find the best price on one certain item for a particular recipe. And they are also correct *if* your purchases are made without comparison shopping the stores, ads, and products on paper first. And *if* you run around in a random manner without first plotting out where to go and what other errands can be accomplished at the same time.

No one is recommending you travel an exaggerated distance to take advantage of a bargain price. Most individuals have a meaningful variety of retail outlets within a reasonable driving distance. A smart money- and time-management plan naturally incorporates other errands into the schedule as well.

> An excited shopping convert reported savings on a single item—hand soap—that allowed her to more than double her buying power. An ad in the paper sent her to a nearby discount drugstore for just one item. She loaded her basket with bars of aloe lotion hand soap that would regularly cost $1.29, on sale for only $.59, a 55 percent reduction! However, her excitement didn't end there. She discovered even greater savings in the same store. A house-brand version of the same style aloe soap was on an unadvertised sale for only $.39 per bar, an unheard-of price at the time. Her savings mushroomed. She purchased 10 bars for only $3.90, as compared to $12.90 for the regularly priced brand name, for a one-item savings of $9!

As a case in point, I live in a suburban city of 90,000 people. Within three miles of my home are at least 12 grocery stores, one membership store (plus one more half a mile outside the three-mile range), seven mass merchandisers (Wal-Mart, K-Mart, and so forth), two drugstores, and three discount stores (dollar-type stores). In addition, there are numerous small specialty shops and countless convenience stores. I can get just about everything I want without ever having to leave my little comfort zone.

On the other hand, not everyone lives in a competitive grocery marketplace with numerous options. For those who live in small towns, immediate options can be limited to a single grocery store or two. But just because your buying options are limited, your buying skills don't have to be.

> Just because your **buying options** are limited, your **buying skills** don't have to be.

Scour the area for nontraditional grocery options, such as discount department stores, drug stores, or even local fruit stands and farmers' markets. Always shop with a plan, even if it is a shortened version. And then rely on the old-fashioned wisdom of doing most of your buying when you go to town, the larger, adjacent community that has a larger shopping base.

A close friend of mine lived in just such a tiny, one-horse town way down on the Texas-Mexico border. With the exceptions of milk and occasionally bread and produce, all of her shopping for her family of seven took place one Saturday each month when she would drive an hour-and-a-half to Corpus Christi. Her lists and plans had to be honed to perfection, because if she forgot anything, they had to do without it for another month.

You may still be doubtful about the economic benefit of shopping more than one store if you are the unfortunate owner of a decades-old, gas-guzzling bucket of compressed rust, held together by duct tape and baling wire, that gets 10 miles to

SAVINGS VS. COST OF GAS

SPEND:	- $3 on gas per trip
SAVE:	+ $25 in grocery savings
NET SAVINGS:	+ $22 per week
x 52 weeks	= **$1,144 per year!**

the gallon on a good day, if it's going downhill, in neutral.

Let's look at the figures in black and white to prove shopping around is a good thing. Say your car gets 10 miles to the gallon, and the route between your top five stores is within three miles of your

home. To go to all or any of your stores, you must drive three miles out, three miles around, and three miles back to your home. That's a grand total of nine miles, or almost a gallon of gas.

Now let's pessimistically assume that gasoline is going to sky-rocket to $3 per gallon. Therefore, your gas cost for the week's grocery shopping is just about $3. If you'll recall, I referenced the U.S. census report in the introduction. The average family of four spends $6,400 to $9,400 per year on groceries, or $123 to $181 per week.

Using this program, you can save at least 20 percent off your grocery bill by shopping multiple stores, or $25 to $36 for an average family. If you spend $3 in gas to save $25 in grocery costs, that seems like an intelligent exchange!

Organize, Divide, and Conquer

Three words that will optimize your buying power are organize, divide, and conquer.

1. **Organize** your shopping strategies with lists and reference pages.
2. **Divide** shopping into quick stops at different outlets.
3. **Conquer** the high cost of eating.

Now if someone asks you, "Where is the best place in town to shop?" you'll know what to tell them!

THINGS TO KNOW

✦ No store has a monopoly on low prices. There is no one best place to shop!

✦ Stores sell more than just groceries. They also sell *image*. However, a store's image may have no relationship to what it charges for groceries.

✦ One-stop shopping offers a combination of food, general merchandise, and services under the same roof. It may be easy and convenient, but it is also more expensive.

THINGS TO DO

✦ There are many places besides supermarkets that sell groceries, and all alternatives should be considered. For the most buying power, shop a combination of outlets rather than shopping in only one place.

✦ Create a store information worksheet by listing all the possible grocery outlets within a reasonable distance that you might visit. Keep this information in your notebook or hand-held planner, and glance at it before you read the ads to refresh your mind about which stores are nearby.

✦ Shopping at several places to get the best bargains doesn't mean that shopping has to be a time-consuming marathon. A smart money- and time-management plan naturally incorporates other errands into the schedule as well.

✦ Organize your shopping strategies with lists and reference pages. Divide shopping into quick stops at different outlets. Conquer the high cost of eating.

3

In-Store Psychology:
Will Shopping Be a Store Decision or Your Decision?

While teaching a seminar in New England, I stayed with a friend who attended my lectures on smart shopping. She listened approvingly to my criticisms of unplanned purchases. On our way home, we stopped at a nearby supermarket to dash in for just a gallon of milk. We left the store 45 minutes later with $68 worth of groceries, including, of course, the milk.

No doubt you've heard that control over impulse buying will trim your budget. But if you are the average shopper, impulse buying probably has a tighter hold on your spending habits than you realize. This is a crucial issue in beating the high cost of eating. As I mentioned earlier, research indicates that 81 percent of all buying decisions are made in the store—we have impulse buying to thank for that statistic.

> In a supermarket parking lot in the Midwest, I began to unlock my car door when a woman, directing a box boy where to put her groceries, opened the back door of a car next to mine. As he began unloading the full cart, she turned to me and commented, "I can't believe it. I did it again. Ninety-nine dollars! And all I came in for was bread and milk. I do this all the time." She's a typical shopper. Maybe the bills from your quick shopping trip don't always total $99, but the consistent unplanned $10, $15, or even $5 can deplete and defeat your budget.

Impulse Buying

Impulse shopping as we traditionally think of it is the last-minute purchase of a candy bar, soda pop, or other junk food while waiting in line at the checkout stand. You must eliminate that limited perception. In fact, the marketers' definition of impulse shopping includes *any* purchase decisions made after you enter the store. Liver or broccoli could be impulse buys! So could shoelaces or laundry soap or Spaghettios.

When you make a choice to buy something after you enter a store, the grocery industry considers that an impulse buy. Most of us have never calculated the overall effect of unplanned, see-and-grab purchases on our grocery bills. After all, a can of this or a package of that now and then will hardly threaten the financial stability of your household.

However, impulse buys can destroy your budget if you're not careful. Small expenditures can quickly add up to thousands of dollars per year. The chart on page 187 in the appendix may help you understand the impact of impulse purchases on your budget—and we've only considered junk-food purchases here. Over the space of a year, just these few impulse purchases each week cost you over $500!

Awareness Can Save You Money

The profits from impulse buying propel the whole merchandising merry-go-round. Supermarkets are designed around impulse. The psychology behind the floor plan of a store, how products are placed on the shelves, the posters and banners that identify each item, the displays at the end of the aisles purposefully encourages spur-of-the-moment spending.

In particular, the front end of the store and the displays crowded around the checkout stand are designed to motivate you to "see and grab." The problem is not these persuasive tactics themselves but how you respond to them. Being aware of the main techniques used by the industry will decrease your chances of succumbing.

Impulse Buying—A New Definition

When we talk about impulse buying, we may think about Aunt Gertrude, who dashes to the store for a pound of hamburger for tonight's dinner, only to return home with three pounds of peaches, two boxes of doughnuts, six cans of peas (on sale), a frozen pumpkin pie (in case the Joneses drop by after church), a can opener, a new ball for Johnny (just like the one the dog chewed up last week), three boxes of breakfast cereal, holiday-motif paper plates (on the clearance table), a couple of candy bars, two magazines, and an umbrella (on display near the checkout stands). She later has to phone Uncle Jack at the office to ask him to pick up the hamburger on his way home.

> *An impulse purchase includes **any** decision you make after you enter the store.*

Remember, impulse shopping is not just grabbing a magazine at the checkout counter. An impulse purchase includes any decision you make after you enter the store. In other words, if you are there to buy something for dinner but haven't decided on the menu, or if you know you want peas but haven't committed yourself to a brand, the grocer is as happy to see you as he is to see Aunt Gertrude!

Impulse purchases can be divided into three categories: generally planned—when a shopper has certain products or product categories in mind but has not preselected a brand; substitute—when a consumer buys a different brand or item than originally intended; and unplanned—when purchases are made that were not even considered before the shopping trip. Since 81 percent of the average shopper's purchases fall into these categories, most shoppers relinquish control of more than three quarters of their shopping decisions to the grocery industry. Other people decide what you're going to buy, and you can be sure that helping you stick to your budget is not their first priority!

Even your wholesome staples can be impulse purchases, if you made up your mind to buy them after you entered the store. They

can sink your budget just as easily as junk food can. The chart on page 188 in the appendix shows the difference preplanned shopping can make on just 10 commonly purchased grocery items.

While these may not be 10 items you personally purchase regularly, the significance is still clear. Impulse purchases, even healthy ones, can nickel and dime your budget to death, without you even being aware of it.

Directed Paths

The entire grocery industry relies so heavily on impulse purchases that everything from packaging and labeling to advertising and promoting revolves around it. Even the floor plan or grid of the supermarket itself is carefully designed to guide you, even manipulate you, to fill your basket with items you had not intended to buy. You enter most stores at a precisely planned point, and your path through the store includes maximum exposure to high-impulse items. Staple items, such as bread, milk, meat, and produce, are never in close proximity to each other. They are placed as far as possible around the store, forcing you to tour the store to find the basics—and providing ample opportunity for impulse buying.

> The entire grocery industry **relies so heavily** on impulse purchasing that everything from packaging and labeling to advertising and promoting revolves around it.

You're probably familiar with the grocery industry's most common floor plan: produce along one sidewall, dairy and baked items on the opposite wall, and meat straddling the back of the store. The space in the middle of the store is striped with a series of long shelving units, forming parallel aisles. Most grocery store experts agree that this layout inspires the most impulse sales, since you are channeled past a multitude of goods as you seek out the few items you actually want.

A Walk through the Supermarket

A walk through a typical supermarket, with an eye open for influences on impulse shopping, can be revealing. Immediately inside the door, you may be confronted with chrome posts—a nice place for parking empty shopping carts, and a subtle way to funnel all shoppers past the display the grocer wants them to see. After grabbing your cart, often the size of a small pickup truck, or so it seems, you are directed into a labyrinth of store gondolas (or tables), piled high with everything you need for the upcoming holiday. Maneuvering your cart through the narrow gaps between the tables is an admirable skill; getting through without succumbing to the pressure to impulse buy raises the skill practically to an art form.

Those tempting seasonal bits and pieces are high-impulse items that are rarely on a shopper's list and may not necessarily be at their best prices. Maybe you were even impressed with the manager's thoughtfulness, putting together such a handy gathering of raisins, chocolate chips, coconut, and candied fruit the first week of November so you wouldn't forget to do your holiday baking early. If every customer emerged from that seasonal bargain corner with a single item in their cart, the display would more than pay for itself! A better plan is to watch the price of these products all year round and buy them when they're most economical.

Mmmmm, Smell the Bakery

If you outwit the seasonal displays, you still have to contend with the bakery. It is usually in the "dead area" in the right or left corner next to the entrance. But you can smell it as far away as the produce section while picking out your onions. The aroma of freshly baked breads, cookies, and pastries makes a peek at the goodies on display hard to resist, especially when you need to pick up a loaf of sandwich bread anyway. The bread, of course, may be hidden on the back shelves, beyond the English muffins, chocolate-covered doughnuts, and jelly-filled breakfast rolls.

Some bakeries offer a free cookie for your little one. Or they sell an all-time favorite cookie or doughnut for a ridiculously low price one day of the week, usually on a slow day like Tuesday or Wednesday when grocers benefit from enticing mothers into the store.

The in-store bakery is one of the most powerful impulse persuaders in the supermarket. Nearly half of all shoppers who come into the store stop there. And 38 to 58 percent of those who stop buy something. For this reason, the flow of heavy traffic is often purposely directed past the bakery's mouthwatering wares.

Delicious Deli

Even more successful than the bakery at loosening purse strings is the deli. After a hectic day at work, when nothing in particular is planned for dinner, its array of delicacies offer exactly what the hungry shopper is looking for. Creamy potato salads, fresh coleslaw and sauerkraut, spicy lunchmeats, cheeses from every country in Europe all display tiny signs with tempting prices that could turn out to be per half pound or half pint. Sometimes sampling trays are set out to encourage would-be buyers. More than half the shoppers who pause at the deli choose something to take home.

A young mother was observed standing in the long line at the butcher counter of the supermarket, waiting her turn, with the number of her turn in hand. She was obviously very pregnant and very tired. Her two children were becoming more and more restless as they tussled around the shopping cart. Finally a voice called out, "55 . . . 55." "Here I am," she replied, waving her number. Her son immediately and emphatically stated, "But Mom, you're not 55." Without a second's hesitation, she responded wearily, "Today I am! Oh boy, today I am!"

Some supermarkets rely on snack bars instead of deli counters. These are often placed in the dead area next to the bakery where sales on ice cream motivate complementary purchases of baked goods. And

like the bakery, the delicious aromas draw customers in, sometimes right off the street. Snack bars, delis, and bakeries are the supermarkets' means of recovering business lost to fast-food outlets.

Scattered Goods

If you are the typical shopper, milk, meat, and produce will be on your shopping list almost every time you enter the store. And if you have the typical shopper's habitual shopping habits, you pass several thousand square feet of meaty dog food, guaranteed cookware, natural vanilla ice cream, and sog-resistant breakfast cereal, not to mention brooms, thread, envelopes, cake mixes, aluminum foil, and much more before you find what you came for. Remember, retailers don't want you to rush in, grab your few needed staple items, and rush out again. They want you to leisurely wander through the store, view as many of their 50,000 items as possible, and hopefully buy a large assortment of those 50,000 items, in addition to your few needed staple items. That's why those few needed staple items are spread as widely as can be throughout the store.

Nonfoods among the Food Aisles

Marketers and retailers have a vested interest in encouraging the sales of nonfood merchandise. The profit on nonfood goods is 10 times greater than the profit on food items. Because of intense competition, food has a markup (profit) of only 4 or 5 percent. Nonfoods, however, have a markup (profit) of about 40 percent. For example, a retailer may purchase a box of cereal from a supplier for $2.40, and sell it to you for $2.49, a mark-up of about 4 percent. The same retailer may purchase glass cereal bowls for 62 cents each and turn around and sell them for 89 cents, a markup of about 43 percent. The retailer has to sell three boxes of cereal to equal the profit of one cereal bowl. No wonder most grocery stores have large nonfood sections; it's a smart marketing practice—for the grocer.

In addition to the nonfood section, you'll also find carefully

chosen, high-profit, nonfood merchandise strategically scattered around the store in several locations, including throughout the food aisles. Some high-profit items may even be displayed in more than one place in the store. Muffin tins may be on the baking goods aisle, as well as in housewares. Bowls and cups may appear next to breakfast foods. You'll find can openers with canned fruit, potholders with baking powder, ice cream scoops with ice cream, and recipe books in the frozen-food section. Impulse sales on these nonfood items boom when they are displayed in several places.

Toys, in particular, have outgrown the toy section and are finding their way into every aisle of the supermarket. In one store, I counted children's coloring and activity books in five separate displays: on the candy aisle, next to the ice cream freezer, alongside breakfast cereals, in dump bins at the back of the store, and on a table next to cookbooks in the center of a summer-seasonal display. Time-starved parents often take advantage of the "convenience" of readily available children's items while grocery shopping.

What retailers like even more, says the vice president of sales for a company that specializes in marketing toys to supermarkets, are the kids who pick out toys themselves and are then unwilling to put them back on the shelves. "A lot of times you have what's called the 'nag factor.' The child chooses the toy, and the parent lets them have it because it'll keep them quiet during the entire shopping trip."[3]

Shelf Positioning

Purposeful shelf positioning is another technique used to increase impulse shopping. As you move up and down the aisles of the supermarket, pausing occasionally to pick out an item you want, you may find yourself inadvertently avoiding items on the top shelf, where removing a single item may cause an avalanche of cans to rain down on your head, or the bottom shelf, where you can't read the unit-pricing labels without kneeling down, sacrificing the knees of your pants and your dignity.

---

3. Joseph Tarnowski, "More Fun in Store," *Progressive Grocer*, February 2004, 61.

Shelf positioning, or the place where a product sits on the shelf, is a highly competitive business within the grocery industry. The placement of products on the shelves encourages the selection of one brand over another. Since shoppers on the whole do not like to stretch or bend and are more apt to take what is directly in front of them, prime products are given prime positioning. Many times, manufacturers pay to have the most desirable position for their products, which is eye level, hand level, or, in the case of items marketed to children, children's eye level. Eye level is buy level!

> In the cereal aisle of a local supermarket, I heard a child laughing and running. Around the corner popped a tousle-headed tot about three years old. She ran up to the shelf, reached out and grabbed a box of a popular sugared cereal. She hugged it and danced around talking to "her friend." Then Dad came around the end of the aisle. "Can I have it, can I have it?" she begged. "No," came the response. "Please, please, please!" "No!" again came the response. She hugged it, gave it a kiss, put it back on the shelf, and said, "Don't worry. I'll get you next time."

Extend your buying power by looking higher and lower for similar products at better prices. The nickels and dimes add up to dollars.

You will stumble onto intentional shelf positioning where you least expect it. In the meat department, for example, you may find bulkier sale items in the well of the case, with smaller packages on the second shelf, and the high-profit items on top.

> **Extend your buying power** by looking higher and lower for similar products at better prices.

A shopper may intend to buy the ground beef, which is on sale, then look up to see ham or specialty steaks displayed appetizingly at eye level. Suddenly, both items are in the cart.

Favorable positioning is always given to impulse items, especially nonfood gadgets. Houseware profits rise 10 to 15 percent when the

right items dangle from J-hooks, fastened to eye-level shelves up and down the aisle. J-hooks are high-impulse fixtures. They sell the things that you rarely, if ever, put on your list. J-hooks evoke a come-to-think-of-it, I-need-one-of-these response, and they are highly successful at selling. Marketers call them profit hooks.

The positioning of products plays a crucial role since the customer, who is likely concentrating on personal matters as much as shopping, has so many products to choose from. By strategically arranging grocery products, marketers can slow customers down so they end up spending more time and money.

A Bit of Help on the Shelf

Doesn't it just drive you nuts that in order to buy a simple box of cereal or bag of macaroni, you have to sort through an entire aisle of cereal boxes or bags of pasta in varying size packages with varying prices—with apparently no rhyme or reason behind either? Because there are no size regulations for the food industry, you may find that the giant economy-size package is more expensive per ounce than a small size. Random pricing and sizing make it difficult, if not impossible, to compare prices and find the best deal for your dollar.

Fortunately, many grocery stores are willing to help you out by placing unit pricing on their shelves. These wonderful little labels help you figure out which items and which sizes are the best deals. To use them, first be sure the items you are attempting to compare are comparable! For example, heat-and-serve soup should not be compared with condensed soup nor should condensed milk be compared with sweetened condensed milk. Unit pricing doesn't take into account quality differences or personal preferences either. What it does do is make it possible to compare similar items of varying sizes and varying brands. For example, macaroni noodles taste pretty much the same, no matter what brand, so you simply want the cheapest kind. Unit pricing is the way to figure that price out.

A unit price tag should always tell you four things: (1) the name of the food, (2) the weight of the package or size of the container, (3)

how much the total package costs, and (4) the unit price, which is the cost for an ounce, pound, pint, quart, or number in a package. This is the number you can compare from one package to another. For example, a 15-ounce box of Frutty-Tutty-O's is $2.79. A 21-ounce box of Frutty-Tutty-O's is $3.49. By checking the unit price tag, you'll find that the smaller box of cereal is 19 cents per ounce and the bigger box is 17 cents per ounce. So, even though the bigger box costs more overall, it costs less per ounce and is, therefore, a better buy.

If your supermarket doesn't offer unit pricing, do the calculations yourself to find out where the best deals are. Simply divide the price of the item by the size of the item to come up with the unit price. The formula even works when an item is on sale. Unit pricing reflects the regular shelf price, not a sale price. But you can figure out unit pricing for sales yourself to see if the sale price on a small box is better than the regular price on a large box.

For instance, imagine that this week only the 15-ounce box of Frutty-Tutty-O's mentioned earlier is on sale for $2.39. Divide $2.39 by 15, and you'll find the cost is 16 cents per ounce on sale, which makes it a better deal than the large box.

Unit pricing is a great help for frugal shoppers. If your store doesn't offer it, speak to the manager and see if you can get it started. Call your neighbors and invite them to help make it a little campaign. One local store manager I spoke with said if eight or ten customers requested the same thing within a two- to three-week period, he generally acted on their requests.

Downsizing the Containers

Unit pricing can help you unmask a sales tactic manufacturers sometimes use that might slip right past you if you're simply a casual shopper. Grocers hesitate to raise prices because customers may turn to other brands rather than paying more. Instead, a manufacturer may downsize its product while maintaining the price.

You may have noticed this happened to ice cream recently. The price remains the same, but now, instead of buying half a gallon, you

are actually buying less.

Tuna is another example. Over the course of a year, the contents of a standard can of tuna decreased from 6½ ounces to 6¼ ounces, then to 6 ounces. The size of the can remained the same, but it contained less tuna. I remember many years back when Mars Inc. downsized the amount of M&Ms in the candy bar-sized package, from 1.69 ounces in the little bag to 1.59 ounces. This is genuinely only noteworthy because on the new bag it proclaimed in bold letters, "NOW EVEN BIGGER PACK!" I guess it's possible that the package was bigger. It certainly didn't hold more M&M's though.

Point of Purchase

You probably do not recognize the extent of your unplanned purchases, which leaves you vulnerable to persuasive tactics. Once you walk into a store, the moment of truth has arrived. You are at the point of purchase (POP). The critical questions are:

+ What are you going to buy?
+ What will and can influence that money decision?

POP refers to all of the devices and displays placed where a product is sold to persuade you to choose a particular brand or item. If you are like most customers, you come into the supermarket with identical feelings toward several brands of any given product. If you need flour, you have probably heard just as much about one brand as another. The brand that grabs your attention as you

> POP displays increase sales **300 to 600 percent**!

approach the baking foods aisle may well be the one you reach for on the shelf. Therefore, marketers take advantage of one last chance to influence your buying decisions with POP advertising.

Window signs that lure you into the store, ceiling banners, mobiles that bring to mind a commercial or jingle, display carts set up in the middle of an aisle or on a counter next to the product—all these are POP materials, as are posters, pamphlets, recipe cards, and

other in-store identification of a commodity or brand. This conglomeration of POP resources directs you to a specific brand at the point of sale and contributes to impulse buying.

One grocery industry report claims that POP displays are responsible for increasing sales almost 300 percent when the display product is offered at regular price and over 600 percent when combined with an advertised sale price.[4]

Usually a customer comes to a store with a grocery list, albeit a short one. She wanders up and down the aisles, selecting items here and there, all the while taking a mental inventory of the cupboard at home and deciding what to purchase. Because her mind is open to what she may or may not need, it is also open to powerful marketing persuasions. The importance of POP cannot be underestimated.

Awareness of POP

You are probably more influenced by point-of-purchase ingenuity than you realize. Let's use Berry Yummy breakfast cereal for an example. As you drive into the parking lot, you see the Berry Yummy logo smiling radiantly in the corner of the supermarket window, above an announcement of the Berry Yummy Coloring Contest. Not two feet inside the door, a banner, billowing in the air conditioning, reminds you that this week is Berry Yummy Eat-More-Fruit Week. The cart you select sports a sign on the flap of the jump seat cheerfully suggesting, "Start your day the Berry Yummy way."

As you reach for your first purchase of the day, a gallon of milk, you meet the Berry Yummy logo eye-to-eye on a shelf strip, across which is printed, "Start your day the Berry Yummy way with Family Farm's Milk." Turning the corner into the cereal aisle, you nearly overturn a life-size figure of your child's favorite cartoon character pointing to a cardboard display case holding coupons and coloring contest entry forms.

At the other end of the cereal aisle, a cheerful salesclerk gives you a free sample of Berry Yummy cereal in a little paper cup and offers a

---

4. "Merchandising Ideas 1990," *Progressive Grocer*, March 1990, 12

recipe card for Berry Yummy Marshmallow Dream Bars made with Berry Yummy breakfast cereal.

Now this may be an exaggeration, but if so, it's only a slight one. Pay attention the next time you're in a store; you'll see some form of all these POP techniques, perhaps not all for the same product, but there, nonetheless.

POP advertising has a proven track record for increasing sales, whether in the form of simple handmade signs or fancy preprinted materials. In one test example, full use of merchandising POP increased sales 413 percent above similar displays on which only price signs were used. Study after study reveals that the brand that makes the strongest impression at the last moment—the point of purchase—is usually the one sold.

Bargains (?) on Display

The most obvious use of POP materials used to ensnare the impulse buyer is the time-honored, ever-present display. Displays are powerful marketing tools. Even simple displays dramatically increase sales because shoppers are much more likely to purchase an item from an end-of-aisle display than just pick up that same item off the shelf. The sales figures for some of the especially clever displays are astounding; they work wonderfully well for getting people to stop, look, and buy.

> ## Price recognition
> *is an essential skill.*

You literally can't miss a good display. If your shopping cart doesn't hook a wheel on a mid-aisle table leg, your child will pull the bottom can of tuna out from under the artistic pyramid at the end of the aisle. Displays are found on tabletops, counters, and shelves; in shopping carts; and in whatever other locations might attract attention. Even shelf extenders, racks and bins, cardboard "dumps," and the fancy J-hooks that dangle useful gadgets from shelves are displays, though most people don't necessarily think of them as such.

These displays have one purpose only: to encourage you to buy

what you see. Often, this is accomplished by implying savings that may or may not be there. The impression is given that anything on display is on sale. Although weekend specials and other true sale items are generally given display space at the end of the aisles, there's no guarantee that prices are reduced on *every* item featured outside of its regular shelf space. Price recognition is an essential skill and the key to making the most of your buying power.

I was teaching a Beating the High Cost of Eating class in Spokane, Washington, a few years ago. I had talked about in-store psychology and the power of displays, in the morning lectures. During lunch, I walked to a nearby supermarket to check out a few things to discuss with the class later. At the end of an aisle was a display of different kinds of coffee beans that you grind and blend yourself, along side a large coffee grinder. Placed on top of the display was a sign that so delighted me that I burst out laughing. I'm sure the deep meaning of the sign was not intended, but it said it all! "We have moved our bagged coffee to the sucker display above the ice cream cones."

Tie-Ins and Related Item Displays

Tie-ins are just that: two items that somehow tie in with each other. The promotion of one encourages the sale of the other. Retailers often take advantage of popular movies, personalities, or events to help sell their products. For example, a breakfast cereal will tie-in to the publicity surrounding the premiere of the latest superhero movie by plastering the front of the box with the superhero's face and printing a half-price admission ticket to the movie on the back of the box.

A tie-in with a manufacturer's contest or coupon promotion is even more lucrative. Occasionally, two manufacturers will promote each other's products to increase sales for both. You might see cookies advertised with milk, or pretzels with beer. Sometimes coupons will be issued that are only valid with the purchase of both items.

Displays and tie-ins are designed to increase impulse purchases. For example, in an ad to grocers, a manufacturer may detail how a display and perceived $1 savings actually promotes sales at the moment, as well as repeat sales later on. Shoppers confront a poster, a display of tuna and mayonnaise, and multiple recipe ideas using these products, along with a sign proclaiming "SAVE $1" in bold letters. "Spur-of-the-moment shopping ideas have proven they attract customers over and over again," the manufacturer declares in this ad. "It takes just a few seconds for interest to turn into a purchase. And that turns into more profits for you."

On closer inspection, the $1 savings turns out to be in coupons, not cash. But by the time you discover that, the display, recipes, and perceived savings have worked their magic: into your cart go the tuna and mayonnaise.

The related-item display works in a similar fashion. In this case, the tie-in is with another product or group of products. Related-item displays may take the form of two or three products posed together on a stand or shelf; they might also take the form of shelf extenders or J-hooks to totally integrate items throughout an entire department. Children's books in the cereal section or women's fashion magazines in the cosmetics area are examples, establishing another point in the store for impulse sales.

Retailers know if they put up the right racks, the related items will sell. As a shopper, you should even be wary of displays that announce prices you know are actual bargains. A favorite industry profit-making trick is to display a price-cut item alongside a high-return moneymaker. You may save a few cents on the bargain item, but you more than make it worth the store's efforts when you impulsively add to your cart a full-priced item from the display.

Sometimes items on display are on sale for good prices. But they don't have to be! Don't be swayed by the displays. Remember, the store's goal is to sell and make a profit. Your goal is to buy and save money.

Check Out the Checkouts

If you're looking for impulse-buying opportunities at their peak, check out the checkout. The closer you get to the checkout, the more temptations you find. Checkout clutter exists for a purpose—everyone must pass through it, so you are a captive audience. Customers waiting in line have plenty of time for the impulse urge to work its magic. While you wait your turn, you see, touch, poke, pick up, smell, look at, read, and buy!

The location of a POP display can influence sales dramatically. Back-of-the-store displays increase sales by 113 percent and in-aisle displays by 274 percent, but neither space holds a candle to the desirability of front-of-the-store displays. Consequently, manufacturers compete intensely for this most advantageous store space. A display at the front of the store will increase sales by a whopping 426 percent.[5]

It's no wonder the competition for front-end floor space is so intense. To help persuade store operators to give them coveted front-floor space, manufacturers supply free racks, bins, and shelf extenders. They also dispatch jobbers regularly to stock these displays with merchandise and the latest advertising gimmicks.

The congestion around the checkout counters testifies that most manufacturers win their bids to set up POP displays in storefront space. The first thing you usually notice as you stand in line is a shortage of checkers, which often leaves you at the end of a nice, long line with 10 or 15 minutes to kill. At least the manager provides a variety of things to look at.

Who would have guessed that there were so many varieties of beef jerky? Key rings in every imaginable style and design twirl on little carousels for your inspection. A dump bin of handy palm-sized accessories, refrigerator magnets, flashlights, calculators, and such (all under $1!) just begs you to sift and discover treasures you may need or want. Even though batteries, emery boards, combs, and razor blades are rarely on your list, they are always useful—and available at checkout stands!

---

5. Ibid., 12.

> A man observed a woman in a grocery store with a three-year-old in her basket. As they passed the cookie section, the child asked for cookies and her mother told her no. The girl immediately began to whine and fuss, and the mother said quietly, "Now Ellen, we just have half of the aisles to go through, don't be upset. It won't be long." The man passed them again in the candy aisle. Of course, the little girl began to shout for candy. When she was told she couldn't have any, she began to cry. The mother said, "There, there, Ellen, don't start crying. Only two more aisles to go, and then we'll be checking out." The man again happened to be behind the pair at the checkout, where again the little girl immediately began to clamor for gum and burst into a terrible tantrum when the mother again said no, adding patiently, "Ellen, we'll be through this checkout stand in five minutes, and then you can go home and have a nice nap." Out in the parking lot, the man stopped to talk to the woman and compliment her. "I couldn't help noticing how patient you were with little Ellen." The mother broke in, "My little girl's name is Tammy. *I'm* Ellen."

The closer you get to the cash register, the more products clamor for your attention. Characters from pocket-size paperbacks stare at you from wire balconies, and when you get close enough, you can read about the authors or what the book reviewers had to say. Magazines and tabloids are even better because, even if you can't read a whole article, you at least have time to look at the "exclusive" pictures of the latest celebrity criminal or see if those "stylish skirts for under $30" are at all your taste. One in-trade magazine estimated that 90 to 99 percent of those who pick up something to read, buy it! One well-known tabloid even credits its vast circulation, far above that of most other newspapers, exclusively to the fact that it is prominently displayed for impulse purchasing.

However, close attention to magazines isn't advised for parents with small children confined to the jump seats of shopping carts. The unwilling prisoners become experts at scooting carts sideways within reach of the cart-high gum and candy. The punch of a small thumb through a weak cellophane wrapper means a sure purchase. And then sister and brother have to be appeased too.

It's no accident that most child-oriented merchandise is displayed

nose-high to a three-year-old. Children create extra sales. One disgruntled mother reported, "Last week, I finally got fed up with the assault at the checkout stand. It almost forces my children's demands. So when my child again opened a package of child-eye-level candy, I promptly took him, and it, to the manager and said, 'You wanted him to buy it, I think you should pay for it!' Sheepishly, the manager replied, 'I'm sorry, but that's the way stores are.'"

Defensive spending skills, or rather, defensive standing and waiting skills are absolutely essential at the checkout.

Your Decisions, Not Store Decisions

These few psychological methods of persuasion are only the tip of the point of purchase iceberg. Many, many other methods exist to coax you to part with your grocery dollars, including spending inducements such as recipes, nutrition information, sampling, in-store TVs, music, and more.

> Your purchases should be **your** decisions, not store decisions.

By the time you work your way down aisle after aisle of POP bombardment, past numerous creative end-of-aisle displays, through the target zone to the checkout stand to unload your groceries and write out your check, you've had plenty of impulse-buying opportunities. The jungle-clutter of well-situated merchandise is carefully planned by the industry for that very purpose. POP is powerful, and it's everywhere. You have to stay on your toes to make sure you don't fall victim to the powerful persuasive influences subconsciously assaulting you on every front. Your purchases should be *your* decisions, not store decisions.

THINGS TO KNOW

◆ Impulse buying can destroy your budget.

◆ Stores are specifically designed to encourage impulse purchases.

◆ Everything in a store, from store layout to shelf positioning to point of purchase materials, is planned specifically to increase sales.

THINGS TO DO

◆ Plan your purchases before you get to the store.

◆ Become familiar with prices. Price recognition is vital in order to combat the psychological strategies that influence your spending.

◆ Recognize persuasive marketing tactics. Awareness of these tactics allows you to develop necessary defensive shopping skills. Be aware of the marketing techniques used by retailers, and don't let them sway you.

◆ Notice unit pricing. If a store offers it, use it. If not, ask a manager to make it available. In the meantime, do the math yourself. Divide the cost of an item by the size of the item so you can make wise decisions.

◆ Carry a small calculator when you shop; it can save you money!

4

Games and Gimmicks:
Are You Playing Games with Your Grocery Budget?

Would you like to win an all-expenses-paid cruise to the Caribbean? What about a year's supply of groceries? Or an instant $1,000? Would that help your budget?

You've seen the ads:

* $10,000 cash!
* Instant winners!
* Win a new car!
* Win your $25,000 fantasy vacation!

Someone has to win, you reason with yourself. Why not you?

Grocery stores offer a legitimate and necessary service to the community. We couldn't get along without them. Most retailers in the grocery business are proud of the service they offer and view themselves as a friend to the consumer, but they are also in business to make a living. To make a business successful, especially a business as competitive as groceries, grocers must use a little resourcefulness now and then to spark customer interest.

Games, contests, giveaways, promotions, and other gimmicks are all are designed with your budget in mind. Their purpose is to draw you back to the store again and again, week after week, because the more you're in the store, the more you're going to spend.

These marketing techniques may appear to be games and gimmicks, but if you look closer, they're not really games at all. They're

big business. By and large, you may not be aware of how sophisticated these "fun" techniques have become in persuading you to part with your money. They are presented in such a way as to appear unrelated to bigger food bills, but don't be fooled. When a store runs a game or contest or promotion, sales increase throughout the store by 15 percent or more for the duration of the game. The word *game* may imply fun, but in relation to your budget, it means *spend*. To be a successful shopper, you must spot a gimmick for what it is. Enjoy it, if you wish. But don't let it increase your grocery bills.

Two Levels of Gimmicks

Two segments of the grocery industry invite you to play and win on a daily basis: the grocers and the manufacturers. While grocers sponsor gimmicks to earn your loyalty to their stores, manufacturers do the same to win loyalty to their brands. Grocers entice you with games, contests, continuity programs, and trading stamps. Manufacturers furnish "instant win" cards, sweepstakes entry forms, coupons, and refunds. Both rely on skillful advertising techniques, and both appeal to the desire to get something for nothing.

> The purpose of games and other gimmicks is to **draw you back** to the store again and again because the more you're in the store, the **more you're going to spend.**

Understandably, the idea of getting something for free is extremely appealing. It represents the ultimate bargain. But to paraphrase a popular quote, "There is no such thing as a free bag of groceries." The purpose of any promotion is not to give things away but to create sales. A "free" gift or contest prize is simply an enticing sales strategy. Don't be misled. The word does not mean *without any cost to you.*

The problem with games and gimmicks is not that someone has

to win but rather that someone also has to pay for the promotion. Often they are the same someone! Whether or not you are a winner, if you are shopping in a store that is playing games and promoting gimmicks, you'll pay extra just for the chance to win.

Gimmicks Used by Grocers

Supermarkets use promises of gifts, savings, or a chance to win to convince you to return week after week. And many consumers do, figuring since they have to buy groceries anyway, they may as well purchase them from a store with a free bonus or fun gimmick. They don't realize they pay for the free bonus or gimmick at the checkout stand in the increased overall prices of groceries necessary to pay for the game. The most common gimmicks used by grocers are listed below.

Supermarket Games

Supermarket games first became popular in the late 1960s. However, they faded from the picture for a while until, after a 20-year hiatus, they began to reappear in the mid-'90s. From versions of Bingo to take-offs on TV shows such as "Let's Make a Deal" and "Wheel of Fortune," supermarket games usually involve collecting small cardboard tickets that you tear open or rub clean to produce a letter or number required to complete a winning sequence. Sometimes tickets reveal instant winners of small rewards such as a loaf of bread or a carton of eggs. Always, however, the game lures you back into the store again and again to try to obtain winning tickets.

Although no purchase is necessary in order to receive a ticket, not many adults (you usually have to be over 18) feel comfortable standing in line at a grocery store just to ask for a free ticket. When several tickets are needed to win, shoppers feel especially embarrassed when they repeatedly ask for game pieces without buying any groceries. Usually, those who want to play a supermarket game do all of their shopping at the store where the game is offered, which is exactly the response retailers want. Supermarkets sponsoring games report an

impressive 15 percent increase in sales for the duration of a game, usually a 13- to 14-week period.

Continuity Programs

A continuity program is any special offer that brings you back to a particular supermarket over and over again to purchase one piece from a set of items each week or month. The set of items can be anything from books to dishes to pots and pans—anything that can be divided into installments. With a continuity program, you need to return again and again to complete the set.

Often, the string attached to completing a particular set is that you must spend a specified dollar amount to qualify for the weekly offering. The lovely cup and saucer needed to complete your china set is only $3.99— with register receipts totaling $30. Volumes QRS of your encyclopedia set are only $5.99—with each additional purchase of $20 or more. And while you're at the store spending that $20, if you decide to buy the rest of your groceries at the same time, Bingo! Chalk one up for the store, because it's the winner.

> Once in a while you can win with store gimmicks. At the time our daughter was to be married, a new supermarket opened up just a mile or so down the road. One of its grand opening come-ons was a continuity program offering stoneware dishes for FREE with cash register receipts showing the required dollar amount spent. Our daughter elicited the support of the whole neighborhood, and with their help she acquired enough cash register receipts to qualify for stoneware place settings for twelve, complete with all of the special serving dishes. That's the only time I have ever seen a continuity program where the weekly special offer was free, and boy, did we take advantage of it!

The goal for the pots, pans, dishes, books, and stamps is to lock you into shopping at one store. The most important purpose of a continuity program is to create store loyalty. The more you come back, the more you become familiar with the store, and the more likely you

are to make it your regular place to shop.

Continuity programs also, in all probability, increase your spending. You repeatedly go back and spend the required amount, and more, to purchase each item before the next piece of the set moves into the featured position—or before the promotion ends. By the time you actually complete the set of whatever it is you're collecting, what kind of a dent have you made in your grocery budget?

Let's take a hard look at how much you're actually spending to collect those promotional prizes. One plan featuring a set of china required the purchase of $1,600 worth of groceries to qualify for a 32-piece service for eight. That would be $1,600 of regularly priced, not-on-sale groceries, since most stores reduce specials during the course of a gimmick to keep costs down.

Retailers can only spend so much money on marketing. If they spend it all to offer pots and pans, they have to make up the cost in the price of hamburger and canned goods. If the continuity program brings a grocer the expected results, he may be able to absorb the cost of the promotion. But if sales don't increase by a healthy margin, costs are passed on to you through price increases on items throughout the store, or through fewer sales.

Is that china something you really need, or are you just caught up in the game? Did you even know that you needed a set of china before you saw it promoted in the grocery store? Maybe you have a hard time passing it up because it seems like such a bargain. Whether or not the featured jewelry, dishes, cookware, or books are a bargain can only be determined by comparison shopping wherever else they are sold. The real issue is whether or not the required groceries are a bargain. Again, comparison shopping is how you can tell.

Fill 'er Up

"Fill up your car after you've filled up your cart" could be the mantra of today's supermarkets. Gas stations are cropping up in grocery store parking lots all over the nation, or at least as a partner program with a gas station down the street, as grocers rush to cash in on this popular loyalty program. When you spend a certain amount

of money in the store, you receive a discount on each gallon of gas. It sounds like a great deal, especially when gas prices soar sky high.

However, grocery store gas programs are designed to promote store loyalty. Like all spend-to-save gimmicks, someone pays for the gimmick. That someone is everyone who pays the grocery price increases necessary to support the gas gimmick, one of the latest in a long line of loyalty programs designed to lock you into one store.

Trading Stamps

If you're older than thirty, you probably remember receiving trading stamps from grocery stores and gas stations when you were growing up. If you were like most of us, you carefully pasted the stamps in their books and pored over the little catalogs, trying to decide what you were going to "spend" your stamps on. It was practically a national pastime. Our family, like many others, saved the books of stamps all year long and redeemed them for Christmas shopping.

> Stamps can be traced back to 1890 when a Milwaukee department store first began offering Blue Chip Trading Stamps. The famous Thomas Sperry and Shelley Hutchinson team began printing S&H Green Stamps several years later.

The 1950s saw an unprecedented boom in the business, and by 1963, an estimated 80 percent of all food stores in the nation distributed stamps! Stamps decreased markedly in popularity during the '70s, due to inflation, the oil embargo, which led to cancellation of hundreds of stamp contracts carried by gas stations, and a growing public skepticism over the supposed savings they represented.

Even then, trading stamps were just an elaborate continuity program, and like all continuity programs, they required spending before saving. When you shopped at a store that promoted them, you received a saver's book, along with one stamp for every dollar you spent. You pasted the stamps in your saver's book, and when you collected enough stamps, you redeemed them at special centers for gift merchandise.

Studies and surveys conducted in the '60s during the heyday of trading stamps show clearly that stamp companies were the only ones that consistently benefited from the stamp craze. Stamps turned out to be a costly promotion, requiring a 12 to 15 percent jump in sales just to break even. Less than 10 percent of retailers were able to absorb the increased costs associated with stamps, and the vast majority of stores compensated by raising their prices, offering fewer specials and/or reducing their advertising expenditures. A wiser, price-conscious public recognized this, and stamps were never able to regain the popularity of their glory years.

However, stamp companies may be on the move again—this time with a few changes in marketing strategies. One intrepid company is concentrating on attracting stores with a high-quality image. Their pitch to grocers claims that stamps (or point programs) appeal to the upscale customer who expects more—and is willing to pay more—for quality. This stamp company also solicits businesses other than supermarkets, including airlines, rent-a-car companies, travel inns, truck stops, pharmacies, bowling allies, and florists, in order to build a family of local businesses where customers can obtain stamps.

As an extra incentive to consumers who collect stamps, the company is also modernizing its redemption centers, now called gift centers, to better convince you that the reward is free. Who knows if it will catch on again. Just keep in mind that no matter how the program is packaged, one fact remains: continuity programs cost money, and the consumer is usually the one who foots the bill.

Smart Cards

Many stores have jumped onto one of the latest marketing bandwagons by offering smart cards, or loyalty cards as they're called in the industry, to their customers. You have probably heard them called reward cards, value cards, or frequent-shopper programs, with the reward being able to purchase certain items at a lower price than those who don't have a card. The card enables you to take advantage of a store's specials, as well as receive notices and offers in the mail or by e-mail.

To receive a value card, you must fill out an application and provide your name, address, zip code, phone number, and other personal information. When the checker scans your card, the sales prices of your purchases are automatically rung up and the information recorded by the computer. In 2000, 70 percent of consumers participated in these frequent-shopper programs.

> *The value of a value card is primarily for the stores.*

The value of these cards is primarily for the stores. First, you give them your personal information. They use that information to electronically track and record what you buy, when you buy, and how much you buy. The stores or manufacturers then use that information, along with the information from the other shoppers in your community, to tailor their sales and promotions both to serve you and to influence your spending. If you don't wish to divulge your private information, and only 3 percent of shoppers chose not to in 2000, you are welcome to shop in their store, but you will pay full price for everything. Sales prices are reserved for cardholders.

The availability of sophisticated technology greatly impacts the way you receive promotional offers. For example, the coupons that used to be printed in a retail store's advertisements have been virtually replaced by electronic discounts available to you through retailer's loyalty card programs. In fact, e-promotions are the number one reason for frequent-shopper programs. These permission-based marketing techniques (you voluntarily gave your information, ergo your permission) are a boon to retailers, who use that specifically targeted information to devise effective promotions aimed directly at you.

I reluctantly have a few of these cards, and I use them occasionally when the stores advertise particularly good bargains. I prefer, though, being able to take advantage of a store's specials without having my choices and habits electronically monitored.

Loyalty programs such as stamps, point programs, and smart cards proliferate during difficult economic times. A recent report

---

6. Richard Turcsik, "A Retailer's Best Friend," *Progressive Grocer*, April 15, 2004, 60.

from the grocery industry boasts of the success of these programs, noting, "Dubbed as a 'retailer's best friend,' the frequent-shopper card and stamp/point programs are proven to increase the number of a store's most faithful shoppers, especially in . . . turbulent economic times."[6] Grocers love these programs, not only because of the valuable customer information they garner, but especially because of the store loyalty they generate. They are considered a "defensive tool against other alternative retail outlets."[7]

The Battle for Your Business

On the surface, indulging in supermarket gimmicks seems unrelated to bigger food bills. Since you have to spend grocery money somewhere, why not spend it where there is an extra feature, such as Smart Cards, or where there is a chance to win something? However, even the simplest and quickest comparison shopping supports two conclusions: (1) stores that spend money on fantastic promotions either raise prices or reduce specials, and (2) no single store has the lowest prices on all products at all times.

Even the stores sometimes admit that they can't pay for games and gimmicks without raising prices. During a grocery store price war a few years ago, one grocery store chain ran a full-page ad proclaiming, "No Games, No Gimmicks, No High Prices. Why we won't play games with your food dollars." The ad continued, "In these days of high inflation, we think our major responsibility is to keep food prices as low as possible. That's why we don't have a supermarket game. Games are expensive, and for every winner there are a thousand losers. Who loses? Perhaps you and your family, in the form of higher prices. If you want lower prices storewide, we invite you to change to [our store]."

---

7. Ibid.

If you are interested in stretching your budget as far as it will go, you'll find that doing all your grocery shopping in one store is never best. This is especially true where gimmicks are offered and over-spending is encouraged to qualify for the rewards.

Manufacturer Promotions

Giveaways are, of course, not limited to the supermarket itself. Manufacturers also use games and gimmicks to entice you to select their products over the competition. From coupons and refunds to in-pack, instant-winner game cards, the idea is to convince you that you enjoy something extra for your money when you purchase a particular product. However, as I've said before, the purpose of any kind of promotion is not to give things away

> The **purpose** of any kind of promotion **is** not **to** give things away but to **sell things**.

but to sell things. A well-executed promotion creates immediate action by the consumer, whether that action is to grab a box of cereal off a supermarket shelf or take a handful of coupons to the store.

Premiums and Games

Premium offers, or a free gift inside a package, continue to be a favorite name-brand company technique for stimulating sales, especially with products that appeal to children. McDonald's has fine-tuned the premium offer, a free toy with every child's meal, into a wildly successful, multibillion-dollar, global marketing stratagem.

Breakfast cereal is also a prime candidate for premium offers. You'll find anything from action figures to CD's to storybooks and more in cereal boxes, targeted right at the little people who influence the shoppers. Children love toys, and if they have a choice between a box of sugar-coated cereal with a toy and a box without one, they go for the toy every time. And often, Mom or Dad buy it because it's easier than dealing with a tantrum in the store.

For adult customers, premium offers often take the form of a free packet of conditioner shrink-wrapped to a bottle of shampoo or a free toothbrush packaged in the toothpaste box. It could be a free salad dressing cruet when you purchase dry salad dressing mix, a coupon for free milk with your package of cookies, or a special package of four markers for the same price as a three-marker package.

When you choose a product with a freebie attached, you have succumbed to a premium. Whether the freebie is actually free is another story. Remember, someone has to pay for these gimmicks. Before you allow yourself to be enticed by a premium, make sure the price on the product itself is acceptable. Marketers find that many consumers are perfectly willing to purchase their products in order to receive a premium, even if they have to switch brands to do it.

Premiums also take the form of instant-win game pieces. You may rub off the silver circle on your in-pack game ticket to discover you've won a $1,000 shopping spree or a trip to the Super Bowl. Maybe it's just a coupon for 15 cents off your next purchase. Either way, you're still a winner!

For a long time, manufacturers balked at using marketing tactics such as instant-win games and contests because, by law, they could not legally require a person to purchase the product in order to enter. Then a government ruling that in-pack games and contests were legal as long as customers could also obtain a card, or entry form, without a purchase changed industry attitudes.

Now instant-winner players have the option of mailing a self-addressed stamped envelope to the company, requesting a game piece or entry form. How many people do you know who will spend 80 cents or so in postage and paper to send for a game piece that will give them a slight chance to win a prize? Not many. Since few shoppers request game cards through the mail, or even realize that the small print on the package advises they can do so, in-pack promotions have become a successful way to spark sales.

Contests and Sweepstakes

As popular as in-pack premiums and promotions are, they take a back seat in popularity to contests and sweepstakes. The prizes sound phenomenal—a dream vacation, a new car, $10,000. Any of us would be thrilled to win. And there is no shortage of opportunities! Hardly a day goes by in the life of any consumer without an invitation to submit your best recipe, match game cards to symbols on packages, spell out the winning phrase, or vote for a favorite ballplayer. You're supposed to be excited by the prizes and anxious to participate. But you aren't necessarily supposed to win. You're just supposed to play and spend, spend, spend.

> You aren't necessarily supposed to win supermarket games; you're supposed to play and **spend**!

Manufacturers are not so concerned with how many people play their games or enter their contests as they are with how many supermarkets decide to feature their contests with in-store displays. Displays mean sales, and sales are the bottom line. An avalanche of entries may be a feather in the cap of the individual who designed the contest, but the thrill for the manufacturer is the markedly increased sales that result from having the company's in-store displays featured in supermarkets. The manufacturer is not really interested in whether or not you play his game, he's interested in grabbing your attention in the aisles and making you look twice at his product. If you look twice at the critical point of purchase, chances are his product is the one you'll buy.

Even though legally a purchase cannot be required, manufacturers work hard to avoid no-purchase entries by inventing contests that strongly motivate you to buy a product when you enter. For instance, in one contest you could mail in an entry form by itself, or you could receive a free holiday-recipe idea book if you include a proof of purchase as well. One household cleaner sweepstakes advertised a prize everyone could win simply by mailing in a proof of purchase.

Complicated Combinations

Meanwhile, there are so many sweepstakes out there these days that it's difficult to come up with truly original contest ideas. In order to be innovative, many manufacturers have moved past sweepstakes and combined several gimmicks into one. For example, a condiment manufacturer offered a contest for a backyard makeover and a chance to appear on a home-and-garden television show, along with recipe offers and coupons worth up to $1.25. From a juice manufacturer you could win a trip to Australia, get a free movie poster for three proofs of purchase, and receive juice coupons. An ice cream company combined a coupon with a chance (hidden at the bottom of the ice cream carton) to be in a movie. Another option encourages you to create a recipe with packaged fruit, purchased with a coupon, of course, and possibly win a scholarship and a trip. Write a creative essay for a margarine manufacturer and win a servant for a day, plus you can check out the website for holiday tips and recipes. A cola drink producer mixed a mystery shopper and coupons with a grocery-giveaway sweepstakes.

Companies not only combine techniques, they also work with each other to organize tie-in promotions. The tie-in can be as simple as a cross-couponing promotion for cereal and milk, or as complex as a multimedia sweepstakes/couponing effort that promotes dozens of brands of canned goods.

The planning, preparation, and execution of such promotions are getting so complicated that the majority of manufacturers simply hire a marketing firm versed in sweepstakes and contests to handle everything from beginning to end. In fact, the whole matter of games and gimmicks has reached big-business proportions, with entire companies built around various aspects. These services, of course, are never free. Millions are spent annually in the industry on a variety of gimmicks, comprising an estimated 60 percent of the nationwide marketing budget! And remember who pays for it, when all is said and done.

Advertising Gimmicks

Although advertising plays an important and necessary role in grocery merchandising, it also increases many individual food budgets and can itself be considered a gimmick. Knowledge of basic advertising techniques should reduce your susceptibility to many ploys.

You must recognize that advertising involves more than blitzing you with a product name in jingles, newspaper ads, mailed coupons, and TV commercials. Advertising is highly professional work with sophisticated research behind it. To make sure a product doesn't gather dust on the grocery shelf, companies employ highly trained and highly paid psychologists who are schooled in motivational analysis or the art of discerning why you buy what you buy. If you happen to belong to the age, sex, or income level targeted for a new product, your buying habits are thoroughly dissected. Scientific marketing research is conducted to further explore the reasoning behind your purchases. The conclusions from this research aid advertisers in designing ads that take advantage of your deepest desires and most protected fears.

By the time advertisers complete their studies, they know whether to attract your attention with a pretty face, a cuddly animal, or a clever phrase. They can also guess whether you worry most about your health or your success with the opposite sex, whether you would rather have more money, more time, or a feeling of superiority. And they know whether putting a recipe or an energy-saving tip on a package will make you feel like you are getting more for your money's worth.

Types of Advertising

You can better arm yourself against psychological advertising techniques if you are familiar with two main types of ads or commercials: institutional and product differentiation. In the first, a company tries to establish a friendly, confident feeling toward an

entire line of products ("You and Betty Crocker can bake someone happy," "L'oreal, because you're worth it," and "Nobody doesn't like Sara Lee") or toward an entire industry (Tony the Tiger telling you to eat a good breakfast).

In product differentiation ads, sellers seek to distinguish their product from all of the others on the market. For example, soap contains a simple ingredient base, lye and fat, that cannot be greatly altered. Yet a manufacturer that advertised "just another good soap" would not likely survive today's competitive scramble. The manufacturer tries to persuade you, therefore, that its soap has something special, perhaps the shape, color, or smell, even though most other soaps will get you just as clean.

Advertising Food

When it comes to food advertising, special techniques are used based on what has boosted sales in past campaigns. For instance, marketers know how important it is to make your mouth water as you watch a commercial. Food is shown in motion (syrup pouring from a bottle) and heard in the background (steak sizzling, popcorn popping). Even newspaper ads are designed with appetite appeal in mind. Food is usually shown temptingly cooked and ready to eat. A raw piece of meat has never made anyone hungry.

Another gimmick used to inspire appetite appeal is borrowing foods that complement the one being advertised. Warm cookies are shown with a cold glass of milk; hamburgers sit temptingly on open buns, garnished with pickles, onions, and tomatoes; a slice of pie is topped with a scoop of ice cream. You are more likely to buy food if you see it fixed the way you would eat it.

To protect yourself from advertising gimmicks, try to determine the angle each ad is coming from. How is the ad trying to appeal to you? Are you really going to feel younger, be more popular, improve your sex life, be more successful, or have more friends if you buy that item? Probably not.

Come back to real life and ask the truly important questions: Is it on your grocery list, and is it a good bargain? The answers to

these two questions are what truly matter when it comes to food, no matter what the advertising industry tells you.

What's the Harm?

When you do your price-recognition homework first and are loaded with self-control, there is little harm in participating in supermarket games and gimmicks. But too many household budgets are undermined by such promotions, usually the budgets of those who can least afford the impact. Dazzled by the prospect of, perhaps this once, becoming the lucky winner, these shoppers consistently overpurchase, both in quantity (buying more than they need simply to obtain the game pieces) and in quality (paying high prices for products that are available for less under competing labels or in other stores).

To protect your budget, watch out for stores offering games; you must be fully armed with price recognition to defend against possible price increases. Watch out for manufacturer gimmicks also. Be sure the price is right first, and check competitive brands for better deals before you buy.

THINGS TO KNOW

◆ When a store runs a game, contest, or promotion, sales increase throughout the store by 15 percent or more for the duration of the game.

◆ Grocers sponsor gimmicks to earn your loyalty to their stores; manufacturers do it to gain loyalty to their brands.

◆ Whether or not you are a winner, you pay extra for the chance to play when you purchase products at stores that offer games and gimmicks.

◆ Stores that spend money on fantastic promotions raise prices, reduce specials or sales, or decrease advertising to compensate.

✦ Manufacturers promote gimmicks to encourage supermarkets to feature their contests with in-store displays. Displays equate sales, and sales are the bottom line.

THINGS TO DO

✦ Be aware of why supermarkets and manufacturers offer games and gimmicks and how those games and gimmicks can impact your budget.

✦ Price consciousness, or the awareness of the actual price of certain products, is your best defense against games and gimmicks.

5

The Brandwagon:
Full of Savings Options

Walking down the aisles of a supermarket, you face an endless sea of food in every style, size, brand, and variety. If I were to send you to the store with only the instruction, "Bring back some corn for dinner," you would have quite a dilemma. Should you buy fresh, frozen, or canned?

In the produce department, you can buy farmer-packed corn tossed haphazardly in a huge bin or a neat shrink-wrapped package of four or five pre-shucked ears. In the frozen foods aisle, you'll discover nine kinds of frozen corn, not counting corn with other vegetables mixed in. The canned vegetable aisle is overwhelming. There are eight kinds of canned corn available—nine more if you include creamed corn, and four more if you count hominy and corn mixed with other vegetables! So with only the instruction, "Bring home corn," you have to select from more than 31 choices.

In a major chain store one day, I counted 23 different brands of laundry detergent. (Not different sizes of boxes, but 23 different brand names.) And at a store down the street, I discovered five more! In every store, you are inundated with choices for how to spend your money. With literally thousands of brands to choose from, how can you distinguish one from the next? It would take a lifetime to try them all.

General Brand Categories

Some of the names on product labels are familiar. Everyone recognizes Del Monte and Pillsbury and General Mills and other national brand names. But what about some of the other brands that you don't recognize? They may be cheaper, but are they as good?

Experience has proven that the cheapest product is not necessarily the best product. If it doesn't taste good, you'll end up throwing it out, and that's no bargain. On the other hand, it may be just as good and a bargain to boot. With so many brands to choose from, your choices can and do affect your budget! It's important, then, that you have some idea of the quality represented by the different brands as you shop. Fortunately, there are guidelines that can smooth the way.

All brands can be broken down into four general categories:

✦ National name brands
✦ House brands and private labels
✦ Economy brands
✦ Generics

Within each category, the brands are essentially equal in quality. But distinctions exist between categories, with each type having clear advantages and disadvantages. Whether you select generics over economy brands or national name brands over house brands depends entirely on your personal preferences after you determine what the options actually are. (See "Brand Quiz" on page 189.)

In 2002 a record number of new products were introduced to consumers. More than 22,000 new products hit the shelves. Some of these will be hits and become staples consumers will buy for decades. Others will fizzle out after a few months or years, either because they're poor quality, poorly marketed, too trendy, not worth buying repeatedly, or just outlive their usefulness. Do you remember these products that are no longer available: Space Food Sticks, Dr. Lyon's Tooth Powder, Prell Concentrate Shampoo, Burma Shave Shaving Cream, Salvo Laundry Detergent Tablets, Rusket's cereal biscuits, Dr. Ross Dog Food, and Brylcreem Hair Styling Cream? Can you name any others?

National Name Brands

National brands are the products that carry the labels and names that are advertised and marketed on a national basis. Most people are familiar with them. How many of you can sing the Oscar Mayer Wiener song? Do you know what goes Plop, Plop, Fizz, Fizz? We know that Frosted Flakes taste Grrrrreat! because Tony the Tiger says so. And what's on a Big Mac? All together: "Two all-beef patties, special sauce . . ." ♪

The advertising for national brands is extremely effective. Sometimes the advertising continues working long after the actual product is out of production. You'll see something that will trigger a memory, and suddenly you'll be humming a long-forgotten tune for a breakfast cereal or cooking oil. My husband can sing a jingle from a dog food commercial from his childhood without missing a word. The Dr. Ross dog food company is no longer in business, but its ad campaign is still working, even after so many years. That's good advertising!

Some products are so tied to a certain name brand that the brand name becomes the accepted name of the product

> Advertising can be a powerful art form, and marketers take it very seriously. Did you know there are international awards given every year for the best commercials and ads? They're called the CLIO Awards, and their mission is: "To provide the international advertising and design industry with the world's best-judged creative competition in the areas of TV, Print, Outdoor, Radio—[and more]—and in so doing, to honor advertising and design excellence worldwide." If you ever get a chance to watch the CLIO awards, you'll find them very entertaining!
>
> (CLIO Awards mission statement, www.clioawards.com)

in general. If you cut your finger, do you go to the cupboard and get an adhesive bandage for it? Neither do I. I get a Band-Aid, no matter what the brand name on the box actually is. We just naturally call them Band-Aids! (See "Do You Remember?" on page 190 .)

A main purpose of this powerful advertising is to convince you, the consumer, that a certain product is superior. There is no

question that brand name products are produced with quality and high specifications. You'll find, almost without exception, that any brand that can survive in today's intensely competitive market is top-quality merchandise. In most cases, years of research and experimentation have generated excellent products in pleasant-to-look-at and convenient-to-use packaging. National brand manufacturers work extremely hard to ensure that their products are consistent and reliable. Each time you buy that product, you can count on the same good taste and quality.

House Brands and Private Labels

Like name brands, house brands and private labels are brands made with consistent, reliable specifications and standards, only without the national advertising and marketing campaigns to promote them. The most familiar labels in this category are house brands, or products that carry the name of a specific store or become identified as that store's brand. For example, Albertson's stores offer Albertson's brand products; Kroger carries Kroger brand. Most supermarkets, discount drugstores, mass merchandisers, department stores, and even membership stores carry a house brand, sometimes more than one. Costco carries Kirkland brand items. Wal-Mart and

"Store Brands Save Consumers More Than Brand Coupons," proclaims the headline in an in-trade magazine. "Even with double coupons, which retailers hate to resort to anyway, national brands aren't a bargain. Instead of wasting their time clipping coupons, consumers should start buying private label." The article goes on to cite a study conducted by National Retail Tracking Index, Inc. Thirty-five items were tracked over a four-month period. When nationally advertised brands were purchased, these items cost $62.55. With coupons, the savings totaled only $2.19, or about 3 percent, for a final cost of $60.36. If double couponing was taken into account, that still left the cost at $58.17. However, when the same products were purchased as quality store brands, the total was only $44.14, for a savings of $18.41, or more than 30 percent over nationally advertised brand prices. (*Private Label Magazine*, July/August 1985)

Sam's Club carry the Sam's Choice brands. You will not see a store-specific house brand for sale in any stores other than the ones they are especially made for.

These brands aren't always easily identified, however. Some supermarkets boast a number of house brands under a variety of names. For example, Safeway carries both the Safeway brand and the Town House brand, as well as Lucerne and Mrs. Wright's.

Private label brands are made with consistent, reliable specifications and standards, but they are available in more than one chain of stores. These brands are marketed to many different stores. For example, Western Family is a private label brand carried by many Associated Grocers stores. Associated Grocers, Inc. (AGI) and Independent Grocers Association (IGA) are two worldwide, wholesale grocery distribution centers that serve large groups of independent retailers.

> House brands and private labels are **money-stretching powerhouses** for beating the high cost of eating.

These stores and store chains are individually owned and operated, but they have banded together to qualify for the same purchasing power as the larger, more powerful store chains. House brands and private label products may range from goods sold exclusively to a certain store or chain of stores to institutional merchandise sold only to hospitals, restaurants, and schools.

If you avoid house brands because you believe they lack the high quality of name brands, you're in for a pleasant surprise. With very few exceptions, house brands equal, and even surpass, name-brand products in required specifications and standards. The quality is every bit as good! You'll find that house brands and private labels could become real heroes for your budget. You can save an immediate 15 to 30 percent over the price of national brand products, even more if the house brands are on sale. House brands and private labels are money-stretching powerhouses for beating the high cost of eating.

Economy Brands

Unfamiliar labels can be confusing at times because many stores carry an economy brand line as well as their house brands and private labels. While economy brands are a form of house brand or private label, they emphasize lower price rather than higher quality, although they still maintain consistent specifications and standards. The lower quality has no effect on nutrition or food value. The difference is essentially esthetics, or appearance.

> If the label is **unfamiliar** to you, ask the store manager to tell you about that brand.

In clothing or soft goods, you'll recognize it as an irregular, a pulled thread or a blur in the die lot, or a crooked seam. The flaw doesn't affect the function, just the appearance. With food, it may mean that the green beans are not all exactly 3/4" long, or the peach slices may have a nick out of them, or some other inconsistent appearance that has no affect on food value. Unless the president is coming to dinner, these items are perfectly acceptable. Even if you can't stand uneven-length green beans on your plate, you can hide them in casseroles or other recipes.

The problem is you may not know how to differentiate economy brands from high-quality house brands simply by looking at the packaging. If the label is unfamiliar to you, the only way to tell the difference is by trying it or asking the store manager to tell you about that brand.

For years, Safeway was the major promoter of economy brands; the company carried Scotch Buy. Now many major stores carry lines of economy brands: P&Q at A&P, Cost-Cutter at Kroger, and Basics at Grand Union are just a few examples. Selling at 20 to 35 percent below national brand prices, economy brands can be a boon to your budget.

Generics or No-Name, No-Brand

Some people mistakenly confuse house brands with generic products. This is a serious disservice to house brands. These two categories of products are not the same at all. No-name products with plain, black-and-white or green-and-white labels came on the scene in the '80s when the economy began its long slide down. Shoppers were screaming for relief from high prices in a time of inflation, so generics were developed and presented as the lower-price alternative to national brands. And, at discounts of 25 to 45 percent, the savings was definitely there. What wasn't there, however, was quality and consistency.

> House brands and generics are **not** the same!

The lower prices were supposedly the result of products made with lower-grade foods, plain labels, and little or no advertising. For instance, canned fruits and vegetables showed gashes or blemishes and may have come in awkward shapes and pieces, sometimes with stems in place. Cleaning products contained more water and less perfume than other brands. No-name pop cans sometimes did not have pull-tabs; tea was sold without tea bags; pasta packages lacked windows, and the pasta was made with white flour instead of semolina flour. Once in a while it was possible for no-name products to simply be overages from a plant producing name brand merchandise, a great bargain at 40 percent savings. But you never knew until you tried one, and it was always a gamble. Since no consistent standard of quality applied, and since whatever was left over was used, generics varied greatly in quality from one purchase to the next.

Generics, or no-names, were created to make national brands look good. In other words, the quality was generally so inferior that shoppers were willing to pay the price for the more expensive, national brand products rather than save money on a food product barely worth eating, or a cleaning product that didn't clean, or aluminum foil so weak it wouldn't contain anything, and so on. Although nutrition and cleanliness standards still had to meet FDA requirements, the inconsistency in quality was pretty hard for consumers to swallow.

Today, many stores guarantee your satisfaction when you purchase generic products, just as with any other product sold in their stores. Use of generics, then, comes down to personal preferences. Some cooks find no-name vegetables fine for casseroles and no-name fruits a great budget stretcher for fruit drinks or fruit salads. Where the taste does not stand alone, or where looks make no difference, generics may not be distinguishable from other brands. How they fit into your buying patterns will depend on what kind of personal preferences you have.

Though generics were introduced years ago, they are still an option in many stores, enjoying varying degrees of popularity depending on the national economy. Generics almost always pop up when the economy is tough. Generic products are a consumer pacifier for difficult financial times.

It's important to realize that *generic*, when the term refers to medicines and pharmaceutical drugs, is completely different than *generic* as applied to food. These are not the same thing at all. New drugs are developed and patented, like all other new products. When that patent expires, other manufacturers can apply to the FDA to sell generic versions of the same drug. By law, these generic drugs must be identical to the name brand drug in dosage form, safety, strength, quality, method of administration, performance characteristics, and intended use.

Although generic drugs are chemically identical to their name brand counterparts, they are substantially cheaper. Generic drugs are a good deal. Generic food—well, it's iffy.

The Production of Food

Before you can wisely compare one brand type to another, you should understand the differences and similarities in the way each type is manufactured.

Basically, all food products have similar beginnings. Vegetables, fruits, and other raw foods are sorted, cleaned, cut, ground, cooked, canned, and packaged in thousands of canneries, mills, bakeries,

and packing houses across the land. Some of these processing plants handle a variety of foods; others specialize in one or two items. Some are owned and operated by national name brand companies, some by supermarket chains, some by independent firms.

The name on the plant seldom has much to do with the labels placed on its products. Basically, any manufacturer can produce an acceptable product for any buyer, provided they can meet the standards the buyer specifies. Name brand companies can provide products for grocery chains, as well as for their own distributors. For example, a Del Monte cannery will produce Del Monte products, but it can also process food for Joe's Corner Grocery Stores.

> If you want to be truly grateful for FDA standards and regulations, read Upton Sinclair's *The Jungle*, written in 1906. This shocking novel exposed the reprehensible conditions in the meat-packing industry at the turn of the century and brought about government reforms that ensure that our food today is processed in clean and sanitary conditions. Thank you, Mr. Sinclair!

Independent processors supply products to both name brand companies and private label companies. For example, Acme Cannery can process food for Best Foods, Western Family, and Joe's Corner Grocery Store. But who processes what for who is not important and may even change from year to year. What matters is how the quality of each product is determined.

Differences Are a Matter of Taste

All products from all manufacturers are subject to FDA standards and regulations. Therefore, any brand that reaches your supermarket shelf has met requirements that protect you from unsafe or unclean foods. As you make your choices and consider what price to pay, let me remind you that differences in quality are based more on aesthetics: how the food looks, feels, or tastes.

Trading Labels

It is logical to assume that in any given company, a first-run product produced for one distributor will be identical to a first-run product produced for another distributor. In fact, there are times when the quality is exactly the same because the product is the same. Sometimes, when a brand quota is filled, a manufacturing plant simply stops its machinery, replaces the labels, and continues processing, rolling out can after can, or package after package, without changing anything but the label. The following are written testimonials from people who work in different processing plants:[8]

"The idea of one manufacturer packaging many brands isn't too new. When I was a young teen, my mother was occasionally called to help a cousin who managed a dairy. This was before too many machines for packaging. Mother would wrap butter! Large square tubs of butter, cut into pound pieces and some into quarter pounds. Paper-package wrappers were there for Meadow Gold, Fred Meyer, Challenge—whatever was used. I remember helping wrap this butter—sometimes changing wrappers with a tub to make the quota each brand supplier had ordered. There was absolutely no difference between brands—except price."

***

"As a quality control inspector at a large potato-processing plant, I witness every day the exact same products being put into different containers being shipped to several different companies. This includes your generic brand as well as the more expensive brands. It is all the same product; the only thing that changes is the container."

***

"I have seen one cannery in a one-month period change labels but never change the food process, only stop the labeling machine, take out the old labels and put in the new one of another company and turn the machine on, all in about 10 minutes' time."

---

8. Letters on file.

***

One of my favorite visual aids to use in my workshops is a collage of 14 labels. These labels all came from the same national brand canning plant, Van Camps. The product during this canning run, corn, was exactly the same for a two-week period. When a brand quota was met, a new label was dropped into the machine, and off the machine would go again. Fourteen different brands, with the exact same corn in all of them!

However, processing food under different brand names is not always just a matter of trading labels. When a company contracts with a cannery to produce its peaches (or stewed tomatoes, macaroni, and so forth), it specifies the standards to be met in each can for that cannery run. Whether the cannery is owned by a name brand manufacturer, a store chain, or an independent organization, the peaches or tomatoes or whatever are prepared according to these specifications, usually under the approval of inspectors sent by the contracting company. In fact, one cannery could conceivably serve

> A grocery store in San Jose, California, was happy to promote its house brand products this way: "Enjoy the quality of national brand products with average savings of 25 percent. Sunny Select products [the house brand] are made for us by some of America's leading food manufacturers. For example, C&H makes Sunny Select cane sugar, Leslie the salt, and Saffola makes Sunny Select cooking oils and salad oils. Sunny Select is lower priced, but you don't have to give up any quality."

many different companies, each requesting first-run products, and each providing different specifications and different inspectors.

Name Brand vs. House Brand Quality

Both name brand and major house brand products are first run, or top quality. One store manager I know, who has worked for three different chains, insists that house brands are sometimes even higher quality than name brands. He told me of a cutting test, or a spot

check for quality, that was run for a regional grocery chain. Several of his store's house brand products were opened and tested for comparison with national brands. In this particular test, the house brands rated superior to the big brands.

Quality vs. Recipe

Some people disagree with me, insisting that they've tried some house brand products and they don't taste the same as the name brand products they're familiar with. Usually, they are confusing quality with recipe. Many national brand products are made with special patented recipes that no other manufacturer can infringe upon. That's what keeps their taste special. Since these popular name brand recipes cannot be copied, other brands either create their own unique taste or imitate the name brand as closely as possible within the law. That doesn't mean the other brand's recipe isn't good, just different.

For example, Hunt's tomato sauce tastes different than Contadina. And Contadina is different than Del Monte. And Western Family tomato sauce, a house brand, tastes different than all of those. All are quality products, yet none of them taste the same. So before you say the house brand soup isn't as good as Campbell's, or house brand spaghetti sauce isn't as good as Ragu, taste it again.

> *Don't confuse* **quality** *with* **recipe**.

Now that you know the quality is just as high, maybe you'll discover you like the taste of the house brand just as much, even though it's not exactly the same.

The High Cost of Name Brands

What's in a name brand? When you purchase a first-run, name brand or house brand product, you buy a promise that your beans will always be sliced in exactly the same manner; your peaches will be the same size, shape, and color; your pears will never be blemished;

and your tomato sauce will taste the same from can to can. With a national name brand, you also buy a colorful label, display materials to encourage you to purchase the product on impulse, and advertising to help you feel familiar and comfortable with your choice.

While most national name brands and house brands are equal in quality, shoppers have, for years, paid as much as 15 to 30 percent more for name brand products. Through well-planned and well-executed advertising, name brand manufacturers have kept their names in the public eye and at the same time have constantly equated high quality with a well-known name. In fact, brand name products are positioned to imply that they provide higher quality than the other choices available to you. It works with non-grocery items also. Add a logo to a pair of $15 shorts, and suddenly, they're selling for $35.

> Most national name brands and house brands are **equal in quality.**

When you go through the checkout stand with your national brand corn flakes, you are not only paying for your cereal, you're also buying the advertising and image associated with those corn flakes.

What these companies never mention is that there are lower-priced products of equal quality on the market, including many house brands. The high prices charged for name brands basically cover the advertising done to make you more familiar with the products. Companies depend on this recognition for survival, since they do not have an automatic distribution system, like house brands do. Instead, they must convince grocers to stock their products by creating consumer demand.

You should be aware that often it is the advertising—not the quality—that raises the price of a product. Take breakfast cereal, for example. Some cereal manufacturers spend more money promoting their product than producing their product! Of the retail price you pay for an average box of breakfast cereal, less than 30 percent covers the food content and less than 15 percent represents net profit to the company. The remaining 55 percent of the price covers commercials,

games, coupons, packaging, ads, and other means of encouraging you to buy the product!

Advertising within the Trade

At the same time manufacturers are advertising to you, they are also making a pitch to the grocers who buy the products to sell to you. Full-page ads are run in trade publications, such as *Progressive Grocer*, to persuade store owners to stock name brand products. Knowing that national advertising brings customers into their stores asking for products by name, and not wanting to be on the spot without the desired merchandise, grocers often opt not only to carry the item but also to join in the campaign to promote it.

Grocers freely admit the profitable influence national brand items have on their sales, and they credit high-powered advertising for name brand sales success. Advertising is recognized not only as the power behind national brands but also behind the supermarket itself. Retailers succumb to pressure from national brand companies because their advertising creates sales the stores can't match on their own. Since most grocers lack the ability and the funds to put on storewide sales and promotions, they let the national brands do it for them, and therefore, the national brands retain undisputed power.

> **Advertising is power!**
> It influences you more than you are aware.

Advertising is power! It influences you more than you are aware. In one marketing-trend report in 2002, this advice was given to marketers: "During a weakened economy with unemployment rising, consumers are looking for ways to save money and are more inclined to switch brands or try a new product. This is the time when marketers should increase advertising and promotional spending to increase their customer bases and market share while their competitors reduce spending and lose customers."[9]

The Trials and Tribulations of House Brands

Although house brands generally represent quality as fine as that of name brand products, they rarely come out ahead in the battle for consumer loyalty. Part of the problem is that house brands and private labels lack the resources to compete with large-scale, name brand advertising; part of the problem is that making fair comparisons between name brands and house brands is very difficult. Many store brands aren't packaged in the same sizes as the name brand products, so it's complicated to comparison shop if a store doesn't use unit pricing. But you can definitely benefit from making the effort to compare. Private labels offer you an alternative to paying the cost of advertising and promoting national brands.

House brands and private label products are increasing in popularity due to continued quality improvements and the growing value consciousness of consumers. "Budget-conscious consumers have two choices for saving money—they can use coupons to receive discounts on branded products, or they can turn to private-label products," says Bob Carter, president of CMS, a promotional redemption services agency. "With the continued quality improvements in many private-label products, brand managers may be concerned that the consumer who tries a private label to save money may permanently switch."[10]

Buying Unfamiliar Brands

When it comes to determining the best value for your money, you must become familiar with which house brands, private labels, or economy brands are available in your area. The chart on page 191 in the appendix will familiarize you with various house-brand and private-label names, as well as some economy brands. Fill out the brand worksheet with the products offered in your local stores. If you

---

9. *Coupon Distribution and Redemption Declined in 2001* (Elmwood Park, Ill.: Santella and Associates, 2002), 11.
10. *2003 Reports on the 2002 Coupon Trends* (Elmwood Park, Ill.: Santella and Associates, 2003,) 23.

don't recognize a brand, take a few minutes to ask the store manager about it: Who makes it? What quality is there? and so on.

Then, before you buy a case, try a can or a box. I know one woman who kept a can opener and a spoon in the glove box of her car. When she came across a great deal on a brand she didn't recognize, she would buy one can and take it out to her car and try it. If it tasted fine and measured up to her standards, she would go back in and buy several to take advantage of the great prices (page 192 of the appendix).

Having so many budget-stretching brand options to choose from in every aisle of every store offers wonderful advantages. The only drawback is that deciding which to take home for dinner may take you longer than you anticipated.

THINGS TO KNOW

- All brands can be broken down into four general categories: (1) national brands, (2) house brands and private labels, (3) economy brands, and (4) generics.

- National brands and house brands/private labels are first-run, high-quality products made to the highest, exacting standards.

- Economy brands are a form of house brand or private label. They emphasize lower price rather than higher quality, although they maintain consistent specifications and standards from one can or package to the next.

- Generics were developed as a lower-price alternative to national brands. Since no consistent standard of quality applies, generics vary greatly in quality from one purchase to the next. What quality there is tends to be low.

- Name brand products are usually more expensive because of the costs of advertising and promotion built into them.

✦ House brands can usually save 15 to 30 percent off the price of name brand products.

✦ Economy brands can usually save 20 to 35 percent off the price of name brand products.

✦ Generics usually save 25 to 40 percent or more off the price of name brands, though the quality of the product will be anybody's guess.

THINGS TO DO

✦ Don't get locked into buying only one brand. Be adventurous and try house brands, private labels, and economy brands to find what meets your standards and works for you.

✦ Try different brands. If you don't recognize a brand, ask a store manager to tell you about it.

✦ If you must have a specific brand for a specific product, buy when the price is right.

✦ There are generally certain times of the year when national brands, such as Dole, Libby, Del Monte, and so on, are promoted. Watch for these times and stock up. (See chapter 8.)

✦ When mass merchandisers, discount grocers, or deep-discount drugstores get a deal on your favorite brand and feature it at a bargain price, that's the time to buy in quantity.

6

Coupons:
Who's Really Getting Clipped?

Coopons or cue-pons? What do you call them? I call them junk!
I realize many shopping experts consider this view akin to heresy, but
I am firmly convinced that coupons are nothing but a savings myth.
Considering how they affect your buying decisions and limit your
buying power, they certainly can't be called a sound shopping con-
cept. They do not save you money, and they were never intended to
save you money. They were intended, rather, to induce you to spend.
And they do.

If you're like most people, you have a miscellaneous assortment
of coupons stashed away in a drawer somewhere with other things
that don't really have a place but that you feel guilty throwing out.

It's certainly not hard to collect them. They show up at the
bottom of flour sacks, on the back of the comics, on the inside of
labels, on the outside of packages, and in the mailbox. They poke out
from bread wrappers, pop up from magazine pages, and pour out
with your morning cereal.

Couponing is heralded as the easy way to save, and today's advice
on cutting your grocery bills often centers exclusively around them.
However, couponing, as it was meant to be practiced, is no more
than a token savings given by manufacturers to motivate you to buy.
There are alternative methods of shopping, based on sound and long-
lasting principles, which are much more reliable ways to save.

The Coupon Boom

Couponing is big business in the United States today. In fact, it accounted for over $3 billion worth of business in 2002, when 336 billion coupons were distributed; that's over 3,100 coupons for every household in the United States.

> Coupons are perceived to be the **next best thing** to money.

Coupon clipping could practically be considered a national pastime. And not all of these billions of coupons are relegated to junk drawers. If you've been at a supermarket checkout counter lately, you know the family scissors have been working overtime.

There is scarcely a more useful promotional tool in all of marketing, and a promotional tool is exactly what coupons are. They are a marketing tactic used to persuade you to buy products—products sold at inflated prices to cover the cost of all the promoting! The *savings* are not real; they are implied. Manufacturers use coupons as a visible way to make price reductions apparent to consumers.

You see a coupon as an opportunity to save 20 cents. Because of that, the coupon is perceived as the next best thing to money. Today, 84 percent of shoppers say they use coupons, and 71 percent believe that coupons save them a lot of money. This, however, may simply be wishful thinking on the part of consumers. "The savings value [of coupons] may be more reflective of the perceived need to economize, than the actual savings offered by manufacturers,"[11] says the president of CMS, one of the foremost promotional redemption service agencies in North America.

Motivating a Change of Habit

The original idea, when C. W. Post issued one-cent-off coupons for Grape Nuts in 1895, was to invite consumers to try a new product at a reduced price, creating an instant demand for it. It wasn't

---

11. *2003 Reports on the 2002 Coupon Trends* (Elmwood Park, Ill.: Santella and Associates, 2003), 5.

long before producers of old products began combating this competition with coupons for items whose popularity they wanted to protect. Couponing has now become the established way to move a product, whether to hasten turnover in lethargic economic times or to generate business for products not selling at all. According to a coupon target-marketing company, "Coupons remain as the only tool available to a manufacturer for motivating immediate purchases by a consumer."[12]

Whatever the specific motivation behind a coupon, its main objective is to stimulate an immediate purchase. Since we, as consumers, are creatures of habit, once in a buying pattern we are hard pressed to make a change. Manufacturers have found couponing the single, most effective tool to date for motivating a sudden change of habit.

Persuading you to make such a change is known in the industry as a *forcing method*. In-trade publications and documents repeatedly refer to coupons as the best forcing method yet conceived by promoters.

The Cost of Couponing

The cost of couponing (almost $7 billion a year) is staggering when you consider that profit has to be made on top of it. If you purchase products associated with couponing, whether you use coupons or not, you help foot this bill. Reimbursement of the coupons' face values accounts for the largest share of the $7 billion, about 59 percent. Distribution of coupons takes the next largest chunk, over $2 billion, or 32 percent of the costs. The costliest method of distribution by far, accounting for 86 percent of the distribution budget, is freestanding inserts—those bundles of coupons that come in your Sunday newspapers. The other 14 percent includes magazine coupons and magazine pop-ups (the coupons on heavy paper that pop up from between the pages), store handouts, in/on-pack coupons, direct-mail advertising, electronic, and newspaper coupons.[13]

---

12. Management Decisions Systems, Inc.
13. *2004 Reports on the 2003 Coupon Trends* (Elmwood Park, Ill.: Santella and Associates, 2004), 3.

Internet Coupons

Online coupons are one of the hottest marketing trends, even though, as yet, they account for less than 1 percent of all coupon distribution. Electronic checkout coupons and shelf dispensers paved the way for the whole new world of electronic promotions opening up to consumers on all sides, from the grocery store all the way to their homes via the Internet.

Consumer Product Goods (CPG) marketers are increasingly devoting more and more of their budgets to online marketing. Their Internet sites offer coupons that you can print out at home and then redeem at the store. Over 992 million coupons were downloaded in 2003. Even so, online coupons account for less than 1 percent of the coupon market. "Coupons are crossing a bridge toward the future. Coupons are offered and redeemed in many more electronic ways than ever before, and the future is expected to deliver new coupon methods that we can only imagine today," states a National Clearing House report on the state of the industry in 1997.[14]

One advantage of Internet coupon sites is that you have access to many more and different coupons than you would otherwise have (if that can be considered a good thing), and often these coupons are directed specifically to you since you have supplied the company with specific personal information in order to have access to any given site. The downside is that it's one more way to track and target you. For the industry, the ability to track statistics is a strong benefit. When you download a coupon, that coupon has a printed code on it that is tied to your individual name, so when it is redeemed, the company knows who redeemed it and where.

One problem with Internet coupons is their susceptibility to fraud. While people have been fraudulently reproducing paper coupons for years, common home technology such as quality copiers, computer scanners, and readily available graphic-design programs make replication easy. And the Web makes it easy to advertise, sell, and distribute quantities of forged or altered coupons.

---

14. *NCH NuWorld Reports on 1997 State of the Industry* (Elmwood Park, Ill.: Santella and Associates, 1998), 45.

"If somebody makes alterations on something that's printed on a $49 printer, how do you know it?" says Louis Ederer, an attorney specializing in intellectual property cases. "It might just look funny because it was a $49 printer."[15]

One coupon-counterfeiting scam perpetrated via the Internet was so pervasive that one major grocery chain (Publix) and many other supermarkets stopped accepting any computer-generated coupons. In the summer of 2003, consumers began streaming into stores in the Atlanta area with phony coupon offers for free cartons of Haagen-Dazs ice cream, Dove soap, and Salon Selectives shampoo, plus coupons for huge savings on products such as Pepsi and Stouffer's frozen dinners. The offers, while not actually online coupons, had been scanned into a computer and then distributed through e-mail, chat rooms, and online auction sites. Instead of the companies distributing a small number of free product coupons, as was their marketing plan, thousands of people fraudulently cashed in on the deal, most without even knowing that they were participating in a scam. Many of the grocery stores were caught in the middle, handing out the free or reduced-price products, then being refused reimbursement from the manufacturers.

However, in spite of the problems, don't look for Internet coupons to disappear from the scene. Rather, you're going to see a lot more of them in the future. A spokesman for a company developing fraud-protected coupons claims, "Coupon fraud has been a problem long before the advent of the Internet. The reality is that the Internet is by far the most cost-effective and targeted method of coupon distribution."[16] Manufacturers are hopping on the bandwagon because, not only do consumers tend to like online coupons, the cost of online coupons is a small fraction of the cost of distributing traditional coupons, approximately $50 million per year instead of $2 billion.

It's important to keep in mind the financial impact Internet coupons may have on you. The statistics are in, and the results don't bode well for your budget. "Internet coupon users are valuable shoppers who spend 30 percent more money on groceries per week than

---

15. Karen Holt, "Coupon Crimes," *Promo Magazine*, April 1, 2004.
16. "Vesdia Responds to Recent Coupon Fraud," *Computer Security News*, August 22, 2003.

traditional coupon clippers (who already spend more than noncoupon users, by the way) and "are more brand loyal."[17]

These problems aside, the main complaints I have against online coupons are the same complaints I have against traditional coupons: They are a coercive, promotional tool for name brand products, and they cost you money!

Target Marketing

The reason coupons are as effective and popular as they are is that marketing companies can direct the right coupons to the right people. The careful compilation of demographic research makes this possible. Although marketers have grouped, divided, categorized, and classified American shoppers for as long as there have been mass producers of products, their ability to pinpoint a prime market has become more sophisticated and more exact over the years. Today's marketing firms control an infinite variety of facts and can cross-reference, in a computer's instant, everything from where chainsaw owners are most likely to live to what income bracket drinks the most orange juice. And they do it with information you have given them.

> Coupons are effective because marketing companies can direct the **right coupons** to the **right people**.

Your so-called junk mail isn't assigned to you arbitrarily. It comes to you because you have made public, wittingly or not, information relating both to your buying habits and station in life.

Use of Census Information

One source of such information is census tracts, which provide over one thousand different demographic measures for every four thousand or so people. These measures include age, marital status,

---

17. "NFO World Group & Cool Savings, U.S. Coupon Trends 2002," *Progressive Grocer*, June 2004.

What are the identifying characteristics of a coupon shopper?

- 48 percent have a household income of more than $50,000.
- 28 percent spend $120+ in an average week on groceries.
- 63 percent are married.
- 38 percent have a college degree.
- 56 percent are book lovers.
- 72 percent read the newspaper.
- 48 percent get coupons from the color coupon booklet distributed in Sunday newspapers.

2003 Reports on the 2002 Coupon Trends (Elmwood Park, Ill.: Santella and Associates, 2003), 12.

---

income, home ownership, product ownership, number and make of vehicles, education, and more. While you donated specific information as confidential, the collective information is available to whoever requests it, in the form of census reports, which are considered public record. Although, technically, your individual privacy has not been violated because no one can associate your facts with your name, the information you give contributes to a portrait of your neighborhood, information greatly appreciated by manufacturers.

You also supply extremely useful targeting information when you apply for grocery-store Smart Cards, when you fill out rebate forms, sign up for online coupons, and any other times you supply information to retail companies. Your information may then be packaged and sold to marketing and information-management companies, who in turn sell it to other companies who use it to woo your patronage.

Targeting works best when marketers can reach and motivate the right audience, so sophisticated marketers use geographic targeting programs and analysis packages to lock in on precise collections of shoppers. Marketers have also learned to effectively use the media to target specific audiences such as brand switchers or competitive buyers. According to the president of one of the nation's leading promotional redemption-service agencies, "Coupons . . . can be distributed broadly to the masses, or be tightly targeted to reach a specific audience—or even a specific consumer."[18]

---

18. *2003 Reports on the 2002 Coupon Trends* (Elmwood Park, Ill.: Santella and Associates, 2003) 2.

Who Receives Coupons?

Although the definition of a prime customer differs for each product, marketing experts have targeted certain consumers for coupons in general. To be counted among this select group, you need to make a healthy income, have at least a high school education, and live near a high-volume supermarket. If you are a woman between 25 and 54 years of age, in a family of at least three members, or have a large family or small children, you are a prime target for coupon packets.

Discrimination

Coupons are discriminatory! Basically, companies distributing coupons are interested in consumers with buying power, or in other words, money. Who does not receive coupons? Male shoppers, single people, younger families, poorer families, and residents of poor areas all use coupons far less frequently than the core audience of more affluent, larger families. Perhaps the reason many of these consumers use fewer coupons is that they are exposed to fewer coupons. Not only are lower income households excluded from mailing lists (I have monitored the university town near where I live, and students and low-income housing areas almost never receive the coupon packets familiar to wealthier members of the community), but they generally can't afford papers, magazines, and other mediums through which coupons are distributed.

> **Coupons are discriminatory!**

Redemption

The second most costly part of a coupon promotion, after face value reimbursement, is redemption, which is done through large clearinghouses. At these clearinghouses, coupons from grocers are sorted and passed on to manufacturers for reimbursement. Grocers are then repaid the total face value of each coupon they turn in,

accounting for 59 percent of the cost of couponing, plus a handling fee, which averages eight cents a piece.

Unfortunately, these reimbursements tempt many people to participate in fraudulent coupon redemption. The cost of such coupon fraud, including Internet fraud, is estimated to be as much as $500 million a year. As with other expenses, this cost is covered in the prices charged for couponed products, which you pay every time you use a product associated with a coupon, whether or not you use the coupon.

"Saving" with Coupons

If you are stuck with the cost of coupons anyway, shouldn't you use them to reduce your grocery bill? Not necessarily. You save money with coupons if you insist on buying only the national brand products for which they are issued, but for most products, there are alternatives that cost less, such as house brands and economy brands.

Coupons can activate an instinctive spend-to-save syndrome. A consumer, anxious about finances and getting the best deal for the dollar, will focus on the coupon savings of fifty cents or a dollar and completely lose sight of the amount he must spend in order to receive that savings. Interestingly, in-trade reports show that shoppers who use coupons tend to purchase items they don't need just to save with the coupons, thus negating any savings they might obtain on the items they do need!

> Coupon users make more **unplanned purchases** than other shoppers and spend significantly **more money** per shopping trip.

In fact, coupon clippers have a reputation in the trade for being big spenders and impulse shoppers. Coupon-redeeming customers tend to buy higher priced items and spend more in the store than customers who do not. Many studies have actually documented that coupon users make more unplanned purchases than other shoppers

and spend significantly more money per shopping trip, regardless of age, education, household size, or income. One study showed that the non-coupon user or occasional user spends an average $16.86 per shopping trip, while the regular coupon redeemer (of equal family size) pays $31.04 per trip, an 84 percent difference!

Repeat Business

Coupons ensure repeat customers. One in-trade advertisement to grocers encourages the use of the company's displays to build store traffic and increase sales. The eye-catching display boldly proclaims "SAVE $1!" But if you look closer at the fine print, you'll discover that your dollar savings comes to you in the form of cents-off coupons, not cash. "First, your customers must buy [our mayonnaise] and tuna," claims the manufacturer to the grocer. "This poster and your display will make sure of that. Then the '$1 refund' gives them three 25-cent coupons on [our mayonnaise] and one 25-cent coupon on any brand of tuna. That assures you of repeat sales." The purposes of coupons are to encourage a specific purchase in the first place, then to get you back into the store to buy again.

Implied Savings

Even if you are the rare person who can limit yourself to only the couponed items you really need, your savings are limited. Coupons are generally good only for name brand products that usually cost 10 to 30 percent more than house brands of comparable quality. Even after the face value of a coupon has been deducted, most name brand products cannot compete with other brands on sale.

Although the face value of most coupons is rising, savings are not necessarily any better. When couponing first became popular, most coupons were redeemed at 10 cents to 25 cents off. In the ensuing years, inflation has caused grocery costs to skyrocket, and the redemption value of coupons has risen substantially also. Now face values of 50 cents up to several dollars are not uncommon. In 2002, the average face value of a coupon was 81 cents.

Yet upon closer examination, many of these coupons require a more expensive purchase. More than one-quarter of all coupons now require the purchase of two or more products. For example, a batch of coupons I collected in February 2004 included these: 55 cents off potato chips, two packages, that is; $1 off specialty yogurt products, when you buy three containers; 40 cents off condensed soup, with the purchase of four cans; 50 cents off egg noodles, two packages, 12 ounces or larger; 50 cents off frozen meals when you buy three entrees. Are you really receiving any more than the original 10-cent to 25-cent savings per product?

Also, while you can usually purchase as much as you want of a house brand or special, you can redeem your coupon only on one item, unless you go to the trouble of collecting identical coupons. Manufactur-

The Top 20 Coupon Distribution Categories in 2002

1. Household Cleaners
2. Prepared Foods
3. Detergents
4. Medications/Health Aids
5. Paper Products
6. Condiments/Gravies
7. Personal Soap/Bath
8. Frozen Prepared Foods
9. Cereal
10. Skin Care Preparations
11. Cough and Cold Remedies
12. Fresheners/Deodorizers
13. Pet Treats
14. Laundry Supplies
15. Toothpaste
16. Oral Hygiene
17. Vitamins
18. Packaged Meats
19. Snacks
20. Canned Vegetables

ers limit you on purpose to discourage you from stocking up at the lower price, depriving them of profits from future sales at the normal price.

Balanced Nutrition

If you are counting on using coupons to feed your family economical and nutritious meals, you're in for a rude awakening. Coupons are rarely issued for basic or staple foods. You could not make a nutritious meal plan solely from products associated with coupons. A typical Sunday's newspaper contains coupons for 43 items, but of those 43 items, only 5 could be considered menu worthy. Eleven were for treats, beverages, or sugared cereals; 5 were pet related; 6 were household items; 3 were condiments; and the remaining 13 were for health and beauty items, nonfoods, or paper goods. Balanced nutrition is not possible using couponed items.

Double Couponing

One day you look in the grocery advertisements and there, emblazoned across the two-page spread, is a bold banner that reads, "Double Coupons!" For that week or month, any coupon you redeem in that store is worth twice the printed value. Quite the deal, right? Yes and no.

Double couponing, plain and simple, is a price war tactic between stores in competition for your shopping dollar. Supermarkets that double coupon often siphon customers away from other stores, so as a defensive measure, when one store begins double couponing, others generally follow in an effort to hold on to their customer base. You would think that double couponing would be a great benefit to the customer, but it isn't so. Double couponing, and the infrequent triple couponing, is frightfully expensive, and very few stores have the marketing budget to maintain it for long.

> **Double couponing** is simply a price war tactic.

While the manufacturer reimburses the stores for the face value of the coupon, the stores pay the cost of the double out of their own pockets. Their hope is to offer double couponing just long enough to

cause customers to switch shopping destinations. If it goes on too long, stores must compensate for the enormous costs by raising the prices of non-couponed items. There is no way for the stores to get around that. They have to offset the cost of double couponing somehow, and it's usually by raising prices throughout the store.

Using double coupons still limits your buying power since you are locked into brand name items and only allowed one item per coupon. However, doubling is one of the few ways

> I was teaching a workshop in Blackfoot, Idaho, a few years ago, and the discussion turned to using double coupons on sale items. A woman commented, "Store A and Store B won't take coupons on sale items. I've tried it and been refused." The murmurs from the audience showed that many others had had her same experience.

that coupons save you money, especially if the store allows you to double coupon on a sale item. (That happens less and less often now.) You need to be aware, though, that the price of other items in a store that offers double couponing will probably be higher to make up for the practice. Think before you do all your shopping there.

But What about the Claims?

Every now and then you'll see astonishing headlines in the tabloids or women's magazines proclaiming, "How to Save 40–60 percent at the Checkout," "She Bought $76 Worth of Groceries for $14—You Can Too," "Free Food—Money Back," and so on. It's a source of frustration to the vast majority of consumers that they aren't able to generate anything like these promised savings, even with the most assiduous use of coupons. And you can't achieve these results simply through sound shopping practices either. These amazing savings are tantalizing, but unfortunately, they're not the lot of the average shopper.

In order to realize these unlikely savings, coupons are not enough. You must participate in a related promotion called "refunding."

While couponing involves a discount at the time of purchase, refunding requires you to first purchase the product at full price, then send in a refund form in order to receive a later reimbursement. The claims made by professional refunders (or coupon queens) are technically true but extremely deceptive. To comprehend how they can accomplish these wildly unlikely, financially miraculous shopping expeditions, you must first have an understanding of how refunding works.

The Basics of Refunding

To take part in a refund offer, you complete three basic steps: (1) find the offers, (2) collect the necessary proofs of purchase, and (3) mail in the proofs of purchase with the refund request form.

1. Find the offers. Refund offers are advertised on e-mail sites, in newspapers, in magazines, at supermarkets, and on the packages of the products themselves. To pull off a shopping trip like ones that are shown in the tabloids, mailing in a refund here and there is not sufficient. You must take advantage of every refund offer you can find. That is best accomplished, suggest refunding pros, by subscribing to several refunding newsletters or Internet sites, for $10 to $30 annually each, in order to access as many refund offers as possible. Since no single newsletter or site can possibly cover all the current offers, your prospects for finding the best bargains improve, presumably, with the number of newsletters and sites you subscribe to.

2. Collect proofs of purchase. No refund is honored without proof you have purchased the correct product(s) in sufficient quantities. Such proof may be anything from a seal, label, or box top to a lid or ingredient panel. Indeed, some manufacturers even demand the whole package! Since it is not unusual for some manufacturers, over time, to make more than one offer on the same product and require a different part of the package each time, many refunders stash and file containers likely to yield future proofs of purchase. In this way they are able to use different pieces from one package to qualify for more than one refund offer. One professional told me she has over 250 cat-

food labels in her basement!

3. *Mail in the proof of purchases with the refund-request form.*
Your proof of purchase must be accompanied by a refund-request
form when mailed to the manufacturer. Pads of these forms are usually provided on the supermarket shelves where refund products are
sold. However, demand for these forms can be great, and stores are
often emptied of them soon after they appear. If these free forms
are not available at the store, you may write the manufacturers for
copies or possibly download copies off the Internet, if you subscribe
to one of the many refunding sites available. One site lets you select
the coupons and refunds you want the most and charges $10 per
year plus 12 percent of the face value of the coupons and offers you
buy from them. So for you to save, you may have to buy the free
forms you need!

Your Reward

In return for your request form and proofs of purchases, you
are mailed your refund, or reward, for trying the product. It may
come in one of several forms: cash (very rare), a free product, or more
coupons. Refunds of more coupons are called bounce backs and are
a manufacturer's way of selling another product to you. The latest
spin on free product rewards is toys or T-shirts or other gimmicky
items. And frankly, do you really need a plastic bobble-headed toy or
a baseball cap with a breakfast cereal advertisement on it, or another
stuffed animal promoting the latest movie?

Some manufacturers even give you a choice of offers. You can
choose the silly bobble-headed toy *or* the breakfast cereal advertisement baseball hat *or* the gimmicky movie-tie-in stuffed animal. How
does one choose from so many fabulous options!

In reality, such a choice merely allows you to make a decision
about what the manufacturer has already persuaded you to do!

How Do the Queens Shop?

The TV super shopping trips and sensational magazine write-ups are unfair to the average shopper. Even though, at some point, they admit, "Savings like these cannot be repeated every shopping trip," the impression is given that everyone could be drastically cutting their grocery bills if they would just learn a few easy techniques. In truth, it is simply not so. It takes time, energy, work, organization, and a monetary investment. These super shopping sprees are planned for weeks or months in advance and involve a combination of refunding strategies. Bounce backs are collected and stored, especially the most desirable ones redeemable for free products. The queens, or whoever is setting up the shopping-trip gimmick, wait for a store to offer double couponing as a special to increase the value of their coupons. By only selecting grocery items for which they have coupons, it becomes possible for these refunders to purchase over a hundred dollars' worth of groceries for $5 or $10. Even the professionals cannot pull off attention-grabbing shopping sprees like this regularly. It takes a long time to gather sufficient bounce backs and free coupons to put on a display sufficient to impress the media. However, the average refunder is more likely to make an eight- to ten-hour-a-week effort for maybe a 25 to 30 percent savings.

> According to one professional refunder at the end of her coupon-shopping spree interview, "A well-rounded shopping trip? No, but it wasn't meant to be. I wanted to buy as much as possible to use doubles and triples, and that's what I did." How long did it take to save all those coupons? "Some of them I'd been holding for at least a year. Some were saved over a six-month period."

Note also that these shopping queens are not going to the store and buying the groceries they need for the week or month. They are buying the things they have coupons for, whether they need them or not. This is one of their main deceptions. When the reporters have gone home and the spotlight is turned off, the coupon queens go back to the store to buy something for dinner, or they

could eat cat food with hand lotion gravy or their four-years' supply of dish soap.

Who Pays for the "Savings"?

In deciding whether or not couponing and refunding might appeal to you as a method of saving, consider one more aspect. Although manufacturers technically pay for the cash refunds and coupons that are returned to the refunder, the money is not cutting into their profit. (If it were, the program would be discontinued.) Payment comes out of carefully planned advertising budgets, which are, in turn, covered in the prices charged for the products. When you buy several products at full price to collect the proofs of purchases that are necessary for a refund, you are, in a sense, paying yourself back. Still, *your* purchases alone do not account for your savings plus the company's expenses plus the company's profit. Who, then, is paying for you to save?

A company offering a refund, or coupon, never intends for everyone who buys the product to cash in on the offer. Of the 335 billion coupons distributed in 2002, only 3.7 billion were redeemed. This return is less than two percent yet is considered widespread redemption by the industry! National brand companies sell many more products at full price than with coupons. Therefore, the people who buy the products at full price pay for the refunds and coupons that allow others to save. According to some university texts, low-income families, which are heavily influenced by television advertising, are heavy purchasers of name brand products. These are the same low-income families that have little or no access to coupons, falling outside the marketing companies' definition of prime consumers. Therefore, the people who need the savings the most are paying for middle- and upper-income families to save.

Consumer Pacifier

> *Coupons are a* **consumer pacifier** *for hard times.*

Coupon promotion and use always increases during economic hard times and times of inflation. According to an in-trade report, "Marketers have historically distributed more coupons when the economy slows in an effort to motivate consumer purchases, and consumers tend to be more apt to respond and redeem during periods of economic decline."[19] People need to see a way out of their financial woes, and coupons have been positioned to fit the bill. They act as a form of consumer pacifier for hard times, lulling people with promises of financial relief on the surface but actually causing more damage than good.

Using Coupons to Your Advantage

Before you hop blindly onto the coupon-marketing/public relations bandwagon, look at your other options first, house brands and economy brands being two of the best. If you use coupons, they should be considered a very small part of the whole, to be used only when they benefit you. To use a coupon to your advantage:

- Use them only for name brand items you can't live without, that you would purchase even if you didn't have a coupon.
- Combine a coupon with a sale. Pay attention as you read the ads for items that you have coupons for and that are also bargain priced.
- Double coupon, and double with a sale, if allowed.

Coopons or Cue-pons. However you say it, they are *not* the answer! They are simply a well-positioned marketing tool, not a sound shopping concept.

---

19. Ibid.

THINGS TO KNOW

♦ Coupons are simply promotional tools that limit your buying power.

♦ Couponing costs over $1 billion a year. If you purchase products associated with couponing, whether you use coupons or not, you help foot this bill.

♦ You receive coupons based on demographic information relating both to your buying habits and station in life that you, wittingly or not, have made public.

♦ Coupon users make more unplanned purchases than other shoppers and spend significantly more money per shopping trip, regardless of age, education, household size, or income.

♦ Double couponing is expensive, and stores usually must compensate for the enormous costs by raising the prices of the other non-couponed items.

♦ While couponing involves a discount at the time of purchase, refunding requires you to first purchase the product at full price, then send in a refund form in order to receive a later reimbursement.

♦ Once expenses are deducted and national brand prices are taken into account, the average refunder is likely to make an eight- to ten-hour-a-week effort for no more than the small savings percentage possible by employing other shopping techniques less troublesome than refunding.

THINGS TO DO

To use a coupon to your advantage:

♦ Use them only for name brand items you can't live without, that you would purchase even if you didn't have a coupon.

◆ Combine a coupon with a sale. Pay attention as you read the ads for items that you have coupons for and that are also bargain priced.

◆ Double coupon, but be aware of the likelihood of store-wide price increases due to the cost of double couponing. Be price conscious and consider purchasing the rest of your groceries at other locations if necessary.

◆ Double coupon with a sale, if allowed.

Section Two
Things to Do

7

Ads:
How to **Really** *Read the Market Report*

One of the most powerful tools you'll find for beating the high cost of eating is delivered right to your home every week: the grocery store advertisements that are included in your newspaper or delivered to your mailbox. These ads are a vital key to putting buying power back in your pocket.

Grocery ads serve several purposes; some are valuable to you, some are valuable to the grocer. If, like most consumers, you are confronted with quite a choice of places to shop, the ads can help you separate the wheat from the chaff. Radio and television advertising may reach a wide audience and successfully promote a grocery store in general, but newspapers are the major link between the grocery industry and you. Only hometown supermarket advertisements provide you with local shopping opportunities, local specials, and a basis for local price comparisons.

By the same token, a grocery ad is not just a listing of products offered at special prices. Grocery ads are a powerful marketing tool, with positioning and marketing behind every ad. These ads are carefully crafted to influence how you spend your grocery dollars and to persuade you to buy! You need to read the ads as if they are the market report and you are a major investor. They are and you are!

A Tool for Grocers and Consumers

Grocers advertise for one main purpose: to establish store loyalty. They want old customers coming back and new customers coming in. In the tug-of-war to get you inside their store, grocers entice you with items offered below normal price. The money grocers invest in advertising, and the profits they forgo on specials, comes back multiple times when you enter the store for a bargain and decide you might as well purchase everything else you need. Grocers know that if your shopping experience is pleasant, or if their specials appeal to you week after week, you may develop a habit of shopping primarily at their store.

One summer I participated in a weekly ceramics class in Orem, Utah. It was common to have group discussions as we worked. One evening the conversation turned to skyrocketing food prices and current economic woes. Knowing my profession and passion for saving money at the grocery store, one woman expressed her disbelief that anything could really make a difference. She doubted that I could offer her any meaningful help. Her family was large (eight children), and her grocery bills were astronomical. She doubtfully and defensively challenged, "Tell me just one thing to do that will cut my grocery bills!"

I asked a couple of questions. No, she didn't read the ads. No, she didn't make a detailed list. No, she never shopped more than one store. She did all her shopping at the small mom-and-pop corner store. I explained just a few shopping concepts, such as reading ads and shopping more than one store, and I challenged her to follow my counsel for the next week.

She came into class the following week, almost running to find me. She had saved $77 by partially following just one concept! Then she enthusiastically added, "What do I do next?"

On the other hand, your main purpose in reading the ads is to find the best price on the groceries you need by noting *all store specials*. Grocers can choose to offer almost any item at an alluring price in an ad. With so much flexibility in pricing, you will seldom, if ever,

see identical specials at all your local supermarkets at the same time. Instead, you may find a low price on meat at one store, a good price on produce at another, and a tremendous buy on frozen vegetables at a third. Next week's selection will likely be just as varied.

That's the beauty of it for the consumer. By shopping more than one store's specials, you immediately obtain substantial savings on several different items that will result in a significantly lower overall bill. Shopping the specials can save you an immediate 23 percent on your grocery bills.

Becoming Familiar with Prices

A working knowledge of prices in your area is essential to reading the ads successfully. Price recognition works as a basic key to buying power. It is how you identify the real bargains in the ads and how you recognize unadvertised specials in the stores. If you don't know what things cost on a regular basis, you won't be able to recognize a good price when you see one. This is a crucial point, and you'll see it many times before we're through.

> *Price recognition is a **key** to buying power.*

Price recognition is an easily obtainable skill. Begin by creating a worksheet like the one titled "Gaining Price Recognition" on page 192 in the appendix. It features several columns where you can record the item, the date, and the prices. Next, list 10 to 20 items that you consistently use. These things should come easily to your mind: bread, milk, oranges, corn flakes, chicken, toothpaste—these types of things. Over the next several weeks, jot down the price of each of these items whenever you see it in the ads or in the stores, even though you may not be buying it at that time. You could also create the worksheet all at once by devoting several hours to this project. Visit several different stores and jot down the various prices on the different brands for the 40 or 50 items you use most. Though prices may fluctuate, you will soon recognize a normal price range for each item.

As you gain confidence in recognizing good prices on those 20 items, move on to a new list of 10 or 20 more and do the same thing again. Keep doing this until you are familiar with the regular prices of all the items you frequently purchase. It won't take long.

Keep track of these pages in your notebook. They will serve as a reference until you are familiar enough with the average cost of each item to read the ads without them. When you see any of these products advertised as specials, you will know immediately whether or not they are actually reduced in price, or whether they are just being promoted.

Recognizing a good price is absolutely crucial to saving money. I can't emphasize enough how critical this one skill is. It's the foundation skill that supports all the other money-saving techniques in this book.

Loss Leaders or Lead Items

Sometimes a store will advertise a certain item at a tremendous price. This is known as a loss leader, or lead item. A loss leader is an item featured in the ad that is priced so low that it lures you into the store. It is a come-on, and it has pulling power. These are immediately recognizable bargains, such as pork and beans, three cans for $1, or canned peaches for 69 cents, or bananas for 25 cents a pound.

> The **purpose** of a loss leader is to get you into the store.

Sometimes these items are priced so low that the grocer doesn't make any profit on them. Once in a while, grocers even lose money on the deal. The purpose of the loss leader for the grocer or retailer is not to earn a profit on that item, it's to get you into the store. Why? If you come into the store for that one item, the chances are good that you will stick around and do the rest of your shopping, filling your cart with nonsale, regularly priced items. That's what makes it a loss leader. Loss leaders are a great deal! Watch for them and use them to extend your budget as far as possible.

Not All Specials Are Bargains

Some items in grocery ads are not loss leaders, but they are sale priced for the same purpose—to encourage you to shop in a store. Other items are not bargains at all; they are promoted at their regular price. But if you haven't done your price-recognition homework, you won't know which is which. And unfortunately, finding bargains in the ads is not as easy as glancing at the items in the largest print.

In any advertisement, a few items will be pictured two or three times larger than other items, often surrounded by frames, sunbursts, exploding skyrockets, or the like. Your eyes are drawn to these items because they are the largest items on the page. This is feature spacing, and it gives the impression of wonderful savings, which may or may not necessarily be there. The positioning on the page suggests that this is *the* featured product, *the* best bargain. Maybe it is. Maybe it's not. The amount or size of ad space given to an item only means that it's featured, not that it is bargain priced.

In a study a few years ago on the value of newspaper ads, over 500 advertised items were compared with their regular shelf price. Eighty-seven percent of the items advertised in large, or feature print (three column inches or more), averaged a 20 percent savings to the consumer, while the remainder were advertised at their regular prices! Among items given secondary ad space (one to three column inches), savings averaged only 10 percent or less on three-quarters of the merchandise. Three percent of the items were actually raised in price for the ad, while the rest were advertised at normal shelf price!

Don't believe the implication that only reduced-price items appear in store ads. Despite their size, placement, or prominence, items pictured may only be featured, not necessarily reduced. In one store's ad, the fine print put a new light on featured items: "Our advertising policy [is] if an item is not described as reduced or a special purchase, it is at its regular price." Not one item in this particular ad was so designated. No wonder grocery ads can be so confusing.

As a general rule of thumb, you can typically expect to find half a dozen good bargains in any one ad, with more appearing during price wars or slow economic times.

Color It Sold

Going through the dull black-and-white newspaper, sometimes you don't stand a chance when you come to a grocery ad. The bright colors and glossy pictures capture your attention like moths drawn to flames. Color is a major head turner, and it influences your spending. Shoppers have been conditioned to recognize red as meaning bargain, on sale, reduced. Because psychological studies show red and black attract the eye more quickly than any other color combination, shades of red, hot pink, and orange fill the ad pages with suggestions of savings. Yellow and black is the second most effective combination for attracting your attention.

> Adding even **one color** to an ad **increases sales** an average of 64 percent.

Color certainly adds to the attention value of an advertisement. This is particularly true in newspapers, where relatively few advertisers use it. The extra cost can be justified on the grounds of increased sales: adding even one color to an ad increases sales an average of 64 percent.

Color combined with words like "Red Hot Buys!" is even more effective in influencing your buying decisions. However, just because it's colorful doesn't mean it's a bargain. Watch out for color, and pay attention to price!

Ad Techniques

Since the physical design of each ad influences your response to a store and its specials, some ads grab your attention with vibrant color and bold print to convey a low-price image. Others use sketches of plump fruit and headlines that curve into soft geometric patterns to project an image of quality and style. Each ad is carefully constructed to convey an image message. For example, an aesthetic, or fancy, ad may employ elegant artwork to imply that better-quality goods are sold at this store. Pleasing-to-the-eye fonts and curved print may

intimate that you are the type to shop at a more exclusive place. It also implies that you are willing to pay more for good quality.

Watch the Wording

As important as the influence of color or artwork is the effect the wording of an ad can have on your judgment of the bargains. One enticingly low-priced sale item in an ad might be limited to "Tuesday Only," while other reductions are offered for the full week. If you don't pay attention, you could overlook the wording and be disappointed.

WORDS THAT IMPLY:

DISCOUNT FOODS: Implies lower prices, prices that are regularly discounted. It's possible but not likely on all items, all the time.

LOWER PRICES: Lower than what? Lower than whose? Lower than next year?

LOWEST PRICE OF THE SEASON: What season? Springtime? Christmas? Flu season? Basketball season? Butterfly migration season? A season could mean anything they want it to, even if it's only a couple of days long.

SUPER-SAVERS: Some might be, but are all the items in an ad really super priced?

PERCENT OFF: Percentage off what price? It implies off the regular price, but is the regular price higher than the store has ever actually charged?

BARGAIN: The word by itself is a lure to price-conscious consumers. It may or may not mean a better-than-normal price.

WAREHOUSE: Warehouse implies a store image with lower-than-regular prices on all things. It implies discounts and greater savings. Remember, no one store has lower prices than all the rest, no matter what image the store portrays.

BUY & SAVE: This implies that in order to save, you need to buy now. It also implies that they have better prices than their competitors and that all items in their ad are sale priced.

> **PRICES SLASHED:** Why? Were they previously too high, or have they been artificially inflated for several weeks to "prove" this store is concerned about your budget? (Believe me, they are! All stores are very concerned that you spend your budget in their store.)
>
> **SALE:** This is a magic word. It has power to draw you into a store. It automatically implies lower prices, but remember, everything is always for sale, but not necessarily always on sale.
>
> **BONUS/IN-STORE SPECIALS:** These are featured as added incentives to insure your return to the store. Price consciousness is the only way to know if the prices really are special.
>
> **CASE LOT:** The rule of thumb used to be that buying by the case during case-lot sales ensured better prices. That is not necessarily the case any more (pardon the pun).

Inflated Claims

The pressure to do all your shopping at one store is great since each store is waging a constant campaign to convince you that you need look no further than what it has to offer. And nowhere is the battle fought so vigorously as in the grocery ads. Increasing inflation increases inflated claims! "Our survey proves we have the lowest prices in town!" states one ad, accompanied by the "proof." As hard evidence, the store may cite a survey with numbers and figures supposedly proving its claim is true.

However, these surveys don't actually prove anything at all. The 30 to 50 carefully selected survey items represent less than 1 percent of the store's inventory. No mention is made of the other 10,000 items because the store could not support a statement insisting that it beats all competition on every piece of merchandise. These surveys are only a marketing strategy to convince you that this particular store is the one-and-only shopping destination for you.

Here's one way these surveys are taken. A store representative will survey a large number of grocery items, maybe 100 to 500 items in all, at a number of stores, including his or her own. With that information, store officials will select 20 or 30 items that their own store sells at a lower price than the others. These 30 items then become the list that proves their store has the lowest prices, no matter what the

prices of the other 470 items may show.

Total Proof Spoof

I know this is true because I did it myself. I call it my total proof spoof. I surveyed 100 items in four different stores. Depending on which items I selected for my final surveys, I proved that all four stores had lower prices than the rest. Anyone can prove anything if they select and slant their survey items from a large enough database.

Not Your Grandmother's Shopping List

On closer inspection, you may notice that grocery ad surveys bear no resemblance to a typical shopping list. Instead of a reasonable assortment of staples, produce, meats, cleaning products, and other items that may appear on your personal shopping list, you'll find line after line of detergents, beverages, junk foods, and paper products, often with more than one size of the same product listed.

Very few people actually read those surveys. Most readers simply see and accept the bold figures at the bottom that prove the store is cheapest, and assume that the list is indicative of a typical shopping experience. Since these surveys don't represent realistic shopping lists, you can naturally conclude that they don't represent realistic savings either.

Faulty Logic

Another favorite ad headline asks you to believe all prices are lower because of one cost-saving feature: "We have no overhead—you know our prices are lower!" These ads employ faulty logic. Whether the store actually has less overhead or it only appears so, it cannot guarantee lower prices on everything. Another example declares, "We sell the greatest majority of generic products. Our prices have to be lower." You may not want to purchase only generics, and prices on other items may be higher than you are willing to pay.

Conditional Ad

Sometimes you'll see an item advertised at a price that seems too good to be true. Before you run to the store to take advantage of it, look a little closer at the ad. What does the fine print say? Some stores make their best specials conditional. Large bold letters proclaim the bargain, trailed by fine print listing the conditions. A conditional ad, while seeming to offer bargain prices, actually limits your buying power and controls your buying decisions. The key words to watch out for are "limit," as in limit one or two or more, and "additional purchase required."

For example, the bold print may advertise eggs for the terrific price of $.59 per dozen. However, at the bottom of the in-store coupon, you'll find that you must buy $5 worth of groceries to take advantage of the deal. Further reading of the tiny print reveals you are limited to one coupon and one carton of eggs. You can't even purchase $5 worth of eggs! The eggs in this situation are not so much a bargain as a come-on, as with the other products in the ad where the same ploy is used. They are used as the loss leader—a very restricted loss leader.

> If an advertised price seems **too good to be true**, read the fine print.

"Limited to stock on hand" is another small-print phrase that can cause frustration when you get to the store. The advertised prices may be wonderful, but if stores routinely stock an insufficient supply of an advertised product without offering rain checks, they are playing an unethical marketing game.

If a popular name brand product is featured, watch out for the statement: "We have the right to substitute." To take advantage of this "bargain," you may need to accept another brand.

These are variations of the old bait-and-switch selling ploy. You are baited into the store with promises of great bargains, only to find when you get there that the bargain is not available, and you are switched to a different brand or product. If you venture to a super-

market to stock up on a special, only to discover the brand is substituted, or out of stock, or your purchase limited, you are thoroughly justified in taking your complaints to the manager and your business to a different store.

Using Other Stores' Ads

Occasionally, you'll find a grocery store that appeals to the loyalty of local shoppers by promising to meet the advertised prices of all its competitors. These supermarkets don't bother to advertise their own specials. Instead, they post the ads of other local stores along with a poster proclaiming, "We assure our customers all of the bargains in town."

Usually stores that ad-match are large, exude a high-quality image, and are laced with high-profit, nonfood merchandise strategically located throughout the food aisles. Anyone shopping only the specials could benefit from shopping here, but shopping for anything else is no favor to your budget. Your price-recognition skills prove rather quickly that unadvertised merchandise is generally priced substantially higher than other stores.

There is an ad-matching store not far from my home. I find it interesting that they actually only match ads of certain select stores. They don't include sale prices from the local store that consistently beats all the competition on canned-goods prices, nor do they match prices with the small, independently owned grocery store that regularly offers great deals on fresh produce. I have gone a few times to take advantage of advertised specials from other stores and found the ad-matching store to be out of stock. Since store personnel don't know what items will be advertised until the grocery ads are published, they are unable to stock an adequate supply of the specials.

Ads as a Power Tool

Now that you're armed *with* price recognition skills and protected against *some* of the psychological marketing influences, you're ready to use the grocery ads as a powerful money-management tool.

Start by gathering the ads from all the stores or outlets where you might possibly consider shopping. You'll want to read every ad, every page. Never pass over the ads for a particular store because you assume they are expensive. Their specials may be worthwhile. A careless perusal might cause you to miss good bargains written in small print.

Devise a standard system for jotting down specials as you come across them. (See the "Ad Shopper" charts on pages 194 to 195 in the appendix.) Choose a format that suits you, and use the same format every week. For each store, note every item of interest that you might possibly buy. Your price-recognition worksheet will help you know which items are on sale for good prices.

> *Grocery ads are a* **powerful** *money-management* **tool**.

Don't try to compare prices or items with other stores at this time. List the item and note the size, the price, and the brand. It's easy to forget which brand you were after when you get to the store if you don't have it written down. You won't shop all of these stores each week or purchase all of the items you write down, but you want to be aware of what your options are and where your greatest buying power is for this shopping period.

When you have reviewed all the ads, it's time to start narrowing down the list. Go through the items for each store and decide if you want that particular item this shopping trip or whether you'll wait for another time. Is the price right? Are you running low? Would you be wiser to spend your money on a different bargain?

Either cross out the ones you don't intend to purchase or circle the ones you want. These will be the items that are at the best prices, which you can stock up on while they're on sale. You can transfer your intended purchases to another paper if you want, though after you're comfortable with this process it may be an unnecessary extra step. (See "Ad Shopper" chart on page 196 of the appendix.)

Compare deals between stores. Are there any similar sales? Which stores have the most and the best sales? Are there some stores in outlying areas with sales that are good enough to warrant driving a little way for the bargains? Keep in mind the items and prices you're

aware of in stores that don't advertise. For example, Store X may have milk on sale for $3 a gallon, but you know the local membership store regularly sells it for $2.29.

Keep these sheets in your notebook as a reference for several months. By comparing each week's specials to past specials, you will begin to recognize several important trends: (1) sale or price-war prices that are even better than regular specials, (2) the items most often offered as loss leaders, (3) stores that tend to confine their specials to certain food groups (one might consistently give good prices on meat, while another uses produce to attract customers), and (4) whether an item consistently appears as a loss leader at the same time of year, or in a monthly pattern.

Poring over the ads week after week requires an investment of time and effort, though as you become more skilled, it becomes less time consuming. However, considering how dramatically this one practice can increase your buying power, it is time well spent!

THINGS TO KNOW

- ✦ Grocery ads are a powerful marketing tool. Grocers advertise for one main purpose: to establish store loyalty.

- ✦ Shopping the specials can save you an immediate 23 percent on your grocery bills.

- ✦ Price recognition is absolutely crucial to saving money.

- ✦ Loss leaders/lead items are items featured in an ad that are priced extremely low to lure you into the store.

- ✦ Psychological tactics used to encourage sales include feature spacing, color, and fancy artwork.

- ✦ Wording in an ad can be influential and deceptive.

- ✦ Surveys, conditional ads, inflated claims, and faulty logic can affect your perceptions and spending.

THINGS TO DO

✦ Cultivate your price-recognition skills. List 20 or so items you buy regularly. Over the next several weeks, record the price of each item whenever you purchase or see it. Though prices may fluctuate, you will soon recognize a normal price range for each item. When you see any of these products advertised as specials, you will know immediately whether or not they are actually reduced in price.

✦ Use grocery ads as a powerful money-management tool. Start by gathering the ads and jotting down all specials at all stores. Narrow the lists down by circling the best deals and the ones that you want. Then, shop the specials for an average 23 percent savings on your grocery bills for this one concept alone.

8

Buying by the Calendar:
Savings All Year Long

Have you ever purchased something you needed, only to discover that a week later the same thing was on sale for substantially less? It's enormously frustrating, especially when your budget is tight. Wouldn't it be great if you had a crystal ball that you could gaze into to see when the things you need were going to be on sale? You may not have a crystal ball, but you can come fairly close with a simple calendar.

> Knowing in advance *when promotions are scheduled enables you to* **take advantage of bargains** *when planning your budget.*

We all know that strawberries are in season in the springtime, and that peaches and nectarines are most plentiful and affordable in the summer months. Fall is the time to buy apples and pumpkins. But maybe you didn't know that fruits and vegetables are not the only foods that have a season or best time to buy.

Many grocery items are seasonal, or calendared to be promoted at specific times. Knowing in advance when promotions are scheduled enables you to take advantage of bargains when planning your budget.

Best Food Buys: In Season and Seasonal

Fruits and vegetables are at their best prices when they are in season, or during their peak harvest time. Other foods and grocery items are not necessarily in-season at any given time because they are manufactured all year long. But they are scheduled for promotion at certain times of year. When those promotions are based on a specific holiday or time of the year, they are referred to as seasonal promotions, which often coincide with significant religious days, culture-related events, manufacturer's promotions, local celebrations, and so on.

> **In-season** means a promotion is due to peak harvest time.
> **Seasonal** means a promotion is based on a specific holiday or time of the year.

Turkeys at Thanksgiving time are a seasonal item, as are potato chips and hot dogs during the hot days of summer when outdoor picnics are a common activity. Christmas, Valentine's Day, tax season, and Super Bowl Sunday—these types of occasions and celebrations have seasonal promotions with bargain prices attached to them. Many times the prices on promoted products are unbeatable because stores buy them in volume and can pass on the good prices. On the other hand, because of limited sale times, exposure, and demand, items could be promoted but at regular prices or even higher. Price awareness is an absolute must!

Calendared Best Buys

You'll find that local products are calendared and scheduled just like those promoted nationally. Keep in mind that local calendaring times may vary somewhat from national trends. For instance, peak strawberry season may be calendared nationally in March or April, but you may find the best prices when local strawberries peak in your area in June.

I suggest you keep track of when the items you use most are on sale. Throughout the year, jot down the major sales events that you see, or file your weekly lists of sales from the grocery ads in your notebook. Since these sale times will often be the same year after year, a review of these sales prices will bring to light local and national trends, which you can then use to plan ahead and take advantage of the best seasonal prices.

For example, every year I buy one or two cases of yams in mid-November when the price comes down. I spread my savings on this item throughout the year by buying it all at once and using it as needed. I also know that a local store near my home has a three-week, case-lot sale with terrific prices on canned goods every July. I put aside a set amount each month so I can stock up during that sale. I may spend several hundred dollars in one fell swoop, but I'll save 30 percent or more over what I would have spent buying the same items throughout the year.

The idea for calendared buying to get the best prices applies to nonfood grocery items and other commodities as well as food. Most nonfood items have "seasons" when they are heavily promoted also. Plan ahead to buy personal hygiene products, household items, beauty aids, and so on before you run out. Prices on nonfood products are definitely affected by calendared promotions and seasonal changes.

Calendaring of Promotions

Seasonal sales are actually part of another type of calendar, the calendar of industry promotions. You are familiar with the obvious reasons for a sale: Christmas, Mother's Day, Thanksgiving, and so forth. The calendar of industry promotions goes far beyond the obvious in providing promotion possibilities.

This calendar of special events, used as the basis for promoting specific products, is based on a variety of things, including holidays, special occasions, current events, sports happenings, manufacturer promotions, manager's specials, or any other reason that might

generate a high level of consumer interest. Accordingly, promotions are planned to feed already existing fires, such as the Olympics or the NBA finals, as well as to create consumer interest where none exists, such as Baby Week or National Pickle Day.

Although prices on some promoted products may be unbeatable, the real purpose of a promotion is often to sell items related to the feature item—related items that are often highly profitable nonfoods or general merchandise. Items that change with the seasons entice you with something different but useful to purchase on each shopping trip, while simultaneously boosting the effectiveness of the grocer's general-merchandise selling efforts. A few calendared promotion ideas with their related tie-in ideas could include mops and brooms for spring cleaning, sun screen and sunglasses for summer vacations, lunch boxes and office supplies for back-to-school month, cough medicine and antifreeze for the dead of winter, and headache remedies

This list of events was compiled from actual industry calendars and advertisements. You will likely see these promotions and others like them in your community:

Back To School * Hawaiian Days * Anniversary Sale * Spring Sale * Harvest Happenings * Mid-Summer Madness * Thanksgiving * Christmas Stocking * New Years * Easter * Holiday Sale * Halloween * Labor Day Picnic Sale * Memorial Day * Ground Hog Day * Dairy Delights * Pre-Holiday Buys * Crazy Daze * Fall Kick-Off * Vacation Time * Travel Days * Manager's Sale * National Pickle Week * May Day * National Grouch Day * National Hot Dog Week * Sandwich Month * National Pet Week * Cat Week or Dog Week * Grandparents Day * Political Themes * Fourth of July * Valentine's Day * National Ice Cream Week * Case Lot Bonanza * Stock-up Sales * Store's House Brand Sale * Truckload Sale * Parking Lot Sale * Indian Summer Sale * Good Nutrition Month * Columbus Day * It's A Small World * National Humor Month * Beach Party Time * Store Birthday Party * Frozen Food Spectacular * World Series Daze * National Singles Week * School's Out * (Name Brand) Sale * National Procrastinator's * National Baked Bean * Promo Days/Week/Month * Bowl Game Widows' Specials *

and antacids the week tax returns are due!

Some calendared promotions are clever and amusing and add interest and fun to shopping. It's possible for annual supermarket promotions to become major community events. For example, the Nash Finch Summer Circus Sale, put on each year in Minneapolis, is a tremendously popular merchandising event, when parking lots and stores take on a circus decor, complete with salesclerks dressed like clowns. Even after years and years of Summer Circus sales, customers look forward to it with anticipation, and so do the people who work in the stores.

Many supermarkets schedule their promotions several months to a year in advance and welcome customer participation. Contact the managers of the supermarkets in your area and ask for details on their upcoming promotional events. You can then work that information into your buying plans. For example, if a case-lot sale or beef sale is scheduled a few months down the road, you can save up now to buy in bulk then.

However, if you're going to shop promotions, plan carefully and practice discipline. A well-executed store event creates excitement and a feeling of festivity that increases impulse shopping. If you want to take advantage of the good buys, free samples, balloons, and activities without breaking your budget, set aside a certain amount of money for impulse purchases, and enjoy your shopping spree!

After the Fact

Sometimes buying soon *after* a promotional event is even better. The concept of clearances works well in all aspects of consumer buying, from groceries to clothing. The items that are overstocked in anticipation of sales may be sold at reduced prices the day or the week after the event. This is particularly true for seasonal- and holiday-related nonfood items. (Food items are sometimes placed on clearance after promotional events end also, but not as predominantly as nonfood items.) If you have the storage space, prepare for next year's holiday immediately after this year's holiday season comes to an end.

As soon as canning season passes, canning jars, lids, and other equipment are reduced for clearance.

At summer's end, picnic supplies may be sold at a good price. After Christmas, holiday paper goods, such as napkins and placemats, candles, table decorations, baking goods, cookie cutters, and candied fruit can be a bargain. After every major holiday, candy and snacks specific to that holiday—pastel M&M's after Easter, Oreos with red filling at Christmas—are sharply discounted. Don't forget to check discount drugstores and other alternatives to the supermarket for these promotions, as well.

Scheduled Buying

Everyone needs holidays, treats, and special occasions to look forward to during the year, and often the joy of such events is expressed in food: serving someone's favorite dish, creating a holiday feast, baking a dessert that's a family tradition. However, when economic times are rough and personal finances are failing, these special treats are often the first thing put aside.

As I discussed calendared buying in one of my workshops, I noticed a woman sitting toward the front of the audience. She appeared to be crying as I explained the details and benefits of scheduled buying. At the end of the segment, when we stopped for a break, she came up to me and said, "I'm crying because I'm so happy. You just taught me one thing that will help my family. We've been having an extremely difficult time financially. My husband lost his job several months ago and all extras, such as special foods and fancy birthday meals, have had to be cut out. But even on our tight budget I can now see how to plan ahead and make a difference."

If holidays are not celebrated in your home due to a limited budget, consider scheduled buying. By starting to plan and buy for those special times several months in advance, you'll find they cost a few dollars a month rather than many dollars all at once. Nonperishable items, from napkins and candles

to baking supplies and candied decorations, can be purchased a few at a time for several months prior to the holiday. Even meats, canned goods, or other parts of a favorite dish can be planned into the shopping list in May, June, and July for an anniversary coming up in August. Start thinking Thanksgiving in June, June birthdays in April, and Easter in January.

Scheduled buying is also the best way to deal with school wardrobes, gift giving, special occasions, and myriad other things that require money and put a strain on your budget. Be alert to sales on items that can be stored and used for future anticipated needs. Assess your calendar to see what upcoming events or occasions need to have purchases scheduled. Prior to compiling your shopping lists, check to see what items are usually available at bargain prices.

Plan your shopping around the calendar so that you buy as much as possible when the price is right! Knowing in advance when seasonal sales and calendared promotions are scheduled enables you to take advantage of the bargains when planning your budget. Combine that with scheduled buying, and your calendar is almost as good as a crystal ball.

THINGS TO KNOW

- In-season refers to fruits and vegetables during their peak harvest time.

- Foods and grocery items are considered seasonal when they are scheduled for promotion. Seasonal promotions often coincide with a specific holiday or time of year.

- The calendar of industry promotions provides retailers with promotion possibilities and ideas for sales events.

- Calendared promotions may be clever and amusing. However, plan carefully and practice discipline when shopping promotions because a well-executed store event creates excitement and a feeling of festivity that increases impulse shopping.

♦ Sometimes buying *after* a promotional event is a cost-saving idea. Items that are overstocked in anticipation of sales may be sold at reduced prices the day or the week after the event.

THINGS TO DO

♦ Keep track of when the items you use most are on sale by jotting down major sales events as you see them or by filing your weekly lists of sales from the grocery ads in your notebook. A review of these sales prices brings to light the local and national trends, which you can then use to plan ahead and take advantage of the best seasonal prices.

♦ Consider scheduled buying. By starting to plan and buy for special times several months in advance, you'll find they cost a few dollars a month, rather than many dollars all at once.

9

A Blueprint for Savings:
Menu Planning and Meal Management

A builder knows better than to construct a house without a blueprint. Before the foundation is laid or a nail is hammered, a builder plans every room in detail and knows what materials need to be purchased according to projected needs. While it is obvious that a blueprint puts the builder in control of his construction expenses, many consumers fail to see planning as a similar key to controlling food costs. Yet, you'll find the time it takes to devise meal management and shopping strategies is repaid in tremendous savings. In fact, complete budget control is impossible without advance planning.

Planning Is Not an Arduous Chore

Perhaps you are reluctant to participate in planning to buy groceries because you mistakenly assume that it involves hours of searching for recipes, figuring balanced meals, and writing out detailed menus. Not so! All it takes is a resourceful mind, an awareness of needs and, after you become proficient, only a little bit of your time prior to each shopping trip.

Menu planning and meal management don't have to be arduous chores. The days of 30-day meal schedules with lengthy coordinated ingredient lists are gone, but that doesn't mean you shouldn't plan meals at all. Menu planning is imperative because you must know what you're going to serve and what you need to buy before you shop.

Your methods of planning, however, are as significant as the plans themselves.

Throw Out Traditional Menu Planning

While planning is generally considered good, some planning methods are actually detrimental. For example, you may be shooting yourself in the foot with a particular habit normally considered good, namely, traditional menu planning. Here's the old, standard way of meal planning and why it's so costly: First, plan a day's or week's worth of meals (usually dinner meals only). Next, find recipes for these menus and make a shopping list from these recipes; include grocery items needed to make the recipes and also the items needed to fill out the menus with side dishes and desserts. Then shop, paying whatever the price is for those items on the day you go shopping, or at best, trying to find good prices on these items.

> *Plan to **eat** the bargains you find, rather than trying to **find** bargains on what you plan to eat!*

This method of menu planning guarantees you will almost always be paying full price for the ingredients for your meals. I say, throw out traditional menu planning! Don't ever pay full price for your meals again.

> The key word is **after**.
> Plan your meals:
> • *After* reading the ads
> • *After* determining the best buys
> • *After* assessing what's in your pantry

Instead, plan to eat the bargains you find, rather than trying to find bargains on what you plan to eat! That means you should plan your menus *after* you have read the ads, when you're aware of what items are on sale and are at bargain prices. Your meals come from the bargains in the ads *and* from your well-stocked pantry.

Before you put pencil to paper, let alone set foot in a store, follow these two vital guidelines for menu planning:

✦ *Plan your meals from the cupboard.* Instead of starting with what you'd *like*, start with what you *have*. Chances are you have on hand many ingredients for meals you commonly prepare. Plan to cook enough meals from the cupboard to free up money to spend on bulk purchases of good sale items. Remember that buying in bulk may mean three or four cans for one person and three or four cases for another.

✦ *Plan your menus from the ads.* As I mentioned above, plan to eat what's on sale. Before you decide on specific dishes, take a look at the ads.

If you are used to traditional menu planning, or if you rarely plan menus at all but just run to the store on your way home from work each day to pick up something to fix for dinner, you'll find you can cut your grocery bill significantly using this one concept alone.

A quick look at the comparison charts on pages 198 to 199 in the Appendix clearly shows how. First, I began by choosing a week's worth of everyday meals. I went to a nearby store and priced the main ingredients for those seven meals. The total for the week's worth of meals planned in the old, traditional way was $61.97. Then I went through the sale ads and found what the bargains were for that week. Knowing those, I chose a week's worth of everyday meals based on these foods.

The main ingredients for that week's worth of meals came to only $27.76, less than half the cost of the old way of meal planning. The savings for just one week, for just one concept, is $34.21. Over a year, that would equate to a savings of almost $1,800!

Calendared buying (see chapter 8) comes into play with menu planning. An awareness of what is going to be on sale enables you to economically plan meals and menus in advance. For example, you could plan to purchase pork and beans during the case lot sales in August, knowing that ham is scheduled to go on sale in the following month or two.

Meal-Management Strategies

Recipe ruts can be so restrictive! Just because a recipe has been in your family for seven generations doesn't mean you can't tinker with it a little or serve it less frequently to make it fit your budget. It's important that you assess your recipes to see which are good choices for your new meal-planning methods and which may need to be moved to the "only for special occasion" section of the file box. When your budget bottom line is on the line, you may need to break free from long-ingrained recipe ruts.

Beyond choosing specific foods to serve in your meals, other general guidelines of meal management can greatly affect your food costs. Try some of the following ideas:

> Here's one of my favorite recipes. It's fast, cheap, and delicious. What more could you ask?
>
> ### Taco Soup
> **Brown** together in a large pot:
> 1 lb. hamburger
> 1/2 medium onion, chopped
>
> **Add:**
> 1 15-oz. can tomatoes w/ juice
> 1 15-oz. can kidney beans (drained)
> 1 15-oz. can corn w/ liquid
> 1 8-oz. can tomato sauce
> 1 pkg. taco seasoning
>
> **Mix** together and simmer 10 minutes. Serve with grated cheese on top and tortilla or corn chips.

1. Be open to new ideas. If the recipes you commonly use don't adapt well to budget-wise cooking, find new recipes. Libraries and bookstores are full of cookbooks for budget-conscious chefs. Many favorite recipes come from friends or family members. When you next meet with your bridge club or church choir, or when you gather at a family reunion or during your lunch hour at work, don't be afraid to ask if anyone has a particularly good, cheap recipe they'd be willing to share with you. It may turn out to be a family favorite.

2. Simplify your meals. Generally, Americans are meat-and-potatoes eaters; that is, we prefer a meal with separate servings of meat, starch, vegetables, and dessert. This system of preparing food is almost always more expensive than alternatives. Dinners can be greatly simplified by serving less costly food mixtures, such as casseroles or soups. Since these items already contain a variety of foods

and nutrients in one recipe, no side dish at all may be necessary. Everyday-fare combination dishes, such as soups, stews, salads, skillet, and slow-cooker meals, will trim your budget and provide good nutrition.

3. Replace expensive ingredients with less-expensive ones. This practice allows you to retain the same nutritive value in a dish for far less money. For example, use chicken legs and thighs instead of chicken breasts, powdered milk instead of fresh milk, broccoli instead of asparagus, and bread in place of rolls. Make a more expensive food, such as meat, go further by using it in casseroles or soups instead of as the main entrée. Return to basic staple foods, such as grains, beans, vegetables, and breads. You don't need to make luxury the daily fare.

4. Use less costly food forms. Substituting different food forms requires you to compare the price of canned, frozen, fresh, and dried foods. For example, the "Comparing of Servings" chart on page 197 in the appendix shows that one pound of fresh asparagus and a 16-ounce can of asparagus both yield three to four servings, while a 10-ounce package of frozen asparagus yields only two to three servings. Compare the price of each form of asparagus by figuring the cost per serving: Divide the price of the item by the number of servings it yields. Although one food form, such as frozen, may normally be cheaper than others, a sale may give a temporary price advantage to a different form. For instance, in-season fresh fruits and vegetables almost always cost less than their frozen or canned counterparts, but the opposite is true during off-season times.

5. Be flexible enough to make last-minute changes. If you are at the supermarket and notice an unadvertised special that could be substituted for a more expensive meal you were planning, don't be afraid to make the switch. However, substituting better priced items as you shop should be carefully distinguished from impulse buying.

There is a world of difference between unplanned purchases and planned unplanned purchases! If you were planning on thawing hamburger for tomorrow's meal and you find chicken at an unadvertised bargain price, buy the chicken, whether or not it's on your list. If your budget is stretched to the penny, you may have to postpone other

purchases until a different time, but it's a wise move if the savings are worth it. Do the same for any item made available at an obvious price break that you know you can use or store for use.

By contrast, don't panic over prices when items you need or want are predicted to skyrocket in price. When a peanut butter shortage was rumored, panic buying helped to inflate the price. However, when sugar prices soared, many consumers quit buying it, and the price eventually fell. If an orange crop freezes, yes, the price of orange juice will go up. If it goes up beyond what you are willing to pay, stop buying it! Another crop of oranges will come along, and in the meantime there are other fruits that supply the same nutrients and taste good. If lettuce is too high, buy cabbage. If hamburger is too high, buy chicken. Do not allow price panic to influence your budget.

6. Don't be afraid to experiment. You often hear mothers tell their children not to play with their food. But I play with food constantly! Willingness to experiment can lead to many original, cost-saving meals. A look at your old, standby recipes may reveal that many of them are based on simple patterns of meal preparation. For example, all casseroles include a meat-grain-vegetable combination with a sauce to hold it all together. Which meat, which grain, which vegetable, and which sauce is fairly interchangeable.

If a recipe calls for green beans and you only have peas, try peas. They are both green vegetables. If it calls for rice and you're running low, throw in egg noodles instead. Even sauces are basically the same—usually tomato-based or milk-based with a little flour as a thickener. By following a basic recipe for white sauce, you open the way to a variety of original gourmet tastes for your vegetables by adding any combination of cheeses and spices.

Observe your recipes closely, comparing recipes for the same types of dishes. Note which ingredients seem to be essential to each recipe in about the same proportions. Beyond that basic pattern, anything goes. You do not need to buy every ingredient listed for every recipe you want to use. Throw in what you have on hand to create more variety for less expense.

7. Trim the use of convenience foods. Time is money, espe-

cially in our current fast-paced society, and there's nothing wrong with planning to use convenience foods when they truly give you more time with your family or more time to finish a project with an encroaching deadline. However, with prices constantly on the rise, many consumers have concluded that money is just as valuable as time. Yet habit or lack of know-how prevents them from exchanging one for the other.

Expensive Conveniences

Very few people would favor a return to growing and harvesting all their own food, grinding their own grain, and making their own bread. Yet many of today's convenience foods have built-in services that would take only a few minutes or even a few seconds for you to perform for yourself. (See "How to Make Grab-and-Go Foods on pages 200 to 201 of the appendix.)

Turning on the Faucet. The principle ingredient in many of our foods is water. Is it worth the extra cost to have someone else turn on the faucet? Unlike some convenience foods that save a significant amount of time and labor, many ready-to-serve soups and drinks only

Just a few words about dry milk. A friend of mine was raised drinking powdered milk, and he swore to himself that when he was grown he would never drink powdered milk again. I suspect that many people share the same sentiment. (I admit to being one of them.) However, when fluid milk prices soar past $3 per gallon in the stores, powdered milk, at around $2 per gallon when reconstituted, can be a money saver. If you can't bring yourself to drink it straight, consider using it in cooking and baking.

save you the few seconds it takes to add your own water. Purchasing them in condensed form is more economical, as you can see in the "Soup's On" chart on page 202 in the appendix. You can purchase other foods in dry or concentrated form as well, including salad dressing, sauces, gravies, pudding, juice, and milk.

Spicing Up the Basics. Rice with seasonings added, oatmeal with

spices, frozen vegetables in butter sauce, or boil-in-a-bag pasta salad usually cost double the price of purchasing the basic food and adding your own flavorings. It isn't difficult to make your own salad seasonings, your own pancake mixes, or even your own prefrozen meals that can later be pulled out and used at your convenience. Simply double your meals when you cook, and freeze the extra one for another day. People who feel they have neither time nor money can create their own convenience by pooling efforts with friends and neighbors. Two or three people working together for a few hours on a Saturday morning could double or triple recipes to make a month's worth of homemade mixes and frozen dinners. Sharing the costs of bulk ingredients can expand savings even more.

> If you love the convenience of sliced cheese for making lunches but aren't willing to pay the extra cost, take a block of cheese to the meat counter and ask a butcher to slice it for you. Most butchers are happy to do this for free.

A Little Extra Labor. You can expect to pay more than double the price to buy your vegetables precut into serving-size pieces, or your salad greens washed, cut, and ready to dump into a bowl. You can pay twice as much to have hamburger made into frozen patties as you do to purchase plain ground beef and form the patties yourself. You also pay half again as much per pound to have cheese sliced, grated, and individually wrapped in plastic. The time it may take to slice your own meat and cheese, or to prepare broccoli florets, chopped nuts, green

> If your children aren't willing to give up their ready-to-eat breakfast cereal, you can still cut the cost (as well as the sugar content) by mixing a box of similar-style plain cereal with a box of more expensive, fancier sugared cereal. (For example, mix Cheerios or Toastios with Fruit Loops or Apple Jacks, or mix corn flakes with any other flake-based cereal.) Mix it in a large bowl and either return it to the original cartons, or store it in an air-tight container.

salad, diced onions, or minced garlic at home is worth it when your budget is on the line.

If you can spare more time, you can cut costs even more significantly. Dry cereals are one of the most expensive purchases you can make at the supermarket. Hot cereals and homemade granola can beat them in taste as well as price. And most hot cereals only take minutes to prepare. Toaster-food items, such as frozen waffles and precooked pancakes, can be whipped up at home for a fraction of the cost. Homemade baking mix is versatile and so easy to make.

Interestingly enough, some back-to-homemade products have been positioned as convenience foods for years. For example, one brand of soup mix requires you to add a pound of meat and let the mixture simmer for an hour and a half. When questioned about the convenience of the soup starter, a representative for the product responded, "It depends on how you define convenience. We feel it's convenient to put it on the stove and ignore it for 90 minutes."[20] Many homemade, slow-cooker meals can be made with this type of convenience and at a much more convenient price.

With your meal-management strategies in place and your menu plans made, the buying blueprint is in order to help beat the high cost of eating.

THINGS TO KNOW

+ Meal management and menu planning are imperative. You must know what you're going to serve and what you need to buy *before you shop*.

THINGS TO DO

+ Plan to eat the bargains you find, rather than trying to find bargains on what you plan to eat. Plan your meals from your cupboard and from the grocery ads. Instead of starting with what you'd *like*, start with what you *have*.

+ Reassess your recipe rut, then simplify your meals by replac-

---

20. "Lack of Promotion Stalls Sales," *Chain Store Age: Supermarkets*, July 1981, 61.

ing expensive ingredients with less expensive ones and using less costly food forms. Be flexible enough to make last-minute changes if you find unadvertised sale prices.

+ Trim your use of convenience foods by adding your own water and seasonings, building around basic staple foods, and being willing to do some of the labor yourself.

10

Sensible Prep Steps:
Running Lists and Balanced Buying Decisions

How many times have you gone to the grocery store, traversed every single aisle, spent several hours and way too much money, only to realize when you got home that you forgot the main thing you went to the store for in the first place? It's easy to do if you go to the store with nothing more than a vague idea in your head of what you intend to purchase. A grocery list, if it's prepared properly, can be a major step in sticking to your budget and saving at the grocery store. Unfortunately, most shoppers lack the expertise to make an effective list in the first place.

A jotted jumble of items on a piece of scratch paper may not be a particularly effective list, but it is a little better than nothing. Unfortunately, it's nearly impossible to remember all the things you've run out of or that you know you'll soon be needing if you're making up your list on your way out the door or, worse yet, as you sit in the car in the store parking lot. Going to the store with only a hazy suggestion of possible purchases leaves you vulnerable to marketing tactics and psychological strategies, which in turn opens you up to impulse buying. Remember, today's shopper makes more than two-thirds of her shopping decisions at the store. Because of that, she is largely a product of in-store influences such as price, new products, and point-of-purchase displays. Impulse shopping equates to squandered budgets and high grocery bills.

The Running List

Avoid most of the frustration of return trips to the store by using a running list—the foundation for a good shopping list. A running list is a page on which you jot down needed items as soon as you notice you're getting low. With a running list, you keep closer tabs on the things you need and decrease your chances of forgetting them, which means fewer return trips to the store. That also means fewer impulse purchases. Keeping such a list updated makes inventorying your pantry and refrigerator unnecessary on the day of your shopping trip. If you post it in a prominent or easily accessible place, such as on the fridge or on a cupboard door, everyone in the family can add to it as ideas occur to them. (I wonder why chocolate is always on my list.)

> *A running list is the* **foundation** *of a good shopping list.*

The running list will probably be a jumble of needs, almost-out-ofs, and wants and wishes. (See page 203 for an example.) When you scrape the last of the peanut butter out of the next-to-last peanut butter jar, peanut butter goes on the list. When you see you are getting low on brown sugar, whether or not it will be gone by shopping day, brown sugar goes on the list. That unusual spice that's called for in several recipes can go on the list too, as can Tommy's favorite flavor of ice cream to serve on his upcoming birthday. However, keep in mind the difference between needs and wants. Sometimes a want may remain on the running list week after week until there is money to buy it.

Balanced Buying Decisions

Balanced buying decisions can facilitate balanced budgets and balanced diets. Even if you're armed with lists of what you need and what's on sale, it's easy to return home from grocery shopping to discover that you don't have the right variety of food to put healthy meals on the table. A great sale on canned goods or frozen foods may

have consumed the majority of the budget for the week, leaving very little to purchase other necessities. And while it seemed wise to have stocked up on sale items, if you are subsequently required to go without, or return to the store repeatedly and spend beyond your budget, it was probably a poor choice.

To avoid overspending on any single food category at any one time, decide how you will break down your grocery budget before going to the store. Start by determining how much money you have to spend in your total grocery budget for the week, or this shopping trip. Allocate

> *Balanced buying decisions* **facilitate balanced budgets** *and balanced diets.*

a specific dollar amount to each of the common categories of groceries: meat, produce, canned goods, and so forth. These amounts may vary from week to week, depending on your needs and priorities. For example, if your grocery budget is $75 for this week, you may allocate $30 for produce, $15 for meat, and $5 for snacks and treats. (See the chart entitled "Balanced Buying Decisions" on page 204 of the appendix.)

Looking at the example in the appendix, you can easily see that after you have read the ads and determined the good buys for the week, you can break down those category allotments into specific stores to extend your buying power. Say hamburger and chicken are on sale in Store A. You might decide to spend $10 of your $15 meat allotment on these, and put $3 toward eggs in Store B, with the remaining $2 going for tuna in Store C.

By setting predetermined budget amounts, you can maintain a balanced diet, expand the number of meals you can create from your pantry, and spread a small amount of money as far as possible without going over your budget.

THINGS TO KNOW

✦ A running list decreases your chances of forgetting needed items at the store.

✦ Balanced buying decisions help maintain a healthy diet when budgets are tight.

THINGS TO DO

✦ Keep an accurate running list of needed items in an easily accessible place.

✦ Decide how to break down your grocery budget *before* going to the store. Allocate a specific dollar amount to each of the common categories of groceries to ensure that you can prepare balanced, nutritious meals.

11

Putting It All Together:
The Shopping Trip Planner

All the pieces to your grocery-shopping puzzle are assembled now; what's left is putting the puzzle together. Each separate puzzle piece helps you save money. The real savings comes, though, when the individual pieces are connected to form a buying power picture. That picture is your Shopping Trip Planner page. (See page 205).

Shopping Trip Planner

Your Shopping Trip Planner page gathers all the planning steps discussed in previous chapters and organizes them to efficiently get the most from each. Before you begin, gather together the current grocery store ads, your running list, your scheduled-buying calendar, your list of predetermined budget amounts, and your notebook with the resource pages you've been filling out. With this information at your fingertips, you're ready to put

> Your Shopping Trip Planner page puts information at your fingertips so you can **stretch your budget** as far as it will go.

the puzzle together and stretch your budget as far as it will go.

Start your Shopping Trip Planner page by specifying the maximum dollar amount you want to spend for any given week. (See chapter 13 for details.) With this number in front of you, you are

more likely to stick to your budget.

First, review your running list before you read the ads. Then your needs will be fresh in your mind so you can watch for good prices on them.

Next, study the ads as outlined in chapter 7. Check the ads for every store within a reasonable distance. Write down information for: (1) any item you consistently use, (2) sale-priced items to stock up on, and (3) any items that are on your needs list. Be sure to include the brand, size, and price of each item.

When you have compiled a thorough list of advertised specials for all stores, review the list one more time and highlight the best deals, the ones you will most likely want to take advantage of. (See chapter 7.)

Now, study and compare the store lists. You should be able to immediately identify which stores are offering the most bargains for you. Select the one to three stores that offer the most and best bargains as your shopping destinations for the week. Don't overlook the stores that don't advertise. The day-old bread outlet or the membership store may have familiar bargains that qualify them as important shopping stops during the week. Your Store Information worksheet will help jog your memory.

While you're learning, transfer the bargains you intend to buy to a separate page. This will avoid confusion when you get to the stores. Eventually, you'll work out your own system for reading the ads and determining purchases. It may be using a highlighter to mark the deals you want to take advantage of or using asterisks on the good choices and scratching out the ones to pass on. Decide what works best for you. But initially, take this extra step so you'll clearly know what to do.

With the grocery bargains determined, quickly peruse your pantry to see what you've already got. Based on what you have and what's on sale, decide on menu ideas. If there are a few items you need in order to finish a favorite recipe or round out a balanced meal, add them to your needs list. A glance at your scheduled buying calendar is also helpful to assess upcoming birthdays, holidays, special occasions, and plans to entertain.

Now, check your needs list again. You'll identify some indispensable items that are not on sale at any of the stores you intend to patronize. Determine where to purchase those items. You don't need to create an additional list. Just jot the items on the list for Store A, Store B, and so forth so that the list for each store includes all of the potential purchases (sales and nonsale needs) for that store.

Next, consider your predetermined budget amounts for maintaining a balanced diet. Plot out approximately how much you will spend on the different sale items and needs items to get the most for your money yet still stay within your predetermined amounts.

And now, for the last step in making your Shopping Trip Planner page a major power tool. You have already identified the stores; now

"We started following your plan [several weeks ago]," one lady wrote. "All of your information has been very helpful. Even without everything in place, we have managed to save over $100 in our grocery budget. Even on a five-week month! The pantry is even becoming nicely stocked. To top it off, we haven't spent money in restaurants 'just because.' It has been great!"

determine the days and times to go, and correlate other errands that fit your route and schedule. Mini-shopping trip strategies fall into place now! (See chart entitleds "Shopping Trip Planner" on page 205.)

Does this seem like too much busy work? Keep in mind it's new. And it's different. Of course, you will need some time to learn the process, but once this process becomes a habit, it doesn't take a great deal of time, and your budget will be the winner. Stay enthused and think positive. In the job market, it takes several months to learn the ins and outs of a new job. If it takes a couple of months to become a competent super buyer, it will be well worth it.

THINGS TO DO

✦ Review your running list.

✦ Read the ads and write down necessary information. Highlight the best deals.

✦ Check your pantry and decide on menu items for the week.

✦ Determine what, if any, other items are necessary. Add these to your needs list.

✦ Determine which store you'll purchase needs-list items from.

✦ Consider predetermined budget amounts.

✦ Decide the days and times to go, and schedule other errands.

Section Three

You Don't Have to Go to the Store!

12

Putting It Away:
The Pantry System

Let's say you've been following the Beating the High Cost of Eating program faithfully for a few months now. Your cupboards are filling up nicely. You're seeing a little improvement in your budget, so you have more money each payday to spend on good deals. Then, one Tuesday evening you open your paper to find the mother lode of case lot sales. You make your lists, squeeze your dollars until they scream, and hit the store to reap the savings. The only problem is that when you get home, you have a mountain of groceries and nowhere to put them!

Next to money, or the lack thereof, insufficient space is the greatest challenge most people face in following the Pantry Principle. Without actual, physical storage space, you can't possibly consider a program that suggests you store quantities of commodities. The success of the Pantry Principle is largely based on your ability to find a place to put it all. Don't be discouraged by this. Lack of space is a problem that can be solved with a little ingenuity and creativity, and the rewards are well worth the effort!

Pantry Search

No matter how small your home or apartment is, or whether you own or rent your home, a pantry is not out of reach. You need to streamline your thinking, replacing yesterday's image of flour bins

and rows of bottled fruit with the twenty-first century concept of an economical support system. The pantry, when functioning properly, is an essential part of sound money management. A pantry, or mini-pantry, is essentially an ammunition stockpile in the battle for the grocery budget. It becomes your springboard for buying power. The better the pantry system, the better the buying backup system. The better the pantry system, the more aggressive buying plans can become. Shelves take on a new significance as they transcend cupboard space to become tangible evidence of purchasing power.

> A pantry is an **essential** part of sound money management.

Very few lucky people will have an ideal situation to work with. For everyone else, a pantry actually consists of a pantry system, meaning a combination of mini-pantries in several nooks and crannies. Generally, there is space enough, even in very small households. The problem is that much of the available space is unrecognized or used inefficiently. Your new goal? Discover how many different places in your home or apartment can be turned into pantries or mini-pantries.

These mini-pantries do not have to be located in one place, nor do they even have to be in areas with optimal storage conditions (dark, dry, and cool), though of course, the more ideal the conditions, the longer your supplies will last. Of course, as you develop your pantry system, it makes sense to keep similar items together. This helps you remember what and how much of each commodity you have. And maintaining an inventory

> A student of mine, a young man who lived with four other bachelors in a small apartment, went home from a class on the Pantry Principle determined to find a place to keep his grocery bargains. After a thorough review of his apartment and ribbing from his roommates, he was totally discouraged. Spare closets and cupboards were not to be found. Refusing to give up, he went out and bought five cinder blocks, placed his bed on four of them, and used the fifth as a step. He had created his mini-pantry—under his bed. He just grinned as he shared his success at our next class.

of what is where makes sense also, particularly if your mini-pantries are spread all over your house. A page or two in your notebook works well for this.

The first rule for finding pantry space: Work with what you have, and look for ways to make it better. The second rule: Don't limit yourself to spaces normally identified as cupboard space or pantry space. Nooks and crannies and unusual places can play a significant role.

Examine each area of your home for hidden potential. Put on your thinking cap and start your creative juices flowing as you look around for different places that can be turned into pantries. Look up, look under, look inside. Rearrange, reevaluate, reprioritize. Where can you find unused or underused space that could be put to work as pantry space?

> ## Rules for finding pantry space:
>
> 1. Work with what you have and look for ways to make it better.
> 2. Don't limit yourself to spaces normally identified as cupboard or pantry space.

To Buy or To Build, That is the Question

When you find a likely looking spot in your home, the next step is to transform it from just an empty space into a working, functioning pantry. That usually means adding shelves, containers, or cupboards of some kind or another. If you are handy with tools, the only thing standing between you and a pantry is a little time and a little money. Check out the ideas and plans included in the "Pantry Search" on page 206 to get you started.

If, however, you were standing in the wrong line in heaven when they handed out the handyman genes, don't despair. Your local home improvement store is loaded with terrific storage and shelving ideas that will work even for people who can't tell a hammer from a hang-nail. I suggest that everyone take a tour through the storage solutions sections of a local building supply store to see what creative options

are available. You may find ideas there that fit your situation, ideas that never would have occurred to you. You can then purchase their supplies, or build your own version of their idea, based on your skill and budget level. Either way, knowing what's available can make a big difference in how you can take advantage of potential pantry space.

Add a Shelf

You'll find as many different shelf options available as there are things that need to be stored on shelves. And there are very few areas in a home that can't be made more useful by adding a shelf or two. Freestanding, ready-made shelving units are available in all sizes, just waiting to be filled with your home-storage supplies. You can also buy freestanding cupboards, rather than just shelves, that will keep all your storage items neatly behind doors. These ideas work great for renters who don't have the option of putting nails in the walls or building shelves.

If you don't have the floor space for a freestanding shelf unit, add shelves on the walls. Metal utility brackets and boards, decorative wooden brackets and shelving, or adjustable shelving tracks allow you to change the height of the shelves to match the items you put on them. Shelves go almost anywhere to take advantage of the smallest spaces.

Rearrange Your Cupboards

The top shelf in many kitchen cupboards is too high to use conveniently every day, especially if your cupboards go all the way to the ceiling. Turn that top shelf into pantry space. Pull out all the extra mixing bowls, Cool-Whip containers, and decorative ice cube trays that are gathering dust and designate the area as a pantry. If it's hard to see what you're storing there, tape a list on the inside of the cupboard door for quick reference.

If you can't create more space on the shelves, add extra shelves or purchase commercial space extenders. A turntable or pull-out drawer in a hard-to-reach corner cabinet makes the space more useable. Sturdy cardboard boxes can be cut to size for custom-built

drawers. I recommend produce boxes that come with tops that slide down over the whole box. Place the box upside down inside the top for a double-strength drawer.

Is there wasted space between the top of your cupboard and the ceiling? Stack pantry items there. Hanging a curtain, about the size of a valance, from the ceiling covers the storage space but still keeps it accessible.

The only catch in maximizing cupboard space is to avoid putting food items over the stove or in any excessively hot area. Use that space for equipment, paper products, or other items that won't spoil.

Do your existing shelves waste space? Is there too much room between shelves? If the shelves are adjustable, arrange them so there is only two inches between the top of the cans and the bottom of the next shelf. Organize your cans and packages so that each shelf holds the same-size items. If you stack cans or packages more than two high, you'll spend too much time restacking fallen goods.

Make Room above the Washer and Dryer

Since many washer/dryer hookups are set back in alcoves, there is usually room to add several shelves, if not a set of cabinets, above them. If the alcove or closet is deep enough, the shelves could be on three walls, forming a U. Although heat and moisture means this is a less-than-ideal spot for food, it can still provide needed space for nonfood items and emergency gear. And if there is absolutely no other space available, it will work for food as well. You'll just need to use the food as quickly as possible.

Convert a Closet

Not many people can spare an entire closet, but even part of a closet—or parts of several closets!—make fine mini-pantries. Inserting several narrow shelves in place of (or above) a common single shelf can maximize storage space at the top of a closet. The side or end of a closet is a good place for a set of shelves or stacked plastic crates. Even if the shelves could only be four feet to six feet deep, you'd find there's a lot of usable space hidden behind your winter coats and galoshes.

Whole Closet

Maybe you have an entire closet you can devote to being a pantry. Assess each closet and evaluate how it is being used, then reevaluate. When we lived in several apartments in California, I simply changed the traditional use of my linen closet. Sheets and blankets were stashed in boxes in the corner of the bedroom closets, and towels and washcloths were relegated to shelves in the bathroom. The entire linen closet was transformed into part of the apartment's pantry system. The floor of the traditional coat closet is another unlikely pantry space, but that's where we kept our buckets of flour and rice and so on.

If you can find a whole closet, put shelves on all three walls, leaving a step-in space in the middle. Don't forget the space on the back of the door where racks can be hung to hold small containers.

A Wall or Two

If you're lucky enough to have a fairly large room in your house that has unused space, turn that into pantry space. Fill one wall, floor to ceiling, with shelves, and hang a curtain in front of them. Just one 10-foot-wide wall, with 12-inch shelves spaced a foot apart, floor to ceiling, holds 1,680 cans, or 70 cases of food![21]

If the room is large enough, build a false wall to form a sort of walk-in closet. This could be as fancy or as simple as you want it to be. If you're not handy with tools, buy tall bookshelves with backs. Line them up side-by-side with the backs to the room and the shelves facing into the little walk-in pantry area, leaving a couple of feet as an entrance. If the pantry area is deep enough, you can greatly multiply your shelf space by putting bookshelves on all sides of the pantry area.

When we were first married, we lived in a small rented home. We weren't allowed to make any permanent changes or mar the walls, but we still wanted to have pantry room. In the bedroom we used as a nursery, we stacked wooden apple boxes, one on top of the other, for

---

21. No. 303 cans, the size of an average can of peas, corn, or green beans. Of course, the shelves will hold more or less, depending on the size.

storage shelves. A curtain, hung from the wall to the boxes, closed off the doorway to this small storage room.

On the back sides of the boxes nearest the bedroom area we tacked up pegboard, painted it to match the nursery furniture, and hung pictures and toys on it for decoration. We placed our children's dresser in the closet, since none of their clothes hung very low anyway, and the space at the bottom of the closet otherwise would have been wasted. The babies could care less that their room was smaller, and our first custom-built pantry was wonderful.

Under the Bed

There are better things to keep under your bed than dust bunnies. Many underbed storage containers are available that allow you to put that space to good use. Some are plastic, some are cardboard. Either one will work fine for an underbed mini-pantry. Several, side-by-side, will maximize the usable space.

Very high beds are quite fashionable. If you have one, you may wish to sacrifice fashion to function, because you could store a lot under a high bed frame. Or for the handy person, take advantage of underbed space by building a simple platform as a bed frame, creating pantry space underneath it. Custom drawers, or custom cardboard box drawers, are a nice touch.

If you have long-term storage foods sealed in gallon cans, such as wheat or beans or dehydrated foods, that you aren't intending to eat for quite a while, stack those in a single layer and use them as a bed frame. A twin-size bed sits neatly on about 70 gallon-size cans (No. 10 cans). It's about the same height as a regular bed frame, and you never see them if you put a dust ruffle on the bed.

A woman who did this reported it worked wonderfully. First, she noted, it was a perfect place to store all those cases of dehydrated food that didn't have anywhere else to go. Second, the underbed space was no longer a hiding place for dirty clothes, dirty dishes, and banana peels. It saved a lot of arguments with her teenager. The same idea will work with five-gallon metal cans or sturdy poly buckets. If you don't have enough cans or buckets to make a solid layer for the

mattress/box springs to rest on, spread out the buckets you have evenly and put a 4' x 8' sheet of plywood on top as a pallet, then place the mattress on top of that.

Under the Sink

There is often dead space under kitchen and bathroom sinks where shelves can be built or set in, even if only to the side of the pipes. Makeshift shelves, balanced on bricks, create room for storing soap, shampoo, deodorant, and other nonfood items. If your bathroom has a sink without a cabinet, consider installing one to serve as a mini-pantry. If you have small children, don't forget to use safety latches if you keep anything down low that could be toxic.

Living Room

While no one wants shelves with soup and tuna lining their living room walls, that doesn't mean the public rooms in your house can't be functional as well as inviting. Pull your couch out two feet from the wall. Stack case goods or equipment in sturdy containers behind it to the height of the couch, put a flat board across the tops of the boxes to even it out, and cover it all with a pretty tablecloth. It makes a slightly unusual sofa-back table for plants or a table lamp. Of course, don't use this space to store items you'll be using all the time, since that could be quite inconvenient. The same idea works for end tables. A pretty tablecloth can cover a multitude of surprises.

One idea I discourage is using dry beans and grains as the filling for beanbag chairs. Food that you are planning to eat needs to be kept clean and stored under the best conditions available. Beanbag filling ends up crushed and filthy after years of being sat on and rolled around on the floor. Besides, it's just not practical. The volume of beans necessary to fill a single beanbag chair would weigh over 200 lbs!

Under the Stairs

Homes with stairwells often have framed-in storage space underneath the stairs. The same concepts apply to this space as to regular closet space. Put shelves on as many walls as possible, or if the slanted

ceiling is too awkward, consider putting shelf units on casters that can be rolled out for convenience.

Garage, Attic, or Shed

Many people think that a garage, attic, or shed is a poor place for a pantry because the areas are too hot, too cold, too accessible to bugs, too dirty, and so on. In many respects, they are right. These places usually are too hot, too cold, too accessible to bugs, and too dirty. However, if this is the only space that you have—adapt!

Creative assessment can get you a workable, wonderful pantry. We spent most of our married lives in California where dark and cool basements, the ideal place for a pantry, are non-existent. We have also moved a lot, so we have had the opportunity to design and create many garage pantries. There is plenty of room in a garage that you may never have associated with a pantry.

Is a garage ideal? No. Does it pose challenges? Of course! Is it an option? Absolutely! It merely requires planning and an awareness that food might not keep as long due to the less-than-ideal conditions.

A garage provides pantry options that range from shelves, to cabinets, to walls-of-cabinets, to a completely insulated, walk-in pantry. In most of our California homes, we've transformed the garage into an extension of the house that contains an entire pantry system of its own including loft, insulated walls, cabinets, and customized shelves.

Having our pantry in the garage usually means our cars are not kept in the garage. It's inconvenient, but it's a choice we've made and a price we've been willing to pay in order to be prepared and live within our means.

Attics are generally much too hot for storing food but perfectly acceptable for nonfood supplies and equipment. If you have an accessible attic that isn't filled with insulation, make sure it's ventilated with good airflow, then use it for blankets and paper goods and things that won't spoil. Pull-down stairs make for easy access to an otherwise inconvenient attic or loft.

Pretty Close to Ideal

An ideal pantry would be a cool basement room dedicated entirely to being just a pantry. Dark, dry, and cool, with shelves on all the walls, this is the kind of pantry everyone would love to have.

A room upstairs works great also. Keep it as dark, dry, and cool as possible by covering any windows, blocking off the heater vent, and keeping the door closed. If you can permanently dedicate a room to being a pantry, consider insulating the walls also.

Creating your pantry system may be a challenge you can't complete overnight. If you are starting at square one, this project might take several months. Set a goal and progress toward it, if only a step, or a shelf, at a time. Continue to improve your system until it functions at maximum efficiency for you. Keep your evaluations and expectations realistic. For more inspiration and ideas, check your library or home improvement stores for books on finding storage space. Some of the ideas you'll find are delightful, as well as creative and functional. Just remember, a pantry in a less-than-ideal spot is better than no pantry at all.

> A pantry in a less-than-ideal spot is **better** than no pantry at all.

THINGS TO KNOW

+ Your ability to stock up on good bargains is largely determined by your ability to find a place to put those bargains once you bring them home. Lack of space is a problem that can be solved with a little ingenuity and creativity.

+ For most people, their pantry will actually consist of a pantry system, meaning a combination of mini-pantries in several nooks and crannies.

+ Your local home improvement store has many storage and shelving ideas.

THINGS TO DO

✦ Find space by adding shelves, rearranging cupboards, converting closets, building false walls, and looking in unconventional places for poorly used or underutilized space.

✦ Don't limit yourself to spaces normally identified as cupboard space or pantry space.

13

Beating the High Cost of Eating:
You Don't Really Have to Go to the Store

In the beginning, I mentioned that the foundation of this money-stretching program is the Pantry Principle—the process of stocking up on commodities and building a supply in your pantry. This is a crucial point. Without a pantry or cupboard of supplies to turn to, you have no choice but to pay full price for all your needs, all the time. The concepts in the preceding chapters are designed to help you stretch your budget to the maximum and use that buying power to stock up when prices are right. When you can turn to your pantry instead of to the store for the majority of things you need, you'll be the winner.

Having a well-stocked pantry is what gives power to all the concepts you've learned. It's what allows you to get to the point where you don't have to go to the store. By now, you've learned some of the things that will impact your budget inside the stores, such as the power of displays and the influence of games and gimmicks. You also know some of the things that you have to *do* to make a difference, such as reading ads and making an effective shopping list. With this background, you're ready to gain complete control of your grocery

> When you do not **have** to go to the store, you have **control** of your grocery budget.

budget. When you do not *have* to go to the store, you have gained that control.

Now, this is not to say that you'll never need to go to a store again, or that you should boycott supermarkets. I frequent them often and regularly. Rather, I encourage proficiency in the skills of shopping, and command of your shopping situation, so that you only go to the store when you want to, not because you *have* to. Some people reach the point where, if they have a financial crisis or some other problem, they can painlessly stay out of stores for a week or a month or two. Some people reach a level of pantry preparedness such that six months could go by without their needing to take a major shopping trip, other than maybe for fresh milk or produce.

> **The benefits of having a full pantry:**
>
> 1. Emergencies lose much of their power over you.
>
> 2. You are not at the mercy of fluctuating grocery prices.

It would be entirely possible for my family to not set foot in a store for a very long time and still eat well. We would miss fresh produce and dairy products, but we could make do with powdered milk and canned produce. However, I couldn't go forever without replenishing my shelves. I would eventually have to start again from scratch and build up my supplies.

The point is, first of all, that when you have a full pantry to rely on, emergencies lose much of their power over you. You are ready, and your grocery budget is available. Secondly, when you are stocked with supplies, you are not at the mercy of fluctuating grocery prices. You take advantage of bargains as you find them and cheerfully stay home when prices are more than you're willing to pay. You choose when, where, and if you go to the store. Your grocery dollars go further and buy more than when you have to pay top dollar.

I was approached by a young woman in Washington, D.C., who wanted to tell me about her success with this program. She and her husband were having a hard time making ends meet on a single income. They had several small children at home and times were tough. She was reluctantly considering getting a job outside the home in order to meet their expenses. She had taken my classes and learned the money-saving/budget-stretching concepts found in this book, and she decided that before she broke down and went to work, she would try diligently applying them to their situation. She was thrilled to relate that she was able to stretch her buying power to the point where she no longer needed to find a job outside the home. Her CPA husband calculated the costs involved had she gotten a job. It would have taken a job earning $18,000 per year to meet their needs, fill the gaps, and cover the expenses!

Shopping as a Business

To reach this point, you must think of shopping as a business. In fact, an argument could be made that shopping *is* a business, with real monetary gains and losses dependent on wise decisions and expertise. If you give it the thought, concern, and organization you give your other businesses or careers, you'll find the returns are rewarding. Your extended buying power can be equivalent to a raise in salary!

However, I don't believe in a book that introduces a new idea without telling you how to start from where you are and make the climb to where you want to be. This chapter, then, is about getting there.

Before the First Payday

Your goal of not having to go to the store can begin on your next payday. (We'll call it your first payday.) As payday approaches, take these steps:

First, inventory your cupboards. Take a close look at what you have on hand. This shouldn't be a hard or lengthy process. Jot down names of items and how many you have of each. You may want to use the categories suggested on the "Example Inventory List" on page 207. A

large family may require more than one page or choose to fill out a separate sheet of paper for each category.

Second, plan menus from foods on hand. Pretend you can't go to the store until the payday after next, your second payday. What meals could you make from what you have on hand? Most people are surprised to discover that, even in a rather empty-looking kitchen, they can usually gather up supplies for several meals. Try to create enough simple meals to last until your second payday, even if you have to eat the same thing several times. (See "Simple Menus from Foods on Hand" on page 208 of the appendix.)

Third, assess your basic needs. You'll find there are some meals you could make if you only had this or that item. Begin a needs list, and add these things to it. Also list other must-have items. Are you out of fruit? Does the baby need formula? Is all the bread gone? What about milk? Make sure you include needs only—those items necessary to nutritiously feed your family from this payday until the next. Also, include essential nonfood items such as toothpaste and laundry detergent.

Do not include wants, those things you would like to have but can live without. Be tough with yourself in determining what is a need and what is a want. When your list of needs is complete, estimate the cost of each item and add the prices together for an estimated total.

> No matter **how small** *your beginnings, this program will* eventually **work for you.**

First Payday Program

You've done the preparation work; now your first payday is here. *Look at your paycheck.* You must first determine what your total grocery budget is. To do this, you subtract from the net amount all the bills and other obligations that need to be paid out of this paycheck, such as rent or house payment, insurance, charitable donations, utilities, car payment, and bus fare. Also, deduct out-of-the-ordinary but necessary expenses (upcoming birthdays, school pictures, and so forth).

What's left is your grocery budget. (See "Your Paycheck" chart on page 209 of the appendix.)

From this grocery budget, subtract the estimated total of your grocery needs. The remaining figure is called your *workable amount.* This is the amount of money you can spend on groceries other than absolute needs. Don't be discouraged if the amount is small. Even a few dollars of workable money will get you started. (See second "Your Paycheck" chart on page 209 of the appendix.)

If your economic situation is such that creating a workable amount each payday seems impossible, consider this option: determine an amount, however small, to pull from each paycheck as if it were another bill. Use this preselected amount as your workable amount. After you have worked at stocking up for several weeks to several months, using a preselected amount as your workable amount, you'll find your grocery budget has achieved some flexibility and you can begin determining a workable amount from your grocery budget as well. No matter how small your beginnings, the entire program will eventually function for you.

The next step is to read the ads. Following the guidelines outlined in chapter 8, look over your local ads. Pinpoint the loss leaders or bargains on items you frequently use that are different from the items you already have on hand. Take a look at your inventory page or your shelves; don't just guess.

If possible, choose foods that combine with those foods you have on hand already to increase the number of simple meals you can serve. If any items from your *needs* list are on sale, be sure to make a note of them. Try to choose those groceries that will stretch your money the furthest.

Now, shop, using your best skills, the skills you've just learned. Buy just enough of your regularly priced needs items to get by until you see a sale when you can stock up. Make it a challenge to spend less on items from your needs list than your estimated amount. Also, buy your selected specials with the workable amount you set aside. Stock up on great deals as much as your space, needs, and money will allow. Then, add your new purchases to your inventory list. You're off to a good start.

As your second payday approaches, *reevaluate your needs* and adjust your lists and menus. At this point, your needs will have changed to some degree since you will have used up some of the commodities that figured heavily in your first menu plan. You may be out of mustard or hamburger or deodorant or some other item that was in stock earlier. Once again, plan simple menus from what you now have in your pantry, including your new purchases, to get you through another pay period.

Second Payday

Your second payday has come, so *divide your paycheck*. Follow the same steps for determining your workable amount as you used the first payday by deducting your grocery needs from your grocery budget. If you were able to plan enough meals from your cupboard the first time to carry you into this second pay period, you should see an increase in your workable amount, even if it's just a small one. If you have a long needs list, freeing money for stocking up on bargains will be a slower process. However, you will eventually see progress. (See Paycheck #2 on page 209 of the appendix.)

Again, *read the ads*. Following the same pattern as last pay period, check the ads for items on sale that you regularly use, and prepare your list of loss leaders and good bargains. Look for the best bargains on a variety of items that will best extend your budget by providing you with well-balanced meals. Perhaps this time you'll want to plan part of your workable amount to take advantage of bulk buys at membership clubs and wholesale outlets. As much as possible, buy *different* commodities from those you have on hand. This allows you to create variety in nutrition as well as menu plans.

Now shop, again using your best skills. Buy necessities and stock up on your choice of bargains. When you put your items in the pantry, mark them on your inventory sheet, and create new meal ideas and menus that include these new purchases. Try to stretch your budget further each paycheck.

Keep the Ball Rolling

Repeat this process until most of your grocery money is being allocated for specials, loss leader items, and bulk buys. Of course, you may choose to go to the store a little more frequently to stay stocked up on fresh produce, dairy products, and other perishables, but even fresh food shopping follows the rules: buy only when the price is right, and stock up as much as possible, using a specific list of items and dollar amounts. Your refrigerator and freezer are definitely part of your pantry system.

Eventually, your pantry should contain a sufficient variety of foods, including perishables, in sufficient amounts that you could serve several weeks of well-balanced meals without going to the store. And the same goes for nonfood items. You should only need to go to the store when you see prices you consider low enough to pay.

> The fuller your pantry grows, the more **in control** you'll feel.

Although it takes different people different periods of time to attain this goal, it can be done. You can make these principles work for you, no matter your income or the capacity of your pantry!

As you work with your new meal planning and shopping skills each pay period, you will gain more and more confidence in your abilities. The fuller your pantry grows, the more in control you'll feel. The habits you develop as you progress are meant to be ongoing. Don't slip back into the old way of menu planning and shopping. Menus should always be planned using what's on hand, combined with what's on sale. Shopping should always be based on specials in the ads and planned before you ever set foot in a store.

If a shopping trip or meal you plan doesn't work out, you now have the flexibility to shift plans and adjust meals at will. You are no longer going to the store each week to buy specific foods for specific meals based on specific recipes. Your meals come out of your well-supplied cupboards. Your grocery budget is devoted almost entirely to buying the best bargains and keeping your pantry stocked.

(See "Paycheck #XX" on page 209 of the appendix.)

Your workable amount should grow larger each paycheck as you progress in following the system until almost all of your grocery money is allotted to purchasing sale items and deals. This is when the other concepts you have learned can be most successfully employed. Since you don't have to go to the store, since you have almost all of your grocery budget to spend on good deals, the supplies on your pantry shelves will increase and grow while your buying power expands. If, during the course of a pay period, you don't see a bargain that meets your current needs, don't buy. In fact, if nothing you want comes along for several pay periods—don't buy. Save the money to really stock up when you see something you want.

On the other hand, if a family member needs a new pair of shoes or a car needs repairs or a doctor bill must be paid, you can use the grocery budget to cover it and still provide well-balanced meals and a snack or two. You don't have to go to the store. Remember—you are now in control.

It can be done! Lynda B., a mother of five in California, attended my classes. The ideas sounded good, but she didn't do much about them for a long time. Then, a financial crunch hit their family: a new baby came along, employment became uncertain, and grocery bills were soaring. Something had to be done!

Lynda's husband suggested that they get out the information and follow the methods they'd learned in my classes but had never tried. They did. After they put the plan and strategies into place, Lynda immediately cut her grocery bills $150 a month over the previous months, and they were eating better, with a greater variety than ever before. They were delighted and doubled their efforts, with even greater success in the months that followed.

It's said that necessity is the mother of invention. This is certainly true with the Pantry Principle. I developed the Pantry Principle program years ago when we decided my husband needed to quit his job and return to the university to finish his degree. We had two teenage children and a gross annual income of only $5,000 per year. Those were tough times, but because of the Pantry Principle concepts, we got through them without ever having to rely on government hand-

outs. We finished school almost out of debt, and we even managed somehow to purchase a small home during that time.

Even though I shared this story at the beginning of this book, I refer to it again because I hope it will encourage you in your efforts to make these ideas meaningful in your life. I know these concepts work because I've lived them. They will work for you too. You can beat the high cost of eating.

THINGS TO KNOW

+ Stocking up on commodities and building a supply in your pantry are the crucial points.

+ Think of shopping as a business.

THINGS TO DO

The preparatory steps for the Beating the High Cost of Eating program are:

+ Inventory your cupboards and plan menus from foods on hand.

+ Determine your basic needs.

+ Add the prices together for an estimated total.

The steps to take on your first payday are:

+ Determine what your total grocery budget is.

+ From this grocery budget, subtract the estimated total of your grocery needs to determine a workable amount.

+ Read the ads and pinpoint the loss leader bargains.

+ Shop, using your best skills. Stock up on great deals. Buy just enough of your regularly priced needs items to get by until you see a sale when you can stock up.

The steps to take on your second payday are:

- Repeat the things you did on the first payday program—determine your workable amount, read the ads, and prepare a list of loss leaders and good bargains.

- Again, buy your necessities and stock up on your choice of bargains, using your best shopping skills.

- As much as possible, buy different commodities from those you have on hand.

On succeeding paydays:

- Repeat these steps until most of your grocery money is being allocated for specials, loss leader items, and bulk buys. Your workable amount should grow larger each paycheck as you progress in following the system until almost all of your grocery money is allotted to purchasing sale items and deals.

Appendix

A Look at Supermarket Image

How important do you consider the following supermarket features? Check the appropriate column for each item.

Store Attribute	Very Important	Fairly Important	Not Important
1. Cleanliness			
2. Good layout for fast shopping			
3. Short wait at checkout			
4. Aisles clear of boxes			
5. Pleasant atmosphere			
6. Convenient store location			
7. Long late hours			
8. Deli and bakery departments			
9. Good parking facilities			
10. Check-cashing service			
11. Frequent sales or specials			
12. Good selection of low-priced store brands			
13. Consistent reasonable prices			
14. Good buys plentifully stocked			
15. Unit pricing displayed on shelves			
16. Separate "deal" or "bargain" section			
17. Large generic section			
18. Unadvertised specials			
19. No overhead, games, or gimmicks			
20. Case lot or special-price section			
21. Racks of free recipe booklets			
22. A home economist in store or on call			
23. Diet-coded shelf tags			
24. Holiday booklets of recipes and hints			
25. Free pamphlets on nutrition and diets			
26. Cashiers that remember your name			
27. Helpful and friendly personnel in each department			
28. Baggers on duty to carry your groceries to the car			

If features 1–5 are most important to you, watch out for stores that claim to make shopping easy. The one-stop shopping image is directed at you if you look for items 6–10. A low-price image is created with features 11–15, while 16–20 go a step further to suggest rock-bottom bargains. If you pride yourself on being an informed consumer, numbers 21–25 may draw you into a store. Features 26–28 suggest a friendly image.

Comparison of Nonfood Items at Grocery Stores and Mass-Merchandise Outlets

Item	Costco	Wal-Mart	Target	ShopKo	Smith's	Albertson's	Macey's
Toilet Paper Charmin Ultra, double roll	(36 rolls @ $11.99) 12 rolls = **$4.00**	12 rolls **$5.78**	12 rolls **$6.99**	12 rolls **$5.99**	12 rolls **$8.99**	12 rolls **$9.49**	(6 rolls @ $3.99) 12 rolls = **$7.98**
Hand soap Dial Gold, 4.5 oz bars	(16 pack @ 5.99) 8 pack = **$3.00**	8 pack **$3.50**	12 pack @$5.89 8 pack= **$3.92**	8 pack **$4.99**	8 pack **$6.29**	8 pack **$6.29**	(3 pack @ $2.49) 8 pack = **$6.64**
Shampoo Pert Plus	(33.9 oz @ $4.79) 25.4 oz. = **$3.59**	25.4 oz. **$3.84**	25.4 oz. **$3.99**	25.4 oz. **$4.99**	25.4 oz. **$7.99**	25.4 oz. **$6.69**	(13.5 oz. @ $3.49) 25.4 oz = **$6.57**
Shampoo Johnson's baby	(40 oz. @ $5.45) 20 oz. = **$2.73**	20 oz. **$3.27**	20 oz. **$3.59**	20 oz. **$3.39**	20 oz. **$4.99**	20 oz. **$4.99**	(15 oz. @ $3.99) 20 oz. = **$5.32**
Laundry Detergent Tide with bleach	267 oz. **$17.79**	(87 oz. @ $7.44) 267 oz. = **$22.83**	267 oz. **$18.99**	267 oz. **$18.99**	(177 oz. @ $14.08) 267 oz. = **$21.24**	(132 oz. @ $13.99) 267 oz. = **$28.30**	267 oz. **$20.99**
Toothpaste Colgate, 8.2 oz.	(4 pack @$6.69 1 tube = **$1.67**	8.2 oz. **$2.24**	8.2 oz. **$2.14**	8.2 oz. **$3.49**	8.2 oz. **$3.49**	8.2 oz. **$3.49**	8.2 oz. **$3.49**
Pain Reliever Tylenol, extra-strength caplets	(325 @ $13.45) 150 = **$6.21**	(250 @ $12.97) 150 = **$7.78**	(100 @ $7.54) 150 = **$11.31**	150 = **$11.99**	150 = **$13.99**	150 = **$13.99**	150 = **$14.99**
Batteries Duracell, AA	(28 pack @ $11.99) 8 pack = **$3.43**	(16 pack @ $7.87) 8 pack = **$3.94**	(10 pack @$5.99) 8 pack= **$4. 79**	8 pack = **$5.99**	8 pack = **$7.99**	8 pack = **$8.99**	8 pack = **$7.79**
Hand Lotion Vaseline Intensive Care	(2/31.8oz. @ $7.79 17.7 oz. = **$2.17**	(24.5 oz. @ $4.17) 17.7 oz. = **$3.01**	(24.5 oz. @$4.39) 17.7 oz.= **$3.17**	(24.5 oz. @ 4.99) 17.7 oz. = **$3.61**	17.7 oz. = **$6.99**	17.7 oz. = **$6.99**	17.7 oz. = **$6.49**
Hair Dryer Conair, 1875 watt, IonShine	**$18.99**	**$19.96**	**$19.96**	**$19.99**	Andi's Brand **$20.99**	**$21.99**	Revlon **$16.99**
Dishwashing Liquid Dawn, 50 oz.	(90 oz. @ $5.99) 50 oz. = **$3.33**	50 oz. **$3.58**	50 oz. **$3.99**	50 oz. **$3.99**	50 oz. **$5.49**	50 oz. **$4.59**	50 oz. **$4.99**

Store Information—Example

Store Name	Address	Business Hours	Miscellaneous Information
Kroger	Market and Butler	24 hours	great anniversary sale in September
Safeway	42nd St. and Main	24 hours	good produce
Giant	Main and Grant Road	24 hours	
Albertson's	State and Center	24 hours	card required
PharMor	8500 So. State	7 a.m. to midnight	
Payless	Homestead and Sunnyvale Road	10 a.m. to 11 p.m.	pharmacy
Long's	King's Road Mall	9 a.m. to 9 p.m.	
Baked Goods Outlet	7th East and Vine	10 a.m. to 8 p.m.	good prices on lunch treats
Scott's Corner Market	8th and 27th	9 a.m. to 7 p.m.	
Costco	3rd East and 72nd So.	10 a.m. to 9 p.m.	membership card, great prices on bulk
Macey's	7th East and also by Kathy's	24 hours, closed Sundays	always great sales

Store Information			
Store Name	Address	Business Hours	Miscellaneous Information

Savings From Shopping Just Two Stores

Item	Store A	Store B
1. Chicken, whole, lb.	$0.47	$1.19
2. Watermelon, lb.	.12	.19
3. Eggs, medium, dozen	.33	.50
4. Hamburger, lean, lb.	1.29	1.69
5. Salmon, frozen fillet, lb.	1.49	1.99
6. Ice cream, Ben & Jerry's, pint	2.00	3.09
7. Hamburger buns, 8 ct.	.33	.89
8. Milk, 1%, gallon	1.89	2.15
9. Corn flakes, Kellogg's	1.69	3.15
10. Chicken breasts, boneless, lb.	1.49	1.49
Sub Total	$11.10	$16.33
11. Peaches, lb.	$1.99	$.59
12. Avocados, lb.	.79	.33
13. Cauliflower, lb.	1.29	.59
14. Bananas, lb.	.39	.39
15. Sirloin tip roast, lb.	3.49	1.99
16. Ibuprofen, Western Family, 25 ct.	2.49	.99
17. Apples, Red Delicious, lb.	.99	.69
18. Cheese, Monterey Jack, lb.	3.99	2.29
19. Lunch meat, Carl Buddig, 2.5 oz.	.33	.33
Sub Total	$15.75	$8.19
Total	$31.50	$16.38

	Store A	Store B
Items 1–10	$11.10	$16.33
Items 11–19	15.75	8.19
Total	$26.85	$24.52

Best of Both	$11.10
	8.19
	$19.29

Impulse Buying: Impact on Your Budget

Item	Cost	Annual Total Per Item
1 bag of potato chips	Only $2.25/weekly	$117
1 package of cookies	Only $2.00/weekly	$104
1/2 gallon of ice cream	Only $3.00/bimonthly	$72
2 2-liter bottles of soda pop	Only $2.00/weekly	$104
4 candy bars	Only $2.00/weekly	$104

TOTAL SPENT IN ONE YEAR $501.00

Planning Makes a Difference

Item	Regular Price	Amount Used	Annual Cost	Planned Purchase	Annual Cost	Savings
Hamburger (85% lean) per pound	$2.49	3 lbs./week	$388.44	Purchased every few months in bulk on sale for $1.89	$294.84	$93.60
Whole grain bread	$2.89	3 loaves/week	$450.84	Bought at day-old thrift shop for $.89/loaf	$138.84	$312.00
Frozen orange juice (12 oz.)	$1.29	4 cans/week	$268.32	Bought extra whenever on sale for $.89/12 oz.	$185.12	$83.20
Toothpaste (6.4 oz.)	$2.79	1 tube/month	$33.48	Purchased in bulk at membership store for $1.43/tube	$17.16	$16.32
Flour (5 lbs.)	$1.99	1 bag/month	$23.88	Bought in bulk during case lot sales (25-lb. bag) $2.99	$7.18	$16.70
Canned green beans	$.89	3 cans/month	$32.04	Bought by case on sale for $.33/can	$11.88	$20.16
Chicken breasts	$2.99	3 lbs./week	$466.44	Purchased every few months in bulk on sale for $1.90/lb.	$296.40	$170.04
Disposable razors (12 pk.)	$6.78	1/2 pkg./month	$40.68	Stocked up when on sale for $3.99/pkg.	$23.94	$16.74
Butter	$3.50	4 lbs./month	$168.00	Bought extra when on sale for $2.50/lb.	$120.00	$48.00
Cheddar cheese	$4.49	5 lbs./month	$269.40	Bought at local dairy outlet for $1.85/lb.	$111.00	$158.40
TOTALS			$2,141.52		$1,206.36	$935.16

Brand Quiz

To measure what you already know about choosing a brand, designate whether you think the following statements are true or false. (All statements refer to grocery products only.)

_____1.   A higher price almost always means better quality.

_____2.   Cheap, low-grade foods may be unsafe to eat.

_____3.   All canneries, packing houses, and other processors of foodstuffs turn out the same products for all of their clients, putting different labels on identical items.

_____4.   No-name, or generic, products are always inferior to national name brand products.

_____5.   The higher cost of nationally known brands is to cover superior ingredients and know-how.

_____6.   Name-brand soups taste different from house brand soups.

_____7.   The same canneries may manufacture goods for both name brand companies and unknown or little-known grocery firms.

_____8.   Brands are available that offer consistently good quality at a reasonably low price.

_____9.   A fancy package and a pretty label raise the cost of a product significantly.

_____10.   House brand products are usually equal in quality to national brand products.

Answers: The first five statements are false, while statements 6–10 are true. Read the rest of chapter 5 for an explanation of the answers.

Do You Remember?

How good are you at remembering advertising jingles and slogans? Take this quiz, based on *Advertising Age* magazine's selections for Top Ten Slogans and Top Ten Commercial Jingles of the 20th Century.

Commercial Jingles
1. You Deserve a Break Today _____
2. Be All That You Can Be _____
3. —— Hits the Spot _____
4. Mmm, Mmm Good _____
5. See the USA in Your —— _____
6. I Wish I Were an —— —— Wiener _____
7. Double Your Pleasure, Double Your Fun _____
8. —— Tastes Good Like a Cigarette Should _____
9. It's the Real Thing _____
10. A Little Dab'll Do Ya _____

Advertising Slogans
1. Diamonds are Forever _____
2. Just Do It _____
3. The Pause that Refreshes _____
4. Tastes Great, Less Filling _____
5. We Try Harder _____
6. Good to the Last Drop _____
7. Breakfast of Champions _____
8. Does She . . . or Doesn't She? _____
9. When it Rains, It Pours _____
10. Where's the Beef? _____

Honorable Mentions
a) Look Ma, No Cavities! _____
b) Let Your Fingers Do the Walking _____
c) Loose Lips Sink Ships _____
d) —— Melt in Your Mouth, Not in Your Hand _____
e) We Bring Good Things to Life _____

ANSWERS:
Jingles: (1) McDonald's (2) U.S. Army (3) Pepsi-Cola (4) Campbell Soup (5) General Motors (Chevrolet) (6) Oscar Mayer (7) Wrigley's Gum (8) Winston (9) Coca-Cola (10) Brylcreem
Slogans: *(1) DeBeers (2) Nike (3) Coca-Cola (4) Miller Lite (5) Avis (6) Maxwell House (7) Wheaties (8) Clairol (9) Morton Salt (10) Wendy's*
Honorable Mentions: *(a) Crest Toothpaste (b) Yellow Pages (c) public service announcement (d) M&M's candies (e) General Electric*

A Few Examples of House Brands, Private Labels, Economy Brands

House Brands and Private Labels

Red Pack	Rexall	Von's
Sacramento	Savon	Ralph's
Publix	Sam's	PS Private Selection
Tuttorosso	Kirkland	First Selection
Aunt Penny's Sauces	Rosedale	Natural Choices
Heart's Delight Nectars	Knott's	First Choice
Western Family	A&P	Trappey's
Springfield	Kroger	Gel
SunLight	Winn-Dixie	Drew
Mary Ellen's	Giant	Archer Farms
Stop & Shop	Finast	Marsh
Giorgio	Cub	Richfood
Lucerne	Fred Meyer	Market Pantry
White Magic	IGA	Thrifty Maid
Truly Fine	Town House	Kash & Karry
Mrs. Wright	Empress	Safeway Select
Harvest Day	Sunny Select	Dunbar
Shopwell	Jewel	Plano d'Oro
Wegman's	Jane Parker	Trader Joe's
Kohl's	Shop Rite	Buena Comida
Farmdale	Nu-Made	Perfect Choice
Lady Lee	Kingston	King Soopers
Piggly Wiggly	Home Best	Raley's
S&W	Flavorite	Splash Sport
Comstock Fruit	Food Lion	Splash Spa
Thrifty	Albertson's	And more . . .

Economy Brands

Bonnie Hubbard	Liberty Gold
Scotch Buy	Geisha
Key Quality	Regal Wrap
Cost Cutter	Lush'Us
Kings Pantry	P&Q
Econo Buy	And many more . . .
F.M.V.	

Local House Brands, Private Labels, and Economy Brands

	House Brands/Private Labels	Economy Brands	Generic available?
Store Name			
Store Name			
Store Name			
Store Name			

Gaining Price Recognition

Items	Date ___ Price	Date ___ Price	Date ___ Price	Date ___ Price	Date ___ Price

Ad Shopper (a)

Store				Store		
How Many?	Item, Size, Brand	Price		How Many?	Item, Size, Brand	Price

Ad Shopper (b)

Store	Macey's	
How Many ?	Item, Size, Brand	Price
	Grapes, red, green, 1 lb.	$ .77
	Chicken breasts, boneless, skinless, 1 lb.	$1.99
	Ice cream, Macey's, ½ gal.	$1.49
	Soda, Shasta, 2-liter	2/$1.00
	Candy bars, Nestle	5/$1.00
	Hot Pockets	3/$5.00
	Eggs, medium, Western Family	2 doz./ $1.00
	Lunch box drinks, Minute Maid, 10-pack	3/$5.00
	Pasta, American Beauty, 16 oz.	2/$1.00
	Paper plates, Hefty, 50 ct.	$.99
	Sugar, Western Family, 25 lbs.	$6.99!
	Cereal, lots of brands	5/$10.00
	Evaporated milk, Sego, 12 oz.	$.59
	Spaghettios	2/$1.00
	Laundry soap, Tide, 175 oz.	$13.99
	Tuna, Carnation and Western Family	3/$.99
	Cheese, Gossner, 2 lb.	$4.99

Store	Smith's	
How Many ?	Item, Size, Brand	Price
	Grapes, red, green, 1 lb.	$ .79
	Chicken breasts, boneless, skinless, 1 lb.	$1.99
	Bagged salad, Dole	Buy1/Get 1 Free
	Milk, Mountain Dairy, gallon	3/$6.00
	Mayonnaise, Best Foods	2/$3.00 with ad coupon
	Corn	3 ears/$1.00
	Bananas	2 lbs./$.88
	Pot roast, boneless, 1 lb.	$3.49 lb.
	Canned vegetables, Smith's, 16 oz.	3/$1.00

Store	Albertson's	
	Sour cream, Albertson's, 16 oz.	$1.09
	Milk, Cream o' Weber, 1 gal.	2/$5.00
	Canned tomatoes, Libby's	$.59
	Bread, Great Harvest, 1 loaf	$2.39
	Hamburger, ex. Lean, 1 lb.	$1.99
	Corn	3 ears/$1.00
	Peaches	$.89

Ad Shopper (c)

Store	Macey's		
How Many ?	**Item, Size, Brand**		**Price**
	Grapes, red, green, 1 lb.		$ .77
	Chicken breasts, boneless, skinless, 1 lb.		$1.99
	Ice cream, Macey's, 1/2 gal.		$1.49
	Soda, Shasta, 2-liter		2/$1.00
	~~Candy bars, Nestle~~		5/$1.00
	Hot Pockets		3/$5.00
	Eggs, medium, Western Family		2 doz./$1.00
	Lunch box drinks, Minute Maid, 10-pack		3/$5.00
	~~Pasta, American Beauty, 16 oz.~~		2/$1.00
	Paper plates, Hefty, 50 ct.		$.99
	Sugar, Western Family, 25 lbs.		$6.99!
	Cereal, lots of brands		5/$10.00
	~~Evaporated milk, Sego, 12 oz.~~		$.59
	Spaghettios		2/$1.00
	~~Laundry soap, Tide, 175 oz.~~		$13.99
	Tuna, Carnation and Western Family		3/$.99
	~~Cheese, Gossner, 2 lb.~~		$4.99

Store	Smith's		
How Many ?	**Item, Size, Brand**		**Price**
	~~Grapes, red, green, 1 lb.~~		$ .79
	Chicken breasts, boneless, skinless, 1 lb.		$1.99
	Bagged salad, Dole		Buy 1/Get 1 Free
	Milk, Mountain Dairy, gallon		3/$6.00
	~~Mayonnaise, Best Foods~~		2/$3.00 with ad coupon
	Corn		3 ears/$1.00
	Bananas		2 lbs./$.88
	Pot roast, boneless, 1 lb.		$3.49 lb.
	Canned vegetables, Smith's, 16 oz.		3/$1.00

Store	Albertson's		
	Sour cream, Albertson's, 16 oz.		$1.09
	~~Milk, Cream o' Weber, 1 gal.~~		2/$5.00
	Canned tomatoes, Libby's		$.59
	Bread, Great Harvest, 1 loaf		$2.39
	Hamburger, ex. Lean, 1 lb.		$1.99
	~~Corn~~		3 ears/$1.00
	Peaches		$.89

Comparison of Servings per Food Form

Vegetables

Fresh Vegetables	Servings per Pound as Purchased
Asparagus	3–4
Beans, lima (in pods)	2
Beans, snap	5–6
Beets, diced (w/o tops)	3–4
Broccoli	3–4
Brussels Sprouts	4–5
Cabbage:	
Raw, shredded or diced	5–6
Cooked	4
Cauliflower	3
Celery, raw, diced	5–6
Kale, untrimmed	5–6
Okra	4–5
Onions, cooked	4–5
Parsnips (w/o tops)	4
Peas (in pods)	2
Potatoes	4
Spinach (trimmed)	4
Squash, summer	3–4
Squash, winter	2–3
Sweet Potatoes	3–4
Tomatoes, sliced	5

Frozen Vegetables	Servings per Package (9–10 oz.)
Asparagus	2–3
Beans, lima	3–4
Beans, snap	3–4
Broccoli	3
Brussels Sprouts	3
Cauliflower	3
Corn, whole kernel	3
Kale	2–3
Peas	3
Spinach	2–3

Canned Vegetables	Servings per Can (16 oz.)
Most vegetables	3–4
Greens, such as kale or spinach	2–3

Dry Vegetables	Servings per Pound
Dry beans	11
Dry peas, lentils	10–11

Fruit

Fresh Fruit	Servings per Pound or Container
Apples	3–4 per lb.
Bananas	"
Peaches	"
Pears	"
Plums	"
Apricots	5–6 per lb.
Cherries	"
Grapes	"
Blueberries	4–5 per pint
Raspberries	"
Strawberries	8–9 per quart

Canned Fruit	Servings Per Can (16 oz.)
Served with liquid	4
Drained	2–3

Frozen Fruit	Servings per Package (10–12 oz.)
Blueberries	3–4
Peaches	2–3
Raspberries	"
Strawberries	"

Dried Fruit	Servings per Package (8 oz.)
Apples	8
Apricots	6
Mixed fruits	6
Peaches	7
Pears	4
Prunes	4–5

Meals from Menus vs. Meals from Ad Sales

Meals from Menus (The Old Way of Meal Planning)
(Not from the Sales)

(Store #1)

1. Baked Chicken and Yams
   chicken, Country Pride, $1.98 lb., package 3.4 lbs. $6.73
   yams, fresh, $.89 lb., 3 lbs. $2.67

   Total   **$9.40**

2. Meatloaf and Baked Potatoes
   hamburger, lean, per lb. $1.29, package 1.3 lbs. $1.68
   potatoes, 10-lb. bag $3.99

   Total   **$5.67**

3. Beef Stroganoff with Frozen Vegetables
   round steak, $2.99 per lb., package 1.6 lbs. $ 4.78
   egg noodles, 12 oz. $ 1.19
   sour cream, 16 oz. $ .89
   frozen veg. medley, Pictsweet, 16 oz. $ 1.99

   Total   **$8.85**

4. Roast Beef and Mashed Potatoes
   rump roast, $3.29 per lb., package 3.1 lbs. $10.20
   potatoes (part of meal 2)   -------
   Total   **$10.20**

5. Lasagna and French Bread
   lasagna noodles, 16 oz. $1.39
   ricotta cheese, 15 oz. $3.99
   hamburger, lean, $1.29 per lb., package 1.3 lbs. $1.68
   french bread, 1 lb. $1.19

   Total   **$8.25**

6. Baked Ham, Roasted Potatoes, and Vegetables
   ham, $1.29 per lb., package 6.68 lbs. $8.62
   potatoes (part of meal 2)   -------
   baby carrots, 2-lb. bag $2.59

   Total   **$11.21**

7. Pork Chops and Rice Pilaf
   chops, regular, $2.59 per lb., package 2.7 lbs. $7.00
   Rice a Roni, 7.2 oz. $1.39

   Total   **$8.39**

   Total for the Week   **$61.97**

Meals from Menus vs. Meals from Ad Sales

Meals from the Ads (The New Way of Meal Planning)

A number in parentheses ( ) indicates a sale price at that store. Store #1, #2, #3, #4

1. Roast Chicken and Parsleyed Red Potatoes
   (#3) chicken, $.47 lb. package, 2.78 lbs. $1.31
   (#2) red potatoes, $.59 lb., 3 lbs. $1.77
   Total   **$3.08**

2. Hamburgers and Baked Beans
   (#3) hamburger, extra lean, $1.49 lb.,
        Package 1.42 lbs. $2.12
   (#1) buns, 3 pkg./$1.00 $ .33
   (#1) baked beans, Bush, 2/$1.00 $1.00
   Total   **$3.45**

3. Chicken Divan
   (#2) chicken tenders, $1.49 lb.,
        package 1.37 lbs. $2.04
   (#4) broccoli, $.59 lb., head 1.34 lbs. $ .79
   Total   **$2.83**

4. Barbecue Ribs and Potato Salad
   (#2) pork ribs, $1.19 lb., package 2.75 lbs. $3.27
   (#2) barbecue sauce, Hunt's, 16 oz. $ .69
   (#3) potatoes, 15-lb. bag, $1.99 $1.99
   (#2) eggs, $.33 dozen $ .33
   Total   **$6.28**

5. Salmon and Rice
   (#2) salmon, $1.59 lb., package 1.8 lbs. $2.86
   (#1) Minute Rice, 2/$3.00 $1.50
   Total   **$4.36**

6. Pot Roast
   (#2) chuck roast, $1.49 lb., package 2.6 lbs. $3.87
   potatoes (from meal 4)   -------
   Total   **$3.87**

7. Stir Fry
   (#1) London broil, $1.99 lb., package .87 lbs. $1.73
   (#4) zucchini, $.59 lb. $ .59
   (#4) broccoli, $.59 lb. $ .59
   (#4) Mushrooms, 8 oz. $ .89
   Total   **$3.89**

   Total for the week   **$27.76**

Difference ($61.97–$27.76) $34.21

How to Make Grab-and-Go Foods Affordable

as Well as Available

Everyone knows that making all your own food from scratch is a great way to save money. Anytime you pay another person to prepare your food you'll pay more than if you do it yourself. This is common knowledge. But what if there just isn't time to cook from scratch? Often there isn't time to cook, period. How do you balance saving time with saving money? The answer, unsatisfying as it may be, is to do the best you can. You save time when you can, and you save money where you can, and with enough effort, hopefully you'll achieve that balance.

One food group that can really put a dent in your budget is grab-and-go foods. Yet, if you need grab-and-go food, your time is obviously at a premium also. To give you an example, I have two grandsons who are involved in everything from sports to music to jobs to you-name-it. Being teenagers, they are always starved and always on the run. They don't have time to sit down to a meal until late in the evening, and they don't have money to grab a burger from a fast-food place if they're hungry in the meantime. There is a shelf in the pantry that their mother keeps stocked with single-serving foods that they can just grab a handful of as they run out the door to keep them going until they have a chance to eat a real meal. But if you have to buy grab-and-go snacks at the store, they'll break the bank in no time at all. What do you do?

First of all, you have to know prices, and you have to know how much you're willing to spend. Set a price for each item (not for a whole package), and then don't spend more than that. You may be willing to pay an average of twenty cents each for granola bars or fruit roll-ups and maybe stretch to 25 cents occasionally for something special, but no higher than that. There are lots of things you can buy that you can eat on the run if money isn't an issue, but if finances are tight they aren't an option. When you see grab-and-go food on sale that fits your budget, buy as much as you can afford, to stretch the

savings through times when the items are only offered at full price. (Just don't put it all out at one time. Find a place to hide the extra supplies that stock your grab-and-go shelf to make them last a little longer.)

Shop around, and look beyond traditional supermarkets. Often membership clubs like Costco or Sam's Club will offer large packages of grab-and-go snacks for prices you're willing to pay. Take advantage of these if you have access to membership stores. Deep discount stores like Wal-Mart and Target can frequently be affordable sources for grab-and-go snacks also. Don't forget day-old bread stores. They will often carry brands of snack foods at discount prices.

Package your own. Buying individually packaged bags of chips or cookies may be out of the picture, but you can make your own quite reasonably. Buy cookies or raisins or any snack food in a regular package, and then divide it up into individual zipper sandwich bags. You can usually get fifteen to twenty little bags of snacks out of a box of cookies, which brings the cost down to a dime or so for each portion. Dividing up a package of cookies doesn't take more than three or four minutes. Even bags of dry cereal make good grab-and-go snacks.

Grab-and-go foods can be perishable items also. String cheese and yogurt are often, though not always, affordably priced. When they are, tape a note to the snack shelf saying, "Yogurt in fridge—don't forget spoon" or something similar. (Buying a supply of plastic spoons when they are on sale is much cheaper than having your good silverware disappear.) Fresh vegetables can be chopped and sorted into zipper sandwich bags so you can take something healthy with you on the spur of the moment. And apples and oranges are always ready to be stuffed in a pocket as you head out the door.

So don't despair if your family eats on the run. With just a little effort, you can be ready as they race by, and you don't have to break the bank to do it.

Soup's On:
Comparative Cost per Serving of Vegetable Soup

	Condensed	Ready-to-Serve	Ready to Serve Microwavable Container	Packaged Dry Soup Mix
Cost	$1.29	$2.19	$1.79	$3.69
Weight	10.5 oz.	19 oz.	10.75 oz.	9 oz.
Add water?	Yes/1 can	No	No	Yes/7 cups
Volume after Water is added	21 oz.	19 oz.	10.75 oz.	65 oz.
Servings per Container (as prepared)	2¹/2	2	1	8
Cost per Serving	**$.52**	**$1.10**	**$1.79**	**$.46**

Running List

N=Need   L = Low, watch for a sale   W = Want, start pricing

Bread	Produce	Dairy Products	Meat

Frozen Foods	Canned Goods	Staples	Snacks/Treats

Cleaning Supplies	Health and Beauty	Miscellaneous	Other Errands

Balanced Buying Decisions

Workable Grocery Budget This Week—$75

Produce	$20
Milk and Dairy	$10
Meat	$20
Bread	$ 5
Snacks/Treats	$10
Miscellaneous	$10
	——
	$75

Further Breakdown

Produce ($20)

Apples @ Harmon's $3
Case of oranges @ Harmon's $8
Vegetables and peaches @ Giant $9

Milk ($10)

Milk @ Costco $6
Cheese @ Giant $4

Meat ($20)

Chicken @ Harmon's $10
Hamburger @ Giant $6
Lunch meat @ Macey's $4

Bread ($5)

Bread @ day-old bread store $5

Snacks/Treats ($10)

Ice cream @ Macey's $6
Granola bars @ Giant $4

Miscellaneous ($10)

Dish soap, shampoo @ Costco $7
Toothpaste @ Giant $3

Shopping Trip Planner

Maximum Grocery Budget for the Week $_____

Things to Gather and Review:

1. Running list (review before reading the ads).
2. Store Information worksheet (check for stores that have good deals but don't advertise).
3. Ad Shopper (mark all potential purchases and attach list to this page).

Decide Which Stores to Shop This Week:

1.
2.
3.
4.

Decide Where to Purchase Needs—List Items That Aren't on Sale Anywhere This Week:

Needs-List Items

Where to Purchase

Additional Errands this Week:

1.
2.
3.
4.
5.

Pantry Search

Walk through your home with this worksheet to see how many different places you can turn into pantries or mini-pantries.

Areas to Consider	How to Improve for Use as a Pantry
Cupboards Space above cabinets Space below cabinets Receding corners Deep cabinets Above stove Above refrigerator	Clean out/rearrange Turntables Double-decker turntables Additional shelves Custom drawers Boxes Step shelves Other
Closets Hall or guest room Bedroom Linen Broom Utility	Rearrange Add shelves/step shelves in space above clothes Use end or half closet for floor-to-ceiling shelves Use crates/bookshelves for shelves Redesign the entire closet solely as a pantry Other
Odd Spaces In laundry room Above washer and dryer Between refrigerator and wall Under beds End or corner of a room Under stairs/stairwells Attic Basement	Rearrange Use space above Add shelves Add vertical drawer Make built-in pantry Use crates for shelves Create pantry space with a false wall (possibly made of the backs of bookshelves) Other
Under Sinks Kitchen Bathroom(s)	Rearrange Add shelves Install or build cabinets/shelves
Out of the House Stairwells Garage Carport Sheds Covered porch Other	

Take this page along with you to your home-improvement store to check out their storage solutions or closet-renovation sections. Let your imagination go, and you'll find you have lots of creative options to choose from.

Example Inventory List

Date:_____

Canned Fruit

Applesauce	39
Mandarin oranges	12
Pears	35
Fruit cocktail	24
Peaches	26
Pineapple, sliced	15
crushed	7
Apricots	9
Cranberry sauce	3
Pumpkin	2
Pineapple juice	2

Canned Vegetables

Corn	10
Green beans	20
Creamed corn	11
Beets	2
Pickled beets	5
Mushrooms	13
Olives	2
Yams	1

Soup

Cream of chicken	16
Tomato	37
Cream of mushroom	24
Chicken noodle	36
Vegetable	32
Spaghettios	5
Clam chowder	2

Beans

Pork and beans	25
Refried beans	28
Chili	7
Kidney beans	20
Small red beans	24
Pinto beans	24

Tomatoes

Tomato sauce	72
Enchilada sauce	10
Stewed tomatoes	28
Diced tomatoes	22
Whole tomatoes	21
Spaghetti sauce	12

Condiments

Ketchup	12
BBQ sauce	6
Mustard	10
Salad dressing	3
Worchestershire sauce	2
Pickles, 46 oz.	2
Pickle relish, dill	1
sweet	1
Mayonnaise	2
Salsa	4
Soy sauce	2

Pasta

Instant rice, brown	4
white	2
Spaghetti, 3-lb. bags	3
Macaroni, 3-lb. bags	5
Lasagna noodles	1
Egg noodles	1
Ramen noodles	45
Cup of Noodles	21
Macaroni and Cheese	15
Pasta-Roni	8
Hamburger helper	1
White rice	20 lbs.
Brown rice	10 lbs.

Oils

Vegetable oil, 48 oz.	3
Shortening, 3-lb. can	5
Spray	2

Baking Supplies

Baking soda, lb.	6
Corn starch, lb.	2
Powdered sugar 2 lb.	6
Brown sugar, 2 lb.	3
Maple flavoring	2
Chocolate chips, semi	3
milk	3
Vanilla,	1
Jello, 3 oz.	27
Pudding, small	3
large	2
Corn syrup, 32 oz.	2
Hot fudge sauce	2
Evaporated milk	25
Jiffy Mix	1
Baking mix	3

Canned Meat

Tuna	52
Corned beef	4
Spam	1
Clams	1
Chicken	1
Sloppy Joe mix	4
Beef stew	1
Beef gravy	1

Hygiene Stuff

Shampoo	4
Baby powder	1
Hand lotion	1
Baby oil	1
Toothbrushes	7
Dental floss	2
Toothpaste	3
Toilet tissue	30
Soap	8

Simple Menus from Foods On Hand

Grilled Cheese Sandwiches and Soup
Tuna Casserole
Baked Potatoes
Pancakes
Spaghetti
Chili
Simple Casseroles
Tuna Sandwiches
French Toast
Macaroni and Cheese
Ramen Noodles
Taco Soup
Tacos

Your Paycheck

							Remainder
			Must Pay				Grocery Budget $100
Housing	Utilities	Credit Cards	Car Payments	Insurance	Other		

Paycheck #1—Grocery Budget $100

Needs		
Bread	$ 5.00	
Milk	$ 6.00	**Workable**
Cereal	$ 6.00	**Amount**
Eggs	$ 2.00	
Produce	$10.00	$100.00
Toothpaste	$ 2.00	-$ 78.00
Soap	$ 2.00	
Misc.	$45.00	**$ 22.00**
Total	**$78.00**	

Paycheck #2—Grocery Budget $100

Needs		
Bread	$ 5.00	
Milk	$ 5.00	**Workable**
Hamburger	$10.00	**Amount**
Produce	$10.00	
Tomato Sauce	$ 5.00	$100.00
Mustard	$ 1.00	-$ 76.00
Toothpaste	$ 2.00	
Soups	$ 3.00	**$ 24.00**
Misc.	$35.00	
Total	**$76.00**	

Paycheck #XX—Grocery Budget $100

Needs		
Milk	$ 5.00	**Workable**
Produce	$10.00	**Amount**
Ice Cream	$ 3.00	
Dish Soap	$ 5.00	$100.00
Misc.	$20.00	-$ 43.00
Total	**$43.00**	**$ 57.00**